EASTER IN ORDINARY

*Reflections on
Human Experience
and the Knowledge
of God*

EASTER IN ORDINARY

*Reflections on
Human Experience
and the Knowledge
of God*

NICHOLAS LASH

University of Notre Dame Press
Notre Dame   London

The Richard Lectures for 1986
University of Virginia

This publication was prepared (in part) under a
grant from the Woodrow Wilson International
Center for Scholars, Washington, D.C. The
statements and views expressed herein are
those of the author and are not necessarily
those of the Wilson Center.

University of Notre Dame Press edition 1990
Published by arrangement with the
University Press of Virginia
Copyright © 1988 by the Rector and Visitors
of the University of Virginia

First published 1988

Library of Congress Cataloging-in-Publication Data
Lash, Nicholas.
     Easter in ordinary : reflections on human experience and the
knowledge of God / Nicholas Lash.
        p.   cm. —(The Richard lectures for 1986, University of
Virginia)
     Bibliography: p.
     Includes index.
     ISBN 0-8139-1150-8
     1. Experience (Religion)—History of doctrines. 2. God—History
of doctrines. I. Title. II. Series: Richard lectures : 1986.
BL53.L27 1988
248.2—dc19   87-23738
                                                                CIP

Printed in the United States of America

For Dominic
without whom this book would have been different

Contents

Preface

This book is an expanded version of the Richard Lectures which I gave at the University of Virginia in November 1986. Among those who helped to make an autumn in Charlottesville a most enriching experience, I would like especially to thank Nathan Scott, Jr., James Childress, Jamie Ferreira, Paul Mendes-Flohr (who was kind enough to read and comment on the material on Buber), and the members of my seminar. I am also most grateful to the late Walker Cowen and his colleagues at the University Press of Virginia for the care with which they helped to see the manuscript through to publication, and also to John Bowden of SCM Press for his encouragement and cooperation.

The greater part of the book was written during seven memorable months, from January through July 1986, which I had the privilege to spend as a fellow of the Woodrow Wilson International Center for Scholars in Washington, D.C. I find it difficult to imagine a more stimulating and congenial setting for such work than that which the Wilson Center provides, and am greatly indebted to the director, James Billington, and to his academic and administrative staff (especially Ann Sheffield and Michael Lacey), to my colleagues at the Center, and to my research assistants Rachel McCleary, David Smalley, and Anne Britton.

Some steps in the argument were tested in discussion with friends and colleagues at Boston College, Colorado College, and Roanoke College. I learned a great deal from those discussions, and hope that the book improved as a result.

I would like especially to thank two people who read through the entire manuscript and whose comments on it were invaluable: David Tracy, of the University of Chicago, and my wife who, as usual, patiently saw each paragraph through each successive draft. I do not know whether my son will ever read the book, but the dedication may remind him of a year abroad during which he and his parents learned much about all manner of things American.

EASTER IN ORDINARY

*Reflections on
Human Experience
and the Knowledge
of God*

1

Where Do We Begin?

Different people browse differently. Some people, finding in a bookshop or a library a book which (perhaps on account of its title, or the name of the author, or even the design on the cover) they think may interest them, turn first to the index, in order to get some idea of topics treated and writers mentioned. Using the index, the browser may "dip," tasting and testing almost at random. Browsing has its uses, and (like all forms of dilettantism) its limits. Sooner or later, a decision has to be made as to whether or not to move on from dipping and to take the risk of serious reading. (It is a risk because all reading, all interpretation, engages the responsibility of the reader.) If one decides to read the book through, from cover to cover, the best place to start is usually the beginning. And most books begin at page one.

Another kind of browsing gets a person to serious reading by a different route. Some people turn first to the table of contents. A table of contents may be treated as a menu, an indication of the courses on offer. Sometimes, as with the case of a collection of essays or short stories, the menu is à la carte. There is no need to take all the courses, or to take them in the order in which they are listed. There are several places at which the reading may begin. Page one is, we might say, no more than *primus inter pares* (that metaphor seems appropriate, since the author presumably had some reason for placing a particular story or essay at the beginning).

The table of contents of a book which, by foreword or format, is presented as a single, unitary whole, may also resemble a menu, but the menu is no longer à la carte. In the case of a novel[1] or of a book (such as this

---

1 Well, most novels: John Fowles's *The Ebony Tower* might be an exception, but then Fowles likes playing with these problems.

one) which purports to contain or to constitute a single argument, the reader is invited to read all the chapters, and to read them in sequence, beginning at the beginning. And most books begin at page one.

But what is it that begins at page one? The obvious answer is that it is the story or the argument. But, for all its obviousness, this answer is much less informative than at first sight it may appear to be. Indeed, in some respects it is quite misleading.

As an indication of why the answer is not very informative, we might change the metaphor and consider the table of contents not as a menu but rather as a kind of map, a printed device that enables one to find one's way around, to see how the parts relate to the whole. Any journey undertaken with the aid of a map will necessarily begin at one of the places that is marked on the map. But there is no one place at which the *map* begins, and it is no business of the mapmaker to tell the traveler where to begin the journey.

It does not, I think, follow that the metaphor of the map is wholly inappropriate. The mapmaker does bear some responsibility for indicating which routes are more direct and trouble free and which, though perhaps more arduous and time-consuming, offer the best rewards in scenery and sight-seeing. From this point of view, the table of contents is a little like the route maps supplied by the Automobile Association. If the traveler wants to get from C to Q, the route map shows the ways in which, for certain indicated reasons, it is recommended that he should proceed.

But, even with this adjustment, the metaphor is still a poor one because, in the matter of human experience and the knowledge of God, I do not know where you (the reader) start from, nor what kind of journey you are prepared to undertake, nor where you think you are going. If you were a traveler, and I a mapmaker (whether of general maps or of recommended routes between particular places), the fact that we were personally un-known to each other would be no disadvantage to either of us. But it is not so when the territory to be mapped out is not physical but linguistic: a matter of words, images, concepts, arguments, "perspectives," and "points of view." The instruments required for the navigation of physical spaces (maps, compasses, sextants, and so on) may, indeed, be tailored to meet a particular traveler's needs, but they remain quite impersonal in character. But it is not always so with the instruments that we require in order to "pursue" an argument or to "follow" a conversation.

There is no problem about the beginning of a general map, because there is no one place at which the map begins. And, in the case of the route map, the decision as to where to begin is taken by the customer. Where the design of a novel, or a history, or a piece of theological or philosophical investigation is concerned, however, no such customer input is possible. Does this matter? Usually, we (that is, writers and readers alike) proceed as if it did not. I suggest, however, that judgments concerning the circumstances in which it matters and the kinds of text in respect of which it might matter, and the extent to which consideration of such questions should influence the writer's decision as to where to begin, all depend (in part) upon the way in which we conceive of the relationships between text and meaning, artefact and interpretation. To such issues I shall shortly return.

Both maps and menus are, we might say, patterns of meaning. But they represent two of the many different ways in which the parts of a text may be related to the whole. My purpose in playing with these two contrasting metaphors for the patterning of a story or an argument was to indicate that there is no universally valid answer to the question of how it is that the parts combine to make a single whole; no one correct account of what it is that gives *unity* to a story or an argument.

This may seem obvious and yet (perhaps because most books begin at page one) we are sometimes tempted to suppose that it is *linear sequence* that gives unity to a story or an argument. It is a factor, certainly: that is why we ask such questions as "What happened next?" or "What is the next step?" But it is by no means the only, or even the most important factor making for such unity. (And, of course, mere sequence, as such, is quite insignificant: neither plot nor argument are ever merely a matter of one damned thing after another.) Where does a story begin? At the beginning. But even the most realistic novelist may begin with the description of events which occur, chronologically, at the end of the tale.

There is, therefore, no such thing as the "obvious" point at which to begin a story, nor is it ever "obvious" how the movement from beginning to end, the movement whose execution constitutes the realization of the story as a *single* story should proceed. And the same is true of an argument, because every argument is a kind of story, and every tale contains some kind of argument. But because most books begin at page one, and are designed to be read in strict sequence, we may be misled into supposing that the uncluttered linearity which is perhaps characteristic of certain highly abstract patterns of inference in logic or pure mathematics can serve as a paradigm of good argument.

Were this the case, then the best way to begin an argument might be by defining one's terms. And yet this is just what it is often impossible, at the outset, to do. I am concerned, in this book, to construct an argument in favor of one way of construing or interpreting human experience as experience of the mystery of God. I hope that the account that I offer will not be lacking in either clarity or "definition." But to define, at the outset, what I take "human experience" and "knowledge of God" to mean would be not only impossible but quite evidently futile.

It would be impossible because what I hope to achieve, at the *end* of this exercise, is some "definition," some particular description, of how these notions work and what they signify. And I clearly cannot begin at the point at which I hope, eventually, to arrive.

Moreover, any attempt to define my terms at the outset would be futile because each reader of this text will bring to it their own account of how these familiar notions work and of the relationships that obtain between them. It will be a highly complex account, the fruit of years of experience, thought, suffering, study, and argument. Many of the elements of the account will have found their way into that complex unity which is your personal identity, self-perception, and narrative without your ever having either explicitly adverted to them or subjected them to sustained scrutiny. And this is probably true, not only of trivial or peripheral features, but of features that are quite central and fundamental to the way in which you think, tick, react, suppose, respond.

As a result, the chances are that any attempt on my part to offer initial summary definition of the notions of human experience and the knowledge of God would probably strike you as abstract, obvious, arbitrary, trivial, perverse, or unintelligible (or some combination of all or most of these).

I remarked earlier that to say that what begins at page one is the story or argument is, in certain respects, misleading. We are now in a position to see why this is so. Beginnings and endings are partial and relative. Texts are produced and read in contexts. Stories are told and arguments elaborated against a background. The context shapes the story or the argument, colors its production and its use, its writing and its reading.

Even of stories as complex and complete as Dante's *Divine Comedy*, or Tolstoy's *War and Peace*, even of arguments as rich and tightly patterned as Hegel's *Phenomenology* or Karl Barth's *Church Dogmatics*, it remains the case that they are but chapters in a library of larger narratives, steps in a pattern of larger arguments. If we were to pursue these considerations (which, at least at this point, I do not propose to do), we might find ourselves, on the one hand, wondering whether it is not the case that every narrative and every argument has metaphysical and theological implications and, on the other hand, wondering how it is possible for us (being the particular, finite persons that we are, exceedingly circumscribed in context, imagination, and experience) ever to hope to do good metaphysics or good theology. We might begin (!) by saying: The Word was made flesh. But how would we *go on?* (For all its importance, I shall treat that question as rhetorical. That is to say, I shall treat it as a question put to you. Rhetorical questions are not questions to which there is no answer, or to which the answer is supposed to be obvious. They are questions to which the speaker or writer neither supplies an answer nor expects an immediate reply.)

At the beginning of this chapter,[2] I spoke of menus and courses, of tasting and dipping. I did so in view of the widespread supposition that texts *contain* their meaning in somewhat the same way that a casserole contains food. When the cook has finished, the dish is complete. Whether we like it or not is a matter of taste. The history of every dish ends with its consumption. Cooking may indeed be a creative art, but this is hardly the case with consumption. Even the most fastidious gourmet would be hard put to it to defend the view that eating was a creative enterprise.

The production and use of texts is very different (though, since the early nineteenth century, the difference has often been obscured by talk of "taste" in literature).[3] Texts do not contain meaning in the way that casseroles contain food. The reader bears a heavier responsibility than the diner, for he or she continues, with every reading, actively to contribute to the history of the "content," the history of the meaning of the text.

We speak of content (and of tables of contents). But texts do not, in fact, contain their meaning. The meaning of the text *occurs* in each act of writing and reading (or fails to do so; it is possible both to write and to read incompetently). Arguments do not exist "in" texts. They occur between people. Argument is a public, intersubjective affair. This is one reason why persuasion plays so large a part in argument. Notwithstanding the illusions of positivism, persuasion plays a considerable part in scientific, philosophical, historical, and theological argument. But, if persuasion is not to degenerate into manipulation and propaganda, the ideological abuses of argument, then it requires patterns and rules of constraint. Rules of evidence, for example. Jurisprudence would be a better model for argument than a string of beads.[4]

The writer, I want to say, does not produce an argument. He produces a text which makes argument possible. Whether it occurs, and what form it takes, depends upon whether anyone reads the text and what they make of it. This is why I earlier suggested that, at least where certain sorts of text are concerned, it may be important for the writer to remember that his readers are unknown to him.

Argument is a kind of conversation. How do good conversations begin,

---

2 A phrase which indicates, of course, that it is not possible even to offer elementary reflections on the problem of beginning an argument without, in practice, taking a decision on the matter. Here, as elsewhere, our practice precedes our attempts at theoretical clarification.

3 See Raymond Williams, "Base and Superstructure in Marxist Cultural Theory," *New Left Review* 82 (1973): 14; on which see my comments in Nicholas Lash, *Theology on the Way to Emmaus* (London, 1986), pp. 82–86.

4 Cf. Stephen Toulmin, *The Uses of Argument* (Cambridge, 1958), pp. 7–8, 15–17, 41–43. "Logic," says Toulmin, "is generalised jurisprudence" (p. 7).

proceed, and reach (when they do) satisfactory conclusions? In practice, we all have answers to these questions, for we all have some experience of fruitful and unfruitful discussion, of satisfactory and frustrating conversation. And if it is difficult to give these answers clear *theoretical* expression, this is perhaps because good conversation is an art, a practical skill, and not a science.

Argument is a kind of conversation. But, when the *medium* of argument is a written text, the differences between this kind of argument and those conducted face to face become so striking that many people would say that the production and interpretation of a text can only metaphorically be called a conversation.

From the author's point of view there is (as I have already indicated) the difference created by the unavoidable silence of the absent and unknown reader. In a live conversation, each move that is made can be enriched, corrected, qualified, clarified, resisted. Live conversation is, we might say, orchestral, whereas the writer is, inevitably, a soloist. He shoulders his responsibilities in solitude.

To a certain extent, a similar solitude burdens the reader. In some accounts of the interpretative process, the reader is said to engage in "dialogue," or conversation, with the text. But the metaphor is somewhat misleading.[5] Texts do not talk. They stay silent, at the mercy of the reader, incapable of interrupting the reading, of correcting it, or of suggesting that something has been overlooked. Nevertheless, the reader does have, in the text, a kind of company that the writer lacks. If the reading is to be responsible and intelligent, the reader cannot do whatever he likes with the text. It does, however mutely, set up a kind of resistance. This is why we sometimes speak, for example, of a reader *struggling* to make sense of a difficult or unfamiliar text.

Finally, it is worth pointing out that it is with the *text,* rather than with the text's producer, that the reader conducts, in however metaphorical or attenuated a sense, an argument or conversation. Quite apart from the fact that writing often sets up possibilities of interpretation of which the writer was unaware, the history of the meaning of the text continues to create fresh possibilities, altogether beyond the writer's imagination or control, as the text continues to be read in different contexts which open up fresh angles of association, implication, and understanding.

In offering these elementary remarks on what it is fashionable to call

---

5 On this, see Bernstein's comments on the work of H.-G. Gadamer, in which the metaphor of dialogue occupies a key role: Richard J. Bernstein, *Beyond Objectivism and Relativism* (Oxford, 1983), pp. 161–63.

hermeneutics (a long word signifying nothing more recondite than the endlessly fascinating problem of what is involved in our attempts intelligently and responsibly to "read," construe, or make sense of texts, and contexts, and circumstances) it is by no means only, or even primarily *this* text, which you are now reading, that I have in mind. Nevertheless, these remarks will (I hope) throw some light on, furnish a kind of context for, my decision to begin a consideration of human experience and the knowledge of God with a discussion of William James's *Varieties of Religious Experience*.

If, as human beings, we have or may have some experience of the mystery of God, and if, on the basis of such experience, we may acquire, even in this life, some knowledge of God, on the basis of what *kind* of experience would we hope to acquire such knowledge? I am assuming that, to this question, many people would reply: "*religious* experience." Not only has William James's description and analysis of the varieties of religious experience acquired something like the status of a classic, and thereby come to exercise considerable influence on twentieth-century treatments of the topic, but, at least in its general approach and broad philosophical and theological presuppositions, it expresses a view of the matter which is, I believe, widely shared by people many of whom have never heard of James, or read his writings, or been directly influenced by them.

I propose, in due course, to argue, on the one hand, that it is not the case that all experience of God is necessarily religious in form or content and, on the other hand, that not everything which it would be appropriate to characterize, on psychological or sociological grounds, as "religious" experience would thereby necessarily constitute experience of God.

In order to render such a story plausible, it will be necessary to build up an account of the relationship between the principal elements of human experience which contrasts quite fundamentally with that proposed and presupposed by James. In my attempt to do this, I shall invoke the help of people as different as Friedrich Schleiermacher and Martin Buber, Karl Rahner and John Henry Newman. This is not, however, a book *about* James or Newman, Rahner or Schleiermacher. Learned studies of all these individuals abound, and I am not attempting to add to their number. It is the issues, or the argument, which interest me, and although I have tried to keep sufficiently close to the texts to avoid serious misrepresentation, I have also tried sufficiently to maintain my distance from them to avoid getting bogged down in details of commentary and exegesis.[6]

---

6 Wayne Proudfoot's careful and intelligent study of *Religious Experience* (Berkeley, Calif., 1985), which includes extensive discussion of Schleiermacher and James, unfortunately

Perhaps we could say (but bearing in mind the limits already indicated to the sense in which writing and reading a text can be said to constitute a conversation) that I am concerned to bring these other people into the conversation between us. My interest in these matters is theological. I want to try to understand the senses in which, and the circumstances in which, our common human experience may be said, from the standpoint of a Christian account of such experience, to furnish us with experience and knowledge of the mystery of God, and to indicate the doctrine of God that is implied in this attempt. And I hope that you may be sufficiently interested to follow and continue the conversation.

---

came my way too late for it to be possible for me to include detailed indications of where our accounts overlap and where they differ. Proudfoot is a philosopher of religion, not a theologian, and his admirable suspicion of "fideism" leads him to offer a less favorable verdict on Schleiermacher and a more favorable (though by no means uncritical) verdict on James than I do.

2

Talking about Experience

In the second of his lectures on the varieties of religious experience, entitled "Circumscription of the Topic," James confronted head-on the apparent arbitrariness of an initial definition of terms. "My lectures," he said, "must be limited to a fraction of the subject. And, although it would indeed be foolish to set up an abstract definition of religion's essence . . . yet this need not prevent me from taking my own narrow view of what religion shall consist in *for the purpose of these lectures,* or, out of the many meanings of the word, from choosing the one meaning in which I wish to interest you particularly, and proclaiming arbitrarily that when I say 'religion' I mean *that.*"[1]

As this passage indicates, the topic that he sought to circumscribe was that of *religion.* The notion of *experience* is not, in these lectures, submitted to close scrutiny. Although it had long been central to his interests as a psychologist, it was only after the turn of the century, as "systematic philosophy" increasingly became his "chief preoccupation," that he gave to it sustained *philosophical* consideration.[2] However, if James had reason to be suspicious of abstract definitions of the essence of religion, how much more reason does any writer have to be slow to attempt a definition of experience!

"'Experience,'" said Michael Oakeshott at the start of his seminal study

---

1 William James, *The Works of William James: The Varieties of Religious Experience,* ed. Frederick H. Burkhardt, Fredson Bowers, and Ignas K. Skrupskelis, introd. John E. Smith (Cambridge, Mass., 1985), p. 32 (his emphasis).

2 See Peter H. Hare, "Introduction" to William James, *The Works of William James: Some Problems of Philosophy,* ed. Burkhardt, Bowers, and Skrupskelis (Cambridge, Mass., 1979), xiv.

Experience and Its Modes, is, "of all the words in the philosophic vocabulary, . . . the most difficult to manage; and it must be the ambition of every writer reckless enough to use the word to escape the ambiguities it contains." On the whole, he managed rather well but, since his time, it has become that much more difficult to escape the ambiguities. I almost inclined to make my own Stanley Hauerwas's admission that "Wittgenstein ended forever any attempt on my part to try to anchor theology in some general account of 'human experience.'"[3]

Almost, but not quite, because "general account" is, in itself, ambiguous. The ambiguity is worth teasing out a little, because it masks disputes and tensions, as ancient as philosophy itself, concerning the philosopher's task.

Each of us knows the names of many things, and the closer to home some particular "district" of experience or activity, the more numerous and nuanced the distinctions that we draw between the different kinds of things that there are. The baker has far more names for different kinds of flour and dough, for different ways of baking, and for the many things he bakes, than does the layman who can hardly tell a bun from a bagel. To most of us butterflies are merely large or small and variously colored (though we can just about tell a red admiral from a cabbage white), whereas the lepidopterist discriminates without a second thought between specimens that we find indistinguishable.

The further things are from the territory of our particular experience and expertise, the broader and more rough-and-ready the distinctions that we draw, and the less sensitive and accurate our capacity for discrimination. The person with no interest in politics, except for a diffuse and deep-seated antipathy to "communism," will take it for granted that Russian, Italian, Nicaraguan, and Chinese socialism are "really" just the same. And, from outside the practices and narratives of Christianity, any suggestion that doctrinal disagreements between Christians might sometimes be about issues that really *matter* will be dismissed as outmoded dogmatism.

Wherever we start from, whatever our background, history, expertise, and interests, we have no alternative but to pattern and order our experience, to find our way around. Chaos and formlessness threaten our identity and sense of direction. We need to put plot and pattern into the confusion that surrounds and constitutes us. From this need there sometimes springs what has been called "the idealising project of knowledge,

---

3   Michael Oakeshott, *Experience and Its Modes* (Cambridge, 1933), p. 9; Stanley Hauerwas, *The Peaceable Kingdom* (Notre Dame, 1983), xxi.

the effort to unify ever more particulars under ever more powerful sub-
sumptive formulas."[4] And so, in quest of clarity and control, in search of
the heart of the matter, we construct ever more general and abstract categories of description.

Pursuing this quest single-mindedly, moving ever further from the thick
unlit undergrowth of unique concrete particulars (*this* fact, *this* feeling, *this*
flower, *this* person), up through ever broader reaches of classification, we
come at last to those uplands of comprehensive description (where the air
may be rarefied but the view, we hope, impressive) which some have
thought to constitute the territory of philosophy or metaphysics or (perhaps) theology. Here all the talk is not of individual things but of "individuals," not of particular statements made on specific occasions but of
"truth" and "meaning," not of what I did on Wednesday or what happened
to Napoleon but of "experience."

On this account (and I hope that those of you with philosophical interests will forgive the crudeness of the caricature), proper names pick out
individuals, particular discourses deal with particular areas of reality
(some large, some small: the language of cooking covers a wider territory
than the language of baking; "science" is a more comprehensive category
than that of "subatomic particle physics"), whereas "philosophy" furnishes us with completely general descriptions of the whole of reality
or, at least, of its most fundamental features. "Metaphysics," said James,
means "the discussion of various obscure, abstract, and universal questions . . . relating to the whole of things, or to the ultimate elements
thereof."[5]

Thus it is that, insofar as we are bent upon the "idealising project of
knowledge," we may be tempted to suppose that it is by abstract argument
that we get to the heart of the matter, that we discover and lay hold of
deepest truth (perhaps even, in the limit, of the truth of God). Against
such pretension, such imperialism of mind, with its implicit underesti-
mation of the significance and value of concrete particulars in all their
bewildering and irreducible diversity, the empiricist raises the cry: "back
to the facts." Or if he is, as William James described himself (for reasons
that we shall consider in due course), a "radical empiricist," then the cry
takes the form: "back to experience." Not, be it noted, back to an *account*
of experience, but back to the real thing. And here we come up against a
difficulty.

The empiricist urges us to eschew speculation, to keep close to the facts,

---

4 Henry Staten, *Wittgenstein and Derrida* (Oxford, 1985), p. 24.

5 James, *Some Problems*, p. 21.

to have our sights set on experience itself, and not to go wandering off, beyond the limits of what we can feel, and touch, and test, into the dreamlands of unchecked imagination. Sensible advice but, in order either to issue or to accept it, there must be some indication of what is to count as "fact" or as "experience." It seems, in other words, as if some general account of human experience is necessary even for those who would pursue a policy of refraining from unwarranted speculation concerning the "nature" of such experience. But what kind of an account might it be? There are at least two different answers that could be given to this question.

Some nouns are names of things. Because of this familiar fact, we may be misled, by the very form of our language, into supposing that to every noun or substantive there corresponds some substance or class of substances, some kind of thing. We do not always fall into this trap. Nobody, I imagine, supposes there to be red admirals and cabbage whites and *also* butterflies (I mean: butterflies which would be butterflies of no particular kind, but *simply* butterflies). Nor do we suppose that "butterflyness," whatever it is that makes a butterfly to be a butterfly and not a beetle, is a kind of stuff of which butterflies are composed. But the discourse of some philosophers concerning "being" or "time" does sometimes give the impression that they suppose there to be some kind of thing, some kind of stuff, which Time or Being is. It is as if the language of philosophy described some "layer" of reality to which only philosophers have access.

We might suppose that our sensible empiricist would not suffer from any such illusion. And yet, where the characterization of human existence is concerned, it is by no means only the "idealists" who sometimes speak as if "mind" or "feeling" or "experience" were the names of entities or kinds of things. Or, to be a little more precise, both empiricists and idealists often speak as if the mind were a kind of thing, and thinking and feeling the names of distinct activities in which this thing from time to time engaged. Some philosophers, caught in this trap, expend much energy attempting to isolate the essence of "pure" thinking or "raw" experience in somewhat the same way as a chemist seeks to isolate an element in its pure form, free from all impurities and all combination with other elements.

We shall have ample opportunity to consider these matters in due course. For the time being, I shall simply assert that any general account of human experience is mistaken, bewitched by the form of our language, if it proceeds on the supposition that there is any such thing as experience. There is no such thing, and hence there is no such thing as pure or raw experience, any more than there is any such thing as pure or raw size or quantity or color.

What alternative view of the matter is available to us? We must, I think, begin by insisting that those concepts which most fascinate philosophers are not the names of *parts* or *slices* of reality. The philosopher is not a kind of scientist. There is no species on which he is the expert, no class of entities about which he has more information than the rest of us. His special interest is with the uses of language, with the ways in which, in conversation, we seek to find ourselves, find each other, and find our way around.

To this kind of account it is sometimes objected that the questions to which philosophers address themselves concern matters of much greater moment than "mere" language. This seems to be true. Peacemaking is certainly not a matter of mere words. It strenuously engages the practical energies of politicians and diplomats, friends and neighbors, parents and priests. Nevertheless, in all their efforts, they will spend much time talking and (it is to be hoped) some time thinking. And if there is a *philosophical* contribution to be made to the making of peace, it will occur through clarifying and purifying the conversation. The objection against the view that philosophy is concerned with language sometimes springs from the mistaken assumption that language is a kind of window through which we look out upon the world. (If it were, then perhaps the philosopher would be a kind of window cleaner, but the metaphor is profoundly misleading.) The words we use—the stories we tell, the images and arguments we entertain—are instruments. They are the specifically human instruments by means of which the kind of animals that we are go about their tasks, construct their relationships, make and destroy the sense and significance of their world. Language, we might say, is always much more than a matter of "mere" words.

Although the flourishing of departments of philosophy, and the obscure technicality of much philosophical discourse, may give a contrary impression, I am almost inclined to say that philosophers have no expertise except disciplined attentiveness and somewhat suspicious curiosity. They may be industrious but theirs is a service industry. They conquer no new territories and fashion no new products. All that philosophers (and, I would argue, theologians) have to work on is other people's conversation.

I have often quoted the definition I once heard offered, by Gerald O'Collins, of the theologian as someone who "watches his language in the presence of God." The philosopher, then, would be someone who watches his language in the presence of other people (which, of course, the theologian should also do). It may seem a small thing to do, but language is an instrument of power, and we would be rash to assume that such watchfulness has nothing to contribute, albeit indirectly, to human flourishing and human freedom. (Totalitarian governments know this, and therefore make a habit of locking up philosophers, along with poets and novelists.) Philosophy does have its uses.

Caught in a web of words, and making some contribution to the clarification and healing of our discourse, it is not surprising that philosophy makes such progress as it does through criticism and disciplined disagreement. The disputes in which philosophers are engaged turn not on questions of empirical fact but on questions concerning the appropriateness and adequacy of the ways in which we use those concepts which form the "framework" of our conversation, concepts which crop up in the course of discussion of almost any subject matter whatsoever, concepts (and the list is endless) such as mind and matter, proof and discovery, good and evil, form and thing, understanding, emotion—and experience.

William James was resolutely opposed to the "idealising project of knowledge," which he took to be the expression, as disastrous in practice as it was mistaken in theory, of a particular temperament or felt need. "It is far too little recognized," he wrote in one of his earliest philosophical essays, "how entirely the intellect is built up of practical interests." Thus, for those people driven by a passion for comprehensive simplification, "more universality or extensiveness is . . . one mark which the philosopher's conceptions must possess. Unless they apply to an enormous number of cases they will not bring him relief."[6] The pursuit of such "extensiveness" leads not simply to the dissociation of concepts from the experience which gave them birth but to the substitution of the abstractness of the conceptual for the concreteness of particular experience. Thus it is that "the intellectual life of man" comes to consist "almost wholly in his substituting a conceptual order for the perceptual order in which his experience originally comes."[7]

There is, however, an alternative project, expressive of a different temperament (though the two impulses may be at odds within the individual): "alongside this passion for simplification there exists a sister passion, which in some minds . . . is its rival. This is the passion for distinguishing; it is the impulse to be *acquainted* with the parts rather than to apprehend the whole. . . . A man's philosophic attitude is determined by the balance in him of these two cravings." Empiricism is the philosophical expression of the second of these two impulses: "Empiricism means the

---

6 William James, *The Works of William James: The Will to Believe and Other Essays in Popular Philosophy*, ed. Burkhardt, Bowers, and Skrupskelis, introd. Edward H. Madden (Cambridge, Mass., 1979), pp. 72, 59.

7 *Some Problems*, p. 33.

habit of explaining wholes by parts, and rationalism means the habit of explaining parts by wholes."[8]

As his thinking developed, however, James came to believe that traditional empiricism fell as thoroughly as monistic idealism into the "intellectualist" trap of attempting "to understand solely in terms of discrete and static concepts the continuity of change in the perceptually given."[9] Hence the "radical empiricism" which he came to espouse embodied his effort to sustain "acquaintance" with the originating flow of "pure" experience.

I have been trying to indicate how it is that resistance to the "idealising project of knowledge" may take at least two very different forms. James would, I think, have found entirely uncongenial my suggestion that the philosopher's task is "grammatical," is an observing and unraveling of the diversity of discourse and of the pitfalls into which language leads us. He would have regarded any linguistic description of the philosopher's task as liable to lead us straight back down the road into the aridities of intellectualism (and it would be difficult to deny that this suspicion has, only too often, proved well founded). He brushed aside, for example, the suggestion that metaphysical problems "result from a misuse of terms in stating them. 'Things' . . . either are or not composed of one stuff."[10] Are we to take this startlingly crude and confused expression of impatience as indicative of the fact that James did, after all, suppose philosophical disputes to turn on questions of empirical fact?

(This question is surprisingly difficult to answer. When A. D. Lindsay reviewed *Some Problems of Philosophy,* he complained that James, by offering three not obviously compatible accounts of what he took philosophy to be, and then proceeding to discuss metaphysical problems in a manner which seemed to correspond to only one of them, had left the nature of philosophy "singularly indefinite." And the introduction to the Harvard edition admits that Lindsay's points "seem well taken.")[11]

---

8 *The Will to Believe,* p. 59; *The Works of William James: A Pluralistic Universe,* ed. Burkhardt, Bowers, and Skrupskelis, introd. Richard J. Bernstein (Cambridge, Mass., 1977), p. 9; see also *Some Problems,* p. 24.

9 Peter H. Hare, "Introduction" to *Some Problems,* xxv.

10 James, *Some Problems,* p. 22.

11 A. D. Lindsay, review of William James, *Some Problems of Philosophy, The Hibbert Journal* 10 (1912): 490; Hare, "Introduction" to *Some Problems,* xxxvi. In the course of his attempt to unravel the ambiguities in James's account of the relationships between philosophy and science, Lindsay insisted that "metaphysics is not a separate science just because it is concerned with the results and assumptions of all the sciences" (491).

It is, moreover, worth noticing that, according to one of the accounts picked out by Lindsay, philosophy would be a collective name for questions that have not been answered satisfactorily enough for the answers to become special sciences. He presumably had in mind a passage such as the following: "As fast as questions got accurately answered, the answers were called 'scientific,' and what men call 'philosophy' today is but the residuum of questions still unanswered. At this very moment we are seeing two sciences, psychology and general biology, drop off from the parent trunk and take independent root as specialties." We are, I think, entitled to suspect that James was tempted to suppose that it was the philosopher's business to become an expert on those districts of our experience which no science has yet succeeded in bringing under control. And perhaps, among such districts, would be that which he described as "religious" experience. Hence his hope, expressed in *The Varieties of Religious Experience,* that philosophy might yet make itself "enormously useful" by transforming itself into a "science of religions."[12]

It is not, therefore, entirely surprising that, when supplying a definition of "experience" for a dictionary, James should have done so in terms which suggest that there is a condition or state of affairs, appropriately described as "raw" experience (with which it is, perhaps, the philosopher's task more closely to "acquaint" us).[13]

It is time to take stock. James's writings on experience in general, and on religious experience in particular, undoubtedly embody a general account of human experience. As a result of his lifelong struggle against "intellectualisms" of every kind, it is an account according to which (as we shall see in more detail in later chapters) *experience* is systematically contrasted with *thought.* It is, moreover, an account the broad outlines and texture of which have found widespread acceptance and are taken more or less for granted in a great deal of the literature on "religious" experience. In taking James's treatment of religious experience as my starting point, therefore, and in offering a by no means entirely unsympathetic critique of that treatment, I hope to provide the elements for a set of proposals

---

12 James, *Some Problems,* p. 12; see *Varieties,* p. 359.

13 "Psychic or mental: the entire process of phenomena, of present data considered in their raw immediacy, before reflective thought has analysed them into subjective and objective aspects or ingredients . . . if experience be used with either an objective or a subjective shade of meaning, then question-begging occurs, and discussion grows impossible" (William James, "'Experience': from Baldwin's *Dictionary,*" *The Works of William James: Essays in Philosophy,* ed. Burkhardt, Bowers, and Skrupskelis [Cambridge, Mass., 1978], p. 95).

concerning the ways in which we might put the notion of experience to rather different use.

It seems to me that a different way of talking about these things, even if we arrive at it indirectly by offering some *resistance* to that view of the matter of which James was so distinguished a spokesman, might be said to constitute a general account of human experience. It will be an account that is formal, heuristic, grammatical in character, and will therefore not, I hope, suck us back into the illusory expectation, characteristic of some forms of the "idealising project of knowledge," that you, or I, or anybody else, could sit in an armchair and announce to other people what their experience is, or should be, like. "Intellectualism in the vicious sense began when Socrates and Plato taught that what a thing really is, is told us by its definition."[14] Taking the world of William James as our starting point should at least offer us some protection against falling into that trap.

There is, however, still one more preliminary task to be performed, and it is that of considering how James's texts are to be taken in a book which, as I have said, is not *about* either him or his work.

---

14   James, *A Pluralistic Universe*, p. 99.

3

Reading
William James

Why was it the varieties of religious *experience* on which James chose to concentrate in his Gifford Lectures? The beginning and the end of the book suggest two rather different (but not necessarily incompatible) answers to this question.

In the first lecture, the decision is explained in terms of competence. "As regards the manner in which I shall have to administer this lectureship, I am neither a theologian, nor a scholar learned in the history of religions, nor an anthropologist. Psychology is the only branch of learning in which I am particularly versed. . . . If the enquiry be psychological, not religious institutions, but rather religious feelings and religious impulses must be its subject."[1] And because, as we shall see, he supposes feeling to be the very heart and essence of personal experience, therefore it is of religious experience that he will treat.

Toward the end of the book, in the lecture on "Philosophy," a somewhat different reason is suggested. There, at one point, he characteristically inveighs against an "intellectualism" which "assumes to construct religious objects out of the resources of logical reason alone, or of logical reason drawing rigorous inference from non-subjective facts." Such intellectualism, finding feeling too varied, too subjective, too evanescent, to furnish secure foundations for religious truth, seeks such foundations in abstract argument, for the deliverances of which its proponents claim "objective," universal significance. But such claims, according to James, are manifestly preposterous. In spite of all the talk of absolute truth, of objectivity and universal import, philosophy "does not banish differences; it founds

---

1   William James, *The Varieties of Religious Experience*, p. 12.

schools and sects just as feeling does." In fact, "the logical reason of man operates . . . in this field of divinity exactly as it has always operated in love, or in patriotism, or in politics. . . . It finds arguments for our conviction. . . . It hardly ever engenders it; it cannot now secure it."[2]

This passage suggests that James has an interest in the banishing of differences and the founding of conviction, and that he supposes intellectualism to be, because divisive, antagonistic to this interest.

A few pages later, stepping up the polemic, he takes as a specimen of intellectualism the treatment of God's "metaphysical" (as distinct from his "moral") attributes in "the orthodox philosophical theology of both Catholics and Protestants": attributes such as the divine necessity, simplicity, omnipresence, and omniscience. "What seriousness," he asks, "can possibly remain in debating philosophic propositions that will never make an appreciable difference to us in action?" For example: "what specific act can I perform in order to adapt myself the better to God's simplicity?" Taking it as self-evident that this question requires no answer he asks, of the philosophical or systematic theologians: "What is their deduction of these metaphysical attributes but a shuffling and matching of pedantic dictionary-adjectives, aloof from morals, aloof from human needs . . . verbality has stepped into the place of vision, professionalism into that of life. . . . What keeps religion going is something else than abstract definitions and systems of concatenated adjectives, and something different from faculties of theology and their professors."[3]

I have quoted this passage at some length for two reasons. In the first place, the sheer verve of the polemic suggests that James's hostility to intellectualism lay deeper than mere disapproval of methodological error. If he sought, in these lectures, to provide the outlines of a "scientific" treatment of religious experience, he did so, at least in part, it would seem, because he saw himself as spokesman and apologist for a practical religiousness which, as living, visionary, engaged with issues of ethics and the meeting of human needs, could fulfil a socially integrative function for which academic theology was singularly ill fitted. In the second place, my impression is that the majority of those who, today, show the greatest interest in matters of religion and religious experience, are likely to find the passage most congenial, and might be surprised to discover that so contemporary a voice speaks from nearly a hundred years ago.

---

2 Ibid., pp. 342, 344, 344–45.

3 Ibid., pp. 349, 350, 352, 352. Or (regarding the last point) as he put it some years later, in his Hibbert Lectures: "Think of german books on *religions-philosophie*, with the heart's battles translated into conceptual jargon" (*A Pluralistic Universe*, p. 14).

James, in other words, wears well. This is borne out, from a different point of view, by a recent study in the sociology of religion. Taking as data the extensive correspondence received by Bishop John Robinson after the publication of *Honest to God,* it examines the varieties of conventional religion in Britain, grouped according to "cognitive styles," that is to say, according to the writers' different accounts of what they took being a religious believer to mean. The sociologist who uses live interviews is faced with the problem that the answers received will be shaped by the questions that are put. The effect may often be to exclude views which those who hold them deem to be "religious," and to make it appear as if the patterns of believing fit quite closely to the inquirer's expectations. And yet, says Towler, "if people who think of themselves as 'religious' . . . hold these views, it is for sociologists to ensure that they do not measure religiousness in such a way as to exclude these people."[4]

According to Towler, "a research method does indeed exist" which goes some way to overcoming this difficulty, and yet "it has been used only rarely in the social scientific study of religion. Its first and most distinguished use was in *The Varieties of Religious Experience,*" which he has taken as a "model," and which he believes to have dated "hardly at all." The feature of James's method which Towler found especially praiseworthy was his use of "documentary material as his data,"[5] because the use of such material prevents the sociologist's questions from exercising undue influence upon the shaping of the replies.

If it is true that James originated so enduringly fruitful a method for the scientific study of religion, this would seem to be yet another good reason for taking his lectures as a way into our topic. And yet, Towler seems to me to praise James for executing a project which he did not undertake. James did, it is true, rely on documentary material, but it was carefully chosen from "literature produced by articulate and fully self-conscious men," people who were "most accomplished in the religious life and best able to give an intelligible account of their ideas and motives." This selection is justified on the grounds that, "interesting as the origins and early stages of a subject always are, yet when one seeks earnestly for its full significance, one must always look to its more completely evolved and perfect forms."[6]

---

4 Robert Towler, *The Need for Certainty: A Sociological Study of Conventional Religion* (London, 1984), p. 37. Towler finds five "cognitive styles," of which the keynotes are hope, assurance, trust, knowledge, and the cherishing of received tradition; see pp. 31, 47, 66, 78, 83.

5 Ibid., pp. 10, 18, 11.

6 James, *Varieties,* p. 12.

James, as we have seen, had little patience with intellectualist assertations of objectivity. Not that he was simply hostile to philosophy: "If she [philosophy] will abandon metaphysics and deduction for criticism and induction, and frankly transform herself from theology into science of religions, she can make herself enormously useful." And he had no doubt that such a science would be, in principle, "impartial."[7] But is not an impartiality secured through so selectively evolutionary an account of what constitutes religion's accomplishment and most perfect forms as questionable as the theoretical objectivity which he excoriated?

That question would not, I think, have greatly troubled James, because the impartiality that he sought was practical rather than theoretical in character. He strenuously resisted the suggestion that scientific or philosophical positions were, or could ever be, value- or interest-neutral. "To speak more seriously," he wrote on one occasion, "the one *fundamental* quarrel Empiricism has with Absolutism is over the repudiation by Absolutism of the personal and aesthetic factor in the construction of philosophy." Philosophers, in other words, have interests, commitments, and agendas, whether or not they acknowledge the fact. If he so frequently focused his polemic on the illusory conviction—characteristic of so much "absolutism," idealism, or intellectualism—that the philosopher, the exponent of "pure reason," has *no* interests and *no* agenda save only the pursuit of "pure truth," he did so, in part, because he believed that these delusions of rationalism were merely the mask for an underlying, unacknowledged, and socially corrosive skepticism.[8]

The impartiality that he sought, therefore, whether in science or philosophy, would be that of a method or perspective which, being sufficiently generous, flexible, provisional, and open-textured to accommodate the broadest possible spectrum of interests and points of view, could contribute to the healing of a social fabric threatened by the factionalism and mistrust which skepticism so insidiously reinforced.

James was not alone in his conception of the philosopher's task. Accord-

---

7 Ibid., pp. 359, 402.

8 William James, *The Works of William James: Essays in Radical Empiricism,* ed. Burkhardt, Bowers, and Skrupskelis, introd. John J. McDermott (Cambridge, Mass., 1976), p. 143. "His antipathy toward skepticism is everywhere evident in *The Will to Believe.* The skeptic in ethics, religion, and human agency may well think that his views, in contrast to those of his fellow philosophers, are objective and scientifically rigorous in their conclusions. James argued, to the contrary, that personal and volitional elements are never wholly absent from anyone's thought" (Edward H. Madden, "Introduction" to James, *The Will to Believe,* xxxviii). Madden goes on to point out, however, that James was equally averse to credulity and that, if he "suffered from anything it was from incredulity rather than credulity. . . . On the whole, James gives the appearance of never having been *quite* sure about anything" (xxxviii).

ing to one commentator, he and his colleagues at Harvard (especially Josiah Royce) "simply assumed that exemplifying republican virtues, especially the virtue embodied in the nation's motto, *e pluribus unum,* was one of their role-specific duties. Such virtues were, at least with James and Royce, religiously felt aspirations." For both men, "religious thought was a kind of socially responsible thought. They engaged in it in order to clarify, among other things, certain duties that everybody owed American society. They saw intellectual statesmanship as a realistic sort of social work, one that could contribute to society's betterment or to the realization of its objectives."[9]

Why, then, was it the varieties of religious experience on which James chose to concentrate in his Gifford Lectures? We are now in a position to see how the two answers indicated at the beginning of this chapter come together. Concepts divide, experience unites. Or, as he put it in a passage which we shall consider in due course: "When we survey the whole field of religion, we find a great variety in the thoughts that have prevailed there; but the feelings . . . are almost always the same."[10] It is hardly surprising that a thinker with James's view of the philosopher's social role should have taken the "varieties of religious experience" to be a most promising field of study.

James's treatment of religion (as of much else) is notoriously individualistic. Almost without exception, he treats of religion as an affair of the private heart. It would, however, for reasons that I have just indicated, be a mistake to suppose that he therefore regarded it as an "asocial concern."[11] His treatment of religion is part and parcel of an overall project which he himself believed to be "essentially a social philosophy, a philosophy of 'co,' in which conjunctions do the work."[12]

There may well be inconsistencies and incoherences here which will require identifying and unraveling as we proceed. But Levinson's remarks on the climate of Harvard philosophy serve as a reminder that, even though it is not my intention to undertake a historical study of James's thought, it is necessary to pay *some* attention to the context in which our text was produced if that text is not to be (perhaps quite seriously) misread.

The same point can be made in more Jamesian terms. For the purposes of this study, my interest is not in James's "experience," but in his

---

9 Henry Samuel Levinson, "Religious Criticism," *Journal of Religion* 64 (1984): 41, 42.

10 James, *Varieties,* p. 397.

11 A point made by Levinson, "Religious Criticism," p. 38.

12 James, *Essays in Radical Empiricism,* p. 99.

"thought" as that thought found expression in a particular text. But to proceed as if the text could be read in complete abstraction from the experiential context in which it was produced would be to give an idealist or intellectualist reading of a text which sought to subvert the pretensions of intellectualism.

It is all of a piece with James's attempted subversion of intellectualist strategies that he is quite extraordinarily difficult to read. That may seem a perverse observation on the work of one who was not only a master of style but who sought to present even the most technical and obscure philosophical problems freshly, concretely, accessibly. The difficulty that I have in mind, however, arises not from undue technicality but from other factors.

In the first place, James is forever coaxing his reader not so much to accept the conclusions of an argument (for any intellectualist may have *this* aim in view!), but rather to come to *see* things in a particular way. "A man's vision," he once wrote, "is the great fact about him." Commenting on this passage, Richard Bernstein insists that "we must take the metaphor of vision quite seriously, especially that sense of vision in which we are aware that what we see—what falls within our field of vision—is more than we can articulate or capture in our conceptual schemes." Hence John McDermott's suggestion that "James's radical empiricism is as much an aesthetic as it is a metaphysics or an epistemology." But, speaking for myself (and for whom else should I speak?), it is much easier to quarrel with an argument than to take issue with a "view." [13]

A second factor making for difficulty arises from the first. There is a great deal of sheer carelessness and imprecision in James's writings. I have much sympathy with Durkheim's caustic comment, in notes to a lecture delivered in 1914, that "what is really characteristic of [Jamesian pragmatism] is an impatience with any rigorous intellectual discipline." James might, of course, reply that this criticism rests upon the assumption that what is to *count* as intellectual discipline is to be decided on rationalist or

---

13 James, *A Pluralistic Universe*, p. 14; Richard J. Bernstein, "Introduction" to *A Pluralistic Universe*, xiii; John J. McDermott, "Introduction" to *Essays in Radical Empiricism*, xlvii. Or, as A. J. Ayer put it: "it would seem that he always had a tendency to look upon philosophy as expressing some general attitude toward the world rather than as seeking and if possible advancing the correct solution to a special set of problems" ("Introduction" to William James, *Pragmatism and the Meaning of Truth* [Cambridge, Mass., 1978], xiv). However, Ayer's (empiricist) distinction between (subjective) "attitudes" and "correct solutions" is perhaps too sharp. On John Henry Newman's notion of "taking a view" as a metaphor, not entirely unlike James's "vision," for an entire educational and intellectual strategy, see Nicholas Lash, "How Do We Know Where We Are?" *Theology on the Way to Emmaus*, pp. 62–65; *Newman on Development* (London, 1975), pp. 34–38, 164–66.

intellectualist criteria. However, even when due allowance has been made for the fact that accuracy, rigor, and discipline may take many different forms, the fact remains that James's admirers have often been nearly as exasperated as his critics by an insouciance in argument that is at least partly explained by the greater store he set on "vision." If we take these two factors together we can see why it should have been said that "radical empiricism's surprising answer" to the tradition of the Cartesian quest for "clear and distinct ideas" (whether in its idealist or empiricist forms) "was, in effect, to praise confusion."[14]

The preference for vision, however, is only a partial explanation of the imprecision because, in the third place, much of the muddle and inconsistency comes from the attempt to combine a sustained attack on particular philosophical positions with a refusal to mount that attack *from* any consistently held or clearly delineated theoretical standpoint (lest the critic of intellectualism should be found guilty of mounting an intellectualist attack).[15] For example, he will sometimes, for a particular purpose, adopt a position which he would, for the most part, have been quite unwilling to endorse. Thus Charlene Seigfried, acknowledging that the Cartesian dualism of *The Principles of Psychology* was "an advertised stratagem, not a conviction," comments: "As is so often the case, James resolutely adopts a position in order to carry out a project that his other methodological principles contradict. The result is ambiguity, if not downright confusion."[16] Such tactics do not make William James an easy man to read.

"I feel," complained James of one of his critics, "as if Mr. Joseph almost pounced on my words singly, without giving the sentences time to get out of my mouth."[17] I earlier acknowledged that, even though it is not my intention to undertake a historical study of James's thought, it is nonetheless necessary to be aware of the context in which he worked. Similarly, even though my interest, in the next few chapters, is in *The Varieties of Religious Experience,* as a powerful and lucid expression of a "view" of religious experience and the knowledge of God with which I wish to take

---

14 Emile Durkheim, *Pragmatism as Sociology,* ed. and introd. John Allcock, trans. J. C. Whitehouse (Cambridge, 1983), p. 64; William Dean, "Radical Empiricism and Religious Art," *Journal of Religion* 61 (1981): 169.

15 The distinction between this and the previous point is, perhaps, a fine one. The two issues are clearly closely connected, but there is a difference between the imprecision that results from a suspicion of premature clarity and the inconsistency that results from the attempt to avoid putting all his eggs into any one theoretical basket.

16 Charlene Haddock Seigfried, "The Positivist Foundation in William James's *Principles,*" *Review of Metaphysics* 38 (1984): 581.

17 James, *Essays in Radical Empiricism,* p. 128.

issue, it will be necessary to pay some attention to James's philosophy as a whole, if the argument of this particular text is not to be misrepresented. I may, from time to time, "pounce" on particular passages, but I shall try not to do so without giving the sentences of their larger context in his thought time to get out of his mouth.

According to Grace Jantzen, the fundamental premise of Leszek Kolakowski's study of *Religion* is that "human persons are not first of all intellectual creatures who map out an intelligible universe and only then begin to act in it and experience it." James would have wholeheartedly approved of this sentiment, and so do I. And a certain shared antipathy to the ravages wrought by what he called intellectualism may help me to consider with some sympathy a text which, in so many ways, I find profoundly uncongenial. In common with many of our contemporaries, James was fascinated by "religion," took no great interest in any particular religion, more or less ignored the New Testament, and took it for granted that (what he took to be) orthodox Christian belief had been rendered "obsolete" by "the vast vistas which scientific evolutionism has opened, and the rising tide of social democratic ideals." To be polemical, we might say that James regarded as almost pure gain what Hegel (of whom James most heartily disapproved) admirably regarded as pure loss: the "shriveling" of religion to "simple feeling, into a contentless elevation of spirit into the eternal." [18]

---

18 Leszek Kolakowski, *Religion* (London, 1982); Grace M. Jantzen, "'Religion' Reviewed," *Heythrop Journal* 26 (1985): 24; James, *A Pluralistic Universe*, p. 18; Georg Wilhelm Friedrich Hegel, *Lectures on the Philosophy of Religion*, vol. 1, *Introduction and the Concept of Religion*, ed. Peter C. Hodgson (Berkeley, 1984), p. 103. James's "view of orthodox theism was actually articulated through study of fairly progressive Old School Presbyterians like McCosh, who accepted a form of the doctrine of evolution. His familiarity with sectarian [i.e., denominational] Christianity was limited to an intimate acquaintance with a kind of religious *thought:* to wit, Calvinism underpinned by Scottish or Common-Sense Realism, already accommodating itself to Darwin's century" (Henry Samuel Levinson, *The Religious Investigations of William James* [Chapel Hill, N.C., 1981], p. 15).

4

What Did James Try to Do?

Just over a year before beginning the Gifford Lectures, James described to a friend the task that he had set himself: "*First,* to defend (against all the prejudices of my class) 'experience' against 'philosophy' as being the real backbone of the world's religious life—I mean prayer, guidance, and all that sort of thing immediately and privately felt, as against high and noble general views of our destiny and the world's meaning; and *second,* to make the hearer or reader believe, what I invincibly do believe, that, although all the special manifestations of religion may have been absurd, (I mean its creeds and theories), yet the life of it as a whole is mankind's most important function. A task well-nigh impossible, I fear, and in which I shall fail, but to attempt it is *my* religious act."[1]

Why should he have supposed the life of religion as a whole to be "mankind's most important function"? The answer is, in part, personal. His hostility to skepticism was no merely academic matter. He had, for long periods, experienced skepticism's seductive power, had lived in the darkness of a pessimism that drew him near despair. "Pessimism," he told the Harvard YMCA in 1895, "is essentially a religious disease" and, in the same address, he characterized "speculative melancholy" as "the sick shudder of the frustrated religious demand."[2] How, then, might that demand appropriately be met? Or, more precisely, what indirect contribution to the meeting of that demand might be made by a Harvard professor of psychology turning philosopher?

---

1   William James, *The Letters of William James,* ed. Henry James (Boston, 1920), 1:127, cited in Henry Samuel Levinson, *Religious Investigations,* pp. 67–68.

2   William James, "Is Life Worth Living?" *The Will to Believe,* pp. 40, 42.

The task that he set himself, in the words of one commentator, was to show: "first, that religion began in despair; second, that it was sustained through encounter with divinity; third, that divine encounter was a non-logical process which restored melancholics to vital emotionality; and fourth, that with such restoration came saintliness or the sort of sociality that exemplified the kingdom of heaven on earth." With this aim in view, James, the philosopher, "turned to a task few religious philosophers have attempted, the study of religion itself."[3] My aim in this chapter is to indicate the strategy that he employed in order to execute his project.

It is hardly surprising that a late nineteenth-century savant with a temperamentally deep-seated passion for the "piecemeal" and particular should have had an almost unbounded enthusiasm for science. But the very empiricism which led him to prefer inductive procedures to intellectualist deductive generalization also rendered him profoundly hostile to the "scientism" that was so prevalent at the time. In other words, he refused to acknowledge the legitimacy of the contention that natural-scientific description and explanation alone could furnish us with true or "objective" accounts of reality, and that religion, or art, or morality, were merely matters of taste, of "subjective" preference, with no real claim to be able to show how things truly are.

"To be radical," he wrote in 1904, "an empiricism must neither admit into its constructions any element that is not directly experienced, nor exclude from them any element that is directly experienced." Hence, "any kind of relation experienced must be accounted as 'real' as anything else in the system."[4] And he saw no reason why the experienced relations between religious feelings and their objects should be treated as exceptions to this rule.

The "interests" (to use his kind of term) which he invested in his project were not only personal and methodological. They were also, as I hinted in the previous chapter, ethical. We inhabit "a pluralistic, restless universe, in which no single point of view can ever take in the whole scene." To live harmoniously in such a world, "we ought . . . delicately and profoundly to respect one another's mental freedom—then only shall we bring about the intellectual republic; then only shall we have that spirit of inner toler-

---

3 Levinson, *Religious Investigations*, pp. 59, 68. There was an element of filial piety in the project. Howard Feinstein, in his study of the influence upon James of his father and grandfather, says that, after his marriage in 1874, "his task would be to explain psychological science with literary grace, while defending the meaning of religious experience (such as his father's) against the tyranny of scientific materialism" (*Becoming William James* [Ithaca, N.Y., 1984], p. 347).

4 James, *Essays in Radical Empiricism*, p. 22.

ance . . . which is empiricism's glory."[5] Dedication to the cause of that republic was, therefore, a further reason for resisting the imperialism of scientific reductionism.

At the risk of begging a number of questions that we have yet to consider, we could say, firstly, that he was convinced that it should be possible to develop as many sciences as there are classes of fact; secondly, that, especially in the years before he brought his doctrine of "radical empiricism" to full development, he was inclined to speak as if all classes of fact fall ultimately into one of two kinds—material and spiritual, outer and inner, physical and mental; thirdly, that mental or psychological facts therefore required, for their proper appreciation, their own kind of scientific treatment. In the Gifford Lectures, he sought to provide the outlines for a scientific treatment of that class of psychological facts which are appropriately described as "religious."

"I do not see," he somewhat optimistically remarked, "why a critical Science of Religion of this sort might not eventually command as general a public adhesion as is commanded by a physical science." Just as the science of optics feeds from, and is verified by, "facts experienced by seeing persons; so the science of religions would depend for its original material on facts of personal experience, and would have to square itself with personal experience through all its critical reconstructions."[6]

There are two things worth noticing about this curious analogy. In the first place, it presupposes that religious experience is such that it is enjoyed by some people and not by others, just as some people are sighted and others blind. This is why he says of his new science: "Even the personally non-religious might accept its conclusions on trust, much as blind persons now accept the facts of optics."[7] In the second place, all this large talk of "facts" uncharacteristically overlooks the implications of the fact that "personal experiences" are not repeatable in the way that optical experiments are.

"Theoretic knowledge," he was to write a few years later, "which is knowledge about things, as distinguished from living contemplation or sympathetic acquaintance with them, touches only the outer surface of

---

5 James, *The Will to Believe*, pp. 136, 33.

6 *Varieties*, pp. 359–60.

7 Ibid., p. 360. Such acceptance may be slow in coming. Blindness is both relatively infrequent and an abnormality, and the blind have better reason to accept the reported "facts" of optics than do the majority of mankind, with their "second-hand" religion, to trust the unusual experiences of those rare privileged specimens who enjoy what James calls "first-hand" religious experience: see below, chap. 5.

reality."[8] I cannot see why this externality of the theoretical should unduly trouble the student of optics but, although James would have been the first to insist that coming to know something *about* religious experience (through reading his lectures, for example) was in no way a substitute for enjoying such experience oneself, the extended quotations from personal reports of "inner" feelings which make up so much of the text of *The Varieties* are surely intended to give us some (albeit indirect) sympathetic acquaintance, not with instances of the operation of a law, but with varieties of "feeling" that lie well below the outer surface of reality.

There is, it has often been said, a powerfully existentialist element in James's thought. He was, that is to say, preoccupied, almost obsessed, by the irreducibility of particular, concrete events and experiences. But it is just this existential uniqueness of individual particulars which no science can directly apprehend. It may be possible to treat any event as an instance of the operation of certain "laws," but no formulation in terms of recurrent regularities can even begin to indicate, let alone to *grasp,* what it is that makes *this* event or experience—this meeting, this pain, this relationship, this joy, this love, this betrayal—unrepeatably, incommunicably, uniquely *itself.* To overlook this would be one way of falling into the trap of "vicious intellectualism" which, in a celebrated formula, he once defined as "the treating of a name as excluding from the fact named what the definition fails positively to include."[9]

I am not suggesting that the project of a "science of religions" was, on his view of personal experience in general and of religious experience in particular, incoherent but simply (and more cautiously) that it would be a science of a rather special kind, whose generalizations would be markedly more fragile and provisional than those of the physical sciences. James comes near to acknowledging this when, concluding the passage which contains the dubious analogy with optics, he remarks that "in the religious sphere, *in particular,* belief that formulas are true can never wholly take the place of personal experience,"[10] but the matter receives no close consideration.

If the study of religion is to be scientific, it must proceed empirically, it

---

8   James, *A Pluralistic Universe,* p. 111. We shall have occasion, in due course, to consider the implications of the fact that James sometimes treats the distinction between "knowledge about" and "knowledge by acquaintance" as if it were equivalent to a distinction between "conceptual" knowledge and "perception": see, for example, *Essays in Radical Empiricism,* pp. 27–28.

9   *A Pluralistic Universe,* p. 32.

10 *Varieties,* p. 360 (my emphasis).

must attend to the facts. James's complaint against academic theology and the philosophy of religion was that they stand too far from the facts, content to remain at the level of "high and noble general views of our destiny and the world's meaning." But those facts to which the study of religion must endeavor closely to attend are matters of intensely personal individual feeling, "immediately and privately felt." "You see now," he says in the conclusion, "why I have been so individualistic throughout these lectures, and why I have seemed so bent on rehabilitating the element of feeling in religion and subordinating its intellectual part. Individuality is founded in feeling; and the recesses of feeling, the darker, blinder strata of character, are the only places in the world in which we catch real fact in the making, and directly perceive how events happen, and how work is actually done. Compared with this world of living individualized feelings, the world of generalized objects which the intellect contemplates is without solidity or life."[11]

It should by now be clear that James's decision, announced in the first lecture, to treat of religion neither historically nor sociologically but psychologically, was grounded in his conviction that living religion is a matter of individual states of mind and their transformation, and that the facts of religious experience must, like all psychological facts, be understood on their own terms. His complaint against "scientistic" strategies of explanation was that, in seeking to account for all phenomena, including the phenomena of consciousness, not on their own terms but in terms of physical causes and antecedents, they failed to respect the facts, and hence betrayed the scientific principle of "proceeding empirically." Tactically, therefore, his objection to attempts to show that emotional states are "'nothing but' expressions of . . . organic disposition"[12] appeals to empiricist principle against what he took to be the prejudices of empiricist practice. (We shall consider, in due course, the dualism of mind and matter implicit in this technique for insulating psychological phenomena from physical explanation.)

Scientistic reductionism or, as James calls that form of it on which he concentrates his polemical fire, "medical materialism," "snuffs out Saint Teresa as an hysteric, Saint Francis of Assisi as an hereditary degenerate. George Fox's discontent with the shams of his age, and his pining for spiritual veracity, it treats as a symptom of a disordered colon." "In the natural sciences," he says, "it never occurs to any anyone to try to refute opinions by showing up their author's neurotic constitution. . . . It should

---

11 Ibid., p. 395.
12 Ibid., p. 19.

be no otherwise with religious opinions." Thus it is that, to use a favorite metaphor of his, the truth and value of religious, as of scientific opinions, is to be assessed in terms, not of their "roots," but of their "fruits." [13] It is the product, not the circumstances of its production, to which we should attend. In other words, the true meaning of religious experience is to be assessed, not in terms of the physical factors that account for its occurrence, but in terms of the *difference* that it makes to human living. [14]

The general background against which he mounted this attack was a particular reading of Darwinian evolutionism. Against the received prejudice that religion is a "mere survival" into the modern world of certain outmoded features from mankind's primitive past, he argued that, on the contrary, the "fruits" of the varieties of religious experience, the harmony and healing that they brought, were evidence of our continual adaptation to meet the needs of our environment. "In general, he pitted his own doctrine of *fit* survival against the anthropological doctrine of *mere* survival to describe and appreciate religion as a human achievement." And he manages to fit his celebration of individual genius (which, as we shall see, influences the choice of material that he considers in the lectures) into this Darwinian pattern. "The causes of production of great men lie in a sphere wholly inaccessible to the social philosopher. He must accept geniuses as data, just as Darwin accepts his spontaneous variations . . . the visible environment . . . *selects* him." He does, in a note, acknowledge that the environment "remodels" the genius, "to some degree, by its educative influence," [15] but this is not where the emphasis lies.

"All our theories are *instrumental,* are mental modes of *adaptation* to reality, rather than revelation or gnostic answers to some divinely instituted world enigma." [16] The reference to adaptation in that passage is an indication of the way in which the Darwinian strand in James's thought is interwoven with his pragmatism, on which a brief word is therefore in order at this point. To insist that thought is instrumental rather than divinatory is to place the emphasis on the testing, or working out of our ideas as a criterion of their truth (hence the emphasis on the fruits, rather than the roots, of religious experience).

The imprecision of James's language is nowhere more notoriously in

---

13   Ibid., pp. 20, 23, 25, 210–11.

14   See *Varieties,* p. 349.

15   Ibid., p. 390; Levinson, *Religious Investigations,* p. 76; James, "Great Men and Their Environment," *The Will to Believe,* p. 170 (this essay dates from 1880).

16   William James, *The Works of William James: Pragmatism,* ed. Bowers and Skrupskelis, introd. H. S. Thayer (Cambridge, Mass., 1975), p. 94.

evidence than in his discussion of the notion of truth. "The two points that do emerge quite clearly," says A. J. Ayer, "are the dependence of truth on experience and the conception of true ideas as being constantly on probation." As James put it in an essay written in 1904: "The pragmatic method starts from the postulate that there is no difference of truth that doesn't make a difference of fact somewhere." So far, so good, but, "for all his attempts to qualify them, James's use of such phrases as 'it is true because it is useful' or '"the true" is only the expedient' was unfortunate."[17]

Thus, for example, the casual assertion, in *Varieties*, that "the true is what works well, even though the qualification 'on the whole' may always have to be added" appears to express a doctrine of pure expediency. That, however, it need mean little more than a general commitment to some form of verificationism is suggested by a passage, written seven years later, in which he insists that "my account of truth is realistic, and follows the epistemological dualism of common sense." With some "reality independent of either of us, taken from ordinary social experience . . . any statement, in order to be accounted true, must agree. Pragmatism defines 'agreeing' to mean certain ways of 'working,' be they actual or potential."[18]

Ayer is, not surprisingly, on the whole sympathetic to James's pragmatism, even if the imprecision of expression irritates him. It is therefore of particular interest, for our purpose, to notice that his final judgment is that it is "only in the domain of morals and theology that the simple equation of truth and expediency for which James has been so widely criticized . . . can fairly be attributed to him." And James himself admitted that he had given "some excuse" in *Pragmatism*, for the charge of having made "the truth of our religious beliefs consist in their 'feeling good' to us, and in nothing else."[19] This is, therefore, an area to which we shall have to return when we come to consider what it might be, in James's view, for a doctrine of God to be true.

---

17 A. J. Ayer, "Introduction" to William James, *Pragmatism and the Meaning of Truth* (1978), xxiv; James, "The Experience of Activity," *Essays in Radical Empiricism*, p. 81 (cf. *Pragmatism* [1975], p. 30).

18 *Varieties*, p. 361; William James, *The Works of William James: The Meaning of Truth*, ed. Bowers and Skrupskelis, introd. H. S. Thayer (Cambridge, Mass., 1975), p. 117.

19 Ayer, "Introduction," xxx; James, *The Meaning of Truth* (1975), p. 5. Where "the domain of morals" is concerned, see Ellen Kappy Suckiel's sensible discussion in *The Pragmatic Philosophy of William James* (Notre Dame, 1982), pp. 45–68. She argues that James "takes the philosophical question, 'What is it that constitutes moral value?' and reduces it to the empirical question, 'What is it that individuals take to be valuable . . . ?' But it should be clear that this reduction is unwarranted" (p. 56).

The somewhat paradoxical character of James's project should, by now, be apparent. It is the attempt, by a philosopher, "to defend . . . 'experience' against 'philosophy'" by displaying the rich diversity of the "more completely evolved and perfect forms" of "religious feelings and religious impulses."[20] By diverting attention away from religious theories and toward religious facts, he sought to supply the elements for a science of religions which, though impartial in respect of competing religious traditions and contrasting patterns of belief, is nevertheless structured, and the selection of evidence determined, by quite specific convictions concerning the individually and socially therapeutic function of the experiences that it describes.

In the intellectual climate of the period, it was a courageously unfashionable project to undertake (going, as it did, against "all the prejudices of my class").[21] And yet, in its concern to commend the facts of religious experience through rich and varied description, its *explanatory* ambitions were, for reasons some of which I have already indicated, exceedingly modest.

In the first place, James regarded it as axiomatic that our explanatory ambitions should, in *any* field of inquiry, be restrained by acknowledgment of that richness and diversity of the facts which no theory can compass or comprehend. "Reality, life, experience, concreteness, immediacy, use what word you will, exceeds our logic, overflows and surrounds it." Because "conceptual knowledge is forever inadequate to the fulness of the reality to be known," his "science of religions . . . would forever have to confess, as every science confesses, that the subtlety of nature flies beyond it, and that its formulas are but approximations."[22]

But if there are, therefore, epistemological reasons for urging that our passion for exhaustive explanation should always be disciplined and held in check, there are also, in the second place, ontological considerations which lead to the same conclusion. Again and again, especially in his later writings, James insisted that "taken as it does appear, our universe is to a large extent chaotic." It is not *simply* chaos: there is an "evolutionary" story to be told "of how a lot of originally chaotic pure experience became gradually differentiated into an orderly inner and outer world." But this achievement is tempered with fragility: what we call "the physical world" is but the precipitate, "the stable part of the whole experience-chaos."[23]

---

20 *The Letters of William James*, 1:127; *Varieties*, p. 12.

21 *The Letters of William James*, 1:127.

22 *A Pluralistic Universe*, p. 96; *Some Problems of Philosophy*, p. 45; *Varieties*, p. 360.

23 *Essays in Radical Empiricism*, pp. 24, 18, 17.

The world, in other words, is never as tidy or controllable as exhaustive explanations of what happens and why would lead us to suppose.

It follows, therefore, in the third place, that all ethical decisions and evaluative judgments are similarly tempered by contingency. James insists on the irreducibility of judgments of fact and judgments of value, but he is equally insistent that "our only guides" in helping us to decide "that *on the whole* one type of religion is approved by its fruits, and another type condemned" will be "our general philosophic prejudices, our instincts, and our common sense."[24]

Against this background, it comes as no surprise to discover, in the fourth place, that James was at pains to emphasize the hypothetical character of all attempts to answer questions concerning "the objective 'truth'" of the "content" of the experiences that he describes. He draws a distinction (which I shall consider in the next chapter) between certain privileged recipients of such experiences and the rest of us. Thus, for example, he says that "mystical states, when well developed, usually are, and have the right to be, absolutely authoritative over the individuals to whom they come." However, "no authority emanates from them which should make it a duty for those who stand outside of them to accept their revelations uncritically." The exceptional states and unusual experiences which so fascinated James could, for those who "stand outside" them, do no more than "point in directions." But point they do: they "tell of the supremacy of the ideal, of vastness, of union, of safety, and of rest."[25] (Notice the choice of epithets.)

Religious experience thus provides not only solace but evidence, and to persuade people seriously to consider such evidence, in a cultural climate in which "the influence of science goes against the notion that religion should be recognized at all," might (or so it seemed to James) be no small achievement on the part of a science of religions. His own hypotheses concerning that in the direction of which the evidence points was in terms, firstly, of the influence of unconscious mind on conscious mental states and, secondly, of the "further" influence of "an altogether other dimension of existence from the sensible and merely 'understandable' world. Name it the mystical region, or the supernatural region, whichever you choose." And he took it for granted that this dimension, or region, this "higher part of the universe" or, as he once described it, this "superhuman con-

---

24 *Varieties*, p. 263; on the irreducibility of fact and value, see ibid., p. 13.

25 See ibid., pp. 402, 401; pp. 335, 339.

sciousness,"[26] was what Christians meant by God. Concerning this supposition, we shall have much to say in due course.

My aim in this chapter has simply been to indicate the way in which James went about the task that he had set himself in writing *The Varieties of Religious Experience*. Before moving on, however, to consider the account that he gave, in those lectures, of what it is that constitutes the "essence" of religious experience, it is necessary to say a preliminary word on a topic which will keep raising its head throughout the next few chapters, because it is quite central to my dissatisfaction with James's account. It concerns the extent to which his treatment is infected by the kind of fundamental *dualism* of mind and matter, subject and object, thought and thing, which is now commonly referred to as "Cartesian."

In his introduction to *A Pluralistic Universe*, Richard Bernstein remarked that "James sees how much of modern philosophy has been trapped within the limiting and distorting confines of Cartesian dualism. . . . This entire framework needs to be challenged and overthrown." Indeed it does, and it is clear that Bernstein believes James to have been, at least in his later work, successful: "The depth of James's criticism of the intellectualist tendency in philosophy should not be underestimated. It is nothing less than a critique of Western philosophic thought." James "turned on the vestiges of dualism in his own earlier work. He advocated a doctrine of 'pure experience' which is the basis of his radical empiricism. According to this doctrine, there is no epistemological duality between the reality known and the knowing consciousness."[27]

"The dualism of Object and Subject and their pre-established harmony are," said James in 1890, "what the psychologist as such must assume, whatever ulterior monistic philosophy he may, as an individual who has the right also to be a metaphysician, have in reserve." In other words, the psychologist has no option but to act as if "'Thoughts' and 'things' [were] names for two sorts of objects, which common sense will always find contrasted and will always practically oppose to each other." By 1904 (when he made the remark I have just quoted) he was convinced that, with the aid of the doctrine of "radical empiricism," he was well on the way to exorcising the Cartesian ghost: "If neo-Kantism has expelled earlier forms of dualism, we shall have expelled all forms if we are able to expel neo-Kantism in its turn."[28]

---

26 Ibid., pp. 386, 406; *A Pluralistic Universe*, p. 140.

27 Richard J. Bernstein, "Introduction" to *A Pluralistic Universe*, xxvi, xxiv, xxi.

28 William James, *The Works of William James: The Principles of Psychology*, ed. Burkhardt,

It is my contention, however, that the ghost is alive and well, and weaving its misleading spells, even in his last writings (and if we can find it *there*, then we shall have every reason to suspect its presence in earlier works, such as *Varieties*). According to Bernstein, "once one makes a separation between consciousness and thing, or between mind and physical reality, then one is forced to some version of the paradoxical notion of a representational theory of mind where ideas 'in' the mind are taken to represent what is 'outside' the mind." I suggest, however, that one is only so forced if one supposes the distinction between mind and matter to be an *empirical* distinction, rather than a distinction that relates to what John Searle calls "two levels of description."[29] We can go on and on discussing whether the kind of stuff that minds are made of is the same kind of stuff that other things are made of, or whether the furniture of the world is made up of one, or two, or more quite different kinds of stuff. But so long as we continue to talk (as James never ceased to do, while vigorously protesting against the implications of the habit) as if "mind" were the name of *any* kind of stuff, then our account will be threatened by the dualisms which we seek to exorcise.[30] This will especially be the case when consideration of problems of cognition is conducted under the influence of analogies of ocular vision.[31] Eyesight entails a spatial relationship between seer and seen and, under the influence of spatial imagery, the Cartesian "ego" remains the best candidate for the experiencing pole of even "pure" experience. Finally, I very much doubt whether our attempts to exorcise the

---

Bowers, and Skrupskelis (Cambridge, Mass., 1981), 1:216; *Essays in Radical Empiricism*, pp. 3, 5.

29 Bernstein, "Introduction", xxi; John Searle, *Minds, Brains and Science* (London, 1985), p. 26.

30 E.g., "there is only one primal stuff or material in the world, a stuff of which everything is composed, and . . . we call that stuff 'pure experience'" (*Essays in Radical Empiricism*, p. 4); "consciousness . . . is fictitious, while thoughts in the concrete are fully real. But thoughts in the concrete are made of the same stuff as things are" (p. 19). Andrew Reck's discussion of *The Principles of Psychology* concludes with the claim that "psycho-physical dualism remains, but it is a dualism not of substances but of processes" ("The Philosophical Psychology of William James," *Southern Journal of Philosophy* 9 [1971]: 311). Quite what we are to make of this remains unclear, however, partly because Reck seems unaware of what the clarifying questions might be, and partly because James himself never thought the issue through, remaining "troubled by the question whether there is an 'I,' a pure ego, functioning as a permanent core of unity within the 'me' and distinct from it" (Reck, 309). It is precisely because James persistently treats such questions as *empirical* in character that I feel entitled to press the charge of residual Cartesianism. Fergus Kerr's admirable study of how we might hope to do *Theology after Wittgenstein* (Oxford, 1986) places James in the anti-Cartesian camp (see pp. 5–7). It is my contention that this is where James sought to be rather than where, in the last analysis, he was.

31 See below chap. 8.

dualisms can ever be carried through from a standpoint as *individualistic* as James's always was. It is the ego, the nervous private "I," wondering whether it can find security and solace in the turbulence and untrustworthiness of our circumstance, that is at the root of the problem. And that ego will not cease to be a problem merely because it supposes itself to be, from time to time, and in certain states of excited feeling, in communion with some "superhuman consciousness" or more comprehensive ego.

5

The "Essence" Of Religious Experience

"**I** think it may be asserted," said James in 1908, "that there *are* religious experiences of a specific nature. . . . I think that they point with reasonable probability to the continuity of our consciousness with a wider spiritual environment from which the ordinary prudential man . . . is shut off." What is it about an "experience" which makes it appropriate (in James's view) to describe it as religious? If we seek for an answer to that question in James's "circumscription of the topic,"[1] we shall discover why he supposed the ordinary prudential man to be shut off from that wider environment to which religious experience may give access.

"The essence of religious experiences, the thing by which we finally must judge them, must be that element or quality in them which we can meet nowhere else."[2] That sounds sensible enough. If there were no such element or quality, then there would be no way of differentiating religious from sexual or political, philosophical or moral experience, no way of indicating what it was that we were studying in studying religious experience.

Nevertheless, the fact that everyone writing on the subject offers his or her own definition of religion, and that these definitions not only differ very widely but frequently conflict, suggests that it will be no easy matter to identify the differentiating element or quality in such a way as to win the kind of widespread acceptance which James sought for his "science of religions." He was, of course, well aware of this difficulty. The very fact that definitions of religion "are so many and so different from one another

---

1   *A Pluralistic Universe*, p. 135; see *Varieties*, pp. 30–50.

2   *Varieties*, p. 44.

is enough to prove that the word 'religion' cannot stand for any single principle or essence, but is rather a collective name."[3] As such, it functions in somewhat the same way as does (to use his own example) the concept of "government."

Definitions of government vary almost as widely as do definitions of religion, but we do not infer, from "the futility of all these definitions,"[4] that nobody knows what is meant by either government or religion, or that the decision to work with one definition rather than another is a matter of sheer prejudice or arbitrary choice. If I understand James correctly, his suggestion is that "religion," like "government" is the name of a complex object the constituent features of which may be found in varying proportion and relationship, and that the different definitions arise from selecting or emphasizing now this, now that, set of features or pattern of relationships.

One difficulty with this view of the matter, of course, is that it encourages the misleading supposition that there is some kind of entity or *thing,* albeit a complex thing, which religion or government always, or essentially is. Thus, for example, it would seem that, on James's account, questions as to whether Christianity, or Judaism, or Islam, or Buddhism, or Marxism, are or not religions would be questions of the kind to which there would be, in each case, a correct answer which could be arrived at simply by inspecting the facts of the case.[5] I would prefer to say that different definitions of religion are simply announcements of a decision to use the word in one way rather than another. Such decisions, if sensibly and responsibly taken, are not arbitrary: there will be reasons, perhaps even excellent reasons, adducible on their behalf.

However, quite apart from the fact that thus to construe the function of definition "grammatically," rather than "empirically,"[6] would go against the grain of James's philosophical style and temperament, his entire strategy for resisting scientistic attempts to explain away religion in nonreligious terms required that there should be at least some "religious facts" which were not only more or less directly observable as such, but which were best accounted for by "religious" hypotheses.

---

3 Ibid., p. 30.

4 Ibid., p. 31, n. 1.

5 For an excellent illustration of why this is not the case, see Trevor Ling, *Karl Marx and Religion: In Europe and India* (New York, 1980), pp. 154–55.

6 Here I have in mind Wittgenstein's famous remark: "*Essence* is expressed by grammar" (Ludwig Wittgenstein, *Philosophical Investigations,* ed. G. E. M. Anscombe [London, 1953], para. 371).

Thus it is that, while it may well be futile to argue about the essence of *religion* (because some people will wish to lay the emphasis upon ritual elements, for example, others upon organizational features or patterns of belief), it is far from futile to inquire as to the essence of religious *experience,* for such experiences are almost as much empirically identifiable bits of (at least some people's) human constitution as are their toes and teeth. The parallel may seem farfetched, but it is not my invention: "It is a good rule in physiology, when we are studying the meaning of an organ, to ask after its most peculiar and characteristic sort of performance, and to seek its office in that one of its functions which no other organ can possibly exert. Surely the same maxim holds good in our present quest. The essence of religious experiences . . . must be that element or quality in them which we can meet nowhere else."[7] In other words, the only accounts of religion which merit serious consideration are those which take seriously the irreducible facticity of religious experiences. Let us, therefore, now follow him as he tries to track down that element or quality in such experiences which pertains to their essence.

This element or quality cannot, he says, be found in any particular feeling, or attitude, or emotion. "There is religious fear, religious love, religious awe, religious joy, and so forth. But religious love is only man's natural emotion of love directed to a religious object . . . religious awe is the same organic thrill which we feel in a forest at twilight, or in a mountain gorge." If, then, religious experience is not specified by its subjective components, is it perhaps (in the second place) specified by its objects? Again, James's answer is no. There is no one subject or set of objects such that the experience of anyone attending to, or considering such objects, would necessarily be appropriately described as enjoying a religious experience. (This seems right, at least in the sense that, were it otherwise, the experience of any philosopher of religion, puzzling away at the question of what, for example, might be meant by "God," would necessarily qualify as religious—not, I think, a suggestion to which most philosophers of religion would take kindly.) In the third place, he suggests, without going into the matter, that there may well prove to be "no one specific and essential kind of religious act."[8]

If, however, there are no specifically religious emotions, objects, or acts, wherein does the specificity of religious experience consist? His answer is that, "as concrete states of mind, made up of a feeling *plus* a specific sort

---

7   *Varieties,* p. 44.

8   Ibid., p. 31.

of object, religious emotions of course are psychic entities distinguishable from other concrete emotions." This account is unsatisfactory for at least two reasons. In the first place, by ignoring those of our feelings that are physical sensations (such as "feeling cold"), the identification of feeling with emotion gives the impression that religious experience is exclusively a matter of *mental* states. In the second place, the suggestion that we should "treat the term 'religious sentiment' as a collective name for the many sentiments which religious objects may arouse in alternation," misleadingly suggests that human beings enjoy a certain range of feelings or emotions which are "aroused," but otherwise unaffected by, their "objects."[9]

However, even if we confine our attention to the narrow band of feelings that he has in view, it is surely the case that our feelings are specified and shaped by their objects and not simply, as it were, "triggered off" by them? Consider, for example, the intolerably abstract character of that reference to "man's natural emotion of love," as if the love of a husband for his wife, the love of rice pudding, the love of Mozart's music, the love of one's country, and the love of God, could all be said to be instances of the *same* emotion aroused by different objects. And the same goes for the other emotions that he mentions, such as the claim that "religious fear is only . . . the common quaking of the human breast, in so far as the notion of divine retribution may arouse it,"[10] as if fear of flying, fear of making a fool of oneself, fear of dentists, and "fear of the Lord," were all but instances of a "common quaking."

If it is true that our feelings are not just emotional states awaiting activation, but that their very form and character is specified by the people, situations, and circumstances to which we respond, then, as not only Proust but every novelist knows, the accurate description of someone's feelings requires a correspondingly accurate and discriminating description of whatever it was that produced, or appeared to produce, the response. Whereas when, as in James's case, feelings are thought to possess an identity of their own, in principle unspecified by their objects, the casualness of the description of the "objective" component of religious experience comes as little surprise. At the end of the day, it was the feeling and its fruitfulness, the temperature and temper of the ego when happily

---

9 Ibid., p. 31. Both these features of his account are influenced by his doctrine of "pure experience," which we shall consider in chap. 6.

10 Ibid., p. 31. The point is well made by Charles Davis, *Body as Spirit: The Nature of Religious Feeling* (London, 1976), p. 32, commenting on the passage which we are considering.

accepting nothing in particular, but just the universe, which interested him.[11] But this is to anticipate.

I see no reason to quarrel with James's insistence that the phenomenon of religion is endlessly complex, consisting, as it does, of so many diverse patterns and permutations of (in his terminology) emotions, objects, and acts. This being the case, it seems hard to quarrel with his decision to select, "for the purpose of these lectures," just one of its many aspects. The aspect selected is that of "personal religion pure and simple." In contrast both to "institutional" religion, which he proposes to ignore "entirely," and also to the realm of religious ideas (about which he will say "as little as possible"), "personal" religion consists of those acts in which, going "direct from heart to heart, from soul to soul, between man and his maker . . . the individual transacts the business by himself alone."[12]

Thus it is that the definition at which he eventually arrives of what, for his purposes, will count as religion, runs as follows: "the feelings, acts, and experiences of individual men in their solitude, so far as they apprehend themselves to stand in relation to whatever they may consider the divine."[13]

At first glance, this restriction of the subject matter is simply a matter of practical convenience, enabling him to concentrate attention on just one aspect of what he has admitted to be a much larger and more complex topic. This impression is, however, misleading. As a first step toward discovering what it was that really led him thus to confine the inquiry, let us consider his defense against the charge that "personal religion," as he has defined it, is more accurately described as conscience or morality than as religion.

He will not waste energy disputing the terminology: "I am willing to accept almost any name for the personal religion of which I propose to treat. Call it conscience or morality, if you yourselves prefer, and not religion." However, his own view is that "it will prove to contain some elements which morality pure and simple does not contain."[14]

"Religion . . . is a man's total reaction upon life," his fundamental way of being and acting in the world, "so why not say that any total reaction upon life is a religion?" We could do so if we wished, and yet there seem to be some fundamental ethical stances which it would be odd to describe

---

11 See *Varieties*, p. 41.

12 Ibid., p. 32.

13 Ibid., p. 34.

14 Ibid., p. 33.

as religious. There are, for example, "trifling, sneering attitudes even toward the whole of life," whereas, for most people, "'religion,' whatever more special meanings it may have, signifies always a *serious* state of mind." There must, he suggests, "be something solemn, serious, and tender about any attitude which we denominate religious . . . and it is precisely as being *solemn* experiences that I wish to interest you in religious experiences."[15]

Even with this specification, however, the distinction between morality and religion is not yet drawn. "At bottom the whole concern of both morality and religion," as fundamental ethical stances or orientations, "is with the manner of our acceptance of the universe." The archetype of *mere* morality, for James, is stoicism, the temper of which he illustrates by a quotation from Marcus Aurelius. Admirable and heroic it may often be, but there is, in stoicism, a certain grimness of self-reliance: "The moralist must hold his breath and keep his muscles tense." This tenseness is in contrast to another "state of mind, known to religious men, but to no others," which has acquired, from some strange source, "a new sphere of power," an energetic, joyful "happiness" or endorsement of the world. If, therefore, "religion is to mean anything definite for us, it seems to me that we ought to take it as meaning this added dimension of emotion, this enthusiastic temper of espousal, in regions where morality strictly so called can at best bow its head and acquiesce."[16] By now, the apparently spare and formal definition of religion from which we began seems to have acquired an unexpected degree of descriptive specificity.

It is worth comparing the passages just quoted with the account which James gave, a few years later, of the "specific nature" of religious experience as "experiences of a life that supervenes upon despair." The phenomenon, "familiar to evangelical Christianity . . . is that of new ranges of life succeeding on our most despairing moments." The emphasis, in these Hibbert Lectures, is on the unexpected, unpredictable character of such psychic "resurrections," such surges of emotion, power, and assurance from the depths of our darkness: "Reason, operating on our other experiences, even our psychological experiences, would never have inferred these specifically religious experiences in advance of their actual coming."[17]

Returning to the Gifford Lectures, what is the outcome of the inquiry which James undertook with the aid of his definition? It is a description of

---

15 Ibid., pp. 36, 37, 38, 39.

16 Ibid., pp. 41, 45, 46, 47.

17 *A Pluralistic Universe*, pp. 137, 138.

the essence of the religious experiences of all "those more developed minds which alone we are studying" in terms of, first, an "uneasiness" and then its "solution." The individual senses that there is "something wrong about us as we naturally stand." This wrongness may be read in moral terms, leading to the acknowledgment of guilt, but also to the recognition of helplessness. But when the second stage, "the stage of solution or salvation" arrives, the person "becomes conscious" that the "higher part" of him "is conterminous and continuous with a MORE of the same quality which is operative in the universe outside of him, and which he can keep in working touch with." Notwithstanding the degree of detail in this description of religious conversion, James claims to have shown it to be "a certain uniform deliverance in which all religions appear to meet,"[18] and *therefore* to be an account of the "essence" of human religious experience.

But what of those people (perhaps the vast majority of the human race) who have never known such experience of conversion, encounter, or release? James really was not very interested in them, and to find out why this should be so, we need to take up the clue provided by that reference to the "more developed minds which alone we are studying."

There are many ways of telling the story of modern Western religious thought. According to one way of telling it (and that by no means the least widespread or influential during the nineteenth century) it is a tale of the gradual liberation of the religious impulse from the cramped particularity of "positive" systems of belief, worship, and organization into a purer, more diffuse, and comprehensive religiousness. In some versions, the tale was thus told as a way of resisting the imperialist pretensions of that narrative of secularization according to which nothing could stop the onward march of scientific rationality in its victorious progress across all the territories previously occupied by religion, "dogma," and superstition. And the place at which religion takes its stand, and builds its redoubt, is the inmost recesses of feeling or "pure experience": "We are so subject to the philosophical tradition which treats *logos* or discursive thought generally as the sole avenue to truth, that to fall back on raw unverbalized life as more of a revealer . . . comes very hard."[19]

In spite of that reference to retreating or "falling back," James does not, for the most part, have recourse to military metaphors. He prefers the language of evolution, of religion's adaptation to meet the demands of changing circumstance. But that the broad narrative which the evolutionary images are intended to serve is along the lines sketched at the start of

18   *Varieties,* p. 400.
19   *A Pluralistic Universe,* p. 121.

the previous paragraph is clearly indicated in the lecture on "Conversion." At least "so far as the religious life is spiritual and no affair of outer works and sacraments . . . the whole development of Christianity in inwardness has consisted in little more than the greater and greater emphasis attached to this crisis of self-surrender." All the way from medieval Catholicism, through Protestantism, and then "outside of technical Christianity altogether, to pure 'liberalism' or transcendental idealism . . . we can trace the stages of progress toward the idea of an immediate spiritual help experienced by the individual in his forlornness and standing in no essential need of doctrinal apparatus or propiatory machinery." We now begin to see why those individuals in whom this "crisis" (a crisis receiving its solution in the experience of "immediate spiritual help") has found the most dramatic expression might be thought to represent the "more completely evolved and perfect forms"[20] of the religious life and, in so doing, to exhibit the "essence" of religious experience.

Even if we have only recently come to *appreciate* that such heightened states of private feeling do, in fact, constitute the true essence of religion, they are in themselves no new discovery or adaptation, but have, from earliest times, occurred and left their traces, being the hallmark of religious "genius."[21]

In religion, as elsewhere, genius held an inordinate fascination for James, who was not much interested in more humdrum personalities. The case studies, in *Varieties,* are not drawn from the ranks of "your ordinary religious believer, who follows the conventional observances of his country, whether it be Buddhist, Christian, or Mohammedan. His religion has been made for him by others, communicated to him by tradition, determined to fixed forms by imitation, and retained by habit. It would profit us little to study this second-hand religious life. We must make search rather for the original experiences which were the pattern-setters to all this mass of suggested feeling and imitated conduct. These experiences we can only find in individuals for whom religion exists not as a dull habit, but as an acute fever." Some like it hot, and James was much more interested in those "intenser experiences" that occur in "the hot place in a man's consciousness . . . the habitual center of his personal energy," and in the type of person who operates from this center at fever pitch, than he was in "the experiences of tamer minds, so cool and reasonable that we are tempted to call them philosophical rather than religious."[22]

---

20 *Varieties,* pp. 173, 12.

21 See ibid., p. 15.

22 Ibid., pp. 15, 44, 162, 44.

This preoccupation with the creativity of individual genius, with the pattern setters whose religious experience is "first-hand," leads him to say that "the *founders* of every church owed their power originally to the fact of their direct personal communion with the divine."[23] He instances Christ, Buddha, and Mohammed and (judging by references to them in other places) he probably had also in mind such people as Luther, George Fox, and John Wesley. Whatever prima facie plausibility this list might seem to give to his suggestion, its exceedingly questionable character, as a *historical* claim, may be sufficiently indicated by pointing out that there are at least some religions (Judaism and Hinduism, for example) the rise of which it fails to explain because they did not have any such individual "founder."

The more fundamental objections to the model, however, have to do with its dependence upon James's general philosophical strategy of sharply *contrasting* "feelings" with both "thoughts" and "institutions." When, in the next chapter, we examine this strategy, with its consequent equation of *personal* experience with individual emotional states,[24] we shall be in a position to ask whether the religion of the pattern setters is ever quite so creative, or that of their followers quite so entirely derivative, as the distinction between firsthand and secondhand religion would have us suppose.

The roots of the dramatic contrast between the vitality and creativity of individual genius and the uninteresting flat-footedness of the common herd are not, however, only to be sought in James's "*philosophic* prejudices," unless the notion of the philosophical is to be extended to cover general social attitudes of a remarkably unsophisticated kind. In his early essay on "Great Men and Their Environment" (1880), James defended the thesis that the "darwinian distinction" between "'spontaneous variation,'" as the producer of changed forms, and the environment, as their preserver and destroyer,"[25] holds just as much in the field of mental as of physical progress. The manner in which he does so is worth quoting at some length.

"It is one of the tritest of truisms that human intelligences of a simple order are very literal. They are slaves of habit, doing what they have been taught without variation . . . devoid of humour, except of the coarse physical kind which rejoices in a practical joke . . . possessing in their faithfulness and honesty the single gift by which they are sometimes able

---

23 Ibid., p. 33.

24 See ibid., p. 32.

25 See ibid., p. 263; *The Will to Believe*, p. 184.

to warm us into admiration. But even this faithfulness seems to have a sort of inorganic ring, and to remind us more of the immutable properties of a piece of inanimate matter than of the steadfastness of a human will capable of alternative choice."[26] James clearly did not have a very high opinion of his servants, even if their doglike devotion was occasionally capable of "warming" him into admiration.

> But turn to the highest order of minds, and what a change! Instead of thoughts of concrete things patiently following one another in a beaten track of habitual suggestion . . . we seem suddenly introduced into a seething caldron of ideas, where everything is fizzling and bobbing about in a state of bewildering activity. . . . According to the idiosyncrasy of the individual, the scintillations will have one character or another. They will be sallies of wit and humor; they will be flashes of poetry and eloquence; they will be constructions of dramatic fiction or of mechanical device, logical or philosophic abstractions, business projects, or scientific hypotheses, with trains of experimental consequences based thereon; they will be musical sounds, or images of plastic beauty or picturesqueness, or visions of moral harmony. But, whatever their differences may be, they will all agree in this—that their genesis is sudden and, as it were, spontaneous.[27]

The picture that emerges is fairly clear. That "element or quality" which constitutes "the essence of religious experiences" is to be sought in the emotional fizzling of the conversion experience of those rare specimens, the pattern setters of religion, whose genius, like that of the New England gentry and the faculty at Harvard, sets them apart from the coarsely physical unimaginative fidelity of the servants and disciples who constitute their environment. Since this is the general background against which James offers his account of what it is for human beings most fruitfully "to stand in relation to whatever they may consider the divine,"[28] the Chris-

---

26 Ibid., pp. 184–85.

27 Ibid., p. 185.

28 *Varieties*, pp. 44, 34. There was no trace of irony in the following passage, which formed part of an argument that, since "the wealth of a nation consists more than anything else in the number of superior men that it harbors" (a claim illustrated by the example of Germany) Stanford University, by paying high salaries, should attract "geniuses" to its faculty: "Geniuses are sensitive plants. . . . They have to be treated tenderly. They don't need to live in superfluity; but they need freedom from harassing care, they need books and instruments; they are always overworking, so they need generous vacations, and

tian theologian is, I think, entitled to view the entire setup with some suspicion.

"What," James once asked, "does it pragmatically mean" to say that "the salvation of the world . . . is possible? It means that some of the conditions of the world's deliverance do actually exist." Given James's particular form of social Darwinism (and however questionable that Darwinism may be, on sociological, philosophical, and theological grounds) his preoccupation with the religious experience of the pattern setters expressed his conviction that, in their experience as nowhere else, something is *done,* some contribution effectively made, toward the world's redemption.[29]

He described his position as that of a "meliorism" which stood midway between "pessimism," according to which the salvation of the world is impossible, and "optimism," according to which it is inevitable. The point is worth developing because it shows that his obsession with heightened states of religious emotion had in it something more serious than a mere hedonism of the imagination. And although the notions of "salvation" and "deliverance" with which he worked were kept studiously vague ("You may interpret the word 'salvation' in any way you like."), the general drift of his thought is not unclear.[30]

"May not religious optimism be too idyllic: Must *all* be saved? Is the last word sweet? Is all 'yes, yes' in the universe? Doesn't the fact of 'no' stand at the very core of life? . . . I am willing that there should be real losses and real losers, and no total preservation of all that is. . . . When the cup is poured off, the dregs are left behind forever, but the possibility of what is poured off is sweet enough to accept." If we set this passage alongside those that we were considering just now, then "election" and "genius" are, I think, brought into disturbingly close conjunction.[31] Nevertheless, the passage does suggest an undercurrent of Augustinian

---

above all things they need occasionally to travel far and wide in the interests of their souls' development" (William James, "Stanford's Ideal Destiny," in *Memories and Studies* [New York, 1911], pp. 363, 365–66).

29 *Pragmatism* (1975), p. 136. In the lecture on "Saintliness" he asks: "Can there in general be a level of emotion so unifying, so obliterative of differences between man and man, that even enmity may come to be an irrelevant circumstance?" If there can, then the individuals "swayed" by "so supreme a degree of excitement . . . might conceivably transform the world" (*Varieties,* pp. 228–29).

30 See *Pragmatism* (1975), p. 137.

31 Ibid., pp. 141–42. Quite how disturbingly is indicated by one commentator's straight-faced remark that "obviously, this universe [portrayed by James] is fit only for the healthy-minded. The needs of the sick soul are left out. James is not totally happy about this, but consistency demands that a choice be made in this matter" (Robert J. Vanden Burgt, *The Religious Philosophy of William James* [Chicago, 1981], p. 95).

seriousness, a capacity for entertaining the tragic, which is quite often absent from those accounts of religious experience which concentrate exclusively on the more comforting or satisfying features of the aesthetic or romantic tradition in which James stands.

I have tried, in this chapter, to provide a reasonably careful account of what it was that constituted, for James, the "essence" of religious experience. There is, however, one element in his definition which I have not yet considered and on which, therefore, some comments are in order by way of conclusion.

"When in our definition of religion we speak of the individual's relation to 'what he considers the divine,' we must interpret the term 'divine' very broadly, as denoting any object that is god*like,* whether it be a concrete deity or not." Leaving on one side the difficulty of deciding quite how "concrete" a concrete deity would have to be, what is it that renders an object "god*like,*" and thus makes it possible for an individual's apprehension of such an object to constitute an instance of religious experience? James's answer is that it is anything "primal and enveloping and real" to which "the individual feels impelled to respond . . . solemnly and gravely."[32]

Many readers, I suspect, have found the studied imprecision of James's theological descriptions attractive and appropriate. Since it is, after all, characteristic of many developed religious traditions to insist that we can more securely say what God is not than what God is, is not imprecision inevitable and accuracy unattainable? Moreover, some such descriptive vagueness will surely be required (so the argument goes) if different religious traditions, each with its own stock of memories, stories, and symbols, are to recognize in each other's patterns of belief a common human effort stammeringly to "name" the one transcendent object of their devotion and aspiration? I suggest, however, that it might be quite important sharply to distinguish, on the one hand, the insistence of the *via negativa* that the image be not taken for the reality from, on the other, a studied lack of interest in accurately naming appropriate objects of faith and worship. The *via negativa* which, as we shall see in more detail later on, is part of the attempt to discipline our propensity toward idolatry, is a very different enterprise from an eclecticism which supposes that it matters not how God is named, provided that the named object provokes us to solemn and grave response. The one tradition is sensitive to the destructive consequences of worshiping false gods; the other supposes that it matters not what you worship provided that your worship brings you peace.

---

32 *Varieties,* pp. 36, 39.

I find little evidence that James ever regarded the question of God as something which demanded serious consideration in its own right. Hence Ayer's judgment, which I quoted in the previous chapter, that, in the domain of morals and theology, the accusation of equating truth with expediency can fairly be leveled against him. My impression is that his description of a certain joyful acceptance of the universe as "religious," and his characterization as "godlike" of that sense of things which provokes such acceptance was, in part, an expression of filial piety.

This is suggested by a report in the text of "the worst kind of melancholy . . . which takes the form of panic fear." The passage is, in fact, autobiographical (though this is disguised in the text).[33] It is a description of a breakdown, set out in carefully imitative contrast to the account once offered by his father, Henry, who had suffered a similar breakdown at about the same age. The contrast is as instructive as the imitation. The passage ends: "'I have always thought that this experience of melancholia of mine had a religious bearing,'" on which Howard Feinstein comments: "How remote from Henry's passionate avowal of 'God's adorable perfection' was his son's 'melancholia' with 'a religious bearing.'"[34]

James's mature position on the matter was that "the only opinions quite worthy of arresting our attention will fall within the general scope of what may roughly be called the pantheistic field of vision, the vision of God as the indwelling divine rather than the external creator, and of human life as part and parcel of that deep reality."[35] The reality or fruitfulness of religious experience was there for anyone to see who was not blinded by scientistic or intellectualist prejudices. There must be *something* which produces these admirable results and, beyond the requirement that this something be a kind of consciousness (because it is on consciousness that it acts), it matters neither what it is nor what we take it to be. There he left the matter and there, for the time being, so can we.

---

33 "Here is an excellent example, for permission to print which I have to thank the sufferer" (*Varieties*, p. 134; see Vanden Burgt, *Religious Philosophy*, p. 27).

34 *Varieties*, p. 135; Feinstein, *Becoming William James*, p. 245.

35 *A Pluralistic Universe*, p. 19.

6

Institutions, Ideas, and Personal Experience

Following James in his quest for that "element or quality" in "religious experiences . . . which we can meet nowhere else," we saw that he found it neither in some particular emotion, or range of emotions, alone (because feelings of love and awe may be aroused by nonreligious objects), nor in some particular object, or class of objects, alone (because any "godlike" object is capable of arousing nonreligious feelings), but rather in the conjunction of godlike objects with appropriate emotions of joyfulness, seriousness, and world espousal. The varieties of states of mind which represent the permutations of suitable objects conjoined with appropriate emotions constituted, for James, "the varieties of religious experience." And we found him confidently asserting that, "as concrete states of mind, made up of a feeling *plus* a specific sort of object, religous emotions of course are psychic entities distinguishable from other concrete emotions"[1] and are, as such, patent of scrutiny by a science of religions specifically established for their consideration.

So far, so apparently clinical, cool, and methodologically dispassionate. However, I have tried to show that his decision to ignore altogether the institutional aspects of religion, and to say as little as possible about its intellectual aspects, far from being merely a matter of organizational convenience (because nobody can be expected to talk about everything at once), had its roots in a particular, highly idiosyncratic view of the nature and function of individual genius. According to this view, the unconvenanted and inexplicable conversion experiences of the religious genius are (notwithstanding the weirdness and eccentricity which often characterizes

---

1 *The Varieties*, pp. 44, 31.

the energetically enthusiastic espousal of the universe) of unique and inestimable significance in the contribution that they may make to the healing, the harmony, the redemption of the world.

In this chapter, I want to concentrate on James's tendency exclusively to identify what he called "personal religion pure and simple"[2] with states of individual feeling or emotion *in contrast* to both the institutional and the intellectual aspects of religion. Having discussed, in turn, these two patterns of disjunction as he handled them in the Gifford Lectures, I shall then consider some passages in his other writings which will help to bring into sharper focus the philosophical presuppositions on the basis of which he was able thus restrictively to characterize the "personal." My hope is that I shall be able, in this way, to give some substance to the charge which I leveled against him towards the end of chapter 4: namely, that, notwithstanding his vigorous and sustained hostility to "dualisms," he was himself deeply trapped in Cartesian dualism of a fundamental and familiar kind.

Persons and Institutions

Although it is James's account of the personal, of what it is that constitutes *personal* experience, which I want to keep centrally in view, it is important to bear in mind that that account was not offered as a merely *theoretical* proposal (or he himself would have fallen into the very intellectualism against which he was struggling). In his view, it is not merely a matter of saying that institutions and ideas *form no part* of the essence of "personal religion pure and simple" but, more practically and more urgently, of arguing that they distort and threaten such religion.

That this is true of religious thought we would, of course, expect. The conviction that "intellectualizing" not only forms no part of the essence of religion but threatens its integrity and very identity is but an instance of his general belief that "the intellectual life of man consists," regrettably, "almost wholly in his *substituting* a conceptual order for the perceptual order in which . . . experience originally comes." Or, as he put it in a passage that I quoted earlier: "verbality has stepped into the place of vision, professionalism into that of life."[3]

The most succinct expression of his belief that the real thing is equally

---

2 Ibid., p. 32.

3 *Some Problems*, p. 33 (my emphasis); *Varieties*, p. 352.

threatened, if not more so, by the institutional aspects of religion, is to be found in the lectures on "The Value of Saintliness": "A survey of history shows us that, as a rule, religious geniuses attract disciples, and produce groups of sympathizers. When these groups get strong enough to 'organize' themselves, they become ecclesiastical institutions with corporate ambitions of their own. The spirit of politics and the lust of dogmatic rule are then apt to enter and to contaminate the originally innocent thing"[4]— which innocent thing was, of course, the extraordinary experience of the individual genius in his "solitude."

This contrast between the "personal" and "institutional" aspects of religion is first spelled out in the lecture, to which we keep returning, on "Circumscription of the Topic": "At the outset," he says, "we are struck by one great partition which divides the religious field. On the one side of it lies institutional, on the other personal religion." The essence of "the institutional branch" of religion is said to consist in "worship and sacrifice," which are construed as "procedures for working on the dispositions of the deity." In contrast, the "center of interest" of "the more personal branch of religion" is said to lie in "the inner dispositions of man himself." The energies of institutional religion are directed toward manipulating the deity whereas, in personal religion—which is concerned with the relation that "goes direct from heart to heart . . . between man and his maker"— the structural element, "the ecclesiastical organization, with its priests and sacraments and other go-betweens, sinks to an altogether secondary place." Thus, personal religion issues in "personal" acts, whereas institutional religion finds expression in "ritual" acts.[5]

There is nothing that is original in this picture. Any student of post-Enlightenment religious thought is familiar with the contrast between priestcraft and prophecy, between "religions of authority" and "the religion of the spirit,"[6] between materialistic religion, with its structures of mediation obtruding between finite and infinite spirit, and religions in which the human individual enjoys a relationship of pure immediacy with whatever is taken to be the divine. And if, to many nineteenth-century thinkers, the elements for this contrast seemed to be simply supplied by the data, objectively *given* in the history of religions (and especially in the history of Judaism and Christianity), the twentieth-century reader of nineteenth-century texts is better placed to notice the influence of more

4   *Varieties*, p. 268.

5   Ibid., p. 32.

6   See, for example, Auguste Sabatier, *Religions of Authority and the Religion of the Spirit* (New York, 1904).

subjective factors. Not to put too fine a point on it, the contrast between material and spiritual, or "external" and "internal" religion, as that contrast was persistently drawn in the dominant narrative of both Liberal Protestantism and its secularized successors, expressed deep-rooted anti-Catholic and anti-Semitic prejudice.[7]

What is to be said, if not about this entire setup (because that would be an unmanageably vast undertaking) at least about James's version of it? There are, undoubtedly, significant differences between a group of people performing a rain dance and an individual holy man, in stillness, beneath the banyan tree; between the complex splendor of pontifical high mass and the silence of a Carthusian cell. But what kind of differences are these, and how might they appropriately be characterized? It is, I think, important to notice that although James sometimes speaks of different "aspects" of religion (a usage in conformity with his formal description of religion as a complex object the constituent features of which are found, in different times and places, in varying proportion and relationship), the thrust of his rhetoric invites us to see "personal" and "institutional" religion not as two aspects of a single complex whole but rather as descriptions of two different kinds of religion. And the contrast, as thus drawn not between aspects of an object but between different classes of object, is surely most misleading?

For instance, how legitimate is his distinction between "personal" acts and "ritual" acts? Are there not innumerable instances of religious ritual the participants in which perceive ritual activity as *the use of a language* at once expressive and transformative of relations of personal communion between human beings and the mystery of God? According to James, religious ritual is, in essence, manipulative. It is difficult to see what sense could be given, on this account, to a notion such as that of ritual *celebration*—for why on earth should we suppose all such celebration to be manipulative in intent? On the other hand, does not the concentration of interest on "inner dispositions," cultivated by the individual in solitude, often take ritualized form—in terms of bodily posture, the repetition of holy words, or the practice of ascetical and contemplative techniques—even if the function of such rituals or institutions of behavior is to enable the devotee in some measure to transcend them?

---

7 Notice how James contrasts "the superior . . . spiritual profundity" of Protestantism with the admittedly impressive structural complexity of Catholic "ecclesiasticism" (*Varieties*, p. 363). On the general issue, and especially on the anti-Semitic strand in the story, see my review, in *Journal of Theological Studies* 37 (1986): 656–62, of *Nineteenth-Century Religious Thought in the West*, ed. Ninian Smart, John Clayton, Patrick Sherry, and Steven T. Katz, 3 vols. (Cambridge, 1985).

It is not the description or classification of branches of religion, however, that is at the root of the problem, but the philosophical anthropology which underlies it. This is easily seen when we consider how it is that domestic social relations in fact function. If there were this "one great partition" between human institutions and individual personal experience, then (for example) birthday parties and rituals of courtship could never be said to be "personal experiences" for their participants. If, however, we are to be prohibited from thus describing them, we shall need better reasons than any that James has so far supplied.

"In critically judging of the value of religious phenomena, it is," he tells us, "very important to insist on the distinction between religion as an individual personal function, and religion as an institutional, corporate, or tribal product." Wondering, as we may, why the "product" might not, in varying degrees, in different hands, and on different occasions, fulfill such a "function," we might suspect the influence of the distinction (which we first considered in the previous chapter) between the "firsthand" experience of the solitary, if eccentric, "genius," and the "secondhand" experience of the rest of us: the unintelligent and unimaginative slaves of habit, who live by suggested feeling and imitated conduct. And we soon discover our suspicion to have been well founded: "The religious experience which we are studying is that which lives itself out within the private breast. First-hand individual experience of this kind has always appeared as a heretical sort of innovation to those who witnessed its birth. Naked comes it into the world and lonely; and it has always, for a time at least, driven him who had it into the wilderness, often into the literal wilderness out of doors, where the Buddha, Jesus, Mohammed, St Francis, George Fox, and so many others had to go." This contention is then illustrated by a lengthy quotation from Fox's *Journal*, on which James comments: "A genuine first-hand religious experience like this is bound to be a heterodoxy to its witnesses, the prophet appearing as a mere lonely madman. If his doctrine prove contagious enough to spread to any others, it becomes a definite and labeled heresy. But . . . when a religion has become an orthodoxy, its day of inwardness is over: the spring is dry; the faithful live at second hand exclusively and stone the prophets in their turn."[8] (That metaphor of newborn "nakedness" is interesting. The implication clearly seems to be—and we shall return to this—that the "clothing" of experience by institutional and conceptual garb corrupts the purity and innocence of the original.)

Now it is, of course, true that the religious innovator, the one whom

---

8 *Varieties*, pp. 268, 269, 270.

we might call the "creative artist" of the religious life, may experience much loneliness, believing himself or herself to tread in isolation a path which none have trod before, finding all existing religious "forms" and customs inadequate to express the freshness of feeling or the force of divine command. It is also true that the originality of the innovator becomes too often and too easily the narrowing routine and hardening prejudice of those who come after. But this is hardly the end of the matter.

In the first place, the emphasis on innovation (required by James's evolutionary explanation of genius) is overdone. Reformers and prophets have often seen their function as that of proclaiming the urgency of a *return* to lost standards of purity and innocence: innovation is exactly what such prophecy deplores.[9]

In the second place, the argument purports to be empirical, historical description. (It must qualify as this, if James is to succeed in his stated intention of providing, by "induction," the elements of his "science of religions.")[10] And yet, the account derives its force and persuasiveness from just those exaggerations and oversimplifications which deprive it of historical accuracy. For example: there abounded, in thirteenth-century Italy, climates and currents of opinion which ensured that Francis did *not* appear, to all who "witnessed" him, as "a mere lonely madman"; nor did the movement which he initiated ever become a "definite and labeled heresy." Or again: however deadening the effects of religious routinization, of what "orthodox" movements can it be said that their "faithful live at second hand *exclusively?*" The point that I wish to stress is that the oversimplifications in James's account are not simply rhetorical devices to heighten the drama of the narrative: without them, the underlying disjunctive contrast between firsthand and secondhand religion, the description of "personal experience" as set *over against* the institutional elements of religion, would simply crumble away. And yet, it is just this disjunction which is central to his whole view of the nature and function of religious experience.

Armed with his romantic image of the genius as one charged up with psychic energy from some strange source "beyond" the public world of social institutions, James exaggerates the pattern setter's originality. Human creativity—whether religious, scientific, or aesthetic—is never absolute. The pioneer is a *product* of the culture and traditions which he or

---

9   James's worship of "novelty" is epigrammatically captured in a late essay: "Philosophy must pass from words, that reproduce but ancient elements, to life itself, that gives the integrally new" (*Memories and Studies*, p. 410).

10   See *Varieties*, p. 359.

she refashions, often (admittedly) in dramatic and unexpected ways. Without the traditions, the cultural and linguistic institutions, of the people of Israel, Jesus could not have had his "personal" experience of the mystery he called Father, in the way that he had it, nor could Paul have had *his* "personal" experience of the mystery of Christ. Had James displayed the slightest interest in Jesus (and that he does not do so is somewhat surprising, in view of the fact that one might have supposed Jesus to be the primary pattern setter for the Christian religion) he would, it seems certain, have been bound to celebrate his genius in terms that sharply contrasted it with the deplorable secondhandness of both the Jewish religion which came before and the new institutions which came after.

On the other hand, the experience of those who come after the innovating genius, and who fashion and inhabit institutions marked by his imprint, is not necessarily secondhand in the sense of being "impersonal," merely a matter of habit and routine, all inwardness departed and all spirit spent.[11] May there not, for example, be a quality of firsthandness (in James's sense) in the experience of listening appreciatively to Mozart, or reading *Anna Karenina,* even for those of us who neither composed the symphony nor wrote the novel? And why should this not also be the case where our use of religious "institutions" is concerned?

There are, I suggest, two fundamental criticisms to be made of James's account of the "personal" as it finds expression in his disjunctive contrast between personal and institutional religion.

In the first place, his identification of personal experience with *individual* experience (as distinct from the experience of individuals) cannot be sustained. Custom *does* deaden and become mechanical. We *may* inhabit the social relations of which we form a part like dead wood drifting down the stream. All such relations, and the domestic, linguistic, religious, moral, and political institutions which embody them, may indeed be reduced by us to matters of "impersonal" habit and routine. And, when this happens, our marriages and friendships wither, our language atrophies with the deadening of our imagination, our religion and our politics harden and fossilize. But it is also possible, not only for geniuses but for ordinary people, continually to seek to *appropriate* these relations, and critically and responsibly to engage in the unending labor of sustaining and transforming the structures and institutions of the human world, and thus to make of that world the context and content of their *personal* experience.

In the second place, our "private" experience is never entirely "naked" (nor is it necessarily as "innocent" as James suggests!). The symbolic, lin-

---

11 Cf. ibid., p. 270.

guistic, affective resources available to us are *given* by prior experience, and by the culture, the traditions, the structures, institutions, and relationships that bring us to birth and give us such identity as we have. The fruit may sometimes surprise us and seem incommensurable with the roots from which it springs (can any good thing come out of Nazareth?), but it is, nevertheless, the *public* world of culture and its institutions which is primary, not whatever "private" world we make or suffer to be uniquely and incommunicably our own. The innocent, naked, newborn "ego" is a figment of the philosophical imagination. If James's account were correct, then the best way to prepare someone for the experience of God would seem to be to abandon them, at birth, in some untracked waste far from human habitation. (It might not work, of course, for who is to tell which baby has the spark of genius, but at least subjection to such thoroughgoing alienation might help the child to develop sufficient feelings of guilt and gloominess to benefit from the experience.)

There are, I think, at least three objections that might be made to my criticism of James's handling of the distinction between the personal and the institutional—the first of which has to do with my reading of James, and the other two with more general considerations.

According to Levinson, James insisted that people "preperceive what they see in the sense that their perceptions are formed by standards of appropriateness they inherit through education . . .[they] are born into languages that they must learn to speak and to speak about if they are to think." [12] Does not this sensible insistence (the evidence for which he cites from the *Principles of Psychology*) run counter to that emphasis on the "nakedness" of firsthand experience that I have criticized? Yes, indeed, but my impression is that not only did James increasingly lose sight of the importance of such considerations as he developed his "radical empiricism," with its doctrine of "pure" experience (which we shall consider in due course), but also that this recognition that *all* human experience is formed and shaped by the institution of language (of gesture and symbol, as well as verbal communication) is incompatible with the account that he gives of the originality of genius, and hence with his description of what it is that pertains to the "essence" of "personal religion pure and simple." His general view of the matter seems to be that, even if we need language in order to speak and to think, we do *not* need it in order to "feel." And feeling, as *contrasted* with thought, is (as we shall see in more detail in the next section) of the essence of "personal" and hence of "religious" experience.

---

12 Levinson, *Religious Investigations*, pp. 96, 97.

More generally, it might be objected that, even if it is ridiculous to suggest that the best way to prepare an individual for the experience of God would be to abandon him at birth in the forests of the Amazon, it is surely significant that many religious traditions, both Eastern and Western, should have laid great emphasis on *solitude,* on flight from the world, on the desirability of finding oneself "alone with the alone"?

Yes, indeed, but those who undertake this journey—whether Jesus or Paul, Buddha, Mohammed, the desert Fathers, or the traveler to High Kailas—carry with them the clothing or baggage of the culture that has produced them, has shaped their personalities and the worlds of their experience. No one goes "naked" into the desert, even though a person may return from it with perceptions purified and simplified by concentration on "the one thing necessary." If there is "nakedness" in the desert experience it comes, not as an initial condition, but as a result that may perhaps be slowly, and partially, and painfully achieved.

It is also perhaps worth pointing out that the function of such experience has been very differently construed in different circumstances and traditions, and that these variations in interpretation correspond to different accounts of the relationship between social relations and the experience of God. In some accounts, the desert experience (whether construed literally or metaphorically) is an ideal goal, even if only attainable by a few; in others, its role is that of representative protest; in yet others, it is to be a staging post from which return is necessary. Perhaps we could say that, according to the first, God is most truly and purely to be found *only* in solitude, in the desert; for the second, he is sought in the desert because his presence has been obscured by the circumstances that obtain in the city; for the third, he is to be sought in the desert in order that his presence may be better discerned, and his purposes more purely obeyed, on return to the city. And these are but random instances, none of which we need suppose to be usually triggered off by the kind of dramatic irruption of raw emotion which James took to be paradigmatic of "religious experience."

Finally, it might be objected that even if James's form of the distinction between private and public, personal and institutional, aspects of human experience, cannot be sustained as an account of our relationships with other people, and of our participation in the worlds of nature and culture, it surely does have something to be said for it so far as our relationships with "whatever we may consider the divine" are concerned?

We shall have quite a lot to say about this question in due course. For the time being, I will simply observe that the plausibility of the suggestion depends upon the assumption that God is one of a number of possible "objects" of human experience, objects that may compete with each other for our attention. According to this view, the purity and authenticity of relationship with God increases in proportion as other objects are ignored and other relationships allowed to wither away. While acknowledging that some such view has undoubtedly exerted considerable influence in the history of Christian spirituality, it is (I would claim) incompatible with what may reasonably be called the classical Christian doctrines of creation, incarnation, and sanctification (a claim, incidentally, which William James would cheerfully and wholeheartedly have endorsed).

Persons and Ideas

Turning now to the distinction between the "personal" and "intellectual" aspects of religion, our treatment can be briefer, because the topic impinges more directly on issues that I wish to consider in the final section of this chapter. As with the distinction between the personal and the institutional, it is not so much the distinction that is troubling as the disjunctive manner in which it is made.

Thus, for example, I have no quarrel with James when he says that "knowledge about a thing is not the thing itself," nor when he continues: "If religion be a function by which either God's cause or man's cause is to be really advanced, then he who lives the life of it, however narrowly, is a better servant than he who merely knows about it, however much." There are many areas of life in which firsthand acquaintance is preferable to secondhand description. Indeed, without the former, whence would the latter be derived? In a world without literature, there would be no literary criticism, in a world without politics no political theory, in a world without scientific practice no philosophy of science. Similarly: "When I call theological formulas secondary products, I mean that in a world in which no religious feeling had ever existed, I doubt whether any philosophic theology would ever have been framed."[13]

When distinctions are drawn between practice and theory, between first-order patterns of behavior and discourse and the second-order patterns of argument and inquiry in which the first-order activities are theoretically reflected, there are important questions to be considered concerning the relationships that obtain between these two orders or "levels" of discourse and apprehension. That these relationships are to be seen in terms of con-

13 *Varieties*, pp. 386, 341.

tinuing interaction, or reciprocal influence, is central to much modern discussion of the "hermeneutical circle." It seems certain, however, that James would have regarded all talk of reciprocal influence with grave suspicion. While he did allow (as we shall see in a moment) that theory, or reason, had a function to perform, his general tendency was to regard it as a threat to the purity of true religion, disruptive of the harmony which true religion might foster.

Thus, in the passage which I quoted just now, the distinction is drawn, not between two levels of discourse, two modes of rational behavior, but between theory (or "philosophic theology") and feeling. Systematically underplaying (when not simply denying) the cognitive element in feeling or emotion, James's general tendency was to identify all "thought" with second-order (or, as he would say, secondhand) theoretical reflection. The impression is thus given that "thought" forms no part of "personal religion pure and simple," and that the less "thoughtful" it is the purer and more personal it will be.

Within this general setup, he gives two rather different answers to questions concerning the relationships between religions and their theologies. According to the first of these, theology is subject to almost indefinite and divisive diversity, whereas religious experience is more or less the same in all periods, all cultures, all religions. "When we survey the whole field of religion," he says, "we find a great variety in the thoughts that have prevailed there; but the feelings on the one hand and the conduct on the other are almost always the same, for Stoic, Christian and Buddhist saints are practically indistinguishable in their lives. The theories which Religion generates, being thus variable, are secondary; and if you wish to grasp her essence, you must look to the feelings and the conduct as being the more constant elements." [14]

I see no reason to dispute the assertion that theological and philosophical theories exist in luxuriant profusion (though the variety is not perhaps as uncontrolled by the subject matter as James seems to suggest). But the plausibility of the claim that, in contrast, "feelings" and "conduct" are "almost always the same" is heavily dependent, firstly, upon his unacceptable account of feelings as autonomous emotional states, unspecified by their objects, and hence, secondly, upon his equally unsatisfactory habit (which we considered in the previous section) of speaking as if the "essence" of personal religion was to be sought in abstraction from all considerations of structure, narrative, history, and social relations.

I suggest, in other words, that "the feelings and the conduct" of "Stoic,

14 Ibid., p. 397.

Christian and Buddhist saints" are, in fact, differentiated by their different modes of apprehending "whatever they may consider the divine," [15] and that these modes of apprehension are specified and determined by varying social, historical, and cultural resources. Consider, for example, how central a determinant of Christian spirituality is the sense of "vocation," which seems quite alien to both the Stoic and the Buddhist traditions (quite apart from the fact that, even on his own account, Stoic "sanctity" rises no higher than "morality" and does not qualify as "religion"). In a nutshell: religious theories are not as varied, nor religious feelings as constant, as he suggests.

His second answer to questions concerning the relationship between religion and rational reflection relies upon his emphasis on the privacy, or incommunicability, of personal experience. One passage in which he places this emphasis is worth quoting at some length.

> Feeling is private and dumb, and unable to give an account of itself. It allows that its results are mysteries and enigmas, declines to justify them rationally, and on occasion is willing that they should even pass for paradoxical and absurd. Philosophy takes just the opposite attitude. . . . To redeem religion from unwholesome privacy, and to give public status and universal right of way to its deliverances, has been reason's task. . . . As moderator amid the clash of hypotheses, and mediator among the criticisms of one man's construction by another, philosophy will always have much to do . . . these very lectures which I am giving are . . . a laborious attempt to extract from the privacies of religious experience some general facts which can be defined in formulas upon which everybody may agree. . . . We have the beginnings of a "Science of Religions." [16]

What are we to make of this? It is undoubtedly true that we often have great difficulty (and by no means only in matters of religion) in giving an adequate account of the events, relationships, and experiences that matter to us most. Knowing what it was actually like to have been *there,* in that place and on that occasion; to love *that* person in the way that we have come, in time, to do; to have experienced *this* particular joy or sorrow, which our friends and relations did not share; knowing these things in the manner that we know them, we rightly resist the breezy intellectualism of

---

15 Ibid., p. 34.
16 Ibid., pp. 341–42.

the philistine "expert," the vulgarian of theory, who rushes in, textbook in hand, and says: "Ah, yes, *this* is what it was like; what you did or underwent was an instance of this class of phenomena which you will find described, with commendable rigor and clarity (though I say so myself) in chapter 3 of my book." No, we say, it was not like that at all and, soon discovering further conversation on the subject to be pointless, we lapse into a silence which the idiot is quite likely to mistake for profundity.

So far, so good. But such sad occasions do not warrant the claim that "feeling is private and dumb . . . unable to give an account of itself." For a start, why on earth should anyone suppose feeling to be capable of self-description? We do not usually expect "feelings" to speak nor "reasons" to shudder, though *people* may do both. The case made by James, in that passage, for the privacy of feeling and the publicity of argument rests, in large part, upon the hypostatization of its elements: poor "Feeling," shivering, inarticulate, in (naked?) privacy, until rescued by the knight errant "Reason," who strides about the place "moderating" and "mediating" (from the privileged stronghold, perhaps, of a Harvard chair).

It is somewhat surprising to find James, of all people, thus hypostatizing "reason." It would surely have been more consistent with his general hostility to intellectualism to have insisted that the attempt to describe, classify, and understand the human phenomenon of religion, in all its bewildering diversity, is made by *people*—people collecting information, listening attentively, elaborating arguments, comparing usages, testing hypotheses. There is no entity called "reason" that orders our affairs. There are, indeed, good and bad arguments, but (as James, when criticizing intellectualism, admirably insists) the users of argument are not as unaffected by personal, affective, and experiential factors as the dichotomous description of reason and feeling would have us believe.

I suspect, however, that even though James might have agreed that "reason's" achievements are less universal than the rhetoric of that passage implies, he would have still wished to stand by his contention that "feeling is private and dumb." There is (it is worth noticing) an element of paradox in the characterization as "dumb" of those feelings, those "personal experiences," which find expression in the torrents of articulate self-description, pouring from people who purport to have had "religious experiences" of the kind that interested James, which fill page after page of his book! As he himself put it elsewhere: "all the various feelings of the individual pinch of destiny, all the various spiritual attitudes," are "as describable as anything else." [17]

---

17 Ibid., p. 394.

The paradox is relieved a little, however, when we remember that, for James, *all* descriptions, of anything whatsoever, are at best pale shadows of the things that they describe. And if one's criterion of complete description is an exhaustive reissuing, in words, of the "things" which the words purport to signify, then spiritual attitudes are, indeed, as describable as anything else because no thing is, in fact, describable. We shall shortly need to consider what kind of "thing" James supposed "experience" to be. For the moment, however, it is enough to suggest that his critique of intellectualism did not, in *fact,* undercut the dualisms of thought and feeling to which he was so opposed. Instead, his strategy was to argue, on the one hand, that since all of "reality" is *really* to be found in feeling or experience, the autonomy of experience must be protected from the unwarranted incursions of intellectualist reason and, on the other, that some more modest and inductive pattern of reasoning might, nonetheless, respect that autonomy while redeeming experience from "unwholesome privacy." It is, however, worth pointing out that James would not have found it necessary to ascribe this liberating task to "reason" had he not himself, by his arbitrary confinement of personal experience to a sphere in which its nakedness was unclothed by language and social relations, locked it into that "privacy" in the first place.

That all the dualisms remain intact, in James's scheme of things, is suggested by his treatment of mysticism. "Personal religious experience," he announces, "has its root and centre in mystical state of consciousness," and "the keynote of all mysticism" is the "incommunicableness of the transport." We are back at "privacy" and it is, I think, of considerable importance to notice that it is *because* of this privacy or "incommunicableness" that "mystic truth" is said to resemble "the knowledge given to us in sensations more than that given by conceptual thought."[18] Surely this combination of a contrast between sensation and thought *as distinct sources of knowledge,* on the one hand with, on the other, the emphasis on the privacy of sensation, suggests that we are in the company of the Cartesian ego, sitting inside the skull and wondering whether it can make reliable contact with the world "outside" the "mind"?

Persons and Pure Experience

We have seen that, according to James, personal religion issues in personal acts. Moreover, the purity of such acts, which constitute the essence of

---

18   Ibid., pp. 301, 321–22.

personal experience, would seem to be threatened both by movements of the body (for bodily movement binds us into rituals and institutions—the patterns and structures of human relationship) and also of the mind (for thinking tends to substitute itself for "the perceptual order in which . . . experience originally comes"). If neither in the body nor in the mind, where then might we search for that "heart," or "soul,"[19] in the hot or heightened condition of which resides the essence of that pure experience in which individuals, in solitude, might know communion with whatever they may consider the divine?

Starting our search with questions of epistemology, of how we may come to know not only God but any thing whatsoever, we will then move to ontology: to consideration of the kinds of thing that there are. Finally, we will ask what kind of people could have the kind of knowledge which James supposes to be the most authentic, pure, and privileged.

"There is," he wrote in 1896, "but one indefectibly certain truth, and that is the truth . . . that the present phenomenon of consciousness exists." (Descartes might not have put it quite like that, but he would surely have applauded the sentiments!) What form might this *now* of consciousness take, and in what directions might it move? "Sensation and thought in man are mingled, but they vary independently. . . . Feeling must have been originally self-sufficing; and thought appears as a superadded function." In the beginning was the feeling. Does this mean that feeling is to be equated with sensation? It would seem so: "'Idea,' 'thought,' and 'intellection' are synonymous with 'concept.' Instead of 'percept' I shall often speak of 'sensation,' 'feeling,' 'intuition,' and sometimes of 'sensible experience' or of the 'immediate flow' of conscious life."[20]

And yet, we must be careful. Experience may "originally come" in perception or sensation, but the latter, at least, is a bodily, organic function. There must, it would be seem, be some kind of receptor, distinct from mere muscular movement, to decode the signals which such movements send and render them the stuff of feeling, or perception, of the immediate flow of conscious life. And (although James does not say so) it is difficult to see what this decoding receptor could be if not some version of the Cartesian ego.

It now seems clear that "feeling" signifies the flow of consciousness, before "thought" has intervened to distinguish between "subjective" and "objective" components of our conscious life and to ask awkward questions about the extent to which the way things seem to be is, in fact, the way that they are. Unfortunately, this impression that we are getting

---

19   *Some Problems*, p. 33; *Varieties*, p. 32.
20   *The Will to Believe*, p. 22; *Some Problems*, pp. 31–32.

somewhere is short-lived. In an early essay, read before the Aristotelian Society in 1884, James defined "feeling" as designating "all states of consciousness considered subjectively, or without respect to their possible function." But, in a note which he later inserted into the text, he said: "If the reader shares the current antipathy to the word 'feeling,' he may substitute for it, wherever I use it, the word 'idea,' taken in the old broad Lockean sense, or he may use the clumsy phrase 'state of consciousness,' or finally he may say 'thought' instead."[21] I am sure that these concessions were intended to be helpful but, frankly, I do not find them so.

I think that the best that we can do is to suggest that, although his general tendency is to *contrast* feeling with thought—inasmuch as the latter refers to a "superadded function" which enters in to complicate and remain distinct from sensation's original self-sufficiency[22]—feeling may nevertheless sometimes itself be spoken of as "thought" inasmuch as, before reflection has come upon the scene, it is feeling, or perception, or sensation which is (we might say) obliged to take the whole weight of the *cognitive* import of "pure experience."

The answer to my first question, then, would be as follows. We come to know anything whatsoever (including God) originally, primarily, and fundamentally by feeling, and only secondarily and derivatively by thought. It follows that our only access to reality, our only window from the ego to the world outside our consciousness, is through feeling or sensation. Objects of thought that have not been first felt are not, therefore, "realities" but merely *candidates* for reality: "ideas" whose cash value remains to be tested by subsequent sensation.

Now let us move to questions of ontology and ask what kinds of things there are and, especially, what kinds of things our feelings and our thoughts might be.

"The only form of thing that we directly encounter," said James, a few years before writing the Gifford Lectures, "the only experience that we concretely have, is our own personal life." Our personal life (which we now know to be, essentially, a matter of feeling, or "pure experience") is, then, a kind of thing. But what kind of thing is it; of what kind of *stuff* is it made? In *Essays in Radical Empiricism,* he moves between two rather different answers to this question. He sets out by saying: "My thesis is that if we start with the supposition that there is only one primal stuff or material in the world, a stuff of which everything is composed, and if we call that stuff 'pure experience,' then knowing can easily be explained as a par-

---

21 *The Meaning of Truth* (1975), pp. 13–14.

22 See *Some Problems,* p. 33.

ticular sort of relation towards one another into which portions of pure experience may enter." Later on, however, he qualifies this quite heavily: "Although for fluency's sake I myself spoke earlier in this article of a stuff of pure experience, I have now to say that there is no *general* stuff of which experience at large is made. There are as many stuffs as there are 'natures' in the things experienced." And how many might that be? Sensibly, he supposes that it does not matter: "Experience is only a collective name for all these sensible natures, and save for time and space (and, if you like, for 'being') there appears no universal element of which all things are made." Hence the conclusion that "thoughts in the concrete are made of the same stuff as things are." [23]

He does not mean, by that conclusion, that the thought of a tree can be cut down and used for firewood—*that* is how you take trees when, for specific practical purposes, you are taking them as "things" and *not* as "thoughts." This, I think, is what he means when he says that the terms "physical" and "mental" do not refer to "two different kinds of intrinsic nature . . . these words are words of sorting." [24]

It seems clear that the strategic intention underlying this manner of treating familiar and fundamental philosophical problems is to *undercut* those dualisms of mind and matter, thought and thing, with which we all tend spontaneously to work. James worked with them himself, and found it more or less inevitable that he should do so, as when he said (in a passage which I quoted earlier) that the psychologist has no option but to act as if "'thoughts' and 'things' were names for two sorts of objects, which common sense will always find contrasted and will always practically oppose to each other." Or, again: "The world of our experience consists at all times of two parts, an objective part and a subjective part. . . . The objective part is the sum total of whatsoever at any given time we may be thinking of, the subjective part is the inner 'state' in which the thinking comes to pass." [25]

Accepting the tenacity of such dualisms, the hold that they have over our imagination, James sought to minimize the damage that they do by bringing us back, again and again, to that sense of engaged and engaging immediacy, that original and primary condition of feeling or consciousness, of which all such discrepancies and alienating contrasts are but the subsequent precipitate. But, if this *was* James's aim, then the strategy that

---

23 *The Will to Believe*, p. 241; *Essays in Radical Empiricism*, pp. 4, 14, 15, 19.

24 *Essays in Radical Empiricism*, p. 76.

25 Ibid., p. 3; *Varieties*, p. 393.

he pursued in order to attain it seems to me to have been, for two reasons, doomed to failure.

In the first place (and this brings me to the third of the questions that I raised at the beginning of this section), what kind of people would we have to be in order to enjoy "experience" in what he took to be its "pure" condition? Certainly not scholars or intellectuals because, however much the educated person seeks to hold in check the intellectualist propensity for substituting analysis and argument for the reality of action, suffering, sight, sound, and relationship, he or she knows that there is no possibility of *return* to some condition of primal innocence which obtained before distinctions had been drawn, differences observed, and choices made. And certainly not the mature individual, of whatever degree of formal education, because maturity is, at least in part, a matter of having "learned from experience" (where that term is taken in the large sense which it enjoys in everyday discourse, and not in the restrictive sense which James sought to impose upon it) all manner of lessons that cannot—for better or for worse—be subsequently *unlearned*. In other words, those who might most closely approximate to the condition of "pure experience" would seem to be either newborn babes or grown-up people whose adulthood had been in some way deferred or dislocated.

There is a striking passage in which James comes close to admitting this. Defining "pure experience" as "the name which I give to the immediate flux of life which furnishes the material to our later reflection with its conceptual categories," he acknowledges that the "purity" of such experience is "only a relative term, meaning the proportional amount of unverbalized sensation which it still embodies." Who, then, might enjoy pure experience in all its purity? "Only new-born babes, or men in semi-coma from sleep, drugs, illnesses, or blows, may be assumed to have an experience pure in the literal sense of a *that* which is not yet any definite *what*." [26] But to set up infantilism, semiconsciousness, or insanity as instances of the ideal condition toward which we should strive, and in which we might stand most fruitfully and authentically in communion with God, seems a somewhat desperate remedy to propose for the ills of intellectualism and institutional sclerosis.

The strategy is doomed to failure, in the second place, for reasons at which I hinted at the end of chapter 4, when I suggested that, so long as we continue to talk as if "mind" were the name of some kind of "stuff" (*whatever* kind of stuff we take it to be), then our Cartesianism remains intact.

---

26 *Essays in Radical Empiricism*, p. 46.

My body is, undoubtedly, a thing. It has size, and shape, and color, holds together for a period of time (until corruption takes its toll) and can be moved from one place to another. But, if we speak as if my mind, or soul, or self (or whatever we take to constitute the *real* me, the heart and center of *my* identity, action, and experience) were *also* some kind of "thing"—perhaps by far the most important bit of the bigger thing that I am—then we shall soon find ourselves supposing that it is, as all "things" are, *located* somewhere. And where else might we find it but "within" me, at my very "center"?

I quoted, earlier, a passage in which James said that "our own personal life" is "the *only form of thing* that we directly encounter." [27] Our personal life consists, according to him, essentially in states of consciousness. Now what on earth could be the "we," the selves, that could come across, meet, bump into, or encounter our own personal lives? Surely the only possible candidate is the elusive "ego," the little person lurking somewhere in my head? All that this little person meets or encounters directly are "his" states of consciousness, feelings, or emotions. With all other "things"—all other persons, facts, events, and circumstances—the little person's relationships are *indirect*, mediated by feeling or sensation.

Notice how, on this account, problems of knowledge are presented as if they were problems of *engineering*—of how the little person might make contact, build bridges, with the "outside" world. The important thing about bridges is that they should be *reliable,* and not suddenly give way beneath their burdens. And the terror of the skeptic (and there is skepticism in all of us, and not entirely without good reason), the heart and center of what Richard Bernstein calls "the Cartesian anxiety," [28] is the fear that the bridges are not reliable, that we cannot be quite *sure.*

Hence the preoccupation with *certainty:* "There is but one indefectibly certain truth, and that is . . . that the present phenomenon of consciousness exists." [29] Here, there hovers the specter of solipsism, the fear that the little person is, in fact, alone in a dark, unreliable, and unmanageable world. Thus it is that the Cartesian presents as *technical* questions (problems of engineering) what are, in fact, questions of *ethics:* of who, and what, and in what circumstances, might responsibly be relied upon. [30]

---

27   *The Will to Believe,* p. 241 (my emphasis).

28   See Richard J. Bernstein, *Beyond Objectivism and Relativism* (Oxford, 1983), pp. 16–20.

29   *The Will to Believe,* p. 22.

30   It is instructive to notice that even Ellen Suckiel, who takes great pains charitably to interpret James's thought and to render his treatment of experience coherent, concludes that "his radical empiricism lacks a way of adequately explaining the commonality of

How might we extricate ourselves from this quagmire of confusion? One thing seems clear, and it is that we shall need a very different account from that offered by William James of what it is that constitutes the "essence" of personal experience. But, before we can begin to build up such an account, we must complete the picture by considering, in more detail than we have done so far, James's treatment of the question of God. It is (as we shall see) very much the kind of treatment that we would have expected. It follows, therefore, that if there are grounds for dissatisfaction with his philosophy of personal experience and (within that philosophy) with his account of what constitutes *religious* experience, we shall eventually be obliged, on these same grounds, to attempt an alternative description of what would count as a doctrine of God, and of the forms that it might take.

---

our experience" (*Pragmatic Philosophy*, p. 142). For a sustained and penetrating treatment of the general epistemological issues, see Stanley Cavell, *The Claim of Reason* (Oxford, 1979). According to Rorty, who has studied James much more deeply than I have, he is to be venerated as one of the first to have "asked us to give up the neurotic Cartesian quest for certainty" (Richard Rorty, *Consequences of Pragmatism* [Minneapolis, 1982], p. 161). Perhaps he did, but he still seems to me to have been caught in the meshes of that quest.

7

The God of
William James

Feeling unites, arguments divide. At a deeper level than that at which we are divided by intellectual disagreement and institutional conflict, we can find ourselves and each other and, in this discovery, find peace.

That version of the gospel according to James makes no mention of religion. Let me, therefore, rephrase it: spirit unites, flesh divides. At a deeper level than that at which we are divided from each other by theological dispute and ecclesiastical tribalism, human beings may "apprehend themselves to stand in relation to whatever they may consider the divine"[1] and, in that apprehension, experience redemption.

Superimpose these two versions of the Jamesian creed, or run them together, and, at first sight, the association of flesh and argument (or "thought") may seem surprising, for there is surely no contrast more profound, no discontinuity more absolute (in the dualist's worldview) than that between "matter" and "mind"? But, as I have tried to show in the last two chapters, it was just because James believed that the division of matter and mind, *once drawn*, cannot be healed or transcended, that he sought, with his doctrine of radical empiricism, to point us back to a state or condition of "pure experience" antecedent to all such separations. Now, *in* that condition (if, indeed, it is attainable) how might the divine be apprehended? Or, to put it another way, what *organ* do we possess for the apprehension of the divine in pure experience? This, as we shall see, is a question which James had some difficulty in answering.

Another thing to notice about my versions of the Jamesian creed is the

---

1 *Varieties*, p. 34.

association of feeling and spirit. James once remarked that, in philosophy before Kant's day, "'spirit and matter,' 'soul and body,' stood for a pair of equipollent substances quite on a par in weight and interest."[2] On such a view of things, "spirit" seems clearly to be lined up with "soul" and "mind" on one side of the dualist's Great Divide. If, therefore, James still wishes to characterize as "spirit" that divinity apprehension of which in feeling or "pure experience" could meet our needs, some very different account of spirit will be required; an account according to which spirit, as the ground and concomitant of feeling, is (to put it crudely) no *closer* to mind than to matter. If he cannot furnish such an account, then his strategy for undercutting dualism will have proved as unsuccessful in his theology as it was elsewhere.

That it is likely to prove unsuccessful we may, by now, expect, and the expectation is enhanced when we notice the Cartesian overtones of the slogan that spirit unites and flesh divides. Flesh divides because it imprisons each little person, each Cartesian self, isolating it from all other selves (and even, perhaps, from God?). As James once put it, in a most revealing metaphor: "We are like fishes in the sea of sense, bounded above by the superior element, but unable to breathe it pure or penetrate it . . . the abstract ideas of which the air consists are indispensable for life, but irrespirable by themselves."[3]

In this chapter, I propose to consider two questions: first, in what manner may the divine be apprehended; second, what kind of divinity, apprehensible in pure experience, would satisfy our needs? (As in the final section of the previous chapter, therefore, consideration of questions of epistemology will precede considerations of ontology.)

As we have seen already, some apprehension of relationship with divinity is required if people are to be brought beyond despair, guilt, or even the somewhat grim integrity of stoicism, to more joyful and peace-producing endorsement of the universe.[4] James believed not only that such apprehension was possible, but that its occurrence was a fact which could be scientifically demonstrated. He therefore had, undoubtedly, a gospel to proclaim, a gospel which has been accepted with enthusiasm by many who have found his treatment of religion not only attractive but persuasive.

---

2 James, *Essays in Radical Empiricism*, p. 3; a remark which suggests a somewhat impoverished grasp of the history of Western thought on these matters before the Enlightenment.

3 *Pragmatism* (1975), p. 64.

4 See above, chap. 4, p. 27; chap. 5, pp. 42–44.

But have they been wise to do so? After all, on James's own account, personal or firsthand experience of relationship with God is the exclusive prerogative of that small handful of human beings who have been the pattern setters of religion. And where does that leave the rest of us?

Consider, for example, his stipulation, in 1895, that a person is religious if and only if he or she is convinced that "the so-called order of nature, which constitutes the world's experience, is only one portion of the total universe, and that there stretches beyond this visible world an unseen world of which we know nothing positive, but in its relation to which the true significance of our present mundane life consists."[5] That stipulation may sound, shall we say, harmless enough, until we ask what kind of conviction this could be.

For the beneficiary of firsthand religious experience, it might, perhaps, be some pure fruit of feeling, some utterly unexpected alteration of emotional state whereby the person "becomes conscious" that "the higher part of himself," which he now identifies with "his real being," is "conterminous and continuous with a MORE of the same quality which is operative in the universe outside of him, and which he can keep in working touch with, and in a fashion get on board of and save himself when all his lower being has gone to pieces in the wreck."[6] But, for the rest of us, the conviction that there *is* any such a "more" could only, it would seem, be a matter of faith in the weak sense that we come to believe the pattern setter, to trust him to be telling it as it is. It may be that the sanctity of the religious genius is so impressive, so persuasive, that we suppose ourselves to have good reason to believe him. But that is not the point. The point is that, for those of us who are not pattern setters, the truth of religion is (on James's account) a matter of evidence rather than experience, of "thought" rather than "feeling."

If this is true, then it leaves the vast majority of mankind as far from God's presence as ever they were when banished into the wilderness by "priestcraft" and the thickets of institutional religion. This does not seem to be quite what James intended, and yet the conclusion appears inescapable. We may be able to throw some light on why it was that James landed himself in this uncomfortable position if we go back to a topic on which I have touched already: namely, the difficulty of knowing quite what we are

---

5 *The Will to Believe*, p. 48.

6 *Varieties*, p. 400. It would, I think, require a chapter on its own to unpack the riot of metaphor in that passage, but notice the implication that it is not *human beings* that are saved, but only that "part" of them which they have learned to identify with their "real" selves.

to make of the fact that, although James usually insists on *contrasting* feeling—as "sensation," or "emotion"—with thought, he sometimes speaks as if feeling were itself a kind of thinking, a mode of thought.[7] Without the contrast, the distinction between firsthand and secondhand religion (and with it, his entire account of "personal religion pure and simple") is in danger of collapse. But, if the contrast is sustained, then most of us are left out in the cold.

"Were one asked to characterize the life of religion in the broadest and most general terms possible," said James at the beginning of his lecture on "The Reality of the Unseen," "one might say that it consists of the belief that there is an unseen order, and that our supreme good lies in harmoniously adjusting ourselves thereto. This belief and this adjustment are the religious attitude in the soul." The surprising thing about this passage is that the very *life* of religion—and this we know to be a matter of the emotions, of feeling, of heart states, of "prayer, guidance and all that sort of thing immediately and privately felt"—is now said to consist of a "belief" and a consequent "adjustment." This is not only to put much greater emphasis on the cognitive character of religious experience than his general account has led us to expect but, by describing the cognitive element in experience as a "belief that" such and such is the case, he seems to be situating it in the order of "conceptual knowledge," of "'knowledge-about' an object not immediately there," rather than in the order of perception, in which "the mind enjoys direct 'acquaintance' with a present object."[8] What, then, has happened to that immediacy of relationship which was supposed to be the peculiar privilege and glory of "personal religion pure and simple"?

In case we had missed the point, the passage from which I quoted just now goes on to insist that religious belief is "belief in an object which we cannot see." How, then, may our relationship with it be apprehended? There are, it would seem, only two possibilities: "All our attitudes, moral, practical, or emotional, as well as religious, are due to the 'objects' of our

---

7 See above, chap. 6, p. 66. As I pointed out in chap. 3, James is difficult to read partly because of the extravagant imprecision of his arguments and the fluidity (or confusion) of his terminology. It was the overall sense of the story, the "vision" he sought to conjure up, which mattered to him more than the details of its presentation. It is, therefore, useless to try to render his terminology consistent. The most that one can hope to do is accurately to capture the *drift* of the argument. It follows, of course, that the thrust of my criticisms is aimed at the drift, rather than at the detail, even if it is only by way of the latter that the target can be reached!

8 *Varieties*, p. 51; *The Letters of William James*, 1:127; *Essays in Radical Empiricism*, p. 28.

consciousness." No surprises here, but then he adds: "Such objects may be present to our senses, or they may be present only to our thought."[9]

There is, as we know, no direct route along the path of mere thought from human beings to the reality of God, at least insofar as we take "mere thought" to mean that intellectual, "conceptual," or reflective realm on the derivative character of which he has been so insistent. The "self" may think what thoughts it likes, but they will not furnish it with materials suitable for the construction of bridges to the outside world. Or, as he himself puts it: "In all sad sincerity I think we must conclude that the attempt to demonstrate by purely intellectual processes the truth of the deliverances of direct religious experience is absolutely hopeless."[10]

It is for this reason that the great majority of the human race, lacking the benefit of such direct experience, are (as we suspected) badly off. "The more concrete objects of most men's religion, the deities whom they worship, are known to them only in idea. It has been vouchsafed, for example, to very few Christian believers to have had a sensible vision of their Saviour. . . . The whole force of the Christian religion, therefore, so far as belief in the divine personages determines the prevalent attitude of the believer, is in general exerted by the instrumentality of pure ideas." So much for the common run of religious believers. But they are no worse and no better off than the theologians, whose religion is "full of abstract objects," such as catalogues of divine attributes, "which prove to have an equal power."[11] As a corrective to academic hubris, to the illusion that erudition or intelligence alone can bring a person closer to God, the emphasis is admirable. The trouble is that all of us, professors of divinity and "simple believers" alike, share a common plight: confined to the realm of "ideas" (whether pictorial, narrative, or abstract in character) we lack all possibility of direct apprehension of relationship with God, and the truth of our religion remains a matter of hypothesis.

But what of the privileged few? If all objects of consciousness are present either "only to our thought" or "to our senses," are we to infer that the pattern setters experience God with their *senses?* Admittedly, religious literature is full of references to "hearing" God, to "seeing" him (if only through a glass, darkly), to "tasting" and being "touched" by him. But surely all these references to sensation are, and are usually taken to be,

---

9   *Varieties*, p. 51.

10   Ibid., p. 359.

11   Ibid., pp. 51–52.

manifestly metaphorical? For it to be otherwise, would not God have to be a material object?

Leaving that question on one side for a moment, it does seem that James had left himself with no alternative but to say that religious experience was a kind of sensation. Hence the hint that at least some Christians (presumably the pattern setters) *have* had "a sensible vision of their Saviour"; hence a reference to "our *sense* of the reality of the religious objects." More explicitly: "We may now lay it down as certain that in the distinctively religious sphere of experience, many persons . . . possess the objects of their belief, not in the form of mere conceptions which their intellect accepts as true, but rather in the form of quasi-sensible realities directly apprehended."[12]

For further light on the matter we must turn, once again, to his treatment of mysticism and, in particular, to the insistence that mystical experience is "incommunicable" (and this incommunicability, we remember, is its "keynote") because "it resembles the knowledge given to us in sensations more than that given by conceptual thought."[13] I can no more have your mystical experience that I can have your pain.

The difficulty with this account is that, on the one hand, our "immediate feelings have no content but what the five senses supply" and yet, on the other hand, the mystics often "emphatically deny that the senses play any part in the very highest type of knowledge which their transports yield." We are, it would seem, forced to the conclusion that mystical experience is quite literally a matter of provision of a sixth sense. The rest of us, lacking this equipment, are "deaf" or "blind" to the truth of mystical experience and are thus incapable of authentic religious faith, for "faith-state and mystic state are practically convertible terms."[14]

Let me see where we have got to. James believed that the route to the truth of religion, and to the reality of God, along the road of pure reason, of argumentative proof, was insurmountably barred. Therefore, if God is to enter the world of our experience, if he is not to remain forever a hypothetical or postulated entity absolutely beyond our ken, then the road to his reality can only lie, in some sense, through sensation. And if this seems a surprising conclusion (and one that James would surely have resisted), my aim in this chapter so far has been to suggest that, in order to avoid it, it would have been necessary for him to unravel just those incon-

---

12　Ibid., pp. 51, 68 (my emphasis), 59.

13　Ibid., pp. 321–22.

14　Ibid., pp. 322, 360 (on which see chap. 4 above), 336.

sistencies and confusions in his treatment of feeling (in relation, on the one hand, to sensation and, on the other, to thought) on which his entire account of religious experience ultimately rests.

What is at issue here, for James, is our apprehension of the truth of religion. It is a matter of the circumstances in which religion could be shown and known to be true. He therefore found himself (as we have seen) obliged to lay unaccustomed emphasis on the cognitive character of religious feeling or experience. In terms of his preferred dichotomy of "thought" and "feeling," he is clear that it is not by thought that the reality of God is to be apprehended. Yet, since it is our knowledge of the truth of religion which is at stake, he is obliged to characterize mystical experience, the pure case and paradigm of religious feeling, as cognitional, "thoughtful," as a mode of knowledge.

It is as if, the arguments for the existence of God having failed, or having been judged to be necessarily inconclusive, James felt obliged to offer the example of the saint as a kind of surrogate natural theology, a demonstration of the reality of the divine not by argument but by eloquent performance. As one commentator puts it: "The attractiveness of religious experience for James lay . . . in the fact that it . . . constitutes a concrete, and possibly persuasive, path to the Deity." That he should have been drawn in this direction is not surprising if we bear in mind how central to the Cartesian anxiety is the quest for certainty, for security and fixed *foundations* to the world: "a God, whether existent or not, is at all events the kind of being which, if he did exist, would form the most adequate possible object for minds framed like our own to conceive as lying at the root of the universe."[15] We may fault the moves made by James (or anyone else) in pursuing this quest but we should not, I think, underestimate the depth of the need which it expresses.

James, we remember, was a pragmatist. If, therefore, the truth of religion is to be shown or established, it will only be established by the demonstrable efficacy of at least some forms of the religious life. As he put it in his postscript: "If asked just where the differences in fact which are due to God's existence come in, I should have to say that in general I have no hypothesis to offer beyond what the phenomenon of 'prayerful communion,' especially when certain kinds of incursion from the subconscious region take part in it, immediately suggests." Turning, then, to the second of our two topics: what kind of God, what kind of being, did James suppose there to be which was, in fact, responsible for such incursion, exert-

---

15 Vanden Burgt, *Religious Philosophy*, p. 61; James, *The Will to Believe*, p. 93.

ing an "influence," raising "our centre of personal energy," and producing "regenerative effects unattainable in other ways"?[16]

"The word 'divine,'" says James in the passage in which he is distinguishing religious from merely moral attitudes, "shall mean for us not merely the primal and enveloping and real, for that meaning if taken without restriction might prove too broad. The divine shall mean for us only such a primal reality as the individual feels impelled to respond to solemnly and gravely, and neither by a curse nor a jest." The divine prompts our respect and loyalty but, as he remarked as early as 1881: "We must not call any object of our loyalty a 'God' without more ado, simply because to awaken our loyalty happens to be one of God's functions. He must have some intrinsic characteristics of his own besides." We must be careful not to say too much about these characteristics, for our concern must be "to keep still living on that subtle edge of things where speech and thought expire." Nevertheless, there are two features that divinity must have if it is to be capable of eliciting our unswerving loyalty: "First, it is essential that God be conceived as the deepest power in the universe; and second, he must be conceived under the form of a mental personality." God, then, is a mind and, going one step beyond Matthew Arnold, he offers as "the definition which I think nobody will be inclined to dispute": "A power not ourselves . . . which not only makes for righteousness, but means it, and which recognizes us."[17]

At this stage, James was a theist, and he saw his theism as standing midway between "agnosticism and gnosticism," holding "to what is true in each."[18] This still seems to have been broadly his position in the Gifford Lectures, which contain some mildly critical remarks on pantheism, and in which, although somewhat attracted by the polytheism which "has always been the real religion of common people, and is so still today," his general conclusion is that "the practical needs and experiences of religion seem to me sufficiently met by the belief that beyond each man and in a fashion continuous with him there exists a larger power which is friendly to him and to his ideals."[19]

By 1908, however, his description of this large and friendly mind, this

---

16   *Varieties*, pp. 411–12 (cf. ibid., pp. 366–67), 412.

17   Ibid., p. 39; *The Will to Believe*, pp. 97, 98, 97, 98.

18   *The Will to Believe*, p. 111. It was, however, a distinctly unspecific theism, signifying "little more than a view situated somewhere between materialism and idealistic monism" (C. Stephen Evans, *Subjectivity and Religious Belief: An Historical, Critical Study* [Grand Rapids, 1978], p. 139).

19   *Varieties*, p. 413. On pantheism, see ibid., pp. 112, 330, 336.

"higher part of the universe" which Christians call God, had moved from theism to a form of pantheism. Acknowledging that "'God,' in the religious life of ordinary men, is the name not of the whole of things, heaven forbid, but only of the ideal tendency in things, believed in as a superhuman person who calls us to cooperate in his purposes, and who furthers our lives if they are worthy," he is nevertheless now sharply critical of "the theistic conception, picturing God and his creation as entities distinct from each other," on the grounds that this conception "still leaves the human subject outside of the deepest reality in the universe." He therefore argues that "the only opinions quite worthy of arresting our attention will fall within the general scope of what may roughly be called the pantheistic field of vision, the vision of God as the indwelling divine rather than the external creator, and of human beings as part and parcel of that deep reality."[20]

Human beings, then, are part of the large and friendly mind, the "superhuman consciousness" (even though only a privileged handful of them can ever personally ascertain this to be the case), and it, in turn, "is finite, either in power or knowledge, or in both at once."[21]

This is not, however, quite the end of the story; for that we must return to the question of evidence. "I myself believe," he wrote in *Pragmatism,* "that the evidence for God lies primarily in inner personal experiences." In the 1890s, he complained that "no part of the unclassified residuum has usually been treated with a more contemptuous disregard than the mass of phenomena generally called mystical."[22] He had a lifelong fascination for the paranormal, and at one time held the presidency of the Society for Psychical Research.[23] His writings show an increasing tendency to describe mystical or religious experience in terms of experience of the paranormal. Thus, when he says: "I think it may be asserted that there *are* religious experiences of a specific nature . . .[which] point with reasonable probability to the continuity of our consciousness with a wider spiritual environment from which the ordinary prudential man . . . is shut off," it is in the "abnormal or supernormal facts" studied by the psychical researcher that he finds "the strongest suggestions in favour of a superior co-conscious being."[24]

20   *A Pluralistic Universe*, pp. 60, 16, 19; cf. *Varieties*, p. 406.

21   *A Pluralistic Universe*, p. 141.

22   *Pragmatism* (1975), p. 56; *The Will to Believe*, p. 223.

23   See *The Will to Believe*, p. 225. The essay just quoted is entitled "What Psychical Research Has Accomplished."

24   *A Pluralistic Universe*, p. 135.

His final view of the matter, expressed in 1909, in an essay entitled "Final Impressions of a Psychical Researcher," was: "Out of my experience, such as it is (and it is limited enough) one fixed conclusion dogmatically emerges, and that is this . . . there is a continuum of cosmic consciousness, against which our individuality builds but accidental fences, and into which our several minds plunge as into a mother-sea or reservoir. Our 'normal' consciousness is circumscribed for adaptation to our external earthly environment, but the fence is weak in spots, and fitful influences from beyond leak in, showing the otherwise unverifiable common connection." [25]

The God of William James turns out, then, to have been not only a creature, but a thing: a large, powerful, fundamentally friendly material object of which our more elevated elements form part. We would hardly have guessed this, and could not have discovered it, were it not for the fact that there has been a privileged handful of human beings who found themselves plugged into it. Caricature? Perhaps; but not misrepresentation: the purpose of a caricature is to highlight the salient features of an object.

That James's God was a creature is evident. It was a finite object, the "higher part of the universe." [26] But any part of the universe, any constituent feature of the world, is most certainly not that world's creator. James's God moves minds and, being actively benign, might even be said to love but, operating as it does entirely on the "mental" or "consciousness" side of the dualist's Great Divide, there is no indication that it could be, as Dante put it, the love that moves the sun and the other stars.

My claim that James's "superior co-conscious being," a being in the order of mind, may nevertheless be said to be a material object may, at first sight, seem more disputable. But, as I have suggested more than once, we cannot talk of "mind," or "consciousness," as if these terms were names for entities of a certain class, made of some kind of stuff, without (by implication, for the comment is grammatical) taking "mind" to be a kind of matter. We may suppose it to be a very thin, attenuated, or gaseous kind of matter, very different from such thicker things as sticks and stones. But, so long as we take it to be a "thing" of any kind, a *part* of something larger (and James's God is *part* of the universe, just as the bit of God in each of us is *part*—albeit the most important part—of the persons that we are) then it is, undoubtedly, a material object.

It could, of course, be objected that such language may be put to appropriate use (whether in respect of ourselves or of God) by insistence on its

25 *Memories and Studies*, p. 204.
26 *Varieties*, p. 406.

metaphorical character and by that strenuous disciplining of the imagination which guards us against mistaking metaphorical for literal description. Not only, however, do the metaphors systematically mislead, by coaxing us into supposing, whenever we are caught off guard, that either the mind or God is, after all, in fact a thing, but James gives little evidence of having felt the need for any such imaginative restraint or discipline.[27]

The reason for this is partly to be sought in his pragmatism. It is pictures and images of God that we require, and the requirement is purely practical: to bring us from anxiety and insecurity into assurance and peace. Whether these images are accurate or adequate, *except* as descriptions of emotional states and their hypothetical concomitants, is not a question in which he showed the slightest interest (hence Ayer's judgment that, in the domain of theology, James simply equated truth with expedience).[28]

There is, however, another reason for James's exuberant use of physical imagery. He sought a science of religions, and every science must have (it seemed to him) its own field of data, its own class of objects, its own segment of the material world, to be investigated and classified.[29] And, since the content of all experience is supplied by the senses, he found himself obliged to speak as if *religious* experiences required a kind of sixth sense. Sensation is a response to physical stimuli, and it is not, therefore, surprising that he should have been quite satisfied with physical images of that divinity which leaks in through the weak spots in our defences.

In most of us, the fences hold; we remain impermeable by the "mother-sea," blind to the sensible vision of our Savior, deaf to extraterrestrial signals. It earlier seemed as though James's tendency to speak as if only a small number of unusual, gifted, or perhaps deranged individuals possessed the equipment that could enable them personally to experience relationship with the divine, left the rest of us out in the cold, cut off from God. But we are not, after all, as badly off as we supposed. For, whatever is to be said about James's "mother-sea" of "co-consciousness," I cannot think of any good reason for mistaking it for the mystery of God.

27 Thus, for example, James shows no "grammatical" interest in why it is that religious literature is rich in paradox and negation. For him, this only indicates that "mystical truth" is best spoken by "music" and not by "conceptual speech" (*Varieties*, p. 333), and the function of music, as indeed of literature, is to stimulate ecstasy rather than understanding. Hence the claim that, "to the poor and unlettered," drunkenness "stands in the place of symphony concerts and of literature . . . the drunken consciousness is one bit of the mystic consciousness" (*Varieties*, p. 307). James, the psychologist, shows no interest in philosophical problems concerning the "naming" of God.

28 See A. J. Ayer, "Introduction" to *Pragmatism and the Meaning of Truth* (1978), xxx.

29 See chap. 4 above.

It is, said James, "the instinctive belief of mankind" that "God is real since he produces real effects." There are several ways in which that remark might be read, and James's position (if I have understood him correctly) is an unstable compromise between two of them. Taken as a straightforward expression of his pragmatism, the production of real effects (and, specifically, of mystical or religious experiences) is what it *means* for God to be real. On this reading, the occurrence of such effects does not contribute toward the *verification* of the truth of the proposition "God is real," but is a factor in its *definition*. The truth of the proposition is made, created, by the occurrence of these effects.[30] To ask whether God is real, or whether he is merely a symbol of human ideals and aspirations, is to ask, and is *only* to ask, whether there are at least some people who *realize* those ideals in the attainment of what James took to count as sanctity.

This reading, however, never entirely satisfied him (perhaps because it failed adequately to assuage the Cartesian anxiety). In formulating, albeit tentatively, what he called his own "over-belief," he also read the remark as a comment on the state of the evidence.[31] The occurrence of those "real effects" which interested him suggested that there was "more" to the world than sticks and stones and human beings. And the best way to test this hypothesis seemed to him to lie in the direction of the investigation of the paranormal.

James's account of what it means for a doctrine of God to be true is, I suspect, the only account compatible with his "rather insouciant expression"[32] of one form of philosophical pragmatism. And the kind of God that he comes up with is the only kind for which there could be room in his particular version of Cartesian empiricism.

A great deal of contemporary discussion of theology and religion takes it for granted that, at least in their broad outlines, these approaches (whether taken together, as in James's case, or, more usually, as alterna-

---

30 *Varieties*, p. 407. See Leszek Kolakowski's remarks on James in "Karl Marx and the Classical Definition of Truth," in his *Marxism and Beyond: On Historical Understanding and Individual Responsibility* (London, 1969), p. 59, and some comments of mine in Nicholas Lash, *A Matter of Hope: A Theologian's Reflections on the Thought of Karl Marx* (London, 1981), pp. 77–87.

31 See *Varieties*, p. 405. "Deeply intrenched" as is James's urge to argue that "morality points to religion" in the sense that, whether or not there "is" a God, ethics requires an *idea* of God as symbolic expression of the more-than-merely-moral world acceptance, "just as deep is the impulse to *peer out* beyond the world of phenomena to find a transcendent reality which shall give human values the highest kind of validity" (Julius Seelye Bixler, *Religion in the Philosophy of William James* [Boston, 1926], p. 117 [my emphasis]).

32 Kolakowski, "Karl Marx and the Classical Definition of Truth," p. 59.

tives) exhaust the possibilities of what the question of God might be. As a result, if we were merely to observe that the worship of James's God would be idolatrous (the form of the idolatry varying from self-obsession to the adoration of a part of the universe), we would not cut much ice. It will therefore be necessary to take a more indirect route. Before setting out, however, it may be useful to try to construct a balance sheet of what we have discovered from our conversation with William James.

8

Taking Stock

The philosopher's task, according to Waismann, is not to advance "proofs and refutations in a strict sense," but to build up a case. "First, he makes you see all the weaknesses, disadvantages, shortcomings of a position; he brings to light inconsistencies in it or points out how unnatural some of the ideas underlying the whole theory are by pushing them to their farthest consequences. . . . On the other hand, he offers you a new way of looking at things not exposed to those objections. In other words, he submits to you, like a barrister, all the facts of his case, and you are in the position of the judge."[1] Having kept close company with William James, during the last four chapters, the time has come to sum up for the prosecution. Only when this has been done shall I be in a position to begin to build up an alternative account, a "new way of looking at things."

In two respects, however, Waismann's metaphor is not entirely apt. In the first place, while any barrister must respect the rules of evidence, I have tried to be not merely accurate but in some measure sympathetic. In the absence of counsel for the defense, therefore, our summing up should at least remind you, the judge and jury, of the strength of James's case. In the second place, the accused in this case is not an individual American philosopher, but a widespread and influential approach to the questions which concern us, an approach for which that philosopher was an eloquent and attractive spokesman. Therefore, after offering some remarks by way of a balance sheet on my reading of William James, I shall take up again, and without reference to the details of James's account, some of the main features of that view of the matter with which I am taking issue.

---

1 F. Waismann, "How I See Philosophy," in *Contemporary British Philosophy*, ed. H. D. Lewis, 3d ser. (London, 1956), pp. 480–81.

James in Retrospect

However much James's sense of the darkness of things, of the fragility of sense and order as construct on chaos, was expressive of his temperament and is explicable, in part, in terms of his personal history, it captures a confusion, bewilderment, and, sometimes, terror that are, a century later, more widely and more deeply felt than they were in 1900. In James's time and place, anxiety could, in some measure, be held in check by confidence in the benefits brought by science and in the possibilities of social progress. In us (where "us" is taken primarily to refer to the middle classes of the Western world, not because this group of people is more important than any other, but because it is the group that I know best and from its ranks are likely to come most readers of this book) such confidence has gone sour. Undreamed-of wealth—in terms of resources, artifacts, skills, and techniques—is either being squandered, as if there were no tomorrow, by that minority of the human race to which we belong, or else is set to the service of insane and insanely extravagant strategies of paranoia the increasingly likely outcome of which is that, one day soon, there *will* be no tomorrow.

Worst of all, we see no way through. Educated to the belief that we were free and responsible moral agents, we now find ourselves (or feel ourselves to be) incapable of countering chaos by constructing, in fact or even in imagination, a human world. Political cynicism expresses our sense of practical impotence, and the poverty of our imagination is evident in the collapse of any common grammar of ends and means, of value and virtue. Instead, we talk of "freedom," but the rhetoric rings hollow, and we have no means of deciding whether "pluralism" prescribes a solution or merely names our predicament.

There is no doubt that we need salvation, but from what direction might it come? Hardly from the public realm of social institutions—we have long lost confidence in *their* redemptive capacity, and the suggestion that it might come through *thinking* harder—that "pure reason" could be our savior—now seems even more ridiculous. And so, numbed by terror and acknowledged impotence, we retreat into varieties of personal and moral individualism, places of private feeling and individual "experience." The increasing extent to which we find some solace in religion, in ill-defined oases of spirituality, may surprise those people who (a few years ago) confidently equated the secularization of the Western world with the imminent disappearance of religion, but at least it helps to explain why Jamesian accounts of religion and religious experience should continue to exercise the attraction that they do.

But, of course, it does not work. However energetically we try to regress into the privacy of "pure experience," we cannot *entirely* disguise from ourselves the recognition that our abdication of social and intellectual responsibility, our attempts individually to tune in to an order beyond the present darkness of our imagination, merely serve to deepen the darkness in the *real* world in which people starve and nuclear policy is pursued.

How then might *actual* chaos be held in check, or some contribution made to its ordering? It would be exceedingly stupid to suppose that these are questions to which there could be *answers*, lying somewhere ready to hand, merely awaiting their implementation (and by whom, and how?). But at least it seems clear that the work of our redemption cannot occur in the privacy of the individual imagination, but would require institutional form and sustained intellectual endeavor. To put it another way: we know our humanity to be threatened, our personal identity fragile and vulnerable, but if we confine the essence of the personal to the territory of the private, we end up by dehumanizing not only ourselves but other people. James's model of pure personal experience, as a condition more fundamental than and originative of institutional forms and reflective procedures, had (as we saw) strangely infantilist overtones.[2] I shall argue in due course, however, that human persons are not what we initially, privately and "inwardly" are, but what we may (perhaps) together hope and struggle to become.

So far, I have done no more than impressionistically indicate why it seems to me that it is precisely the more questionable features of the Jamesian account which help to explain its enduring popularity. It does, of course, possess great strength. "The depth of James's criticism of the intellectualist tendency in philosophy," expressed with sustained energy and power, undoubtedly accounts for his impact as thinker of impressive and fruitful originality, even if there is more than a touch of hyperbole in Bernstein's claim that what James offered was "nothing less than a critique of Western philosophic thought."[3] And because the intellectualism that James deplored has done at least as much damage in theology as in philosophy, we can wholeheartedly welcome his insistence that reality is richer than reflection; that it is not by pure reason alone that we can take our bearings and find our way (quite apart from the fact that reason is never as pure, as devoid of passion and particular interest, as its advocates suppose it to be);

---

2 See my discussion of "Persons and Pure Experience" in chap. 6.

3 Richard J. Bernstein, "Introduction" to James, *A Pluralistic Universe*, xxiv. For a lucid and provocative defense of the view that such a claim is *not* hyperbolic, see Richard Rorty, *Consequences*, xiii–xlvii.

that quality of feeling is no less important to our well-being than quality of argument; that imperialist pretensions on the part of particular ideals of explanation are always to be resisted; and that the life of religion (as, indeed, of much else) is ever under threat from that passion for law and order, for tidiness and clarity, which is a feature of the internal dynamics both of institutional power and of reflective or theoretical curiosity.

Where the pragmatist strand in James's thought is concerned, it is surely possible to deplore the casualness of his tendency, in matters of theology and ethics, to equate truth with expediency, while yet acknowledging that experience is the test bed of truth and that "there is no difference of truth that doesn't make a difference of fact somewhere"? The pragmatist tradition of which James was so eloquent an exponent does, at the very least, serve as a corrective to the tendency to suppose that, in order to make a case for the truth of (for example) Christian belief, all that one has to do is to show, on the one hand, that at least some versions of the Christian doctrine of God are not demonstrably incoherent and, on the other, that christological claims can be furnished with sufficient historical warrant to merit their being given serious consideration. Even when these indispensable tasks have been successfully performed, the pragmatist (and something of the pragmatist lives in all of us, if we have our feet on the ground) will say: "that is all very well, but does it *work?* does it make any difference?" He will insist that, in order to make a case for the *truth* of Christianity, it is necessary that the redemptive transformation of the world, by the agency of a loving God, which Christianity proclaims, should at least be in some measure *indicated.* He says, in effect: "don't talk of love, show me." In other words, even though it would be quite improper to *define* the "true" as "what works well—on the whole,"[4] that remark might still suggest a useful criterion to call in aid when seeking to test the truth of the claims and proposals that we make. However, as soon as we ask the further question: "works well for *whom?,*" James's account runs into serious difficulties.

Religion, on James's account, works well or, at least, works best, for that small company of its creative artists, the pattern setters who fulfill, in matters of religion, the evolutionary function of genius. By their uncovenanted appearance, as "spontaneous variations," geniuses ensure the survival in religion of whatever it is that is "fittest" to survive, and they thereby make some contribution to the redemption of humanity. And if it seems, on this account, that few are called and even fewer chosen, this (he might well say) is not an outcome for which he can be held responsible: it

---

4 James, *Essays in Radical Empiricism*, p. 81; *Varieties*, p. 361.

simply indicates within what tightly tragic limits chaos can, in fact, be ordered and destructive darkness held at bay.

The emphasis on the indispensability of genius is but a striking expression of James's thoroughgoing individualism: "in his religion, as in his philosophy, it is the individualistic note that is struck. . . . His is not primarily a gospel of social righteousness or of service." [5] Not that this gospel is lacking in social implications. It is, we might say, the religious form of "trickle down" theories in economics. Allow a handful of select individuals to accumulate great wealth and, when their cup is full to overflowing, the parched generality of mankind may receive at least some modicum of refreshment.

In their persistent and obsessive individualism, "his writings furnish a refreshing contrast to the prevalent over-emphasis on the social origins and social values and functions of religion." [6] Perhaps, but, in religion as in economics, it is possible to invoke pragmatic considerations and to ask on the basis of what evidence, and in the light of what assumptions and practical estimations, such a judgment is arrived at. In James's case, we have seen that, even if we leave theological considerations entirely to one side, his preoccupation with the pattern setters, with those who live their religion at "firsthand" and not (like most of us) merely at "secondhand," depends upon quite arbitrary and unsustainable disjunctive contrasts between, on the one hand, personal and institutional existence and, on the other, personal experience and intellectual activity.

It is these disjunctive contrasts and, with their aid, the confining of the territory of the personal to the realm of individual, private feeling and emotion, which renders the Jamesian account at once so seductive and so dangerous. The situation is not lacking in tragic irony. By calling us back from the death-dealing rigidity of institutional order, and from the divisiveness of intellectual debate, to some primordial realm of pure experience in which the individual may "apprehend" himself to "stand in relation" to that "continuum of consciousness" of which we each form part,[7] James sought to secure firm foundations for religious truth, prospects for progress, and a basis for social harmony. And yet, the foundations turn out to be nothing firmer than the fragile optimism of an excited ego entertaining dubious hypotheses concerning the paranormal. Moreover, by banishing the institutional and intellectual orders to the wastelands of the *im*personal, both politics and theory are reduced to matters of

5 Bixler, *Religion in the Philosophy of William James*, p. 107.

6 Ibid., p. 107.

7 See *Varieties*, p. 34; *Memories and Studies*, p. 204.

mere mechanism or technique, unconstrained by considerations of personal responsibility. And so, by seeking for sense and safety in the wrong direction—at some center of our individual privacy rather than in the public realm of common action, common understanding, and shared experience[8]—we merely succeed in bringing nearer the day when darkness and destruction have the last word. To put the point theologically: if we would find ourselves in the presence of God, we are ill advised to pursue strategies which exacerbate the conditions of his absence from our world.

James's doctrine of radical empiricism was an attempt to overcome the dualisms which kept intellectualism alive even in the empiricist tradition in which he stood. In this sense, we could say that the *aim* of radical empiricism was to bring us back into our bodies, back to perceived particularities of flesh and feeling.[9] I have tried to show, however, that the attempt was unsuccessful because, by continuing to treat of "mind" as if it were some kind of thing, made of some kind of "stuff," he left in place that obstinate and anxious little person, the Cartesian ego.

We do, undoubtedly, have good reason to be anxious, and James was correct in supposing that our anxiety will not be overcome by argument alone, nor merely by altering our arrangements of social order. That argument alone might bring us healing, might bring us closer to God, is (as in some uses of arguments for the existence of God) one of the illusions of that intellectualism against which James valiantly protested. (And the twentieth century has surely provided us with sufficient evidence that transformations of social structure are not alone sufficient to bring about corresponding transformations of consciousness and morality.)[10] I have tried to suggest, however, that James's brand of Cartesian individualism inhibited him from discovering that, if anxiety is to be redeemed at all, such redemption could only occur through the abolition of egotism in the establishment of patterns of mutual trust. But if we were to follow that train of thought, we would soon be brought back from what *James* called "religion" to consideration of the ways in which we might construct and reconstruct the body politic.

That last remark may also serve as a reminder that our judgments in these matters are always, and unavoidably, ethical or political as well as

---

8 On these constitutive features of human community, see Bernard J. F. Lonergan, "*Existenz* and *Aggiornamento*," in his *Collection*, ed. F. E. Crowe (New York, 1967), pp. 245–46.

9 This seems to be the drift of Wild's careful discussion of what was at issue in James's rejection of "transcendentalism"; see John Wild, *The Radical Empiricism of William James* (New York, 1969), pp. 111–14.

10 See Nicholas Lash, *A Matter of Hope*, pp. 273–80.

theological in character. Where the specifically theological components of such judgments are concerned, it is important not to decide *in advance* what "the question of God" might be or how it should best be explored. How we *take* the question of God, the kind of question that we suppose it to be, and how we handle it, will always depend upon the way in which we take "the question of the human." To put it more concisely: our theology is always correlative to our anthropology.

The correlations may, and indeed should, be mutual. But it is a further criticism of the Jamesian treatment of religion that the correlations can, in his kind of system, only work one way. The Jamesian God is always a function of previously specified human need. Anyone interested in finding out why Karl Barth was so hostile to what *he* called "religion," has only to read William James!

The possibility conditions for the redemption of the world—for the illumination of darkness and the ordering of chaos into "form," for the healing of anxiety and of the circumstances that give it rise—do not lie to hand *within* our confusion and disorder, nor can they be brought to hand by the strenuous exercise of will, feeling, or fantasy. Where then *do* they lie, and how might their recognition be brought to speech? I do not believe that these questions can even be properly formulated until we have undertaken what Karl Barth once called an "energetic revision of our anthropology." [11]

The "Little Person" and Its God

James's radical empiricism served, in its day, as an original and powerful corrective to one strand in the classical empiricist tradition. [12] In our own day, that tradition, though no longer as dominant as once it was, is still active and influential among philosophers of religion both in versions of its classical form and in versions variously affected by the Jamesian corrective. And if we look further afield, to the broader constituency of those who read, rather than write, studies of religious experience and essays in

---

11 See Karl Barth, *Church Dogmatics,* vol. 3, *The Doctrine of Creation,* ed. G. W. Bromiley and T. F. Torrance, trans. Harold Knight, G. W. Bromiley, J. K. S. Reid, and R. H. Fuller (Edinburgh, 1960), 2:390.

12 For a brief but discriminating account of the different strands in the tradition, see D. M. MacKinnon, "Introduction" to John Henry Newman, *Newman's University Sermons* (London, 1970), pp. 9–23.

the philosophy of religion, the same (perhaps not surprisingly) seems to be true. In other words, many people with an interest in these matters would probably agree that speculation is suspect and experience reliable, that "religious experience" is more like the real thing than are religious theories, that "institutional religion" is oppressive, tedious, or irrelevant, and that feelings are more fundamental than the "beliefs" in which those feelings are expressed. If, to some readers, this all sounds rather vague and imprecise, so much the better: my interest, for the rest of this chapter, is more with a general, often diffuse, *climate* of discourse and perception than with the detail of particular claims and arguments.

My focus of interest is in what it is that people usually seem to be talking about when they talk about religious experience. After commenting on (*a*) what I shall call the "contraction" of the concept of experience, and (*b*) on the role played by metaphors of "sight" or "vision," I shall (*c*) consider what it is that religious experience is generally taken to be experience *of:* in other words, I shall say something about the *objects* of religious experience. Finally, (*d*) I shall offer a summary sketch of the less than satisfactory *theological* options that (were we to think things through more thoroughly and consistently than we usually do) we should discover alone to be available to us within this general setup. As we proceed, William James's specific contribution to the discussion will recede into the background.

(*a*) In most of the contexts in which we talk about our "experience," we are talking about whatever it is that we have undergone and done, and of the ways in which we have *learned* something from what we did and underwent: *experientia docet*. Both these aspects of the notion are usually in play when we describe someone as an "experienced" teacher, parent, or politician, or when we ask: "Is this how you have found it to be, in *your* experience?"

For some reason, we usually talk quite differently about *religious* experience. In this area (not uniquely, perhaps, but characteristically) the talk tends to be of experiences, in the plural; of brief and isolated moments of heightened awareness or profound emotion, moments which occur unexpectedly, interrupting the ordinary conduct of our affairs and having little directly to do with it (in somewhat the same way that attendance at Sunday services interrupts the business of the week).

The interesting thing to notice is that, in so speaking, we talk of religious experience in something like the way in which philosophers (of a certain temper) talk of all manner of "experience," whereas in most other areas our everyday discourse is at variance with this tradition of philosophic usage.

Richard Swinburne, for example, introduces his account of the argument for God from religious experience by *defining* experience (any experience, mark you) as "a conscious mental going on."[13] In most contexts, this definition would probably strike us as rather odd. We would not usually describe toothache or indigestion as mental goings-on, yet most of us have some experience of these things. And even if we take a more complex example, such as the experience of personal betrayal, it would seem odd to describe being betrayed as something which went on in our minds, even if adverting to the fact that we have been let down is a major factor in the painfulness of the experience (which will also include all manner of physical features, such as opening letters, finding the door closed in our face or—if the Judas was a business partner—a significant diminution in our bank balance). For *human beings,* experience, at least in the vast majority of its forms, includes a great deal more than mental goings-on. For the Cartesian "ego," on the other hand (which, being itself not bodily, can only enjoy nonbodily or "mental" experience), Swinburne's definition seems entirely appropriate: the little person inside the skull observes or notices its body's indigestion.

Reflecting on the history of modern English-speaking philosophy, Stephen Toulmin has commented that "everyday terms having a familiar sense in the public domain of joint actions, pooled understandings and interpersonal meanings have been projected into the private, individual domain of hidden thoughts, sensations and feelings; and the corresponding abstract nouns (consciousness, thought, mind and experience) have been given a certain 'false concreteness,' as the supposed *names* for the content of basic sensibility."[14] Quite why this "contraction" of these concepts from the public to the private realm should have taken place is a question of considerable historical and sociological interest. At the beginning of this chapter, and at one earlier point in the discussion,[15] I offered some hints as to why this contraction should have been especially marked in matters of religious sensibility. But the point that I now want to make is simply that if (as I believe) there is very little to be said in favor of, and a great deal to be said against, retaining a contracted account of experience *in general,* then there is even less to be said in favor of retaining a contracted account of *religious* experience which is quite at variance with our healthier and more sensible habits of speech in regard to other aspects of our existence.

---

13 Richard Swinburne, *The Existence of God* (Oxford, 1979), p. 244.

14 Stephen Toulmin, "The Genealogy of 'Consciousness,'" in *Explaining Human Behavior: Consciousness, Human Action, and Social Structure,* ed. Paul Secord (Beverly Hills, Calif., 1982), pp. 66–67.

15 See above, chap. 5, p. 44.

(b) The more contracted our use of concepts such as "thought" and "experience," and the more Cartesian the model at the service of which the contraction is employed, the more difficult it becomes to give a satisfactory account of what might be meant by *knowledge* of God. As an indication of why this should be the case, I now want to suggest some reasons for supposing that metaphors of "sight" can be most misleading as descriptions of human knowledge and understanding.[16] (We noticed the pervasiveness of these metaphors in James's writings, all the way from his general insistence that "a man's vision is the great fact about him," to matters of more detail such as the analogy between the "science of optics" and that "science of religions" which he sought to construct, and his characterization of God as the "Unseen.")[17] Because we are bodies, physical objects equipped with sense organs, in a world of other physical objects, with some of which we interact—we are produced by them, we bump into them, we notice them, eat them, count them, care for them, wonder about them, marry them, are hurt and eventually destroyed by them—it is hardly surprising that descriptions of human understanding should be saturated with metaphors of sensation.

Where all the senses save sight are concerned, the metaphorical character of such description is usually so obvious as not to be misleading. We do not need to sniff in order to "smell a rat" when someone starts to act suspiciously, nor do we suppose that shouting louder will help in circumstances in which another person obstinately refuses, for whatever reason, to "hear" what we are saying.

Where metaphors of ocular vision are concerned, however, the situation is less straightforward. In the first place, these metaphors occur more frequently, and exert much deeper influence on our descriptions of human action, and specifically of our quest for knowledge and understanding, than do metaphors drawn from the operation of our other senses. We use them all the time to describe such activities as noticing where an argument is going (do you "see" why I am laboring the point?), or trying to understand something (can you "see" what I am driving at?).

But, in the second place, just because their use is so widespread, we may fail to advert to their metaphorical character in circumstances in which it would be prudent to do so. Among such circumstances would be those in which we allow ourselves to be misled by the *spatial* character of ocular

---

16   The following paragraphs can be only hints and headings, because the exploration of these metaphors, and the paradoxes to which their use gives rise, has been an endless source of difficulty and fascination, at least since the days of Plato and the author of the Fourth Gospel!

17   James, *A Pluralistic Universe*, p. 14; *Varieties*, pp. 359–60, 51.

vision into creating all sorts of false problems concerning the relationship between subject and object, between "subjectivity" and "objectivity,"[18] or between ideas "in" the mind (like images on the retina) and the real world "outside" it. The little person comes to think of itself as a kind of camera and, before we know where we are, practical problems concerning the reliability of information, and ethical problems concerning the reliability of other people, get turned into pseudomechanical problems of "mental engineering."

Another way of putting the point would be to say that, even if "seeing an object" may often do no damage as a metaphor for what we might call the technical aspects of understanding—by which I mean the skills required in order to be able to follow or "see the point of" an argument—its use encourages us to lose sight (!) of the fact that a great deal of our understanding of almost anything, and especially the kind of understanding which is a major factor in personal relationships, requires not simply skills of alertness and intelligence, but also some sort of sympathy and the incurring of the risks of friendship. There are aspects of understanding which are the fruit, and not the precondition, of love.

The model of the mind as a kind of inner eye has the further disadvantage that it misleads us into supposing that knowledge is merely a matter of understanding information, of getting the picture into focus. It thus reduces knowledge (almost literally) to the possession of "bright" ideas. Of bright ideas and intelligent hypotheses there is, of course, no lack: "New books pour forth annually by the thousands; our libraries need ever more space. But the vast modern effort to understand meaning in all its manifestations has not been matched by a comparable effort in judging meaning. The effort to understand is the common task of unnumbered scientists and scholars. But judging and deciding are left to the individual, and he finds his plight desperate. There is far too much to be learnt before he could begin to judge. Yet judge he must and decide he must if he is to exist, if he is to be a man"[19] (or even, lest the dated terminology distract, if she is to be a woman!). There is a sense in which the knowledge that we need, if we are to negotiate our circumstances responsibly and fruitfully, is more like wisdom than it is like expertise. And *this* aspect of the matter

---

18 Cf. Bernard Lonergan, "Cognitional Structure," in *Collection,* pp. 231–36. Few people have devoted as much effort as Lonergan did, over fifty years, to demythologizing "the myth that knowing is looking" (p. 233). This may be one of the reasons why he is not widely read. But the interest aroused by Richard Rorty, *Philosophy and the Mirror of Nature* (Princeton, N.J., 1979), much of the early argument of which is aimed at the same target, is perhaps encouraging.

19 Lonergan, "Dimensions of Meaning," in *Collection,* p. 266.

metaphors of ocular vision merely serve (if the paradox be permitted) to obscure from view.

No one has ever seen God. Why should this be so? Recalling some uses of the metaphor that I mentioned earlier, we might want to ask: is it because no one has ever *noticed* him?[20] Or is it because no one has ever understood him, has "seen the point" of God? And if we insist, with the greater part of the tradition, that whatever can be fully understood, or "comprehended," cannot be God, does it follow that God can never be seen? The same question would arise if we approached the matter from another angle and, remembering that we sometimes speak of *moral* "blindness," asked whether even the saints, in this life or the next, may *straightforwardly* be said to "see" God? If not, then why do we speak of beatific "vision" and, if so, with what *organ* would they see him?

I have two comments on this cluster of questions. The first is that the less alert we are to their metaphorical character, the sillier they seem, and the second is that, cumulatively, they suggest that the fundamental ground of God's invisibility lies not in our limitations or incapacity, but in the nature of God. God is not simply (as it happens) invisible: he is, in James's phrase, "*the* Unseen." I suggest that, the more firmly our consideration of the matter is rooted in the contractions of Cartesian dualism, the more we shall be inclined to suppose that God is, in principle, invisible because he is a person without a body, constituted, as all persons are, of some non-bodily, immaterial kind of stuff ("spirit," perhaps?). All "persons" or "selves" are, on the Cartesian model, *in* themselves invisible: personhood or selfhood is *inferred* from bodily behavior. It is through such inference that we come, insofar as we do, to know other persons. Small wonder, then, that the idea of *knowledge* of God is so problematic, because God has no body.[21]

But if God is a person without a body he is, presumably, a kind of mind. Not, perhaps, an instance of pure reason, but a non-embodied instance of thought and will and kindness to an infinite degree: pure, perfect, unre-

---

20 If we were to introduce christological considerations at this point, matters would be further complicated in perhaps quite interesting ways. We might say, for example, that Jesus was noticed to be a nuisance, but that most people did not notice that he was God. But that cannot be quite right: surely the disciples' faith was not a matter of "noticing" something about Jesus which other people failed to see? What, then, was it that they alone saw in him? It all depends, you might say, on what we mean by "see." But that is precisely what we are considering!

21 "Insofar as the notion of knowledge relies primarily on metaphors of sight, i.e. on a notion of knowing as seeing, it remains a problematic notion for theology" (Ronald F. Thiemann, *Revelation and Theology: The Gospel as Narrated Promise* [Notre Dame, 1985], p. 153).

stricted consciousness or selfhood. But suppose we were to agree with Anthony Kenny that "'the self' is a piece of philosopher's nonsense produced by misunderstanding of the reflexive pronoun," and that "to ask what kind of substance my *self* is is like asking what the characteristic of *ownness* is which my own property has in addition to its being mine."[22] Does all our talk of God's invisibility, then, rest upon the fragile foundations of grammatical confusion? I am inclined to say that the answer is yes *to the extent* that, under pressure from the Cartesian contractions, we construe as literal description the metaphors of ocular vision. In order to talk less nonsense about God than we sometimes do, it is not different metaphors that we require, but less contracted frameworks for their use.

Finally, I would draw attention to the fact that the *spatial* character of ocular vision frequently misleads us into treating the "distance" between ourselves and God as an epistemological problem. If it were so, then the gap might be narrowed by intellectual ingenuity (and this hope keeps alive some of those forms of philosophical theology against the intellectualist pretensions of which James would quite properly protest). However, as Augustine put it a long time ago, we are separated from God "not by intervals of space, but by difference of affections."[23] But this, as I suggested earlier in a slightly different context, is just the kind of consideration which metaphors of ocular vision, when handled within the framework of the Cartesian contractions, systematically obscure from view.

(*c*) Next, what is religious experience experience *of?* James's answer, as we know, was that, in such experience, we become conscious that the "higher" part of ourselves "is conterminous and continuous with a MORE of the same quality which is operative in the universe outside" us. Shortly after James's day, sociologists of religion, under Durkheim's influence, came up with a rather different answer and suggested that the object of such experience was, in fact, society and the pressure which it exerts antagonistic to our individual or domestic interests. However, according to Robert Towler, Thomas Luckmann's *The Invisible Religion,* published in 1967, "was the last major contribution to the sociology of religion to use the word 'religion' to denote beliefs and ideas with no super-empirical or

---

22 Anthony Kenny, "The First Person," in *The Legacy of Wittgenstein* (Oxford, 1984), p. 81. Kenny was commenting on G. E. M. Anscombe, "The First Person," in *Mind and Language,* ed. S. Guttenplan (Oxford, 1975), pp. 45–66.

23 Augustine, *De Trinitate,* bk. 8; chap. 7. The translation is that of Arthur West Haddan, rev. W. G. T. Shedd, in *A Select Library of the Nicene and Post-Nicene Fathers of the Christian Church,* ed. Philip Schaff (Buffalo, 1877), 3:122.

supernatural reference, as Durkheim had done." For more than twenty years, then, "there has been a move to restrict the word 'religion' to beliefs and practices with a supernatural referent." [24]

This contention is borne out by a recent, wide-ranging study of mystical experience, the author of which asserts that "experience of the transcendent is common to all religious traditions. It is from such experience that all the more general manifestations of man's religious behaviour are primarily derived." Towler agrees: "Every religion and every type of religiousness has a conception of some order of reality which transcends the material world of tables and chairs." [25] At this point, however, anxious as I am to learn from empirical studies undertaken by the social scientists, I begin to feel confused. Or, rather, I begin to suspect the confusing influence of familiar dualisms. For, surely, most people suppose there to be in the world not only physical objects such as tables and chairs but also such things as thought and kindness and integrity? But supposing the furniture of the world to contain such items as these does not make most people religious. It begins to look as if the Jamesian model is still intact. There are, in the world, tables and chairs, and there is also another order of reality: namely, the order of mind and consciousness. The religious person, then, is the person who purports to have experience of a "more of the same quality," a larger or superior realm of consciousness which transcends, or lies "beyond," the familiar world of everyday experience.

James's pioneering efforts to construct an empirical study of the phenomenon of religious experience lay fallow for many years until the zoologist Alister Hardy, who regretted that, since James's day, there had been "little organized knowledge of this phenomenon," "set up a research unit to find out more about it." Hardy's description of his project is so strikingly Jamesian as to be worth reporting in some detail. "Over the years," he and his colleagues "collected together over four thousand first-hand accounts . . . which show that a large number of people even today possess a deep awareness of a benevolent non-physical power which appears to be partly or wholly beyond, and far greater than, the individual self." Some people call this power "God," but Hardy himself did "not believe in a deity with an anthropomorphic image—an old gentleman 'out there'— but I take 'theism' to mean at least a belief in a contact with a power which *appears to be* greater than, and in part to lie beyond, the individual self."

24 James, *Varieties*, p. 400; Robert Towler, *The Need for Certainty*, pp. 3, 4–5.

25 Philip C. Almond, *Mystical Experience and Religious Doctrine: An Investigation of the Study of Mysticism in World Religions* (Berlin, 1982), p. 5; Towler, *The Need for Certainty*, p. 68.

For Hardy, "the 'personal God' is not a power *out there* but has none the less an equally important *personal* reality of a psychological nature." At the end of his study, he announces that "the spiritual nature of man is, I believe, being shown to be a reality. We now need a new biological philosophy which will recognize both this and the need to study consciousness as a fundamental attribute of life."[26]

All the features are familiar: "psychological" as the name for the nature of something; the equation of the "personal" with "consciousness"; the physical imagery used to describe both the "non-physical" entity some call God (e.g., "power") and the manner of our apprehension of it (e.g., "contact") in privileged moments of heightened emotion. It is perhaps more disturbing in 1980, than it was in 1900, to find a scientist of distinction offering such detailed descriptions without a trace of what we might call hermeneutical curiosity. In order to sharpen the conceptual focus a little, therefore, and also to inquire further both as to what might be meant by "theism" and as to why the language of "spirit" should be thought appropriate as a general characterization of the entities and experiences under discussion, let us turn back from the scientists to the philosopher: "By a theist," says Richard Swinburne, "I understand a man who believes that there is a God. By a 'God' he understands something like a 'person without a body (i.e., a spirit) who is eternal, free, able to do anything, knows everything, is perfectly good, is the proper object of human worship and obedience, the creator and sustainer of the universe.'"[27]

Anyone at all familiar with either Jewish and Christian literature, or with the uses of the concept of spirit in everyday English (which range all the way from gin to genies, and from high spirits to the spirit of an age) is likely to be somewhat surprised that Swinburne should not only offer "person without a body" as a *definition* of "spirit," but should do so without providing either justification for the definition or any further discussion of it. Expressing such surprise, Patrick Sherry suggests two possible explanations for the casualness of Swinburne's parenthesis. On the one hand, he points out, "definitions like his have been common in philosophy at least since Locke's time" and, on the other, "some such definition is

---

26 Alister Hardy, *The Spiritual Nature of Man* (Oxford, 1979), pp. 2, 1, 2 (his emphasis), 3 (his emphasis), 142. In the light of my remarks, at the beginning of this chapter, on some of the implications of James's contraction of the "personal" to the realm of private feeling, it is worth noticing that those whose "experiences" Hardy reports showed little interest in either "contradictory theological theories" or in "institutional religion" (pp. 131, 132).

27 Richard Swinburne, *The Coherence of Theism* (Oxford, 1979), p. 1.

current in ordinary language" inasmuch as "people often speak of ghosts, and indeed of the dead generally, as 'spirits.'"[28]

The first explanation suggests that Swinburne's account of the personal, and hence his description of what it is to be a theist, is situated somewhere within the broad framework of the Cartesian contractions, and the second reminds us of James's interest in the paranormal. In order to follow up these hints I now propose, by way of conclusion, to offer a broad and impressionistic sketch of the narrow and unsatisfactory theological options that alone are open to someone whose notion of God, and of what it is to believe in God and to have experience of his reality, are worked out on the basis of one form or another of the Jamesian model. It will, I admit, be a caricature but, as I remarked on a previous occasion, the function of a caricature is to highlight salient features of whatever it is that is being caricatured.

(d) If there is, as we are told, a "fallacy of misplaced concreteness," there is also, perhaps, a fallacy of misplaced abstractness, which consists in mistakenly supposing that reverence before the mystery of God is best displayed by a studied avoidance of linguistic precision. It is not the *practice* of religion which is the culprit here—the liturgies and service books of most major religious traditions are rich in material crafted with the disciplined care and precision which characterizes all great poetic and narrative literature—but those commentaries on, or interpretations of, religious practice which (especially since the latter half of the nineteenth century) have supposed that accuracy, or concreteness of imagery, is the hallmark of superstition, unacceptable anthropomorphism, or sectarian narrowness, and that vagueness is a requirement of religious liberality in an age of reason. There are, I think, few better illustrations of this than the uses, vague to the point of vacuity, of the notions of "transcendence" or "the transcendent."

The fogginess of the terminology may also, I suspect, be sometimes due to a reluctance to face up to some of the implications, unpalatable for religious belief, of the ramifications of Cartesian dualism. Let us, therefore, now ask what kind of experience would count (within the Cartesian framework) as experience of God, and try to work out the answers in a manner that is, if flat-footed, at least frank.

If, in answer to our question, we were told that experience of God is a particular kind of "spiritual" experience, this answer would be likely to

---

28   Patrick Sherry, "Are Spirits Bodiless Persons?" *Neue Zeitschrift für Systematische Theologie und Religionsphilosophie* 24 (1982): 41.

reflect the twofold assumption that, on the one hand, all "experiences" are mental events and that "spiritual" experiences are a particular kind of mental event (distinguishable, perhaps, from "merely intellectual" mental events) and, on the other hand, that all the objects of which we have experience are of one of two kinds: there are physical (or material) objects, and there are nonphysical (or spiritual) objects.

Professor Swinburne's definition of experience as "a conscious mental going on"[29] would, of course, be an example of the first assumption at work. And, under the influence of the analogy of ocular vision, the second assumption supposes that the objects of knowledge and experience must be composed of *some* kind of stuff (or how else could they be seen?), even if some of them are such that (perhaps on account of their immeasurable distance from the little person's gaze) they remain forever out of sight (or "unseen"), with the result that all talk of our experience or knowledge of such objects runs up against considerable difficulties. This general setup can be represented diagrammatically, as follows:

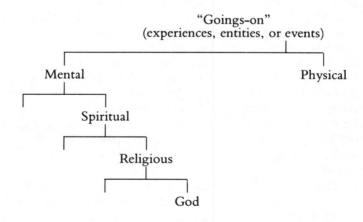

---

29 Swinburne, *The Existence of God,* p. 244. Swinburne is puzzled by the fact that some kinds of "religious experience" purport to be of perceptions of God "not mediated via any sensations." It is, he suggests, to such experience that the mystics lay claim when they speak of experiencing God "in 'nothingness' or 'darkness.'" How are to understand such claims? The best analogy that Swinburne can think of (in striking confirmation, as it seems to me, of the triviality to which a certain kind of empiricism, when working hand in hand with insensitivity to literary considerations, reduces the entire discussion) is that of it seeming to him that "my hand behind my back is facing upward rather than downward, yet not because of any sensations" (Richard Swinburne, "The Evidential Value of Religious Experience," in *The Sciences and Theology in the Twentieth Century,* ed. A. R. Peacocke [Notre Dame, 1981], p. 185).

If we take this diagram as it stands, it seems that we have no option but to admit that, since spiritual entities are a subclass of mental entities (and are therefore composed of whatever stuff the mind is made of), therefore God is also made of mind stuff. To put it more simply: if the "spiritual" is to be located on the "mental" side of the Great Divide, then it follows that God, since he is a spirit, is a kind of idea. Perhaps an enormously powerful, good and impressive idea, but an idea nonetheless. And, if God is an idea, then he is *only* an idea.

According to some people, it is nevertheless important for us to continue to entertain this idea, because it spurs us on to nobler deeds and loftier ambitions. We saw that William James was drawn in this direction, which is the defining characteristic of all purely *functional* accounts of religious belief. Sometimes, of course, the idea is kept alive not to wake people up, but to render them docile and subservient (as Lenin saw when he altered Marx's description of religion as "the opium *of* the people," the tranquilizer which they need to ease their pain, to "opium *for* the people,"[30] administered by the state to keep the people quiet).

However, according to others (such as Feuerbach, Marx, and the mainstream of the Marxist tradition), the sooner we *stop* having this idea, and get on with the business of shouldering our responsibilities for the making of humanity and the transformation of the world, the better off and more authentically human we shall be.

In other words: if God is an idea, then he is only an idea, and the dispute between theism and atheism is merely a dispute as to whether this idea is a useful or a harmful fiction.

There is, however, another direction in which (still operating within the Cartesian framework) we might move. Resisting the suggestion that "spiritual" events are only events "in" the mind, we might explore the possibility that there is mind stuff, "consciousness," or "spirit," to be found "outside" the mind and even, at least in part, outside *all* human minds, "beyond" the world of familiar, mundane reality.

As William James and Alister Hardy both found, it is not easy to win support for such exploration among the enlightened, because it runs counter to the claim, frequently made on behalf of modern science (though often not by scientists), that only physical or material entities exist. This claim, though monist in content, is often dualistic in form.

---

30 See Karl Marx, "Contribution to the Critique of Hegel's Philosophy of Right," in *Early Writings,* introd. L. Colletti (London, 1975), p. 244; V. I. Lenin, "Socialism and Religion," in V. I. Lenin, F. Engels, K. Marx, *On Historical Materialism* (Moscow, 1972), p. 411.

Thus, for example, it might be agreed that there could, in principle, be only two kinds of stuff: physical and mental, or material and spiritual. The point is (so the story goes) that, as a matter of actual, empirical *fact,* the latter class is empty. There are, in fact, no spiritual entities.

Against such prejudice, therefore, the research gets under way, in the hope that we might establish, scientifically, the existence and operation of that nonphysical or "spiritual" side of the universe which natural-scientific description leaves out of account. Before we know where we are, religious experience is associated with experience of the paranormal: of phenomena for which there is some evidence but which are inexplicable by the canons of contemporary science. It is, as Patrick Sherry has pointed out, a striking fact that "many philosophers of religion," within the empiricist mainstream, "look to parapsychology" for analogies for the being and action of God.[31] It is but a small step from here to the assumption that the explanation of religious experience is to be sought in the same direction as explanation of the occult. As any film producer or best-selling novelist knows, our Western imagination is currently obsessed with the occult and with stories of visitations from realms extraterrestrial. The entities in question range from the malign and destructive through the trivial to the impressively beneficent, but it is all, is it not, a matter of "spirit"? And does not our fascination with the spirits arise, in part, from our recognition that they enjoy an existence which transcends (that word again!) the limitations of matter and which, as a result, evades our attempts scientifically and technically to *control* them? And is not God the supreme spirit? Thus it is that, in current English usage, the concept of the supernatural, which once referred to that which, by God's redeeming grace, his sinful creatures were enabled to do—namely, to realize their humanity in truthfulness and love—now refers to entities from outer space.

This, then, is our bleak inheritance from the Cartesian worldview and its concomitant contractions of the realm of the personal. Religious experience, on the run from painful and public fleshly fact, from the terrifying inexorability of impersonal institutional processes beyond our control, and from the pressures, risks, and uncertainties of the mind's inquiring, contracts into those private temples of the heart in which, unwittingly, we worship either an idea or a ghost.

Looking back over the route that we have traveled so far, some readers may feel that a certain amount of demolition has been done, and that we are now surrounded by rubble. But this state of affairs need not unduly dismay us: building sites often look like that.

---

31 See Sherry, "Are Spirits Bodiless Persons?," 42.

I do not have to hand a plan for our building (or map of our route, or menu for our meal!), but it may be helpful to indicate, by way of conclusion, the general direction in which the argument will lead. As Christians, we can dispense with theism. We shall not do so in order to become atheists. Most modern atheisms have been constructed as negations of forms of theism. I am not suggesting, however, that theism should be contradicted, but rather that we try to avoid falling into the trap of accepting some of the assumptions on which it is constructed.

Swinburne's description of what it is that the theist understands by "God" is followed by the assertion that "Christians, Jews and Muslims are all in the above sense theists. Many theists also hold further beliefs about God, and in these Christians, Jews and Muslims differ among themselves." I find that account unacceptable. The things which Christians, Jews, and Muslims characteristically (and to some extent differently) believe about God cannot be divided, in the way that Swinburne does, into a "central core" with variable penumbra, without doing fundamental violence to Christian, Jewish, and Muslim belief. The belief (for example) that God is his Word, eternally uttered and addressed to us in time; or the belief that God is his self-gift, his life, his joy, animating, transforming, and reconciling all nature and history; these beliefs are not, as Swinburne claims, "further beliefs" which may be "added to" and, by addition, "complicate," a prior set of convictions concerning an entity with all the interesting characteristics listed by him.[32]

According to the Oxford English Dictionary, the terms "theist" and "theism," originating with Voltaire, make their first recorded appearance in English in 1662 and 1678 respectively. There they joined "deist" which had arrived, also from France, a few years earlier (in 1621) and, in 1682, "deism" appeared to complete the set. At the outset, both "deism" and "theism" were used, interchangeably, to denote "belief in the existence of a Supreme Being as the source of finite existence, with rejection of revelation and the supernatural doctrines of Christianity," and it would be many years before the senses separated and "theism" came to be used without connotations intended to be pejorative of Christian doctrine.[33] In other words, what Swinburne (and, I suspect, many English-speaking philosophers of religion today) takes to constitute a common "core" of belief originally designated a set of beliefs, and a mode of believing, *alternative* to what were thought to be the beliefs and procedures of traditional Christianity.

---

32 See Swinburne, *Coherence of Theism*, pp. 1, 222.

33 See *Oxford English Dictionary*, s.v. "Deism," "Deist," "Theism," "Theist."

Theologians had, of course, discussed "divine attributes" for centuries. But, in an older tradition, the discussion was not descriptive but grammatical: the attributes were attributes of "divinity," indications of what might and might not be meant by "godness." And, because we do not know God's nature, they served as protocols against idolatry, reminders that anything whose nature we *do* know, anything that we can imagine, consider, or come across as an individual object among the other objects that there are, is not God and is not to be worshipped—whether it be a statue, a person, an institution, or an ideal, and be it ever so beautiful, impressive, attractive, or powerful. In the tradition which runs from seventeenth-century deism to contemporary philosophy of religion in the empiricist tradition, however, the divine attributes are (in marked contrast) taken to be specifying characteristics, identifying properties, of an individual entity, a being called "God."

Originally, therefore, the theist supposed that orthodox Christianity related to God improperly, by having recourse to authority rather than to the deliverances of reason. And if, nowadays, the theist more modestly supposes that he is confining his attention to the "central core" of Christian (or Jewish, or Muslim) belief, he nevertheless lays claim to quite a lot of detailed information concerning the nature of God.

In suggesting, then, that we dispense with theism, I am suggesting that we try to offer an account of Christian experience and the knowledge of God which owes nothing to the assumption that the divine attributes are "essential properties" of a being called God, to the list of which *other* "properties" may be added according to taste or tradition.[34] However, the attempt can only be successful in the measure that we first provide the elements of an account of the *human*—of what it is that might be meant by *personal* action, suffering, thought, and experience—significantly different from the account that I have been criticizing. The suggestion is, in other words, that we dispense with theism (and also, by implication, with those atheisms which are constructed as theism's antitheses) not by attacking it head-on, but by undertaking that "energetic revision of our anthropology" which would render the question of theism redundant. We might then find ourselves in a better position to consider the question of God.

---

34 See Swinburne, *Coherence of Theism*, p. 296.

9

Contemplation
And Piety

In order to start the conversation all over again, we need to move to some context in which consideration of the ways in which human beings may find themselves to be in relation to God is confined neither to some one particular "district" of human experience nor to the experience of isolated individuals. It would be a context in which relation to God is considered in terms of the ways in which our human experience—construed as whatever it is that human beings achieve and suffer, feel, think, enact, and undergo—is shaped, disciplined, informed, and transformed by particular traditions of practice and symbolism. It would be a context in which the redemption of the world would be taken to occur, not through the irruption into our world of "external" forces and energies, but, by God's graciousness, through the reconstruction of the world and the reshaping of discourse, relationships, and institutions. It would, accordingly, be a context in which the account given of what it is to be in relation to God was not locked into feeling at the expense of thought, or into private, individual states of mind at the expense of public behavior and intersubjective patterns of thought and inquiry. It would, finally, be a context in which—if the distortions of intellectualism (in James's sense) are to be avoided—the heart is known to be no less important for the attainment of truth than the head, and in which the test bed of truth is acknowledged to be experience.

In order to discover such a context we could, of course, go back to the Fathers of the Church, or the medieval Schoolmen, or the Reformers of the sixteenth century: to almost any period of Christian history, in fact, before the late seventeenth century. But we are so obsessed by the *differences* of our modern world from every world that went before that the interpretative labor required in order to show that—notwithstanding the profound and dramatic differences that there undoubtedly are—the Christian conversation of an Augustine, or an Aquinas, or a Calvin, was such that, in *their* place, it met the kind of requirements which I have stipulated for *ours*, would be enormous. And anyway, we do not need to go so far: we need go no further than the early nineteenth century. Not only is the world of the early nineteenth century close enough to us to be recognizably "modern" (thus rendering the conversation easier) but the principal protagonists—Kant, or Hegel, or Schleiermacher—continue to exercise a direct and powerful influence on the philosophy and theology of our own day.

I therefore propose, in this chapter, eventually to consider one or two well-known passages from the first chapter of Schleiermacher's *The Christian Faith,* passages which will enable us to take the first steps toward the construction of an alternative account. However, I shall approach Schleiermacher indirectly by way, firstly, of some further remarks about mysticism and, secondly, of some discussion of Hegel's criticism of Schleiermacher in his *Lectures on the Philosophy of Religion.*

Mysticism and Theology

"The early decades of this century," says Rowan Williams, in a fascinating essay on Cuthbert Butler's *Western Mysticism,* "abounded in . . . woolly accounts of what mysticism meant." And if, by now, innumerable attempts have been made to introduce some precision into the discussion, we seem no nearer agreement as to what the concept of mysticism might mean. Thus, for example, there are (I suspect) still quite a number of people who, even if they were reluctant to go so far with William James as to say that "faith-state and mystic state are practically convertible terms," would nevertheless agree with him that "personal religious experience has its root and center in mystical states of consciousness." In contrast, a recent study set out to show that "mysticism need not necessarily be regarded as a part of religion" at all. It is simply the name of a cluster of psychological states and conditions, and its exploration is the business, not of the theologian, but of the psychologist.[1] It is interesting to notice,

---

1 Rowan Williams, "Butler's *Western Mysticism:* Towards an Assessment," *Downside Review* 102 (1984): 199; William James, *Varieties,* pp. 336, 301; Frits Staal, *Exploring Mysticism* (London, 1975), pp. 4, 198.

however, that this author thereby showed himself to be in fundamental agreement with James inasmuch as both men take the concept to refer to some set of psychological phenomena, "experiences," or states of mind.

What's in a word? Why should this usage be contested? Principally, I suggest, because it renders it that much more difficult to discover what it was that people were talking about when they talked about mystical or contemplative experience *before* the concept became thus contracted.[2] If the concept of mysticism (and, more generally, the notion of religious experience) is still to be of service to the Christian theologian—part of whose task it is to render ancient texts intelligible to our time—then such concepts will need to be so taken as to allow us, for example, to make sense of the claim that "the ecclesial dimension of mystical experience is of fundamental importance; for the whole Church is always involved in the process of conversion." Thus it is that, drawing on a recent symposium on *Mysticism and Philosophical Analysis,* Williams suggests that mysticism should be taken to describe "not a cross-cultural, supra-credal specific experience, but a jumble of attempts to perceive how consciousness is drastically 'reconditioned' by the living-out in depth of a particular religious commitment," be it Christian, Jewish, Islamic, or Buddhist. "'Christian mysticism' is therefore the cluster of such attempts which assembles around the central symbols of Christian speech and action. It may take a variety of experiential forms, and the theologian will sometimes be engaged in assessing how far . . . certain of these forms distort or obscure the human goal as Christian faith perceives it—because they are self-indulgently consolatory, infantile, or whatever. And it is here, through the critical evaluation of experiences in the light of a comprehensive theological vision of the human destiny or the 'human project,' that Christian contemplative practice finds its intelligible unity."[3]

To say that the integrity and authenticity of Christian practice requires that such practice be "contemplative" in character is to be talking a very different kind of language from that according to which contemplation,

---

2 Thus, Rowan Williams indicates how deeply Augustine and John of the Cross are misunderstood when their consideration of these matters is construed as a discussion of particular "experiences" in a Jamesian sense (see "Butler's *Western Mysticism,*" 204–6), and I shall have occasion, in a later chapter, to point out how misleading, in terms of current psychological usage, is the title of von Hügel's study of *The Mystical Element of Religion.*

3 Benedetto Calati, "Western Mysticism," *Downside Review* 98 (1980): 209, quoted by Rowan Williams, "Butler's *Western Mysticism,*" 214; Williams, ibid., 209. See *Mysticism and Philosophical Analysis,* ed. Stephen Katz (London, 1978).

or mystical experience, are names for some specific, unusual, transient states of individual feeling.[4] One of my reasons for moving, in this chapter, back to Schleiermacher is that his account of "piety" is, in this respect, ambiguous. It can be read, and has been read, as lending support to both these contrasting accounts of what it is that we are speaking about when we speak of religious experience.

Hegel

There are two reasons for stopping next, on our journey, at Hegel's lectures on the philosophy of religion. In the first place, the remarkable renaissance of Hegel studies that has taken place, during the last fifteen or twenty years, has made it easier for us to appreciate how much he *shadows* the work of such twentieth-century theological giants as Karl Barth and Karl Rahner (and I shall have something to say about Rahner in a later chapter). In the second place, Hegel's account, in those lectures (and especially in the second series, of 1824) of the "concept" of religion, was worked out by way of contrast to the views of Kant, on the one hand, and of Schleiermacher, on the other. On both fronts, his concern was with religious consciousness as a mode of knowledge. It seemed to him that the denial of the knowledge of God was disastrous, not only for Christianity but for the culture as a whole, whether that denial took the form (with Kant) of insistence on our ignorance or (with Schleiermacher) of a non-cognitive account of devotion, feeling, or piety.

Before 1821, Hegel had never lectured on the philosophy of religion. Why did he begin to do so on the thirtieth of April that year? Although he was not in direct contact with Schleiermacher, he would have got wind of the fact that the latter's *Glaubenslehre* was about to be published (the first volume appeared in June) and he "may well have concluded that it was necessary to provide a counterweight to a theological position about which he had reason to believe he would have deep reservations."[5]

In the introduction to this first series of lectures, he deplored the fact that "the doctrine that we can know nothing of God, that we cannot cog-

---

4 See *Varieties*, p. 302.

5 Peter C. Hodgson, "Editorial Introduction" to Georg Wilhelm Friedrich Hegel, *Lectures on the Philosophy of Religion*, vol. 1, *Introduction and the Concept of Religion*, ed. Peter C. Hodgson (Berkeley, Calif., 1984), p. 2. (To reduce the risk of confusion I shall, in this chapter, refer to Hegel's text as *LPR* and to Hodgson's editorial material as Hodgson, *LPR*.)

nitively apprehend him, has become in our time a universally acknowledged truth, a settled thing, a kind of prejudice," something that we
simply take for granted. "It is no longer a grief to our age that it knows
nothing of God; rather it counts as the highest insight that this cognition
is not even possible." For Hegel, of course, if there is no possibility of the
knowledge of God, then the prospects for human self-knowledge, and the
quest for human freedom and integrity, are thereby placed under grave
threat. The task of philosophy of religion, therefore, is to give "to religion
the courage of cognition, the courage of truth and freedom." It is, indeed,
courage that is required, not merely intellectual ingenuity: hence he will
seek to demonstrate "the reconciliation of the heart with religious cognition, of the absolutely substantial feeling with intelligence."[6]

In the light of our discussion of the Jamesian tradition, there are three
points worth picking out from the treatment, in this first series of lectures,
of the "concept" of religion. In the first place, Hegel may have been a
rationalist in the sense that, for all his insistence on the reciprocal character
of the relationship between religion and philosophy, between narrative or
symbolic modes of discourse and pure "thought," even his most sympathetic commentators admit that, "in the final analysis," he is "not as clear
about the reciprocity" between symbolic representation (or "Vorstellung") and thought "as he is about the sublation of religion in philosophy."
However, neither in these lectures or elsewhere was he ever an intellectualist in the sense that James deplored: "religion is precisely the true content but in the form of representation, and philosophy is not the first to
offer the substantive truth. Humanity has not had to await philosophy in
order to receive for the first time the consciousness or cognition of truth."[7]

In the second place, we are a long way here from any idea of "raw" or
contentless experience: "The essential point is that religious sensibility
["Empfindung"] immediately and on its own account advances to consciousness, to representation. . . . There is no sensibility that is not also
representation."[8] Or, as we might put it, there is no human experience
that is not, *as* human experience, a matter of the making of pictures and
the telling of tales.

In the third place, we are even further away from the Cartesian ego, the

---

6 *LPR,* pp. 86, 109, 104.

7 Peter C. Hodgson, "Georg Wilhelm Friedrich Hegel," *Nineteenth-Century Religious
Thought in the West,* ed. Ninian Smart, John Clayton, Patrick Sherry, and Stephen T.
Katz (Cambridge, 1985), 1:108; Hegel, *LPR,* p. 251.

8 *LPR,* p. 217. The term "Empfindung" "points to 'sensations' (*Empfindungen*) . . . which
are *received* in a mode of immediacy, received as they are *found (finden)*" (Hodgson, *LPR,*
p. 269).

little person locked away "inside" its body. Commenting on the relationship between the immediacy of feeling, or sensation, and the element of distance, of standing back to consider the matter, which is found in all thoughtfulness or reflection, Hegel insists that "I am the relation of these two sides; these two extremes are each just me, who connect them. . . . In other words, *I am the conflict.* . . . I am not *one* of the parties caught up in the conflict but am both of the combatants and the conflict itself."[9] The sense of the "self," here, is not that of some thing, some part of me (the relationship of which to *other* parts of me proves strangely resistant to satisfactory description), but rather of how it is that I find out who I am, and become who I am, through negotiating—in action, suffering, and reflection—the circumstances of my existence. The personal pronoun is used, not to *name* some "thing," but to indicate that I am able to tell some story as *my* story: to produce an autobiography.

By the time that Hegel next lectured on the philosophy of religion, in 1824, Schleiermacher's *The Christian Faith* had been long enough in print to have aroused considerable controversy, much of which focused on his use of the concept of "feeling," and it is this which Hegel takes as his target in a lengthy section of his treatment of the "concept" of religion.[10] The topic is touched on, however, in the introduction, and it is to that that we first turn.

As in 1821, Hegel declares his resolute opposition to the view (associated with Kant) "that reason is limited to objects of sense experience" and, equally, to the view (associated with Schleiermacher) "that religion has its proper domain in the realm of feeling. The two views share in common the conviction that God cannot be known cognitively."[11] But, if God cannot be known cognitively, then the concept of God is reduced to the status of a mere idea, a hollow abstraction. If God cannot be known, all that we are left with is an empty notion of a "supreme being." It is interesting to notice that Hegel appears to be leveling this last charge, not only against eighteenth-century theism, but also against Schleiermacher. And the heart of his complaint is that the theologians have neglected the Christian doctrine of God, which is a doctrine of God's Trinity.[12]

---

9   *LPR*, p. 213 (his emphasis).

10 See ibid., pp. 258–314.

11 Hodgson, *LPR*, p. 62.

12 "The doctrine of the Trinity, in Hegel's view, is the 'central point' and 'absolute truth' of the whole of philosophy, the 'fundamental determination' of the Christian religion" (Hodgson, "Georg Wilhelm Friedrich Hegel," p. 100). According to Schleiermacher, in a passage from the first edition of *The Christian Faith* which does not appear in the

"It is just this definition of God by the Church as Trinity that is the concrete determination and nature of God as spirit; and spirit is an empty word if it is not grasped in this determination." In other words, outside the context of the doctrine of the Trinity, and of that doctrine as employed in defining, determining, or shaping Christian life, prayer, action, and suffering, "spirit" is simply an abstraction. "But when modern theology says that we cannot have cognition of God or that God has no further determinations within himself, it knows only that God *is* as something abstract without content, and in this way God is reduced to this hollow abstraction. It is all the same whether we say [with Kant] we cannot have cognition of God, or [with Schleiermacher] that God is only a supreme being." [13]

We can only imagine, or "represent," the reality or being of God by speaking of him as *a* being, perhaps a supreme being. As soon as we do so, however, we are tempted to suppose that God is available (as all "things" are) for our inspection or abstract consideration. But, as Hegel remarks later on, "God does not offer himself for observation." Therefore, "in order to find the ground of religion we must abandon the abstract relationship of observation." [14] It is God himself who *initiates* the reality of religion, which consists essentially in the *relationship* between himself and us. That God is only to be known *in* this relationship "and is not to be known simply abstractly . . . is what it means to say that God is *spirit*." [15]

Hegel seems to be saying something along the following lines. God can only be known as he *is:* that is to say, he can only be known in that *movement* of utterance and love which he eternally is. God is to be known, not by "gazing" at representations of that movement (whether these be pictorial, narrative, or abstract in character) but by *participating* in it. And it is this participation which constitutes the reality of human life and history, a reality which achieves representational expression in Christian symbolism, and which it is the task of philosophy to express in thought. [16]

---

revised edition of 1830–31, even if the idea of God were not available from any other source, "pious excitations would be available, so that the effort would arise, when thoughtful reflection has advanced far enough, to form the idea of a *supreme being* by means of considering these excitations" (quoted from Hodgson, *LPR*, p. 127 [my emphasis]).

13   *LPR*, p. 127.

14   Ibid., p. 313.

15   Hodgson, *LPR*, p. 68. "Stated cursorily," says Hegel in the third (1827) version of the lectures, "religion is our relation to God" (*LPR*, p. 448). Hodgson's careful unpacking of the complex Hegelian permutations of the verb "to be," in consideration of the senses in which God may and may not be said to "exist," is most helpful; see pp. 57–58, 415.

16   See *LPR*, p. 141.

The charge against Schleiermacher, then, is that, by locating religion in the realm of feeling to the exclusion of thought, he has blocked the way to the knowledge of God: "nothing remains but the realm of contingent subjectivity; that is the realm of feeling." The result, according to Hegel, is "atheism. God is thus a product of feeling, of my weakness—a product of pain, hope, fear, joy, cupidity, and so forth." We may form what abstract ideas we will of some supreme being, but these ideas remain our inventions and our playthings, deprived of objective reference: "What is rooted only in my feeling *is only for me.* . . .It seems necessary therefore to show . . . that God is not simply rooted in feeling, is not merely *my* God." [17] We are not, I think, stretching things impossibly far if we say that Hegel saw in Schleiermacher something not unlike a German version of William James!

Atheism, for Hegel, cuts far deeper than any mere matter of disbelief in a supreme being. It is the condition of those who (whether as individuals or as societies) are so locked into narcissistic self-absorption as to be cut off from relationship with God, deprived of that redemptive knowledge of God which is our human participation in the reality of God's self-movement. Atheism, then, is the condition of those who get *stuck* in their finitude, where "finitude" means, not contingency, but egotism. They may, of course, continue to *talk* of "God": "Over and against [the] finite subject there is another, in which it has its terminus. This other, which is called God, is a beyond, nothing else for us but what, in the feeling of our finitude, we yearn for, this and nothing more; for we are fixed in our finitude absolutely." [18]

In this condition of abstract, indeterminate yearning—the unknown and unknowable terminus of which we call God—we have no basis on which to make plans, formulate policies, arrive at and implement responsible moral and political judgments. Behind page after page of brilliant polemic against the myth of pure feeling, or of a contentless sense of dependence, one detects the horror of anarchy which had shaped his diatribe, in the *Phenomenology,* against that "absolute" freedom which, *as* absolute, as devoid of content and determinacy, unleashed the destructiveness of the French revolutionary terror. [19] "We see," he says with bitterness, "that we must of necessity face up to a revolution that has occurred in Christendom. The religious consciousness [i.e., unstructured "piety"] contains the

17 Ibid., pp. 136, 137 (his emphasis).

18 Ibid., p. 284.

19 Cf. G. W. F. Hegel, *Phenomenology of Spirit,* trans. A. V. Miller (Oxford, 1977), pp. 358–63.

root of everything through which humanity has its truth, the root of all duty for it; all other rights and duties depend on the form of this inmost root," the feeling of dependence. And so, deprived of all basis for thoughtful consideration of rights and duties, there can be, for "this variety of self-preserving subjectivity, this I," no religion, but merely "a general cultivation of [unthinking] consciousness."[20]

We shall consider Schleiermacher's own presentation of the matter in due course. For the moment, all that we need to ask is: how did Hegel arrive at this reading of Schleiermacher? There seem to be two components of the answer: the first has to do with the concept of "feeling," and the second with Schleiermacher's doctrine of "utter dependence."

"The view that religion has its proper place in feeling (*Gefühl*) was widespread in Hegel's time and took different forms." Hegel himself sometimes distinguished quite carefully between "Empfindung," or sensibility (which we have come across already) and "Gefühl," or feeling. The latter term connoted, not primarily sensations, but "the activity of the *self,* which integrates these sensations in a 'reflected totality.'" In the 1821 lectures, his preference had been for "Empfindung" as a general term for feeling, prescinding from such distinctions. In the 1824 and 1827 series, however, he usually uses "Gefühl" instead. This shift is doubtless to be explained by the fact that, by then, Schleiermacher had made this term into a major theological category, and it was against Schleiermacher that his polemic was directed. The ironic consequence, however, is that, "in order to sharpen his polemic against the theology of feeling, he seems to downplay the extent to which feeling is an act of consciousness and not merely a sensation."[21] In other words, Hegel's own use of the term "Gefühl" now seems not only to ignore distinctions he himself had drawn but, in so doing, to give to the term a sense much closer to "Empfindung." To put it another way: Hegel's attack on Schleiermacher seems partly to depend upon the assumption that the latter was *mis*using the term "feeling" to refer to sensation.

Why should Hegel have supposed that religious piety, on Schleiermacher's account, was, as it were, mere doglike devotion, and not at all a matter of responsible, thoughtful *human* behavior? The root of the problem seems to lie in a proposition in the first edition of Schleiermacher's text (a proposition which, as we shall see, he rephrased more carefully in the second): "The common element in all pious excitations, and therefore the essence of piety, is this: that we are conscious of ourselves as utterly dependent,

20 *LPR*, pp. 300, 310, 301.

21 Hodgson, *LPR*, pp. 136, 269.

that is, we feel ourselves dependent on God." On which Hegel commented, witheringly: "If we say that religion rests in this feeling of dependence, then animals would have to have religion, too, for they feel this dependence." [22]

Kant and Fries

The relationship between Hegel and Kant is not our concern (which is just as well, for this is a field in which it is most imprudent for anyone to enter who is not an expert in the complex and tortuous history of German idealism). Nevertheless, I propose to make a short detour, en route to Schleiermacher, in order to collect one or two useful clarifications concerning what Schleiermacher might have meant by "feeling."

Hegel's impatience with Kant's form of the doctrine that we can have no knowledge of God was matched by William James. "Immanuel Kant," said James, "held a curious doctrine about such objects of belief as God, the design of creation, the soul, its freedom, and the life hereafter. These things, he said, are properly not objects of knowledge at all." Kant, according to James, offers us, in "this particularly uncouth part of his philosophy . . . the strange phenomenon . . . of a mind believing with all its strength in the real presence of a set of things of no one of which it can form any notion whatsoever." [23]

Uncouth indeed, were it not for the fact that Kant supposed that it was *people,* and not "minds," that believed things. For James, the only objects that can be known are things that can, in some manner, be *gazed at* by the mind's eye. But suppose we approach the matter rather differently and ask: whence might our ideas of God be *derived?* One thing at least is clear, according to Kant, and that is that they cannot be immediately derived from any intuition, felt need, or pious feeling. Whatever the role of religious experience (in something like James's sense of this notion), such experience cannot itself supply us with *ideas* of God or rules for their appropriate use. According to Emil Fackenheim, "Kant repudiates, not religious feeling and its role in the religious life, but the belief that religious feeling can be speculatively or morally cognitive. And he attacks as 'mysticism' and *Schwarmerei,* not all religious experience, but merely the kind

---

which believes itself to be in the sort of direct contact with the Deity which would supersede theoretical and moral concepts alike."[24]

The point at issue can, I think, be quite sharply indicated by asking: if some people feel themselves to stand in relation to whatever they consider to be God, how do they know that it is *God* with whom they are in relation? It must surely be on the basis of an idea of God obtained from somewhere else that they decide that *this* experience, this feeling, is experience of God? Kant himself put it like this: "The concept of God and the conviction of His existence can be met with only in reason; they can come from reason alone, not from either inspiration or any tidings, however great their authority. Even if an immediate intuition befalls me of such a kind as nature, as far as I know, cannot afford, a concept of God must still serve as the rule for deciding whether this appearance conforms to the characteristics of divinity . . . it is at least clear that in order to judge whether that which appears to me and which affects my feeling either externally or internally is God, I would have to test the appearance by comparing it with my rational concept of God."[25]

James sometimes gives the impression, firstly, that individual, private feeling contains within itself the elements required for the description of its object; secondly, that a variety of such descriptions are, as it were, simply lying around the place, and that from this variety we then select the one which best matches the "content" of our feeling. Kant's point seems to be, firstly, that if we suppose ourselves to find, in the immediacy of feeling, some idea of God, then all that we in *fact* find "are the products of [our] imagination mistaken for divine";[26] secondly, therefore, that we have no way of knowing how to *use* the term "God" unless we have at hand some *rules* on the basis of which to discriminate between appropriate and inappropriate uses, and that the acquisition and application of such rules is a procedure of reason.

What, then, of the other emphasis in Kant's doctrine, the emphasis on the fact that pure reason—abstract or speculative argument or inference—cannot, of itself, furnish us with knowledge of God? Here, we need to remember Kant's stress on the primacy of "practical" reason—of consideration of what is to be, not merely thought about or hoped for, but done,

24 Emil L. Fackenheim, "Immanuel Kant," *Nineteenth-Century Religious Thought* 1:31.

25 Immanuel Kant, "What Is Orientation in Thinking?," in *Kant's Critique of Practical Reason and Other Writings in Moral Philosophy*, trans. L. W. Beck (Chicago, 1949), p. 301. We need to bear in mind the breadth, in Kant's use, of the concept of "reason," which stands opposed to the *arbitrariness* of both sheer authoritative "fiat" and unreasoned emotional "conviction."

26 Fackenheim, "Immanuel Kant," 32.

aimed at, and intended. It is in the dialectic of action and reflection, of willing and thinking, that we truly have such knowledge of truth (including the truth of God) as may be accessible to us. If this is on the right lines, then we may say of Kant, as I earlier remarked of Hegel, that he may have been in some sense a rationalist, but he was not, in James's sense, an intellectualist.

This, I think, is the burden of the following observation by Karl Barth:

> Does not man always exist at the invisible intersection of his thinking and willing? Did not Kant's doctrine of the primacy of practical reason at least put forward a reminder of this unity in man? Was it not this with which Schleiermacher's teaching of the central significance of feeling was truly concerned? It was a reminder—Hegel was right in this—which should of course not be allowed, by discrediting thinking, to lead to a vitiation of the notion of truth, but one which must protect the notion of truth from one-sided theorizing. Is a theory of truth which builds itself up upon the inner logic of a thought which is divorced from practice still the theory of man as he really is, the theory of his truth? Can the theory of truth be any other theory but the theory of human practice?[27]

If Barth is right, then Schleiermacher's account of "the central significance of feeling" has something in common with Kant's insistence that the notion of truth be protected from one-sided theorizing (or what James called intellectualism). In which case it begins to look as if Hegel's criticisms of Schleiermacher were quite seriously wide of the mark. As the next step, therefore, toward finding out quite what it was that Schleiermacher meant by feeling, I turn to Jakob Friedrich Fries.

Fries published the text known in English as *Dialogues on Morality and Religion* in 1813, eight years before Hegel's first lectures on philosophy of religion and the appearance of the first edition of Schleiermacher's *The Christian Faith*. Fries is important for our story because his account of feeling as a matter of *aesthetic* appreciation or judgment—of the recognition, we might say, of the truthfulness of the beauty of things—serves as a link between, on the one hand, Kant and Schleiermacher and, on the other, between early nineteenth-century German thought and the phe-

---

27 Karl Barth, *Protestant Theology in the Nineteenth Century,* trans. Brian Cozens and John Bowden (London, 1972), pp. 417–18.

nomenological tradition within which stand James, Husserl, and Rudolf Otto.[28]

Fries, who had been educated in the tradition of German pietism, was convinced that "the one-sidedness of the conceptual, scientific culture of our day must be resisted." This concern we have already met in both Hegel and Kant. According to Fries, however, if such intellectualist one-sidedness is to be resisted effectively, then "warmth of spirit must once more be won for the life of the nation." He saw himself as continuing Kant's work by adapting it. In particular, he sought to transpose Kant's transcendental critique of knowledge into a phenomenological analysis of the elements of conscious experience.[29]

Among these elements, he devoted particular attention to that felt awareness, that presage or presentiment of the *unity* of reality behind the diversity of the forms of its appearance, which is the defining characteristic of aesthetic sensibility. Through such presentiment, "a pure and disinterested feeling akin to the experience of the beautiful and the sublime, we are given the assurance that the world of appearance and the real world are not two worlds but one, and that the former is a manifestation of the latter—a finite projection of the infinite into the finite."[30]

If, therefore, warmth of spirit is to be won for the life of the nation, there are two conditions that must be met: the fostering of such presentiment and its purification. This is the background against which, in the *Dialogues,* he discusses the nature and function of those "distinctively religious institutions"[31] which are necessary, in addition to institutions of government and scholarship, if the life of the state is to develop fruitfully and harmoniously.

Religion, according to Fries, consists of three elements, "the first and most essential of which . . . is the emotion of enthusiasm, submission to

---

28 Jakob Friedrich Fries, *Dialogues on Morality and Religion,* ed. D. Z. Phillips, trans. David Walford, introd. Rush Rhees (Oxford, 1982). "There is . . . an obvious but quite unexplored analogy between Fries's psychological method and Husserl's phenomenology" (Alexander P. D. Mourelatos, "Fries, J. F.," *The Encyclopedia of Philosophy,* ed. Paul Edwards [London, 1967], 3:255). On Fries, Schleiermacher, and Otto, see Almond, *Mystical Experience,* pp. 114–15. For Otto's own discussion of the treatment, by Fries and Schleiermacher, of "feeling" as a matter of aesthetic judgment, see Rudolf Otto, *The Idea of the Holy* (Oxford, 1923), pp. 150–54.

29 Fries, *Dialogues,* p. 82. On the last point, see Frederick Copleston, *A History of Philosophy,* vol. 7, *Fichte to Nietzsche* (Westminster, Md., 1963), p. 248.

30 Mourelatos, "Fries, J. F.," 253.

31 Fries, *Dialogues,* p. 101.

God, and the devotion in which piety consists." As the phrasing suggests, this first element, of emotion, takes "three forms" in which "the serious basic moods of religious feeling manifest themselves." "Submission to God" is the form in which "consciousness of guilt" induces humility and the ideal of self-sacrifice; "enthusiasm"—the "true source of life in the moral life of man"—induces ideals of friendship, of "zeal for the spirit's progress to art and science" and for "the unified life of the nation." It is, however, the third form on which he lays the greatest emphasis. "Devotion in the pure thought of God is the most distinctive emotion of religion . . .[it] is the vital power of piety and of religious virtue: its pure and simple guidance of feeling, through the most powerful and the most sublime idea, is best able to resist the headstrong drives of the emotions. . . . Only devotion is capable of thoroughly purifying us. In this is to be found the whole importance of religion." [32]

This first element of religion, the element of emotion or "the religion of the heart," is complemented by the other two: on the one hand, by "the doctrine of faith," the fostering of knowledge; on the other hand, by the rendering *communicable* of our "most serious feelings of the beautiful and the sublime" through the establishment of "consecrated metaphorical language and consecrated rites." [33]

Religion, then, according to Fries, is constituted by a threefold interest: in the *good,* for "the task of piety is that of . . . moral education"; in the *true,* for "the doctrine of faith is . . . directed to human knowledge"; and in the *beautiful.* [34]

If, however, the aesthetic interest is to be fostered in a manner conducive to social harmony, one indispensable task of public pedagogy will be to liberate people from the tendency to confuse "the metaphor which is embodied in symbol and myth with the thing itself." "The chief thing for the true and beautiful advancement of positive religion is that, in public life, image and symbol should no longer be confused with eternal truth." [35]

These complex constructions of the Romantic imagination may seem confusing and their development into proposals for social policy obscure. For our purposes, however, the important thing to notice is the suggestion, firstly, that the "one-sidedness" of intellectualism requires the fostering of "feeling," or "emotion" and, secondly, that if feeling is to be

---

32 Ibid., pp. 100, 99.
33 Ibid., pp. 100–101.
34 Ibid., p. 101.
35 Ibid., pp. 69, 106.

fostered in a manner conducive to the attainment of that harmony of which it contains some presentiment, it will require both the *internal* purificatory discipline of that "devotion in which piety consists" and the external discipline of rational instruction and aesthetic criticism (lest symbols and metaphors be misidentified with the reality that they express).

If the strategic switch from transcendental critique to phenomenological description sets Fries on the road which leads to William James, it is, nevertheless, clear that—in common with all his contemporaries—Fries's interest is in religion as a public, social phenomenon. I have quoted him at some length in order to show how far we are from those *contracted* accounts of private, individual experience, which we considered in earlier chapters. Indeed, notwithstanding the strangeness of the language and conceptual framework, it is not (I think) fanciful to suggest that Fries's account of piety has more in common with Rowan Williams's description of Christian contemplative practice than with the Jamesian accounts of mystical experience.

There is, however, one crucial difference between them. Williams emphasized the importance of "the critical evaluation of experiences in the light of a comprehensive theological vision of the human destiny." This suggests a standpoint from which the criteria of criticism are *theological* in character, whereas for Fries the dominant criterion is that of the attainment and preservation of social harmony. Fries's program is, politically, profoundly conservative. Its theological liberalism is entirely set at the service of sustaining social cohesion: "For, once people are clearly convinced that there is no disagreement about sacred truth, but only a diversity of opinion relating to the choice of suitable images and symbols, then every good citizen will happily make a concession to his neighbour, for the sake of patriotic love."[36]

Fries, in other words, is quite as unconcerned as James ever was with the question of God *in its own right*. There seems no way in which, within his system, we could take seriously into account Kant's warning that, if it is *God* whom we would worship, and not some figment of pious imagination or patriotic sentiment, we require some *rules* on the basis of which to discriminate between appropriate and inappropriate "consecrated metaphorical language and consecrated rites." We shall need to keep this issue in mind when we consider Schleiermacher's identification of the feeling of "absolute dependence" with "being in relation with God."[37]

---

36 Rowan Williams, "Butler's *Western Mysticism*," 209; Fries, *Dialogues*, pp. 118–19.

37 Fries, *Dialogues*, p. 101; see Friedrich D. E. Schleiermacher, *The Christian Faith*, ed. H. R. Mackintosh and J. S. Stewart (Edinburgh, 1928), p. 12.

Schleiermacher

Turning, at last, to Schleiermacher, I shall concentrate on the third and fourth paragraphs of the revised (1830–31) edition of *The Christian Faith*. I do so, not because these perhaps overworked pages can be understood in isolation from either their immediate context in the introduction as a whole,[38] or the broader context of the development of Schleiermacher's thought, but because they do provide a brief and condensed expression of his mature understanding of how it is that human beings are in relation to God. Having ascertained, from these texts, what Schleiermacher meant by "feeling," by "piety," and, especially, by the feeling or consciousness of "utter" or "absolute" dependence, we shall be in a position to reconsider Hegel's criticisms of the first edition of *The Christian Faith,* and to say something about the notorious identification of the feeling of absolute dependence with "being in relation with God." Finally, I shall stand back from the detail of the text, and consider where Schleiermacher fits into the larger picture that I am attempting to sketch.

The propositions which these two paragraphs expound are among those listed as being "borrowed from Ethics."[39] Ethics, for Schleiermacher, was at once historical and normative: it was, in a lapidary phrase, "the science of the principles of history," the study of how human societies, and individual members of society, attain what is taken to be their highest good.[40] When the theological discipline of dogmatics "borrows" propositions from ethics, it borrows them from *Christian* ethics. In other words, these early paragraphs are a consideration of the way in which human beings move, in history, toward the attainment of what Christian faith takes to be their highest good: namely, communion with God in the communion of saints. Piety, we might say, is the stuff of sanctity. This, I suggest, is the context in which to read the proposition which heads the third paragraph: "The piety which forms the basis of all ecclesiastical communions is, considered purely in itself, neither a Knowing nor a Doing, but a modification of Feeling, or of immediate self-consciousness."[41]

---

38 Warning us that this is not so, see Richard Crouter, "Rhetoric and Substance in Schleiermacher's Revision of *The Christian Faith* (1821–1822)," *Journal of Religion* 60 (1980): 295, 297.

39 Schleiermacher, *Christian Faith,* p. 5.

40 F. D. E. Schleiermacher, *Brief Outline on the Study of Theology,* trans. and introd. Terrence N. Tice (Richmond, 1970), p. 27; see Richard Reinhold Niebuhr, *Schleiermacher on Christ and Religion* (New York, 1964), pp. 92–105.

41 Schleiermacher, *Christian Faith,* p. 5.

Schleiermacher's father had experienced, in an intensely personal way, the tensions between the rationalism of Enlightenment theology—Christianity-in-the-head, and the anti-intellectualist pietism, a Christianity of the heart, of the Moravians.[42] Schleiermacher's account of feeling was the fruit of his attempt to achieve, not a compromise between these two traditions, but their reconciliation. Thus he rejected, on the one hand, the rationalism which regarded feeling, or conscious pre-reflective experience, as a kind of muddled or primitive form of thinking. On this account, pure thought, with its characteristic clarity and definition, is the ideal toward which, in all matters (including religion) we should permanently strive. On the other hand, he equally rejected the tendency of pietism, in its concern to protect the autonomy of feeling, so to press the *contrast* between feeling and thought as to come up with an account of feeling as noncognitive. Against the first of these approaches, Schleiermacher sought to emphasize the primacy and autonomy of feeling; against the second, he insisted that feeling is neither mere sensation, nor blind emotion, nor conscious experience *minus* its intellectual component.[43]

In case it seems, up to this point, as if Schleiermacher's notion of feeling had certain affinities with James's account of "pure experience," it must at once be insisted that there is, in Schleiermacher's world, no place for the Cartesian "little person," no "nucleus of the self shut up in inviolable privacy." We find ourselves to be wherever we are before (and the "before" is not temporal) we are in a position to think about the matter, or to do something about it. We are *recipients* of our identity, our world, our circumstances, our relationships, before we are agents in, or transformers of, that world. "To be an ethical, historical agent means to suffer (in the widest sense) and, in response, to do; to be determined and to determine."[44] Dependence is, in this sense, prior to freedom. Whether or not we can be conscious of "absolute" dependence (and this is a matter we shall consider in due course), "there can . . . be for us no such thing as a feeling of absolute freedom." Whatever our capacity for creativity, however exalted our intelligence or our power, we never create "ex nihilo" (for this, it would seem, would be what it would be to be *absolutely* free). "The self Schleiermacher outlines . . . is through and through a determined and dependent being." And the concept of feeling, or "Gefühl," refers to "the mode through which this inner *givenness* of the self achieves expression

---

42 See Martin Redeker, *Schleiermacher: Life and Thought* (Philadelphia, 1973), pp. 8–9.

43 See Robert R. Williams, *Schleiermacher the Theologian* (Philadelphia, 1978), pp. 24–26.

44 Niebuhr, *Schleiermacher*, pp. 122, 115.

and enters into consciousness."[45] We can, of course, consider this givenness of the self, make of it, in "self-contemplation," an object mediated by thought.[46] Because it is not this aspect of the matter which concerns him, Schleiermacher insists that what he means by "piety" is feeling as *immediate* awareness of the givenness of the self.

It follows, on this account, that all our thinking and willing, our considering and deciding, our "Knowing" and "Doing," are aspects of human *agency*. Moreover, from the standpoint of ethics, even the things that *happen* to us, the circumstances that we suffer and undergo, are aspects of our agency inasmuch as, by shaping and reshaping us, they furnish us with fresh tasks and responsibilities.[47]

If everything that we think and do, consider, enact, and undergo, is an aspect of our agency, it follows that there can never be moments or instances of *pure* feeling, for feeling "belongs altogether to the realm of receptivity." It is, rather, that—if we would think, act, and suffer responsibly, sensitively, appropriately—then what is required is, we might say, the continual disciplining and purification of our feeling, of our consciousness of receptivity. As R. R. Niebuhr puts it: "On Schleiermacher's terms, life uninformed by religion"—that is, by piety—"is life without style or art; it is mere mechanical involvement in the reciprocal motions of thinking and acting." Nor are we mistaken in being reminded, at this point, of that aesthetic approach to the pedagogy of the spiritual life which we came across in Fries. Karl Barth refers, at one point, to "the capacity of feeling, as Schleiermacher put it, or that of 'presentiment,' as de Wette preferred to express it, linking up with the philosophers Jacobi and Fries."[48]

Finally, it is important to bear in mind that Schleiermacher's account of piety as feeling is resolutely theological in character, even though this is not immediately apparent on the surface of this text. If "piety did consist in Knowing," then it would follow that "the most perfect masters of Christian Dogmatics would always be likewise the most pious Christians. And no one will admit this to be the case." On the other hand, it can hardly be the case that "piety consists in Doing . . . for experience teaches that not only the most admirable but also the most abominable . . .

---

45 Schleiermacher, *Christian Faith*, p. 15; Niebuhr, *Schleiermacher*, pp. 113, 121 (my emphasis).

46 See Schleiermacher, *Christian Faith*, p. 6.

47 See Niebuhr, *Schleiermacher*, p. 110.

48 Schleiermacher, *Christian Faith*, p. 8; Niebuhr, *Schleiermacher*, p. 131; Barth, *Protestant Theology*, p. 92.

things, are done as pious and out of piety." There is, indeed, "both a Knowing and a Doing which pertain to piety, but neither of these constitutes the essence of piety."[49] All knowing and all doing are, as we have seen, aspects of agency, and human beings are not saved by agency or, as it is more usually put, by "works."

According to one commentator, an interpreter of Schleiermacher "must decide whether a Calvin or a Tillich is the proper 'model' to have in mind when reading Schleiermacher." As one who is no expert in these matters, I cannot see why one should be obliged to make the choice. Could it not be that the manner of presentation is "Tillichian," but that all that is said is said, from start to finish, as a restatement or interpretation of the Calvinist "sola gratia"? For is it not in relation to the graciousness of God that we learn, in the purification of feeling or piety, more deeply and accurately to acknowledge our existence as belonging "altogether to the realm of receptivity"?[50]

Having established that piety pertains to the realm of givenness, dependence, or receptivity, Schleiermacher focuses more specifically on that aspect of piety which differentiates it from all other features of feeling. The proposition at the head of the fourth paragraph runs: "The common element in all howsoever diverse expressions of piety, by which these are conjointly distinguished from all other feelings, or, in other words, the self-identical essence of piety, is this: the consciousness of being absolutely dependent, or, which is the same thing, of being in relation with God."[51]

We have already noticed the asymmetry between givenness and agency; between being determined by, and determining, our world and its constituent circumstances and relationships; between dependence and freedom. This asymmetry arises from the fact that the *reciprocity* which characterizes our relationships with all people and all objects in the world (for, where our "co-existence with the world" is concerned, there is nowhere "to be found in this whole realm" either an "absolute feeling of dependence" or an "absolute feeling of freedom") is not the whole story. And it is not the whole story because, although there is "for us no such thing as a feeling of absolute freedom,"[52] there is, he maintains, such a thing as the feeling or consciousness of utter or absolute dependence.

If there is such a feeling then, of course, it can no more occur on its

---

49 Schleiermacher, *Christian Faith,* pp. 9, 10.

50 Crouter, "Rhetoric and Substance," 285; see Schleiermacher, *Christian Faith,* p. 8.

51 Ibid., p. 12.

52 Ibid., p. 15.

own, in a pure state, than can any other aspect or "modification" of feeling. Nevertheless, as is the case with all feeling, all recognition of the givenness of the self, it may exist, in counterpoint to the all-pervading "realm of reciprocity," in a more or less clear or clouded form. (Using this metaphor, we could say that, for Schleiermacher, the unclouding or clarification of consciousness is the work of our redemption, the discipline of discipleship: there was only ever one man in whom it existed in pure, unclouded form, and the condition of our consciousness can never do more than approximate to the condition of the consciousness of Christ.)

We misunderstand what Schleiermacher is getting at if we suppose him to be speaking only of a recognition of contingency, of an acknowledgment that here, and thus, is how we happen to be: "he has more than simple contingency in mind"; the feeling of absolute dependence expresses "the *unity of the self* for which not even the sum of the world's influences upon the individual can account."[53]

The difference, we might say, is that between contingency and human creatureliness. Everything that happens or exists or occurs in the world does so as the outcome of the confluence of the multiple influences that contribute to its occurrence or production. It is possible (and often useful) to concentrate upon describing and explaining the forces of production (as scientists and historians do). It is equally possible (and often interesting) to concentrate upon depicting the uniqueness, the *haecceitas* or "thisness," of some particular product or occurrence (as poets and artists sometimes do). But it is also worth adverting to the fact (and the implications of the fact) that there are some things that can *recognize* their identity-in-thisness; some things that can say "I." I am suggesting, in other words, that the ability to use the first person singular pronoun (and this is also the ability to tell the story of the unity of one's self: to produce an autobiography) arises from what Schleiermacher calls "the feeling of absolute dependence."

Niebuhr points out that "one of the difficulties encumbering Schleiermacher's discussion of feeling arises from his failure to distinguish between the formal and material aspects of the phenomenon." Formally, the feeling of absolute dependence is the same in each of us; materially, however, it "has for its content in each man his life unity or particular way of existing":[54] no two of us can truthfully produce identical autobiographies.

But what has all this got to do with "being in relation with God"? "As regards the identification of absolute dependence with 'relation to God' in

---

53 Niebuhr, *Schleiermacher,* p. 123 (my emphasis).

54 Ibid., pp. 123, 124.

our proposition: this is to be understood in the sense that the *Whence* of our receptive and active existence, as implied in this self-consciousness, is to be designated by the word 'God,' and that this is for us the really original signification of that word."[55]

For Schleiermacher, all conscious experience is "determined by and dependent on its distinctive object."[56] Our experience, insofar as it pertains to the realm of receptivity, *comes* from somewhere. It has what he calls a "whence." We are moved by a piece of music, bruised by a piece of furniture, provoked by a question, challenged by some situation which calls for our attention and action. We may, as we reflect upon the matter, correct our first impressions of what it was that "determined" us, revise our description of it, and so on. And we may, in some contexts, call such reinterpretation "proof," but to do so is to construe proof as a matter of furnishing the warrants for revised description; it is not a matter of trying to build bridges between our nervous loneliness and objects "outside" ourselves which we did not experience but merely inferred.

I am suggesting, in other words, that the only sense in which Schleiermacher's identification of the "whence" of the feeling of absolute dependence with God could be said to indicate the outlines of a "proof" of God would be a sense (which might have affinities with Anselm's form of the ontological argument) according to which proof was a matter of furnishing better and more secure descriptions or conceptually clarified interpretations of the world of our experience. Schleiermacher himself put it this way: Anselm, he said, "proceeds from the indubitable, invariant God-consciousness given in self-consciousness, and he postulates that this is to be made explicit in concept."[57]

We shall shortly return to this question. At this point, however, I propose to interrupt the direct exposition of Schleiermacher's text in order to reexamine Hegel's criticisms of the first edition of *The Christian Faith*.

We saw earlier that Hegel's criticisms of Schleiermacher were focused, firstly, on his founding of religion in feeling and, secondly, on his use of the concept of absolute dependence. Where the first of these criticisms is concerned it should, by now, be clear that Hegel simply misunderstood Schleiermacher. Whatever may have been the case some years earlier, in the *Speeches on Religion*, it requires a singularly careless or willful misreading of *The Christian Faith* to suppose that "feeling," for Schleiermacher,

---

55 Schleiermacher, *Christian Faith*, p. 16.

56 Robert R. Williams, *Schleiermacher the Theologian*, p. 23.

57 Schleiermacher, *Geschichte der Philosophie* (Berlin, 1890), p. 184; quoted from Robert Williams, *Schleiermacher the Theologian*, p. 49.

and (especially) that aspect of feeling which he identifies with "piety," connotes some thoughtless condition of consciousness.[58]

Where Hegel's second criticism is concerned, the situation is somewhat less clear-cut. When we read the first edition of Schleiermacher's text in the light of the revised edition of 1830–31, we find the crucial *contrast* "between *religious* feeling and the feelings of reciprocity that we experience in relation to finite objects" indicated by the description of piety as a matter of being "conscious of ourselves as utterly dependent." But, in the first edition, that contrast, though thus mentioned, was not emphasized and spelled out with anything like the clarity that it was in the second.[59]

As a result, Hegel can hardly be blamed for not having noticed the importance of this contrast, and for supposing that, for Schleiermacher, "God" was a particular object of some sense of dependence in more or less the same way in which a dog's master is an object of its devotion. At least in the revised edition, however, Schleiermacher is insistent that "any possibility of God being in any way *given* is entirely excluded, because anything that is outwardly given must be given as an object exposed to our counter-influence, however slight this may be."[60] But it is precisely this element of *reciprocity* of influence which the notion of *absolute* dependence is intended to exclude. With this, however, we are brought back to the problem that we were considering earlier: what is Schleiermacher's *justification* for identifying this non-objectifiable[61] "whence" of the feeling of absolute dependence with God?

The first point that needs to be made is that, whatever the grounds on which some people (including Schleiermacher) *name* the "whence" of the feeling of absolute dependence as "God," it is not necessary to have heard the word "God," or to know how to use it, in order to be conscious of

---

58 Admittedly, the matter is made slightly clearer in the revised edition, which includes, in the third proposition, the important qualification "*immediate* self-consciousness," which was absent from the original (on this, see Hodgson, *LPR*, p. 136).

59 Hodgson, *LPR*, p. 280. Thus, for example, the important sentence spelling out how the "identification of absolute dependence with 'relation to God'" is to be "understood" (*Christian Faith*, p. 16) is absent from the first edition (see Hodgson, *LPR*, p. 279).

60 Schleiermacher, *Christian Faith*, p. 18.

61 Except by uses of metaphor that we *know* to be such: "The transference of the idea of God to any perceptible object, unless one is all the time conscious that it is a piece of purely arbitrary symbolism, is always a corruption" (*Christian Faith*, p. 18). "*Purely arbitrary*" overstates the case and, if taken at face value, would render otiose that labor of discriminating theological interpretation of which Schleiermacher himself was a master. But the general point is clear: anthropomorphism in religious and theological discourse does most damage when we fail to advert to its anthropomorphic (and hence symbolic) character.

and to acknowledge our absolute dependence. The proposition heading the fourth paragraph "is intended," says Schleiermacher, "to oppose the view that this feeling of dependence is itself conditioned by some previous knowledge of God."[62]

Many people, perhaps, unschooled in "piety," undisciplined (through no fault of their own) in contemplative practice, may never be brought to any heightened sense or recognition of their absolute dependence. And, even if they are so brought, they may not try to give its "whence" a name. (There are, indeed, good reasons for not doing so: the feeling of absolute dependence is not a feeling of dependence on any particular person or object and, in the ordinary way, it is only to people and objects that we give names.)

Nevertheless, the point that I want to emphasize as strongly as possible is that, if we *do* attempt to name—to give an account of, to say something about—the "whence" of the feeling of absolute dependence, then the name that we give, the content of the account that we offer, must be *derived from elsewhere:* it is not, and it can never be, given in or furnished by the feeling itself.

Too many of the commentators (it seems to me) overlook the importance of Schleiermacher's remark that the designation by the word "God" of the "whence" of the feeling of absolute dependence "is *for us* the really original signification of that word."[63] He is, in other words, simply stating that this is, or should be, the way in which Christians use the word "God": they use it to designate the "whence" of the feeling of absolute dependence. The remark, therefore, is what Wittgenstein would have called a "grammatical" remark; it does *not* constitute an *empirical* claim of any kind. To put it another way (with our discussion of Kant in mind) Schleiermacher is indicating one of the *rules* according to which the word "God," which we have inherited, is appropriately to be used.

The word "God" is inherited from our culture and our history. It is by reflectively and critically appropriating and interpreting the cultural, historical processes which produced us, and in which we find ourselves situated, that we acquire the use of the language or languages by means of which we attempt to give an account of our human experience. It is from this process of critical remembrance that Schleiermacher acquired his use of the term "God." It is only by this process, therefore, that he is able to

---

62 Schleiermacher, *Christian Faith*, p. 17.

63 Ibid., p. 16 (my emphasis). I cannot therefore accept Proudfoot's contention, commenting on this passage, that "the word *God* . . . derives its meaning solely from the feeling of absolute dependence" (*Religious Experience*, p. 20).

designate the "whence" of the feeling of absolute dependence as "God."
It may not be a very good designation (since we do not know what it
means). But we know what we are trying to name when we use it.

I have labored the point at some length, not only because it is of quite
fundamental importance, but also because many theologians and philosophers of religion schooled in the empiricist tradition seem to have some
difficulty in grasping it. Thus, for example, according to one recent (and
highly intelligent) critic of Schleiermacher, "the feeling of absolute dependence removes one from the world or particular times and places . . . and
allows an immediate relation to God through the transparent tissue of feeling." [64] Not only does this description incorrectly presume that the feeling
of absolute dependence can be had *on its own,* can occur in some state
"removed" from the realm of reciprocity, but it operates under the influence of the familiar assumption that conscious apprehension of whatever
kind (whether feeling or thought, for example) is to be described in terms
of ocular vision: as a matter of "gazing" at an "object" (for what else are
we to make of that reference to "transparency"?). [65]

It therefore comes as little surprise when the same commentator, describing the feeling of absolute dependence as a "self-authenticating experience of God," goes on to ask: "What warrants [Schleiermacher's]
identification of the experience of absolute dependence with an experience
of God? What warrants the move from a self-referential claim to a refer-
ential claim concerning a distinct other?" [66] The second of those two
sentences clearly indicates that the author takes it for granted that Schleiermacher's identification constitutes an *empirical* claim. And this, I have argued, it most certainly does not.

Almost all modern discussion of religious experience proceeds on the
twofold assumption that, firstly, the notion refers to some particular kind
or category of "experience" or psychological state which may be phenom-
enologically distinguished from *other* kinds of conscious experience and,
secondly, that "God"—or "whatever we may consider the divine" [67]—is
the name of a particular object or thing which we encounter or come

---

64 Thiemann, *Revelation and Theology,* p. 29.

65 The danger, therefore, of talking, as I have done, of "contemplative practice," is that
    "contemplation" is likely to be misunderstood as a kind of "gazing." But, as Hegel said,
    "God does not offer himself for observation" (*LPR,* p. 258). However, in view of the
    central place occupied, in the history of Christian spirituality, by the notion of contem-
    plation, I do not see that it is possible to do more than continue to use the term while
    warning against this particular misconstrual.

66 Thiemann, *Revelation and Theology,* pp. 29, 30–31.

67 *Varieties,* p. 34.

across in enjoying the kind of experience which is called "religious." It might make things easier if, in developing the kind of account of Christian existence as contemplative practice, and of Christian theology as critical interpretative reflection on such practice, which I have begun to sketch in this chapter, we were simply to dispense altogether with the notion of "religious experience" (for reasons closely connected with those that led me to suggest, in the previous chapter, that we try to dispense with "theism"). This may not prove possible, but at least I hope that my suggestion that our human experience of the mystery of God—or, as we might now prefer to put it, our being in relation with God—is not necessarily a matter of religious experience may, by now, seem less paradoxical than when I first made it.[68]

At the beginning of this chapter, I said that Schleiermacher's account of piety could be read as lending support to each of the two very different accounts of what religious experience might mean that I have been trying to pry apart. If this is so, then I have perhaps been guilty, in the last few pages, of pressing him too firmly into service on my side of the issue. A few remarks on this question may serve to bring a somewhat lengthy chapter to a close.

Richard Crouter, commenting on the differences between the two editions of *The Christian Faith,* says that "in paragraphs 15–19 of the later version . . . the idea of the rootedness of dogmatic language in the original proclamation of the church is repeated so often as to become a dominant theme." This is to read Schleiermacher's project, as I have done, within an interpretative or "hermeneutical" tradition of theological discourse. On the other hand, Robert Williams, an equally distinguished commentator on Schleiermacher's theology, while allowing that "Schleiermacher's thesis concerning feeling as immediate self-consciousness cannot be adequately understood against the background of continental rationalism or British empiricism," goes on to suggest that "it is best understood as an anticipation of the thought of Edmund Husserl."[69] Do we then, after all, have to choose, if not between Calvin and Tillich, at least between Schleiermacher the hermeneutical theologian and Schleiermacher the philosophical phenomenologist? And does not my dragging of Fries into the discussion suggest that the latter alternative may be the more correct?

Karl Barth (not, one suspects, without a touch of irony) spoke of Hegel, "the great perfecter and surpasser of the Enlightenment," as having

---

68   See above, chap. 1.

69   Crouter, "Rhetoric and Substance," 301; Robert Williams, *Schleiermacher the Theologian,* p. 26.

"brought the great conflict . . . between a purely worldly awareness of civilization and Christianity . . . to a highly satisfactory conclusion." The Enlightenment had "widened the rift" between Christian faith and secular culture which appeared in the seventeenth century, and Hegel briefly succeeded, after a fashion, in healing that rift. Moreover, the manner in which he did so was not entirely dissimilar to Schleiermacher's project of reconciliation: "At the back of Schleiermacher's proposed treaty" between discipleship and culture "was admittedly something quite similar to the Hegelian declaration of solidarity. . . . But Schleiermacher, with his teaching of the feelings as the seat and basis of religion, remained too deeply rooted in Romanticism to be able to make clear the unity he too had in mind."[70]

Perhaps that is as near as we can get. I have little doubt that Schleiermacher's *intentions* were "hermeneutical" in the manner that I have indicated. But the tools that he used to implement that intention were such as to enhance the plausibility of the claim, made by a later generation—when the language of "feeling" and "experience" had contracted into empirical description of individual psychological states—that all he was *really* talking about were "subjective," psychic phenomena.[71]

---

70 Barth, *Protestant Theology,* pp. 409, 410, 411.

71 An influential instance of this would be Otto's criticism that Schleiermacher's account of the "feeling of absolute dependence" made relation with God a matter of "inference" from a merely "subjective" psychological fact; see Otto, *The Idea of the Holy,* pp. 10–11.

10 🦋

Newman and
Some Triangles

"Exclusive"
and "Inclusive"
Treatments of
Triangles

The differences between Kant and Hegel, Fries, Schleiermacher, and William James, are so striking that it is worth emphasizing two things that all of them had in common. Each of them sought, in a different way and from a different standpoint, to supply correctives to intellectualist one-sidedness in matters of religion; and each of them worked with a tripolar or "triangular" model of the things that people do and undergo. The terminology is as varied as the treatment. Thus, for example, James, leaving on one side the institutional branch of religion, and saying as little as possible about religious ideas, concentrates on sentiment or feeling, on "concrete emotions"; Fries considers the relationship between devotion, "the doctrine of the faith," and "consecrated metaphorical language and consecrated rites"; Schleiermacher explores the permutations of knowing, doing, and feeling.[1]

As a reminder of the antiquity of such "triangular" arrangements for the consideration of what Paul Tillich called "the intrinsic dialectics of experienced life," it is worth mentioning that the themes of Kant's three critiques—of the negotiation, in knowledge, desire, and feeling, of the

---

1   See William James, *Varieties*, pp. 32, 47; Fries, *Dialogues*, pp. 100–101; Schleiermacher, *The Christian Faith*, p. 5.

"realms" of nature, ethics, and art—can be construed as a rereading, a reformalization, of the medieval "transcendentals" of truth, goodness, and beauty. (This is also suggested by Fries's statement, following Kant, that religion is constituted by a threefold interest in the good, the true, and the beautiful and, in our own day, by the language in which Hans Urs von Balthasar, with an eye on Kant, announced his program for a theological aesthetics.)[2] And, of course, further back, behind the medieval patterns, we are reminded of the way in which many of the Fathers, and especially Augustine, patterned their consideration of the Christian experience of God in incessant permutation of (for example) memory, understanding, and will.[3]

It might, at first sight, seem as if these threefold patterns are so ancient, so deeply embedded in the Western memory and imagination, that they are no longer worth noticing or commenting on. Are they not, or have they not become, simply the way in which we happen to handle things? Perhaps, but it is also possible that, as an heuristic alternative to patterns dependent upon one form or another of Cartesian dualism, they might still prove to be of considerable theological interest. Thus, for example, according to Walter Kasper, "the history of modern thought" (by which, being a German, he means the history of modern German thought) is, at one level, "a history of the many attempts made to reconstruct the doctrine of the Trinity." Not that these attempts were made, for the most part, either by theologians or with explicitly theological considerations in mind. According to Kasper, "the credit for having kept alive the idea of the Trinity belongs less to theology than to philosophy," and he mentions Spinoza, Lessing, Fichte, Schelling, and Hegel, all of whom, he says, "were trying to revitalize what the theologians were treating," either by mechanical repetition or scholarly disdain, "as a dead object."[4] And even if the experts were to decide that Hegel's interest in these matters was

---

2 Paul Tillich, *Systematic Theology* (Welwyn, 1968), 3:312; see Immanuel Kant, *Kant's Critique of Judgement*, ed. J. H. Bernard (London, 1931), p. 42; Fries, *Dialogues*, p. 101; Hans Urs von Balthasar, *The Glory of the Lord: A Theological Aesthetics*, vol. 1, *Seeing the Form*, ed. Joseph Fessio and John Riches, trans. Erasmo Leiva-Merikakis (Edinburgh, 1982), pp. 151–52.

3 On pre-Christian "ternaries and triads," see Walter Kasper, *The God of Jesus Christ*, trans. Mathew J. O'Connell (New York, 1984), pp. 236–37. Kasper points out, incidentally, that "a Christian use of the triangle as a symbol was, however, rendered impossible for a long time because the triangle was originally also a sexual symbol, and as such contained a reference to the primordial, maternal ground of all being. Only since the fifteenth century has the triangle served as a symbol of the Trinity" (p. 237). But perhaps triangles are no more dangerous, in this respect, than images of "monopolar" theism!

4 Ibid., p. 264.

theological as well as philosophical, the same could hardly be said of his most influential successors—such as Feuerbach and Marx.

In this and the following two chapters I shall be considering a further variation of the pattern in the work of Newman and Friedrich von Hügel, but it will be some time before I can develop in any detail the suggestion, at which I have been hinting in the last few paragraphs, that we might find in these ancient and pervasive triads or triangles, material on the basis of which (having, so far as possible, "dispensed with theism") we might recover and reformulate a Christian account of what it might mean for human beings to be in relation to God.

It is when we concentrate on the strategies adopted for the correction or dethronement of intellectualism that the differences between the authors whom we have so far considered become most apparent. These strategies are of two kinds which (borrowing, as we shall see, a distinction from von Hügel) I shall call "exclusive" and "inclusive." Thus Kant, Hegel, Fries, and Schleiermacher (as I have suggested that he may be read) all pursued *inclusive* strategies according to which no account of human experience is adequate which fails to treat knowing, doing, and feeling, or ideas, emotions, and institutions, as integral constitutive elements of human experience in general and hence (insofar as it is under consideration) of religion, religious experience, or being in relation with God. On the other hand, William James, and Schleiermacher (as he is sometimes read, and as Hegel read him) pursued *exclusive* strategies, identifying the "essence" of piety, or personal experience, or "personal religion pure and simple,"[5] with feeling or emotion *in contrast* to thought and organization, to ideas and institutions.

The exclusivist pursues a quest for essences, for the *essence* of personal or religious experience, and finds that essence in "inner," individual states of mind or emotion which are cherished and exalted at the expense of the "outer" world of structures and arguments. (In order to be an exclusivist, it may not be *necessary* to be a Cartesian, but it certainly helps!) The inclusivist, on the other hand, while he or she may deem some things to be essential and others of less importance, does not suppose the quest for essences to be a profitable enterprise.

The exclusivist characteristically treats useful distinctions between aspects of human behavior as dichotomous descriptions. Thus, there can be no objection to drawing distinctions between feeling and thinking, as a way of reminding us that there are significant differences between (for example) responding to a piece of music and constructing an argument. It

---

5 *Varieties*, p. 32.

is when such distinctions are hardened into dichotomies that the trouble starts: for when did you last find yourself *simply* "feeling," without the slightest play or engagement of the mind, or *simply* "thinking," without the slightest interest, excitement, or distaste?

When, as often happens, the exclusivist identifies the essence of the *personal* with individual, private, states of mind or feeling, the public world of institutions and arguments is perceived as a threat to the purity of the personal. The inclusivist, on the other hand, takes personal integrity and maturity to be the fragile fruit of dialectical interplay between the forces and factors which are represented by the three corners of the triangle.[6]

In matters of religion, the tendency of the exclusivist is not merely to concentrate attention on those aspects which, alone, he deems to pertain to the essence of religion, but also *thereby* to exclude from personal relation with God that great majority of the human race who do not enjoy those "experiences" with which that essence has been identified. Exclusivism, in other words, far from being merely a matter of method, has (as I have already indicated) far-reaching implications for both theology and social policy. Thus it was, as we saw, that James's high estimation of individual genius (and his concomitant contempt for "human intelligences of a simple order") led, quite naturally, through his distinction between firsthand and secondhand religion to the assertion that "there *are* religious experiences of a specific nature" which "point with reasonable probability to the continuity of our consciousness with a wider spiritual environment from which the ordinary prudential man . . . is shut off."[7]

The French Jesuit theologian Léonce de Grandmaison believed (like William James) that "the mystical sense" was "a rare endowment, a very real exception" to the ordinary state of things. Accordingly, in his review of the first edition of von Hügel's *The Mystical Element of Religion,* de Grandmaison took von Hügel to task for "more or less assuming that the mystical sense . . . was, if not universal, at least common among mankind." Reflecting on this criticism in 1923, in his preface to the second edition, von Hügel remarked that it now raised in his mind, "not so much the question as to any awareness or experience which could properly be called mystical, and which we could nevertheless hold to be universally prevalent, but the question as to the implications of *all* our knowledge . . . as to whether we do not all, as a matter of fact, act and think in ways fully explicable only as occasioned and determined, in some of their most strik-

---

6 I shall shortly be developing this last point, with the help of Newman and von Hügel. We have already (especially in chap. 6) considered an exclusivist strategy in some detail.

7 See William James, *The Will to Believe,* p. 184; *A Pluralistic Universe,* p. 135.

ing features, by the actual influence of the actually present God."[8] Von Hügel was, as we shall see, an inclusivist.

Friedrich von Hügel, once described by Bishop Gore as "the most learned man living," was ten years younger than William James, and *The Mystical Element of Religion,* which Archbishop Temple regarded as "the most important theological work written in English during the last half-century," was published in 1909, seven years after James's *Varieties.*[9] The full title of the book, *The Mystical Element of Religion as Studied in Saint Catherine of Genoa and Her Friends,* is misleading. For all his fascination with Catherine and, more generally, with the Italian Renaissance which he described as "those early modern times . . . environed by the priceless boon and starting-point of a still undivided Western Christendom," this particular person, place, and time serve simply as a *way in* to the exploration of more general issues. As he puts it in the preface: "The book has, throughout, a treble interest and spirit; historico-critical, philosophical, religious . . . it is the most certain of facts that the human soul is so made as to be unable to part, completely and finally, with any one of these three great interests."[10]

In order to discover the perspective from within which von Hügel approaches his treatment of the "three elements" of religion, I now wish briefly to consider their treatment by one of the long list of individuals to whom, in the preface, the baron expresses his indebtedness. This list includes Plato, Eckhart, Nicholas of Cusa, Fénelon, Spinoza, Leibniz, Kant, and Kierkegaard—"that certainly one-sided, yet impressively tenacious rediscoverer and proclaimer of the poignant sense of the Transcendent essential to all deep religion";[11] it continues up to the present, mentioning (among his friends) Eucken, Troeltsch, Blondel, and Bergson, and concludes with a reference to the "stimulation and help" of another friend whom he had first met when he was a young man: John Henry Newman.

---

8 Friedrich von Hügel, *The Mystical Element of Religion as Studied in Saint Catherine of Genoa and Her Friends,* rev. ed. (London, 1923), 1:xi, xii (the first reference being to von Hügel's quotation from de Grandmaison's review).

9 The remarks by Gore and Temple are quoted from Bernard Holland's introductory memoir to Friedrich von Hügel, *Baron Friedrich von Hügel: Selected Letters, 1896–1924,* ed. Bernard Holland (London, 1927), p. 53. The first copy of the *Mystical Element* "landed on the baron's desk on 25 November" 1908 (James J. Kelly, *Baron Friedrich von Hügel's Philosophy of Religion* [Leuven, 1983], p. 97). Von Hügel read James's *Varieties* in the summer of 1902, and jotted inside the front cover of his copy that he found the first chapter "simply admirable" (cited from Kelly, ibid., p. 80). He had also, two years earlier, read *The Will to Believe* (p. 76).

10 Von Hügel, *Mystical Element* 1:xxi, xxiii.

11 Ibid., xxix.

The Three Offices
of Christ

In a chapter of *The Mystical Element* which we shall later be considering in some detail, von Hügel acknowledges that one of the sources of his description of "the three elements of religion" was the essay which Newman included, in 1877, as a preface to the third edition of his study of *The Via Media of the Anglican Church*.[12] That preface was the mature statement of an account of the three elements which found its first expression in a sermon preached by Newman in Oxford, in 1840, on "The Three Offices of Christ."[13]

In that sermon, Newman described "the three . . . principal states in which men find themselves" as "endurance, active life, thought." The account rests on a description of society as made up of three classes or "aspects of mankind": firstly, "the sufferers . . . the oppressed, the poor, the sick, the bereaved, the troubled in mind"; secondly, a ruling or administrative class: those "who are full of business and engagements, whether for themselves or for others"; and, thirdly, those whom he describes as "the studious, learned, and wise." These three aspects of the human condition find their representation in Christ's three offices: as priest, king, and prophet. Christ on the Cross represents human endurance; as "the embodiment of God's rule," he represents the active ordering of human affairs; as teacher, or prophet, he represents "learning" or "wisdom." Christian existence, according to Newman, displays this threefold pattern both at the social level—for "knowledge, power, endurance, are the three privileges

---

12 John Henry Newman, *The Via Media of the Anglican Church*, 3d ed. (London, 1877), 1:xv–xciv. See von Hügel, *Mystical Element*, 1:53. Von Hugel also acknowledged another source: "I have found much help towards formulating the following experiences and convictions in Professor William James's striking paper, 'Reflex Action and Theism,' in *The Will to Believe*" (p. 51). "From a study of this essay von Hügel concluded . . . that all man's knowledge and activity begins with sense-impressions, then moves through a central process of reflection and ends finally in the discharge of will and action" (Kelly, *Von Hügel's Philosophy of Religion*, pp. 201–2). However, I shall suggest that, especially where matters of religious experience are concerned, the differences between von Hügel's account of experience, and that offered by James, are at least as striking as the similarities. It therefore seems to me that Kelly's suggestion that the two accounts are more or less the same (see p. 142) is misleading.

13 John Henry Newman, *Sermons Bearing on Subjects of the Day* (London, 1869), pp. 52–62. For fuller discussion of this sermon, and of the preface to the *Via Media*, see Richard Bergeron, *Les Abus de l'Eglise d'après Newman* (Paris, 1971); Nicholas Lash, "Life, Language and Organisation: Aspects of the Theological Ministry," *Theology on Dover Beach* (London, 1979), pp. 89–108.

of the Christian Church," and in the life of each individual, for "all His followers in some sense bear all three offices."[14]

Such pictures are easy to paint, but the interest of Newman's account arises from the twofold insistence, firstly, that, as a description of the natural order of things, of unredeemed humanity, each aspect contains within it the seeds of its own corruption and, secondly, that each aspect becomes (or should become) transformed by its coincidence with the other two.

Thus, on the one hand, *mere* endurance is simply suffering, passion without prospect; "mere learning," the condition of those whose social circumstances immunize them from pain and poverty, while not burdening them with the responsibilities of power, is, as he says (in Oxford!) of the "philosophers of this world," the "most despicable" of "all forms of earthly greatness";[15] while mere power, without wisdom and endurance, is blind tyranny.

On the other hand, each of these aspects, as it is found in Christ (and, by implication, as it ought to be found in the lives of his followers) is dialectically transformed: Christ's endurance was, in fact, the manner of his kingly rule; his wisdom was that of the despised product of Nazareth. And the Christian thinker, bearing the "prophetical office" as Christ bore it, will not be a rationalist or idealist, who supposes thought to be autonomous in respect of either suffering or organization: he will be one who thinks out of endurance, who reflects on action.

In the 1860s, endurance, active life, and thought were replaced (in point of terminology) by "devotion" or "passion," "party adherence" or "fellowship," and "philosophy" or "science."[16] Within the framework of the distinction drawn in 1870, in the *Grammar of Assent,* between religion and theology, religion (which pertains to the realm of personal appropriation, of "real" apprehension and assent) finds focus in "devotion," while theology, as "notional," is the Christian form of "thought" or "philosophy." In other words, by the time that Newman came to write his preface to the third edition of the *Via Media,* he was in possession of a model, patterned on the three offices of Christ, in terms of which he could consider the dialectical relationships, within Christianity, between personal experience, intellectual inquiry, and the ordering of a movement or institution.

There are evident affinities between Newman's account and Schleier-

---

14   Newman, *Subjects of the Day,* pp. 54, 56, 55.

15   Ibid., p. 60.

16   See Newman, *The Philosophical Notebook of John Henry Newman,* ed. Edward Sillem; rev. A. J. Boekraad, vol. 2, *The Text* (Louvain, 1970), p. 167; Lash, *Theology on Dover Beach,* pp. 94–95.

macher's treatment of the relationships between feeling, knowing, and doing. For both men, although the distinctions drawn between the three corners of the triangle are irreducible, a certain primacy is accorded to devotion or piety, passion or feeling, as pertaining to "the realm of receptivity."[17] Unless thought and organization, "knowing" and "doing," express such receptivity, unless their exercise and operation is modulated and purified by what I have called contemplative practice, their products are corrupted by an unfeeling and oppressively "unreal" rigidity. Nevertheless, both men were equally insistent that devotion or piety unshaped and unconstrained by ethical and intellectual considerations is thereby no less disastrously corrupted. And it is this threefold tendency toward corruption, and the checks and balances by which it is constrained, which form the theme of the 1877 preface.

"Christianity," says Newman, "is at once a philosophy, a political power, and a religious rite. . . . As a religion, its special centre of action is pastor and flock; as a philosophy, the [theological] Schools; as a rule, the Papacy and its curia."[18] As always with Newman, the concepts find flesh in narrative description. Rather than reflect, in the abstract, on the relationships between individual and domestic piety, reflective thought, and public organization, he evokes three *images:* of patterns of worship and intimate relationship in particular communities of devotion and pastoral care (we might, according to taste, supply the image of a "basic community" or an English village church); of university departments of theology; and of a center of ecclesiastical administration (Newman's "Papacy and its curia" can also stand for Church House, Westminster, or some office in Geneva).

Having provided us with the pictures, he proceeds to draw out the ideas: "Truth is the guiding principle of theology and theological enquiries; devotion and edification, of worship; and of government, expedience. The instrument of theology is reasoning; of worship, our emotional nature; of rule, command and coercion." And then, in order to remind us that each aspect of Christianity, left to itself, is corrupted by the operation of its own constitutive principle, he goes on: "In man as he is, reasoning tends to rationalism; devotion to superstition and enthusiasm; and power to ambition and tyranny."[19]

Newman, in other words, was just as conscious as was William James of the vulnerability of religion to the aridities of intellectualism and the

17 Schleiermacher, *The Christian Faith,* p. 8.

18 Newman, *Via Media,* xl.

19 Ibid., xli.

oppressive deadliness of structure and routine.[20] But, whereas James supposed that the purity of religion was to be sought in private states of feeling, and that it required for its survival the cherishing of rare blooms of individual "genius," Newman lays particular emphasis on the fact that the *health* of religion is to be sought in the continual, costly, practical, public quest for an appropriate balance or harmony between its constituent elements.

There is in the life of the individual, as in the life of society, unceasing struggle between three fundamental forces or impulses, any one or two of which—if allowed to dominate the rest—corrupt the whole by the pursuit of that which is, in principle, an indispensable constituent of human (and hence of religious) identity and excellence. Thus it is that Newman speaks of the "chronic collisions or contrasts" between Christianity's "three several departments of duty,—her government, her devotions, and her schools—from the conduct of her rulers, her pastors, her divines or her people," and of the "collisions and compromises" between the three offices or aspects of the Church "in consequence of their respective duties and interests."[21] The pattern of relationships between "endurance," "active life," and "thought" is, for him, inherently *unstable,* and such stability as is fitfully achieved is the fruit, not of human ingenuity, but of the abiding presence of God's sustaining and redeeming grace. His analysis of the way in which the dialectic between the three "offices" works itself out, as changing circumstances call forth changing styles and strategies of conduct and operation, is a *historian's* analysis rather than a philosopher's. And, as a historian, he sees no prospect or guarantee of the interplay of elements finding stable resolution within the historical process which they constitute. If, nevertheless, he retains his confidence that no one or two of the elements of religion will succeed in definitively crushing or obliterating the others, this is a confidence born of the conviction that, however fragile and unstable the pattern, that pattern is, nevertheless, the sacramental expression of the vector of God's action in human history. In *that* sense (even if in that sense alone) Newman's view of the matter is not unlike Hegel's belief that human history is an expression and obscure transcription of God's eternal self-movement.

But perhaps the difference between Newman's position and that of Wil-

---

20 James would not, one feels, have taken violent exception to Newman's remark that "there may indeed be holiness in the religious aspect of the Church, and soundness in her theological, but still there is in her the ambition, craft, and cruelty of a political power" (ibid., xlvi).

21 Ibid., xliii, lxxxii.

liam James can be most sharply indicated by noticing that, whereas the residual Cartesianism in James (which led him to identify the "personal" with *one* of the three elements of religion) found expression in his preoccupation with *certainty,* Newman (though he wrote a large book on religious certitude) places at the center of the picture Christianity's unceasing quest for and fitful attainment of *integrity.* Though, as we shall see, it is von Hügel who explicitly makes the move to take the concept of the "personal" to refer to the appropriate outcome of the interplay of all *three* "elements," Newman undoubtedly helped to provide him with the materials on the basis of which this move could be made.[22]

---

22 The point may be illustrated by laying out diagrammatically the terminology favored by Schleiermacher, Newman, James, and von Hügel (whom I have included for the sake of completeness, although it will only be in chap. 12 that we shall consider his treatment of the "elements of religion"). Only in James's case does the category of the "personal" figure as *one item* in this table of the elements.

Schleiermacher	Newman	James	von Hügel
Feeling	(1840) Endurance	PERSONAL	"mystical"
	(1860s) Devotion Passion		
	(1877) Religion (Devotion) (Feeling)		
Doing	(1840) Active Life	Institutional	Institutional
	(1860s) Fellowship		
	(1877) Rule or Organization (Expedience) (Command)		
Knowing	(1840) Thought	Intellectual	Intellectual
	(1860s) Philosophy		
	(1877) Theology (Truth) (Reason)		

11

Von Hügel:
Three Forces

Friedrich von Hügel, according to Patrick Sherry, was "one of the few modern thinkers to have been concerned equally with philosophy, theology and spirituality." Sherry suggests that the lack of serious interest in von Hügel's work since his death (which is in striking contrast to the respect shown in his lifetime, by philosophers and theologians alike) may partly be attributable to the fact that "a re-awakening of interest in spirituality," in recent years, has not, for the most part, gone hand in hand with an interest in either theology or philosophy.[1] Since I happen to believe that an appreciation of the interconnectedness of these three forms of activity is necessary for the health and accuracy of both theology and spirituality (I leave it to the philosophers to stipulate the requirements for the flourishing of their enterprise), it is thus hardly surprising that I should give some space to the consideration of von Hügel's *Mystical Element of Religion.*

On von Hügel's account, the varieties of religious experience arise from the permutations of what, in the first chapter of his book, he calls "the three chief forces of Western civilization" with the "three elements of religion" which are discussed in the second.[2] A summary of that first chapter will, therefore, not only provide indispensable background to his treatment of the elements of religion, but will also serve to indicate the flavor of the unusual style of a neglected thinker.

While helping von Hügel to revise the manuscript of *The Mystical Element,* George Tyrrell (who was a close friend) protested to Maud Petre

---

1 Patrick Sherry, "Von Hügel: Philosophy and Spirituality," *Religious Studies* 17 (1981):1.
2 See von Hügel, *The Mystical Element,* 1:3–49, 50–82.

that it was "a hopeless book; a battery of heavy artillery to bring down a flea." Or, as Tyrrell more tactfully put it when reviewing the book: "There is a chapter in many a sentence, and a volume in many a chapter." Von Hügel's craggy and mountainous style, with rambling clauses and accumulation of contrasting epithets, was the aesthetic expression of a central and abiding philosophical conviction: "Pray get this point quite definite and firm,—that to require clearness in proportion to the concreteness, to the depth of reality, of the subject-matter is an impossible position,—I mean a thoroughly unreasonable, a self-contradictory habit of mind."[3]

In his passionate determination to sustain attention to the *givenness* of concrete reality in its irreducible diversity and complexity, and his refusal to take refuge in premature (and ultimately illusory) theoretical clarity, there are striking affinities between von Hügel's literary strategy and that of James's radical empiricism. In von Hügel's case, however, the execution of the strategy is not thwarted by residual Cartesian assumptions concerning the "self" and the problem of knowledge. This comes across in a passage which is worth quoting at some length because, for all its characteristic lack of technical precision, it shows him putting his finger on a number of issues that we have already come across more than once.

> Now doubtless not only Luther but Kant also intended thus to find certainty concerning God within their own souls, and so to escape that lapse into doubt and self-delusion which they considered to attach to all seeking of such assurance in social traditions and external proofs and practices. Yet the modern idealist philosophy, as first clearly formulated (between Luther's time and the time of Kant) by Descartes in his fundamental principle, was so eager to make sure of this kind of interiority and sincerity, that it started, not from the concrete fact, viz., a mind thinking *something,* and from the analysis of this ultimate trinity in unity (the subject, the thinking, and the object), but from that pure abstraction—thinking, or thought, or a thinking of a thought; and, from this unreal starting-point,

---

3 George Tyrrell to M. D. Petre, 1 April 1908, quoted from Kelly, *Von Hügel's Philosophy of Religion*, p. 96; Tyrrell in *Quarterly Review* 211 (1909): 105, quoted from Kelly, *Von Hügel's Philosophy of Religion*, p. 97; Von Hügel, *Essays and Addresses on the Philosophy of Religion: First Series* (London, 1921), p. 100. As he put it on another occasion: "the cultivated modern man is still largely arrested and stunted by the spell of Descartes, with his insistence upon immediate unity of outlook and perfect clearness of idea, as the sole, universal tests, indeed constituents, of truth" (p. 70).

this philosophy strove to reach that now quite problematical thing, the object.[4]

In von Hügel's case, moreover, the mistrust of premature conceptual clarity is motivated (as it never was for James) by specifically theological considerations. "Life, after all, at its deepest," he says, in a passage critically appreciative of the British idealists, "is a stretching out of faith and love to God into the dark." It is this stretching out into the dark which he missed in T. H. Green and the Caird brothers, of whose work he asked: "Gethsemane and Calvary, are they truly, fully here?" Or, as he put it elsewhere, in a passage with audible christological overtones: "God is the God of the body as He is of the soul; of Science as He is of Faith; of Criticism and Theory as of Fact and Reality. And thus, in the long run and upon the whole, man will, even qua spirit, have to grow and to be through conflict and temptation, through darkness and humiliation, and through a triumph hardly won."[5]

Autodidact and polymath, von Hügel, for all his erudition, was not a specialist in any one particular academic discipline. Everything that came his way was grist to his mill, and it seems likely that his tendency to lumber, like some unchained beast, across the neatly cordoned gardens of academic specialization, partly accounts for the neglect from which he has suffered in recent decades (though this is, perhaps, just another way of making Patrick Sherry's point). "We religious men," he once wrote, "will have to develop, *as part of our religion,* the ceaseless sense of its requiring the *nidus,* materials, stimulant, discipline, of the other God-given, nonreligious activities, duties, ideals of man, from his physical and psychical necessities up to his aesthetic, political and philosophical aspirations."[6]

---

4 Von Hügel, "On the Specific Genius and Capacities of Christianity. Studied in Connection with the Work of Professor Ernst Troeltsch," *Essays and Addresses: First Series,* p. 186. Von Hügel's immense respect for the thought of his friend ("Professor Ernst Troeltsch considers himself as largely a successor of Schleiermacher; yet it is impossible not to realize . . . the great superiority of Troeltsch" [von Hügel, *Eternal Life: A Study of Its Implications and Applications* (Edinburgh, 1912), p. 199]), which he had studied in considerable detail ("Possibly no Englishman, probably no American, knows his mind and works as intimately as I know them myself" [*Essays and Addresses: First Series,* pp. 145–46]), never amounted to unqualified agreement and, in these two papers on Troeltsch (i.e., ibid., pp. 144–69, 170–94), first written in 1914, he distinguishes between the admirable insistence of "the religious Troeltsch" on the " *givenness*" of things and the tendency of "the philosophical Troeltsch" to remain too close to the "idealism" of the Kantian tradition (see p. 187).

5 *Eternal Life,* pp. 222, 223, 332.

6 *Essays and Addresses: First Series,* p. 62 (his emphasis).

What he has to say, therefore, cannot be located on any standard map of the disciplines: whether in apologetics or systematic theology, in philosophy or the psychology of religion. And although the chapter which we shall shortly be considering is some kind of a sketch in the history of ideas, its range and scope is such as to make the professional historian understandably uneasy. The great scholar knows how little even the greatest scholar knows, and he suspects such sweeping narrative as vulnerable to illusion and unrestrained mythopeia.

This distaste of the professional craftsman for the products of the ambitious amateur is important, if only as a restraint upon fantasy and self-deception. Most of the past is dead, silent, invisible—and few of us have closely considered more than the minutest fragment of the little that remains. To suppose that we can tell the whole story is to mistake wish fulfillment for memory, narrative construction for discovery. And yet, our concern accurately to depict the few twigs visible, our sensible suspicion of impressionistic descriptions of the forests of the past, should not lead us to overlook the fact that present self-understanding is shaped and influenced (whether we acknowledge it or not) by *general impressions* of the way that things have been, of how things fell out to bring us to where we now are. Attempts to tell the whole story are undoubtedly hazardous, but a fastidious refusal to take the risk, far from freeing us from illusion, may merely leave us in bondage to an unacknowledged narrative. And one of the things that von Hügel was trying to do in this opening chapter was to call in question what he took to be the dominant received account of the relationship between rationality and emotion in the history of Western civilization.

The Fringe
of Feeling

In all our darkness and confusion, our sense of impermanence and the inbreak of chaos, how might we hope to make some sense of things, find some stability in memory and relationship, some reliable springboard for effective common action? Such questions, according to von Hügel, confront us with what seems to be the "most radical and abiding of interior antinomies and conflicts experienced by the human race and by individuals." On the one hand, it appears to be the case that "reasoning, logic, abstraction," are the necessary instruments of "the Universal and Abiding"; and yet such reasoning does not move the heart or prompt us effectively to action: "Reasoning appears but capable, at best, of coordinating, unifying, explaining the material furnished to it by experience of all kinds." On the other hand, what does thus "move or win the will," namely, "Instinct, Intuition, Feeling, the Concrete and Contingent," is too particular, too evanescent, to furnish the continuity, the communicable stability that we seek. It is "by the fringe of feeling, woven out of the past doings and impressions, workings and circumstances, physical, mental, moral, of my race and family and of my own individual life; it is by the apparently slight, apparently far away, accompaniment of a perfectly in- dividual music to the spoken or sung text of the common speech of man, that I am, it would seem, really moved and won." And yet, this "fringe of feeling" is "not merely untransferable, but also unrepeatable . . . it never was before, it never will be again." Hence the antinomy, the "initial enigma: the apparently insurmountable individuality of all that affects us, and the equally insurmountable non-affectingness of all that is clearly and certainly transmissible from any one man to another."[7]

(This emphasis on the incommunicability of the fringe of feeling re- minds us of James's insistence on the privacy of individual experience. But von Hügel is describing how things *seem* to be. James, confronted by a dilemma similar to that expressed in von Hügel's antinomy, tried to cut the knot by declaring the universality of reasoning to be illusory and in- dividual feeling to be, in fact, the more constant element. Von Hügel's strategy does not entail outright denial of either claim; instead, as we shall see, he tries to construct an account of the pattern of relationships between feeling, knowing, and doing—between memory, understanding, and will—which is equally resistant to both idealist intellectualism *and* its Jamesian antitheses.)

Especially in matters of morality and religion, incommunicable feeling and intuition seem not only to play a dominant part, but to be "fraught with every kind of danger." Nothing, it appears, "can equal the power of strong feeling or heated imagination to give a hiding-place to superstition, sensuality, dreamy self-complacent indolence, arrogant revolt and fanata- cism." Nothing seems "better calculated than such emotion to strain the nerves . . . to blunt commonsense and that salt of the earth, the saving sense of the ridiculous," and to bring us "close to where sanity shades off into madness" and "ethical elevation breaks down into . . . depravity."[8]

Nor is it only in the experience of individuals that this is how things appear to be, for "the secular experience of the race would seem fully to bear out such suspicions." That age-old experience appears to consist of

---

7 *Mystical Element*, 1:3, 4, 5.

8 Ibid., 5, 6.

"a double series of personalities, events, and movements": a "light" series, in which order, clarity, reason, and practical skill have been in charge, and have flourished "in the cultivated, well-drained plains of human science and strict demonstration"; and a "dark" series, in which feeling and emotion, sprung from the "obscure, undrained, swampy places of ignorance and passion," have broken in to take the upper hand.[9]

As instances of the latter phenomenon, he offers: the flourishing of Neoplatonic mysticism at the breakup of the Roman Empire, medieval sectarianism, the rise of Anabaptism and Quietism, and the emergence of German Romanticism "as a reaction against . . . eighteenth-century Rationalism."[10] (We might extend the list and add the growth of the counterculture, vulnerability to the peddlers of drugs and pornography, and renewed fascination with Eastern mysticism on the one hand and, on the other, with the occult, as belief in scientific and technological development as media of redemption turns sour in the aftermath of the Holocaust, the prospect of nuclear annihilation, and the seeming impotence of industrialized societies to assist in meeting even the most elementary needs of three-quarters of the human race.)

It looks, says von Hügel, "as though the experimental-emotional strain could only thrive fitfully on the momentary check or ruin of the clear and 'scientific' school; as though it were a perhaps inevitable disease breaking in occasionally upon the normal health of the human mind." If this is how things have been, then it would seem that "the verdict of history" is "fatal to any type of religion in which . . . individual experience and emotion would form religion's core and centre." And thus, of the three strands in Western Christianity—the "Historical" (which he associates with "the High Church party" in the Church of England), the "Experimental" (of which Nonconformity and Anabaptism are taken as examples), and the "Rational" (illustration of which includes Unitarianism and Socinianism)—it is surely the second which has "proved itself decidedly the weakest for good, the strongest for evil, of the three." This, at least, is the received account, the way that the story is told in the dominant narratives of our culture—"at the Universities and amongst the thinking, ruling classes generally"—in respect both of Christianity and the history of society at large. However, "this first aspect of things" will, he says, turn out, on closer examination, "to be largely deceptive."[11] It is already clear that one of von Hügel's strategic concerns in these meandering volumes will

---

9 Ibid., 6.
10 Ibid., 7.
11 Ibid., 7, 8, 9, 10.

be to rehabilitate the contribution which feeling or emotion—the "mystical element"—might make to the integrity and fruitfulness of human and religious experience.

Hellenism, Christianity, and Scientific Method

Von Hügel's sketch of the three forces whose interplay has produced the cultures of the Western world begins with an account of the way in which the antinomy from which he set out "has been explicated for us" by "Hellenism," the earliest of these forces to appear upon the scene, whose characteristic "thirst" was for "richness and harmony."[12]

In Greek thought, with the pre-Socratics, Plato, Aristotle, and Plotinus picked out as representatives, "philosophy" stands, not for some one particular academic discipline or intellectual enterprise, but for "the totality of all mental activity, the nearest approach to an adequate realization of the reasonable nature of man." In Plato, this Greek quest for wisdom included "an unfailing faith in an unexhausted, inexhaustible, transcendent world of Beauty, Truth and Goodness, which gives itself, but never gives itself wholly, to that phenomenal world which exists only by participation in it." But the antinomy stands, and von Hügel notes with regret Plato's "saddening aloofness from and contempt for all trades and handicrafts, for all the homely tastes, joys, and sorrows at all peculiar to the toiling majority." With Aristotle, "the purificatory . . . deeply religious tone and drift of Plato's philosophy . . . has disappeared." At every turning point in Aristotle's thought, "we get a conflict between the General, which is alone supposed to be fully true, and the Particular, which is alone supposed to be fully real."[13]

We do not need to think as far ahead as Hegel's dialectic to notice that we are being invited to consider the ways in which this conflict between actuality and truth will still endure, even when this first force has been overlaid, or complicated, by the emergence of the other two. This "ideal of an ultimate harmonization of our entire life and of its theory we must never lose, more and more difficult though its even approximate realization has of necessity become." It has become that much more difficult

---

12   Ibid., 11, 10.

13   Ibid., 18, 19, 16–17, 22.

because, at least insofar as Hellenism "identified abstractions with realities, and names with things, and reasoning with doing, suffering, and experience," this "clear, conceptual, abstractive Greek method" has been superseded by two other forces which, at least at first sight, appear "even more antagonistic to each other than either appears to be to the Greek view," namely, Christianity and scientific method.[14]

If, for von Hügel, the essence of scientific method is to be found (as we shall see) in the submission of all claims whatsoever to empirical testing, the "essence of Christianity" is, for him, to be found in the revelation of "personality" and in the fostering and production of "persons."[15] The category of the personal is so central to von Hügel's understanding of Christian spirituality that it might seem surprising that he nowhere provides a definition of it. But abstract definition was not his way: his preference was for *depiction*, for the weaving (even with abstract terms) of a concrete description which, he hoped, his readers would recognize as containing the sense of that which they sought and struggled to become.[16] And it is the person that Christ was who always serves as focus and paradigm for such descriptions.

The quest for the "essence of Christianity" has often taken the form of a search for some distinctive, central, *doctrine* or set of doctrines: the fatherhood of God, incarnation, justification by faith, or whatever. For von Hügel, however, "its originality consists not so much in its single doctrines, or even in its teaching as a whole . . . as in its revelation, through the person and example of its Founder, of the altogether unsuspected depth and inexhaustibleness of human Personality, and of this Personality's source and analogue in God."[17]

Christian experience, on this account, is experience of participation in what we might call *a school for the production of persons*. It is a school whose pedagogy is structured in suffering negotiated and interpreted after the pattern of the suffering of Christ. For von Hügel, "the philosophers or

---

14 Ibid., 48, 25.

15 According to Joseph Whelan, what emerges from his study of von Hügel is "a view of Christian spirituality as the production of personality through a pervasive incarnationalism that is at once profoundly theocentric in character and deeply affirmative of secularity" (Joseph P. Whelan, *The Spirituality of Friedrich von Hügel* [London, 1971], p. 13).

16 As Whelan puts it: von Hügel "constructs the meaning" of his concept of personality "eclectically—not be defining it *a priori*, but by designating it the synthetic term embodying all that man already is as gift, and all that he must do and be as freedom" (ibid., p. 144); see Margaret Lewis Furse, "A Critique of Baron von Hügel and Emil Brunner on Mysticism" (Ph.D. diss., Columbia University, 1968), 2.

17 *Mystical Element*, 1:26.

systems before Him"—whether their mood was that of a "pessimism, seeing the end of life as trouble and weariness, and seeking escape from it into some aloofness or some Nirvana," or of an "optimism" which ignored and explained away "the suffering and trial, which as our first experience and as our last, surround us on every side"—were, in the last resort, escape routes from the pedagogy of the personal. And so, a lyrical description of Jesus as one in whom we find, "for the first and last time . . . an insight so unique, a Personality so strong and supreme, as to teach us, once for all, the true attitude towards suffering," ends in a characteristic note of disciplined celebration: "But with Him, and alone with Him and those who still learn and live from and by Him, there is the union of the clearest, keenest sense of all the mysterious depth and breadth and length and height of human sadness, suffering, and sin, *and,* in spite of this and through this and at the end of this, a note of conquest and of triumphant joy." [18]

There follows a distinctly dated sketch of the New Testament material the interest of which (for our purposes) consists in the claim that, in each of the three major blocks of that material (Synoptic, Pauline, and Johannine), we find "the two chief among the three modalities of all advanced religion: the careful reverence for the external facts . . . (so far as these are known), and for social religious tradition and institutions; and the vivid consciousness of the necessity and reality of internal experience and actuation, as the single spirit's . . . assimilation of the former." (The implication would seem to be that what is *missing* from this second "force" is that which was Hellenism's distinctive contribution: the pursuit of "an ultimate harmonization of our entire life and of its theory.")[19]

If the emphasis in his account of "Hellenism" was on wisdom sought in terms of truth and beauty, the emphasis in the account of "Christianity" is on the mystery of human identity and integrity in relation to God, glimpsed and schooled in suffering. "But now," he says, "athwart both the Hellenic and the Christian factors of our lives, the first apparently so clear and complete and beautiful, the latter, if largely dark and fragmentary, so

---

18 Ibid., 26–27. According to Whelan, "little that he writes, before or after, is not a commentary upon [this] passage" (*Spirituality of von Hügel,* p. 33). Notice that the note of joy sounds not *only* "at the end of this," but *also* "through this." If "there is in Jesus a note of joy which accompanies, indeed informs, the whole temper, the speaking, doing and being—a joy from and about God" (von Hügel, *Essays and Addresses on the Philosophy of Religion: Second Series* [London, 1926], p. 192), this is because joy, for von Hügel, comes close to serving as a *definition* of the divine nature: see "Suffering and God," pp. 167–213.

19 *Mystical Element,* 1:29, 48.

deep and operative, comes and cuts a third and last factor, that of Science, apparently more peremptory and irresistible than either of its predecessors. . . . *They* evidently cannot ignore *it; it* apparently can ignore *them.*"[20]

Von Hügel's immense, perhaps excessive, *reverence* for the scientific spirit led him somewhat uncritically to endorse a positivistic conception of scientific method which was on the wane even at the time that he was writing. It also led him almost entirely to neglect the cognitive character of art and literature. And yet, in both respects, his was a view which continues to exert deep and widespread influence, and by no means only on the popular imagination.

The scientific spirit, he tells us, has "three main characteristics, which are indeed but several aspects of one aim and end." There is a passion for clarity, which finds expression in the identification of the knowable with the quantifiable; there is "the great concept of Law, of an iron Necessity running through and expressing itself in all things, one great Determinism"; and, thirdly, there is "a vigorous Monism," both of means—"the reckoning Intellect, backed up by readily repeatable, directly verifiable Experiment"—and of end: a view of "the Universe within and without [as] a strict unbroken Mechanism."[21]

We inhabit a culture in which the forces of "Hellenism" and of "Christianity" have been overlaid and in some respects obliterated by the scientific spirit and by structures and procedures in which that spirit is embodied. In this situation, the devotees of Hellenism and of Christianity have often accepted (with varying degrees of enthusiasm or regret) the relegation of the forces which they represent to the margins of social and cultural experience. Thus art and religion are reduced to affairs of the private heart and individual feeling, while philosophy becomes an esoteric and autonomous academic discipline, the pursuit of which is the prerogative of a breed unknown until two hundred years ago: the "professional" philosophers.[22]

All such fragmentations of the human spirit were abhorrent to von Hügel, who completed his sketch of the third "force" constitutive of our civilization by considering the "place and function of such science in the totality of man's life." His first question concerns the contemporary inad-

---

20 Ibid., 39.

21 Ibid., 40.

22 I hasten to add that, for distinct but related reasons, the idea of the "professional" theologian is, or should be, similarly problematic: see Nicholas Lash, *Theology on the Way to Emmaus*, pp. 4–9.

equacy of prescientific worldviews. "The mistake in the past," he suggests, did not lie "in the doctrine that the Visible cannot suffice for man and is not his mind's true home; nor in the implication that the Visible cannot directly and of itself reveal to him the Spiritual world." Both these contentions can stand. But what is now ruled out is, on the one hand, the view that "what can be known of [nature] can be attained by Metaphysical or Mystical methods" and, on the other, the view that "strictly quantitative . . . scientific method and investigation can, even in the long run, be safely neglected by the human soul, as far as its own spiritual health is concerned."[23]

The first of these points appears to amount to the stipulation that there is no feature of the natural (including the human) world which is not, in principle, amenable to scientific exploration. Neither philosophy nor feeling can function as routes providing access to reality which *bypass* the laborious, tentative, and permanently unfinished work of scientific inquiry and testing: "We encounter everywhere," he says, "both within us and without, both in the physical and the mental world, in the first instance, a whole network of phenomena,"[24] amenable to scientific interrogation. Thus, for example, Christian believers who say (as well they may) "I know that my redeemer liveth," may not stop their ears to the awkward questions, concerning the sources and veracity of this knowledge, which come from (for example) the historian, the psychologist, or the social scientist.

The second point is perhaps the more original in its insistence that something of the scientific temper is *required* for the health of the spiritual life, inasmuch as it "will help us to discipline, humble, purify the natural eagerness and wilfulness, the cruder forms of anthropomorphism, of the human mind and heart." The world has been, in Weber's sense, "rationalized," and to become "persons" in *this* world requires the discipline of submission to the fact of its *im*personal bleakness. If God, and his joy, are to be found in this world he will, as it were, only be truthfully found on the other side of this form of the desert experience. Thus it is that "we have permanently to take science in a double sense and way. In the first instance, Science is self-sufficing, its own end and its own law. In the second instance, which alone is ever final, Science is but a part of the whole . . . a necessary yet preliminary function, of the whole of man. Crush out, or in any way mutilate or de-autonomize, this part, and all the rest will suffer. Sacrifice the rest to this part, either by starvation or attempted

---

23 *Mystical Element,* 1:43–44.

24 Ibid., 44.

suppression, or by an impotent assimilation of this immense remainder, to that smaller and more superficial part, and the whole man suffers again, and much more seriously."[25]

On this account, it will not be surprising if the relationships between the scientific spirit—even forms of that spirit which are sensitive to the limits of science's scope—and forms of philosophy or discipleship which acknowledge that they can neither have the first word nor stand as competing, alternative routes to wisdom, are marked by continual tension or, as von Hügel would say, "friction." Thus, summarizing this first chapter, he says of his three "forces or conceptions of life," not only that they "are still variously operative in each of us," but that they find "their harmonious interaction in but few men, their full theoretical systematization in none." "The facts of these last four centuries," he concludes, "bear out the contention that neither can the religious life suppress or do without the philosophical and the scientific, nor can either of these other two lives suppress or permanently do without its fellow or without religion."[26]

My extensive use of quotations in this chapter may seem unduly to have slowed down the pace of our discussion. It seemed to me, however, that this leisurely way of proceeding was called for not only by von Hügel's own style, and not only in virtue of the fact that most readers are likely to be less familiar with his writings than with those of James or Schleiermacher, but, above all, because he was, as we have seen, deliberately writing *against the grain* of a number of assumptions still deeply rooted in our culture.

Von Hügel was fighting, simultaneously, on several fronts. Alongside William James, he resisted the suggestion that the work of our redemption can either be executed by pure thought or looked for in "the network of phenomena" (of physical and mental facts, and their ordering in natural or social structures and institutions). Alongside James, he sought to rehabilitate the realm of feeling. But, whereas James saw this realm as constituting an autonomous district of private "persons," von Hügel regarded it as but one thread to be woven into a larger and more complex tapestry. The hero, in James's story, is evolution's rare gift, the individual genius or

---

25 Ibid., 44, 45. Von Hügel would, I think, have viewed with some suspicion the gnostic tendency in certain recent contributions to the philosophy of science (such as Fritjof Capra, *The Tao of Physics: An Exploration of the Parallels between Modern Physics and Eastern Mysticism* [London, 1975]) which are at least in danger of ignoring his warning that "all this preliminary work and knowledge does not directly require religion nor does it directly lead to it; indeed we shall spoil both the knowledge itself, and its effect upon our souls and upon religion, if religion is here directly introduced" (*Mystical Element*, 1:44).

26 Ibid., 48, 49.

pattern setter, the recipient and transmitter of necessary and unusual energies. In von Hügel's account, the central figure is Christ, the bearer of God's joy, brought to the darkness of Golgotha (for whom, therefore, heroic epithets are not obviously appropriate). For James, pure experience or "personal" existence is to be protected, in privacy, from the ravages of ideas and institutions; for von Hügel, personal existence is to be sought, or hoped for, as the outcome of appropriate engagement with, and immersion in, all the the forces and elements, relationships, enterprises, and institutions, which actually and concretely constitute the public human world.[27]

The contrasts between the two accounts (and their implications for what it might be to be in relation with God) will become clearer when, in the next chapter, we consider von Hügel's analysis of the three elements of religion. For the time being, the thing to notice is that Christianity, as a concrete fact (i.e., the Church or worshiping community), is not to be identified with the "force" of that name, for Christian experience, in the concrete (and the ideas, feelings, institutions, and relationships that go to make it up) is formed by the strenuous, fragile, and permanently unstable interaction of all three forces.

---

27 "Here," as von Hügel put it with uncharacteristic succinctness, "the human person begins more as a possibility than a reality" (ibid., 76).

12

Von Hugel:
Three Elements

A few weeks after the publication of *The Mystical Element*, von Hügel, at the invitation of the Norrisian Professor of Divinity at Cambridge, F. C. Burkitt, read a paper to the Cambridge Theological Society on "Three Laws and Forces Operative in the Growth of Religious Biography." The reference to growth was indicative of his overriding preoccupation with the conditions required for the attainment of that *maturity* which alone can preserve us from the disastrous consequences of the various forms of "one-sidedness" to which, as individuals and as social formations, we are ever vulnerable.[1]

Where the religious biography of the individual is concerned, there is a sequence to the order in which the three elements come to exercise a certain dominance. For the child, religion is "above all, a Fact and Thing," a matter of "sight." The child "believes whatever it sees and is told, equally, as so much fact, as something to build on." "At this stage the External, Authoritative, Historical, Traditional, Institutional side and function of Religion are everywhere evident." For the adolescent, "the time . . . of questioning, first others, then oneself, has come . . . the facts seem to clamour for reasons to back them. . . . Here it is the reasoning, argumentative, abstractive side of human nature that begins to come into play." The world of the adult, finally, is a world of action and suffering, of interiorized, personally appropriated experience and responsibility. The adult does not live by unquestioned reception of what is seen and heard, by sight or tradition, authority and brute fact. But neither does the adult live by

---

1 A preoccupation which is evident throughout the chapter on "The Three Elements of Religion" (*Mystical Element*, 1:50–82) and, especially, throughout the two complex and wide-ranging final chapters (*Mystical Element*, 2:309–96). On the Cambridge occasion, see Kelly, *Von Hügel's Philosophy of Religion*, p. 97.

inquiry and analysis, criticism and speculation. Received tradition and critical analysis, fact and theory, are set to the service of action and decision undertaken as the expression of personal responsibility. Here, in the world of the adult, religion, he says, "is rather felt than seen or reasoned about, is action and power, rather than either external fact or intellectual verification."[2]

There are three things worth noticing, by way of introduction, about this somewhat stereotyped little sketch. In the first place, the concept of *religion* could be substituted, throughout, by such concepts as politics or ethics. The "elements of religion," formally considered, are elements common to all aspects of our growth to maturity as social animals.[3] This is why, throughout the concluding summary to the whole work, he speaks of the three elements as "corresponding" to "the three great forces of the soul."[4] It follows, of course, that, far from the "mystical element" constituting the *essence* of religion, it is (as are the other two elements) but the religious instance of an element equally indispensable to political or moral maturity. This view of the matter requires (as we shall see) that the concepts of "religious experience" and of "mysticism" be construed very differently from the way in which they are taken in the Jamesian tradition.

In the second place, although, in common with many nineteenth-century writers, von Hügel takes his story of the growth of the individual to serve as a model, or heuristic analogy, for the construction of larger narratives of social history, he does not fall into the trap of making his model a procrustean bed, an artificially rigid interpretative framework into which, willy-nilly, the evidence is to be pressed. Moreover, his story tells, not of the triumph of knowledge or reason, but of *the possibility of wisdom* and, in contrast to evolutionary uses of the analogy (whether Hegelian or other), he insists on the indispensability, for social as for individual health, of all *three* elements being kept fully and permanently in play.[5]

---

2 *Mystical Element*, 1:51, 52, 53.

3 Von Hügel's position here, if I understand him correctly, seems close to Newman's when the latter said, in 1829: "When faith is said to be a religious principle, it is . . . the things believed, not the act of believing them, which is peculiar to religion" (John Henry Newman, *Parochial and Plain Sermons* [London, 1868], 1:191).

4 *Mystical Element*, 2:387. In the opening chapter, these were said to be the "three chief forces of Western civilisation." The shift of terminology is significant. In his ambitious final sketch of the "endless combinations and conflicts" (ibid., 392) of forces and elements, the account of the "forces" floats ever more free from historical specifics. "Ideas of history" are, notoriously, even more difficult to control than "histories of ideas."

5 For the Comtean version of the analogy (by way of contrast) and its eighteenth-century roots in Turgot's "law of the three stages," see Edmund Leach, "The Anthropology of Religion: British and French Schools," *Nineteenth-Century Religious Thought in the West*, 3:219, 227.

In the third place, although, on the whole, von Hügel's fluidity of terminology, as he accumulates epithets descriptive of each of his three "elements," suits rather well his impressionistic purposes—his concern to
depict rather than analytically to define—there is one interesting apparent
exception. Following leads indicated by James's paper on "Reflex Action
and Theism," von Hügel says that "man is necessarily a creature of action,
even more than of sensation and reflection." It is, therefore, in the realm
of "action" that he locates "the third side of Religion, the Experimental
and Mystical side," in which our "emotional and volitional powers" are
"met and fed."[6] To one critic, this description was simply confusing, because "the will to believe and the active, volitional, practical expression of
religion are as far removed from the mystical form of religion and belief
as they are from the intellectual." This criticism rests upon the assumption
that "mystical" religion is essentially *passive*. But the fact of the matter is
that von Hügel is at pains to show that *each* of the three elements takes
active or passive form, depending upon the circumstances in which it is
brought into play, either on its own or in conjunction with one or both
of the other two elements. Hence his insistence that each element has
a double character, and his final naming of them as "Historical-
Institutional," "Critical-Speculative," and "Mystical-Operative."[7]

My impression is that what von Hügel was *after* (even if he never expressed himself on the matter with unambiguous clarity!) was nearer to
Schleiermacher than he knew. For Schleiermacher, as we saw, all action
and passion, everything that we do and undergo may, from the standpoint
of ethics, be considered as aspects of human agency and, *as* such, require
disciplining and purifying by "feeling" or "receptivity."[8] Similarly, for
von Hügel, the role of the mystical element is that of integrating, through
disciplined personal appropriation, the elements of "fact" and "thought,"
of "sensitivity" and "reflection." If it is true that, for Schleiermacher, "life
uninformed by religion . . . is mere mechanical involvement in the reciprocal motions of thinking and acting," something similar could be said (in
von Hügel's terminology) of religious behavior and thought uninformed
by the mystical element. On this reading, both Schleiermacher and von
Hügel were concerned with the *quality* of what I earlier called contempla-

---

6 William James, "Reflex Action and Theism," *The Will to Believe*, pp. 90–113 (on which,
   see *Mystical Element*, 1:51); *Mystical Element*, 1:52, 53.

7 J. B. Pratt, *The Religious Consciousness: A Psychological Study* (New York, 1921), pp. 13–
   14 (quoted from Kelly, *Von Hügel's Philosophy of Religion*, p. 203); see *Mystical Element*,
   2:393–94.

8 See above, chap. 9, pp. 121–22.

tive practice and, from this standpoint, von Hügel was not guilty of inconsistency when he referred, in one breath, to the religion of the adult as "felt" and as "action and power."[9]

Obstacles to Maturity

There are affinities between the store set by William James on firsthand religious experience and von Hügel's insistence on the indispensability of the mystical element. For both men, religion that is simply inherited, lived, or inhabited, or that is mere matter for intellectual consideration, is (as it were) religion by proxy and, as such, is but a pale shadow and distortion of the real thing. But whereas, on James's account, in order for religion to be firsthand, in order for the individual to enjoy "direct personal communion with the divine,"[10] he or she must be the *original* recipient of something that impinges from "outside" all times and places, stories and circumstances, on von Hügel's account we *make* our experience firsthand in the measure that we personally appropriate, interiorize, and take decisions about, whatever it is that we have received, inherited, or understood.

Thus, according to von Hügel, a "preliminary difficulty" that stood in the way of the task which he had set himself arose from the fact that, whereas "evidences of a predominantly individual, personal, directly experimental kind . . . have hitherto been all but completely overlooked by trained historical investigators . . . now the opposite extreme is tending to predominate, as in Prof. William James's *Varieties of Religious Experience.*"[11]

---

9 R. R. Niebuhr, *Schleiermacher on Christ and Religion,* p. 131; see von Hügel, *Mystical Element,* 1:53. Von Hügel is usually very critical of Schleiermacher for staying (as he saw it) too close to Spinoza. It is all the more interesting, therefore, to notice the warmth of his acknowledgement that Schleiermacher "pierces to the very core of the facts by representing religion as normally occupied," not only with deeds and ideas, but "*also* (he attempts to make it *only*) with contemplation and recollection; and as alone furnishing sufficiently deep motives, and sufficiently vivid environment, for the steady persistence of such difficult, precious dispositions as love, humility, contrition. How immensely deeper does Schleiermacher see than Kant!" (*Eternal Life,* p. 192).

10 James, *Varieties,* p. 33.

11 *Mystical Element,* 2:309. On 10 May 1909, von Hügel sent William James a copy of *The Mystical Element,* accompanying it with a letter (the only one he ever wrote to James) which combined generous appreciation for the latter's work with a threefold criticism.

The contrast between their approaches is neatly illustrated by comparing their comments on George Fox's *Journal*. For James, the *Journal* was eloquent testimony to the truth that "first-hand individual experience" comes "naked . . . into the world and lonely." Von Hügel's comment, as he takes the *Journal* as "springboard, sample-book, and test" of "the sterilising and unjust practical consequences of this 'pure' spirituality," is more caustic: "that 'Christ is the light of every man that cometh into the world,' was *not,* as Fox will have it, simply a direct inspiration of the living God to the living Fox, discovered later on, by this same Fox, to have also been vouchsafed to the writer of St. John's Prologue fifteen centuries before." [12]

This suggests (and it is a suggestion to which I shall return in the following section) an account of religious experience as intrinsically, or constitutively, interpretative or "hermeneutical" in character. Growth in the knowledge of God is indeed, for von Hügel, a function of experience, but (in a description which is in striking contrast to some of the *contracted* accounts and definitions that we came across in earlier chapters) he says that "real experience" and "real knowledge" are the fruit of "the endless contacts, friendly, hostile, of give, of take, between ourselves and the objects of all kinds which act upon us, and upon which we act in some degree or way." [13]

It follows that the "three sides of the human character," and the corresponding "three elements of Religion, are never, any one of them, without a trace or rudiment of the other two; and the joint presence of three such disparate elements ever involves tension, of a fruitful or dangerous kind." [14] Maturity, in religion as elsewhere, is a matter of deepening and sustaining this potentially fruitful and risk-laden tension.

The enterprise is dangerous because, in the history of an individual, as of a religion or society at large, there is no guarantee of success. The

---

As his first "dissatisfaction" he noted: "I continue to feel your taking of the religious experience as separable from its institutional-historical occasions and environment and from the analytic and speculative activity of the mind . . . to be schematic, *a priori,* not what your method, so concrete and *a posteriori,* seems to demand" (James Luther Adams, "Letter from Friedrich von Hügel to William James," *Downside Review* 98 [1980]: 230). His second criticism concerned the relevance of the paranormal (see below, n. 28) and the third the inability of James's pragmatism to take seriously into account "what I think is, in proportion to a religion's depth and delicacy, religion's primary conviction and unalterable insistence, viz. the predominance of its Object . . . over the Subject, the apprehending finite spirit" (234).

12 James, *Varieties,* p. 269; von Hügel, *Essays and Addresses: Second Series,* pp. 61, 75, 77. The title of the address in which these comments occur was, significantly, "On the Place and Function, within Religion, of the Body, of History, and of Institutions."

13 *Essays and Addresses: First Series,* p. 52.

14 *Mystical Element,* 1:53.

history of Christianity, as of the other world religions, can be told as a story of the shifting relationships and imbalances between all three elements. Thus, he says at one point, "the human race at large has evidently been passing, upon the whole, from the exterior to the interior, but with a constant tendency to drop one function for another, instead of supplementing, stimulating, purifying each by means of the other two."[15]

There is no clear correlate to maturity in the history of a religion or of a society. A social group may attain some measure of harmony between its constitutive forces and elements, but such harmony is fragile and impermanent: hence von Hügel's reference to the "*endless* combinations and conflicts" between forces and elements which "can and do appear in every possible variety of combination with, and of opposition against, the others."[16] In the case of the individual, on the other hand, it would seem that, in the measure that all three elements are brought into play, they can—with discipline, difficulty, and watchfulness—be *kept* in play. We do not *expect* the wise to regress to infantilism or adolescence, whereas even the richest and most humane civilization can decline into one-sidedness—and certain kinds of one-sidedness lead straight to barbarity.

Nevertheless, von Hügel's remark about how it has been with the history of "the human race at large" and "upon the whole" does suggest that he sees some analogy between the larger narratives and the story of the crises which an individual must surmount on the way from infancy to adulthood.

The crisis of adolescence can have two unsatisfactory outcomes: the individual may either refuse this first tricky venture toward maturity, and seek to remain in the child's world of "external," unintellectualized fact, or that world may—instead of being sustained to supplement the developing power of the critical and inquiring mind—be obliterated, suppressed, by the one-sided development of the second, intellectual element.

In the first case, the individual may be tempted "to cling exclusively to his existing, all but simply institutional, external position, and to fight or elude all approaches to its reasoned, intellectual apprehension and systematization." The effect of this resistant absolutizing of particular facts, events, places, authorities, images, narratives, texts, or formulas, is to contract and shrivel a person's religion: to make of it "a something simply alongside of other things" in life, and to reduce its object to some one

---

15 Ibid., 59. It seems clear, from the context, that he does *mean* "the human race," but his brief comments on Hinduism, Buddhism, and Islam (see 56–57) suggest that his attention is, in fact, focused on modern Western Europe.

16 Ibid., 2:392 (my emphasis), 393.

particular feature of the world "outside" the individual. The tendency, in other words, is toward "superstition" and idolatry.[17]

This contraction of religion into exclusiveness may take one of two forms. Synchronically, religion comes to "be conceived as [one] thing amongst other things, or as [one] force struggling amongst other forces; we have given our undivided heart to *it*,—hence the other things must go. . . . Science and Literature, Art and Politics must all be starved or cramped. Religion can safely reign, apparently, in a desert alone." Alternatively, the contraction may take the form of what he calls "*successive exclusiveness*," such that religion comes to be conceived as "a thing fixed in itself, as given once for all, and to be defended against all change and interpretation, all novelty and discrimination."[18]

When, at the end of the book, he takes a final glance at the ways in which religion becomes "destructive of itself" when this first element "is allowed gravely to cripple, or all but to exclude, the other forces and elements," it is the second alternative on which he concentrates. Accordingly, superstition is now defined as "an oppressive materialization and dangerous would-be absolute fixation of even quite secondary and temporary expressions and analyses of religion."[19]

Returning to the story of the development of the individual, the crisis of adolescence may also be unsatisfactorily resolved in the *opposite* direction. The individual, rejoicing in the power and play of rational inquiry and argument, may allow the world of the intellect simply to "supplant" the institutional, historical element. In this case, religion, assimilated "to Science and Philosophy," will "grow hard and shallow, and will tend to disappear altogether." This time, the tendency is not toward superstition, but toward "rationalism and indifference." More generally, whenever our capacity and need for intellectual analysis is "allowed superciliously to ignore, or violently to explain away, the other kinds of approaches and contributions to religious truth and experience," the outcome is an agnostic rationalism the fruits of which amount to no more than "a petty, artificial arrangement by the human mind of the little which, then and there, it can easily harmonize into a whole."[20]

(Polemically, by keeping the analogy between the individual and society in play, he encourages us to see fundamentalisms and "traditionalisms" of

17 Ibid., 1:54, 55.
18 Ibid., 71.
19 Ibid., 2:387.
20 Ibid., 1:55, 2:389.

every kind as infantilist in character, and to regard intellectualism or rationalism as the hallmark of a culture stuck in an unsatisfactorily resolved crisis of adolescence.)

Returning once more to the story of the individual: even if both the dangers so far mentioned are avoided, and the person "passes well through this first crisis," and thus achieves the "collaboration" of the "external" and "intellectual" elements, there is "a final transition, the addition of the third force, that of the emotional-experimental life, [which] must yet be safely achieved." This final transition will be differently resisted by each of the first two elements: "To the external force this emotional power will tend to appear as akin to revolution; to the intellectual side it will readily seem mere subjectivity and sentimentality ever verging on delusion."[21]

It is, of course, integral to his account that neither fear is simply groundless. The "mystical element," the force of feeling and emotion, may indeed be tempted to "sweep aside . . . the external, as so much oppressive ballast, and the intellectual, as so much hair-splitting." Thus, whereas William James regarded the emergence of a religion of pure feeling, standing in no essential need of intellectual expression or institutional embodiment, as proof of the progress of religion, von Hügel sees it as the degeneration of unrestrained subjectivity toward "emotional fanaticism."[22]

In order to complete the picture, we would need to consider what happens when the mystical element combines with one, and only one, of the other two, to the attempted exclusion or suppression of the third. Perhaps because von Hügel was at heart a philosopher, or perhaps on account of the circumstances of Catholic Christianity at the time that he was writing, he regarded the collusion of the "institutional" with the "emotional" against the "intellectual" element as posing "now the great central difficulty and pressing problem of more or less every degree and kind of religious life."[23] This emphasis, it seems to me, is quite consistent with his overall concern, as a thinker and writer, to rehabilitate the mystical element, because, according to "the treble interest and spirit" of the book, the *integration* of the intellectual element with the other two is necessary for both the production and the sympathetic reception of an exposition

---

21 Ibid., 1:55. He is writing, we remember, at the height of the Modernist crisis.

22 Ibid., 1:55; see James, *Varieties*, p. 173; von Hügel, *Mystical Element*, 2:391.

23 *Mystical Element*, 2:367. "Inasmuch as the feeling clings to historical facts and persons, it will instinctively elude or attempt to suppress all critical examination and analysis of these its supports. Inasmuch as it feeds upon its own emotion . . . it will instinctively fret under and oppose all that slow discrimination and mere approximation, that collection of a few certainties, many probabilities, and innumerable possibilities, all that pother over a very little, which seem to make up the sum of human knowledge" (1:75).

such as his of (as he puts it in his final sentence) "the character and necessity, the limits, dangers and helpfulness of the Mystic Element of Religion." [24]

"Inclusive" and "Exclusive" Mysticism

I have spoken of maturity, health, and the possibility of wisdom. But, of course, the Christian term for that which von Hügel sought to recommend, and the conditions for the hazardous, strenuous, risk-laden attainment of which he described in such detail, is *sanctity*. To say that Christianity is a school for the production of persons is to say no more and no less than that it is a school for the production of saints. Von Hügel can therefore refer (with a matter-of-factness which some will find surprising and others—assuming an exclusivist account of religion and religious experience—unintelligible) to the mature and purified "religious imagination, mind, heart, and will,—*that is to say,* the complete, fully normal human being at his deepest." [25] That remark certainly does not indicate any conflation of Christian criteria with whatever are taken, in any particular social context, to count as criteria for sanity or mental health. [26] It simply serves as a reminder that, however eccentric saints may often be, holiness after the pattern of Christ is (from within the perspectives of a Christian anthropology) the goal and standard of personal—which is *not* to say simply individual—human existence.

Contracted accounts of "mysticism" and the "mystical" have, in recent decades, become so widespread as to make it that much more difficult for even the sympathetic reader not to set out with misleading expectations of what von Hügel was talking about. He was not unaware of the problem and therefore sought, in a number of passages, clearly to distinguish be-

---

24 Ibid., 2:396. In the preface, that "treble interest and spirit" is said to be "historico-critical, philosophical, religious" (1:xxiii).

25 Ibid., 2:378 (my emphasis).

26 If only for the very "Hügelian" reason that "the soul cannot attain to its fullest possible spiritual development, without the vigorous specific action and differentiation of forces and functions of a not specifically religious character" (ibid., 393). On the place of considerations derived from "theoretical and clinical psychology . . . within the wider range of spirituality," in von Hügel's account, see Whelan, *Spirituality of von Hügel,* pp. 147–48.

tween what he called "inclusive" and "exclusive" mysticism. Taking the term "mysticism" to refer, in general, to "both the right and the wrong use of feeling in religion," he described *inclusive* mysticism as simply a matter of allowing, in the practice and theory of religion, "the legitimate share of feeling in the constitution of the religious life," whereas he took the mistake of the *exclusive* mystic to be that of continually attempting to make feeling, or emotional states, the essence or "all of religion."[27]

In the light of James's assertion (made the year before the publication of von Hügel's study) that "there *are* religious experiences of a specific nature [which] . . . point with reasonable probability to the continuity of our consciousness with a wider spiritual environment," it is hardly surprising to discover that the baron regarded "Prof. James's in many respects valuable *Varieties of Religious Experience*" as "seriously damaged" by a "tendency to treat Religion, or at least Mysticism, as an abnormal faculty for perceiving phenomena inexplicable by physical and psychical science." And his own answer to the question: "Is there such a thing . . . as specifically Mystical experience or knowledge?,"or as "a specifically distinct, self-sufficing, purely mystical mode of apprehending reality?," was: "I take it, *distinctly not.*"[28]

Mysticism "as such," when allowed to flourish in isolation from reciprocal, purificatory, corrective interaction with the other two elements, has, he says, "ever tended to deny all positive character to evil," and thus to breed an evasive and unreal optimism. Mysticism "as such" tends to be in flight from the darkness of the world. But flight leads neither to self-knowledge nor to the knowledge of God. It is not, he says, "the smoother, easier times and circumstances in the lives of individuals and of people but, on the contrary, the harder and hardest trials of every . . . kind," that "have ever been the occasions of the deepest trust in and love of God to which man has attained."[29] This is neither stoicism nor masochism, but a reminder that, for the Christian, Gethsemane and Calvary stand as paradigms of religious experience and of the deepest and most fruitful forms of the human experience of God.

---

27 *Mystical Element*, 2:291.

28 William James, *A Pluralistic Universe*, p. 135; von Hügel, *Mystical Element*, 2:308, 275, 283. It is clear from the context that by "psychical" von Hügel means "psychological." He is not referring to that investigation of the paranormal which fascinated James but of which von Hügel remarked: "I have so far . . . never come across any subject, or rather any result, of "Psychical Research" which has appealed to me as of any spiritual, religious worth" (James Luther Adams, "Letter from Friedrich von Hügel to William James," 231).

29 *Mystical Element*, 2: 293, 291–92.

There is, in all mysticism, a "turning-away from all multiplicity and contingency, from the visible and successive," in single-minded quest of the one thing necessary, the pearl of great price, the glimpsed simplicity and stillness, the eloquent silence of the mystery of God. But whereas exclusive mysticism makes of this "turning-away," this asceticism or other-worldliness, the one sole movement and standard of perfection, it is characteristic of inclusive mysticism that it acknowledges the mystical element to be but one factor in what von Hügel calls a "larger asceticism."[30]

Whereas exclusive mysticism perceives, in the "multiplicity and contingency," the fragmented character of human existence—the varied and endless demands made upon time, attention, energy, responsibility, and affection by family, friends, work, and society—simply a distraction from and threat to the development of personal wholeness, a "larger and wider"[31] asceticism recognizes, in the discipline of these relationships and demands, the workshop in which personal wholeness and identity are forged.

Similarly, whereas exclusive mysticism perceives in the bewildering pluralism of the objects and methods of intellectual inquiry, and in the insurmountable tentativeness and provisionality of the results of such inquiry, a distraction from and a threat to the singleness and purity of its passion, the "larger asceticism" recognizes the indispensability for personal maturity of that "courage, patience, perseverance . . . self-oblivion . . . and willing correction of even one's most cherished views," which characterizes the scientific temper. This is why von Hügel believed that scientific disinterestedness, far from being irreconcilable with religious commitment, may serve, in our culture, as the "special channel and instrument for the preservation and acquisition of [that] absolutely essential temper of detachment" which is the very soul of this "larger asceticism."[32]

He was well aware of the fact that the structures of social existence, and the modeling of that existence (in discourse and public policy) in terms of scientific laws and regularities, do tend to crowd out, diminish, and eliminate the "personal"—thus reducing the person (in fact and imagination) to the status of an impersonal instance, an ant in the ant heap, a speck of dust in the movement of matter. But whereas the exclusive mystic there-

---

30 Ibid., 348, 351.

31 Ibid., 348.

32 Ibid., 351, 380. For von Hügel (who read more widely in German than in English), the concept of "science" refers as much to historical study as to natural-scientific inquiry. Hence his remark that "History is essentially necessary to Religion if only as a corrective, probably the sole efficient corrective, against the delusions of a false Mysticism" (*Essays and Addresses: Second Series*, p. 53).

fore supposes that religion has nothing to do with politics, nor faith with intellectual abstraction, what von Hügel pleaded for is the recognition that personal identity (the Christian construal of which is personal relationship with a personal God) is not secured or sustained by *opting out* of the worlds of science and society but, on the contrary, by continual submission to the *purification* which engagement in the affairs of these worlds entails.

At one level, of course, what is at issue here is the relationship between love of God and love of the creature. The exclusive mystic, supposing these loves to be, in the last analysis, mutually exclusive, opts for what he takes to be the love of God. In doing so, he reflects what von Hügel calls the "first, easier, more popular conception" of the relationship: a conception according to which God is "practically thought of as the First of Creatures, competing with the rest for man's love and . . . placed alongside of them." God, on this view, is "not loved perfectly, till He is loved alone." [33]

But there is also a "second, more difficult and rarer conception," according to which "God is placed, not alongside creatures but behind them, as the light which shines through a crystal and lends it whatever lustre it may have. He is loved here, not apart from but through and in them. . . . The love of Him is the 'form,' the principle of order and harmony; our natural affections are the 'matter' harmonized and set in order." [34]

It does not follow, he argues (with the monastic life in mind) that there is no place, within the Christian "organism," for a "minority" the pattern of whose life will "represent a maximum of 'form,' with a minimum of 'matter.'" But, though he admired the "first plan" of Plato's *Republic,* he had harsh things to say about the effect of "late changes and additions in that great book, especially as these have been . . . still further exaggerated, by Plotinus and Proclus." In these later versions, we are confronted, "in its most perfect and most influential form," by "that ruinously untrue doctrine of the separation of any one set of men from the mass of their fellows." [35] There is, therefore, in von Hügel's scheme of things, no place for distinctions between first-class and second-class Christians—between an elite corps of geniuses and pattern setters and the slaves of habit who live their religion simply at secondhand.

His instinct here was admirable. It sprang from the conviction, central to his incarnationalism, that all human experience and thought, all secularity and all religion, exist and flourish only as "*socially* appropriated gifts

---

33 *Mystical Element,* 2:353.

34 Ibid., 353. Von Hügel is paraphrasing George Tyrrell, *The Faith of the Millions* (London, 1901), 2:49–53.

35 *Mystical Element,* 2:355, 356, 357.

and achievements." Unfortunately, however, this admirable instinct never found adequate expression, either in his perception of the implications of his own doctrine or in his private life. "The deeper layers of his spiritual insight, and consequently his deepest feelings, do not seem to have been reached by the moral and material catastrophe of the first world war, nor indeed, perhaps, by any of the socio-moral and politico-moral problems which since that war have so grievously tortured our generation and affected the whole Christian outlook." And a friend who lodged with him for some years "recalled the squalor in which the baron's servants lived." We are poignantly reminded of his own warning that the forces and elements on whose dialectical interdependence he so splendidly insisted find "their harmonious interaction in but few men, their full theoretical systematization [and, we might add, their full practical actualization] in none."[36]

Clarifying the Sense of God

If there is, in fact, no such thing as "specifically Mystical experience or knowledge," no "specifically distinct, self-sufficing, purely mystical mode of apprehending reality,"[37] then it would seem to follow that the content of the accounts that we offer of our experience of God must be derived from elsewhere than the mystical element of religion. My formulation may be awkward, but I am trying to indicate that there are similarities between von Hügel's view of the matter and that which we came across earlier when considering Schleiermacher's account of what is "for us" the signification of the word "God."[38]

Thus, according to von Hügel, "man's dim, but deep, his 'confused' sense of God . . . does not, of itself, or directly, furnish any definite, clear, stable conception or even image, of a Perfect Being." In itself, this "ob-

---

36 Whelan, *Spirituality of von Hügel*, p. 221 (his emphasis); Michael de la Bedoyère, *The Life of Baron von Hügel* (London, 1951), quoted from Kelly, *Von Hügel's Philosophy of Religion*, p. 211; ibid., p. 211; *Mystical Element* 1:48.

37 *Mystical Element* 2:275, 283.

38 This was not how von Hügel himself read Schleiermacher, for whom (according to the baron) God, even in *The Christian Faith*, "is just the unity of the multiplicity which appears as world" (*Eternal Life*, p. 197; cf. ibid., pp. 180–98, on which see Kelly, *Von Hügel's Philosophy of Religion*, pp. 170–71).

scure, not transparent" sense might "be 'explained' as purely immanental in its origin and end. But . . . this dim sense is met, in real life, by the clear conceptions, the historic incorporations, the traditional training schools, the visible institutions of the great world-religions."[39] It is, in other words, in these schools that we learn to use the languages in which the sense of God is clarified—languages the disciplined use of which restrains us from naming as "God" any particular fact, object, thing, image, institution, or idea. These schools are not academic seminars, for the purpose of their pedagogy is to enable us to continue to worship (and, for von Hügel, the fact and possibility of adoration is the first and last word about religion)[40] without identifying the object of our worship either with ourselves or with the world or with any constituent feature of the world.

It might at first sight seem as if this emphasis on nonidentity, on divine transcendence, would bring von Hügel close to Kierkegaard. And indeed it does, but with crucial qualification. He is gently critical of Kierkegaard for so "exalting" the "difference of nature between man himself and God . . . as to cut away all ground for any experience or knowledge sufficient to justify him in even a query as to what God is like or not like." And he adjusts Kierkegaard's account by suggesting that any such single-minded celebration of divine transcendence is, in fact, parasitic upon acquaintance with divine reality. It is, he says, "this dim, deep experience which ever causes our reflex knowledge of God to appear as no knowledge at all."[41]

Convinced that the sense of God is—however dimly or inchoately, and in whatever bewildering variety of histories and narratives, institutions and patterns of thought—an actual and operative factor in all mature human experience, this vigorously uncompromising Christian criticizes (with uncharacteristic asperity) those theologians who seek to depreciate the authenticity and significance of non-Christian religions. Thus Wilhelm Herrmann's resolute insistence that, although "'everywhere outside of Christianity, Mysticism will arise, as the very flower of the religious development . . . the Christian must declare such Mystical experience of God to be a delusion,'" is put firmly in its place: "such an exclusive amalgam of Moralism and History . . . is a sad impoverishment of Christianity."[42] And if "inclusiveness" of temperament (and friendship with Ernst

---

39 *Essays and Addresses: Second Series*, pp. 143, 144.

40 See Whelan, *Spirituality of von Hügel*, p. 81.

41 *Mystical Element*, 2:287, 290.

42 For the Herrmann passage, see *Mystical Element*, 2:332; ibid., 333. Karl Barth had similar misgivings about "mysticism," and Herrmann, we remember, was Barth's teacher.

Troeltsch) were factors facilitating von Hügel's positive assessment of non-Christian religions, he saw himself as standing in a tradition of precontracted early modern Catholicism represented by the seventeenth-century Spanish Jesuit Cardinal de Lugo, according to whom "the ordinary method by which God offers and renders possible his salvation" is neither through "miracle nor by the sheer efforts of individuals, but by traditions, schools and churches"—Jewish, Muslim, or "heathen."[43]

Moreover, if the sense of God is given, however "dimly," in all mature human experience, then we would expect to find some correlate, in our secular experience, of that ceaseless dialectic of supply and demand, of gift, clarification, and request, which is sustained by the interactions between the three elements of religion. Thus it is that in what von Hügel calls "the abiding difference between even this its present experience and the great Reality thus experienced and revealed," the experience of religion is said to be precisely *like* (and not, as its apologists too often urge, *unlike*) the experience of science, art, philosophy, and ethics. It is, therefore, hardly surprising that we find him charging William James with having overlooked "the fact that, even in the most individual experience, there is always some intellectual framework or conception, some more or less traditional form, which had previously found lodgement in, and had been more or less accepted by, that soul; so that, though the experience itself, when at all deep, is never the mere precipitate of a conventionally accepted traditional form, it is nevertheless, even when more or less in conflict with this form, never completely independent of it."[44]

Von Hügel's twofold emphasis—on the pervasiveness of the sense of the presence of God and on the fact that this sense is always sustained with recognition of "the abiding difference"[45]—raises two important questions. On the one hand, "the experience of God, as described by him, is so general that it is not clear what it would be like *not* to have such an experience." On the other hand, although (according to Sherry) von Hügel is correct in supposing that, "in every perception and reflection there may be an implied contrast," a felt and recognized "difference," which provokes that hunger and restlessness of which Augustine spoke so eloquently, "the problem is as to the ontological weight to be put on this." How does von Hügel know "that what he experiences is in fact infinitely good, powerful,

43 *Essays and Addresses: First Series*, pp. 252, 253; cf. ibid., pp. 63, 92, 234–35, *Eternal Life*, pp . 350–51.

44 *Essays and Addresses: First Series*, p. 63; *Mystical Element*, 2:309.

45 See *Essays and Addresses: First Series*, p. 22.

loving and so forth. In particular, how does he know that it is the Creator of the world?"[46]

Although more carefully phrased, Sherry's question is similar to that put by Thiemann to Schleiermacher concerning the latter's warrants for identifying experience of absolute dependence with experience of God. And, in von Hügel's case as in Schleiermacher's, my own view is that the most satisfactory answer is to be sought in terms of what I called a hermeneutical account of human experience.[47] Although von Hügel (more evidently than Schleiermacher) does seem to suppose that assertions concerning the sense of the presence of God constitute empirical claims, for which empirical warrants can be furnished, the fundamental thrust of his treatment suggests a recognition that the *articulation* of our "dim" sense of the reality of God in specifically Christian theistic terms is the fruit of that educational process in which Christian discipleship consists. In other words, learning to designate the "true originator and the true end" of "that noblest, incurable discontent with our own petty self and . . . that sense of and thirst for the Infinite and Abiding, which articulates man's deepest requirement and characteristic" as *God* is more like learning to use a language than it is like verifying the truth of a particular factual claim. It is in acquiring the use of this language that we become acquainted with him "who, even now already, is our Peace in Action, and even in the Cross is our abiding Joy."[48]

Learning how to use the word "God" is largely a matter of learning how not to *mis*use it. In von Hügel's view, adoration is as natural an activity as are remembering or understanding. Reverence, wonder, adoration are evoked from us as spontaneously, and as dangerously, as are the operations of the other two elements. Dangerously, because adoration is as easily misplaced as memory and understanding are misguided. To say that God has certain attributes (such as those mentioned by Sherry) is to deny the propriety of attributing infinite goodness, almightiness, or whatever, to any particular fact, idea, person, institution, or state of affairs. And it is in this unceasing dialectic between spontaneity and skepticism that the

---

46 Patrick Sherry, "Von Hügel: Philosophy and Spirituality," 9. We shall take up this aspect of the problem in a later chapter, when considering Karl Rahner's account of experience of God. It is, however, worth noting that the form of Sherry's question seems to presuppose that, in order for us to be able sensibly to talk about human experience of God, there must be some particular *category* of experience to which such discourse refers.

47 See our discussion at the end of chap. 9.

48 On the supposition that empirical warrants can be furnished, see (for example) *Mystical Element*, 2:338; ibid., 395; *Essays and Addresses: First Series*, p. 96.

purificatory discipline of contemplative practice proceeds. This, I think, is why von Hügel once remarked (with Hegel's rationalism in view) that the "root motives and deepest substance of the great Trinitarian movement," as the Christianity of the early centuries sought to sustain its recognition of the identity and difference between Jesus and the mystery that appeared in him, arose from the need "to protect this richness of the life of God as against all absolute co-ordination with the world."[49]

The difficulty that I have with Sherry's question concerning how von Hügel knows that what he experiences is the creator of the world is that the form of the question suggests that God is the name of an object which we may or may not come across in the world, or (at least) whose existence and specifying characteristics may be inferred on the basis of our experience. To set the question up that way, however, seems to presuppose that we can make no headway toward the knowledge of God until certain epistemological issues have first been resolved. And I have already tried to set question marks against that familiar cluster of assumptions. Von Hügel could be very critical of Hegel, but he would certainly have agreed with Hegel that "God does not offer himself for observation."[50]

Nevertheless, Sherry does have a point. Von Hügel's central and overriding, insistent conviction that "religion, in proportion to its genuine religiousness . . . ever affirms Reality, a Reality, *the* Reality distinct from ourselves, the self-subsistent Spirit, God," does seem (at least in the bewildered climate of contemporary conversation) remarkably *assured*. It is true that his insistence that "the central conviction and doctrine of Christianity is the real prevenience and condescension of the real God" is christological in focus: "God's nearness is straight out of the heart of Jesus." It is also true that, according to him, our *recognition* of God's prevenient reality springs not from a "perception of the Infinite," but is rather the fruit of engagement, in suffering and striving and thought, with personal and social conditions which seem to betoken God's absence: "What is a sense of God worth which would be at your disposal, capable of being comfortably elicited when and where you please?"[51] And yet, however admirably von Hügel sustained, in his writing, a disciplined dialectic of presence and "abiding difference," he does seem to find it surprisingly (I

---

49   *Essays and Addresses: Second Series*, p. 152.

50   Hegel, *Lectures on the Philosophy of Religion*, 1:258.

51   *Essays and Addresses: Second Series*, p. 59; ibid., p. 107; von Hügel, *Letters from Baron Friedrich von Hügel to a Niece*, ed. and introd. Gwendolen Greene (London, 1928), xxxi; *Mystical Element*, 2:340; *Letters to a Niece*, p. 87 (cf. *Mystical Element*, 2:338–39).

am almost tempted to say naively) easy to handle the language of affirmation.

On the other hand, if we therefore allow (to Sherry) that von Hügel seemed unduly confident that it was indeed *God* of whose presence and reality he spoke, at least he never suffered from the illusion (not unknown in the standard literature on the philosophy of religion) that theological discourse could ever settle into some single, straightforward register of description. On the contrary, his doctrine of God, and of our relationship with God, is always in *tension* (reflecting the dialectic of affirmation and denial) between pantheism and agnosticism, both of which he describes as "always plausible and most nearly true."[52]

Thus, for example, he insists that there is "a legitimate agnosticism. And it grows large in direct proportion to God's gift of himself to man." Only those who know not God suffer from the illusion that they know what God is like. He quotes with approval John of the Cross's dictum that "one of the greatest favours of God" is the "ability to see so distinctly, and to feel so profoundly," that we "cannot comprehend him at all."[53] Those who use the word "God" without difficulty, who find it easy to state exactly what it is that they want to *say* about God (whether from the standpoint of belief or of unbelief) are, on von Hügel's view, in danger of losing touch with reality. Here, as elsewhere, it is one-sidedness that is dangerous. Correlatively, it is only one-sided (or, we might say, undialectical) agnosticism, unchecked and uncorrected by the influence of other considerations, that is ruinous of religion.

Similarly, although he regards the "theories" of Spinoza (whom he always takes as the classical exponent of pantheism) as "largely ruinous," he writes with great sympathy about his "deep and noble . . . instincts and intuitions." If one-sided agnosticism wrongly equates our recognition of the incomprehensibility of the mystery which we worship with simple ignorance, one-sided pantheism renders worship impossible. A passage in which he makes this point is worth quoting at some length because it shows how much more appreciative he was of the element of truth in pantheism than it is possible to be if one takes it for granted that "God" is the name of a real or illusory particular being outside our world. "'What is the harm, religiously, in such an identification of God and man?' If it is only man's ' *depths* which are God,' is 'not the difference . . . one simply of words? I think not. For such a view, if it were fully to determine the

---

52 *Essays and Addresses: Second Series*, p. 136.

53 Whelan, *Spirituality of von Hügel*, p. 105; *Mystical Element*, 2:258.

imagination, reason, emotion and will, would make adoration—the very centre of the religious life—impossible . . . I cannot, in all sober, consistent conviction, adore myself; indeed in my *deepest* moments I shall be *most* removed from all such fantastic feelings.'" His own position (on this side of the matter) he described as "panentheist": "If Panentheism, the doctrine that God is in all things, is . . . in the right; Pantheism, the doctrine that God is *equally* in all things, is . . . profoundly false."[54]

It should be clear that the *pattern* of a doctrine of God which thus seeks continually to sustain the dialectic between pantheism and agnosticism, presence and absence, identity and difference, affirmation and denial, and which finds the resources for doing so in continual reappropriation of the gospel narratives, will be trinitarian in character (and, in that sense at least, will have dispensed with theism). It is therefore no surprise to discover that von Hügel's treatment of the elements of religion, and of the doctrine of God implied by the interplay of those elements, is trinitarian from start to finish. The doctrine of God's trinity is, we might say, the *figure* in relation to which von Hügel, as he read and reread the New Testament, sought to bring his imagination, understanding, and action into nearer conformity with the ideal of sanctity.

Interpretation, Grace, and Fruitfulness

By way of conclusion, I would like briefly to mention three topics the first of which we have already touched on more than once: firstly, the notion of a hermeneutics of experience; secondly, the question of where the doctrine of divine grace fits into a theology such as von Hügel's; and thirdly, what von Hügel calls "two conditions of the fruitfulness of the entire process"[55] of Christian growth in experience and knowledge of God.

I suggested earlier that, for von Hügel (as for Schleiermacher) the *content* of the accounts that we offer of our human experience, as experience of the mystery of God, must be derived from elsewhere than the mystical element of religion. But this way of putting the matter is not quite satis-

54 *Essays and Addresses: Second Series*, p. 153 (cf. *Mystical Element*, 2:375); von Hügel, "The Relations between God and Man in 'The New Theology' of Rev. R. J. Campbell," *Albany Review* (1907): 656–57 (cited from Whelan, *Spirituality of von Hügel*, p. 109; cf. *Eternal Life*, p. 366); *Essays and Addresses: Second Series*, p. 39.

55 *Mystical Element*, 2:394.

factory, inasmuch as it could be taken to imply that we bring our accounts, our stories, our interpretations, to—or more or less arbitrarily impose them upon—some independently given occurrence or unshaped state of affairs, known as "experience." Von Hügel, however, defined "real experience" and "real knowledge" as being "conveyed" by "the endless contacts, friendly, hostile, of give, of take, between ourselves and the objects of all kinds which act upon us, and upon which we act in some degree or way."[56] But to say that not only "knowledge" but also "experience" is *conveyed* by such contacts would seem (correctly) to suggest that interpretation—the accounts that we render of the way things are—is a constitutive element in what we take *experience* to mean.

The recent literature is (happily) saturated with suggestions of this sort. If I pick out just one example, I do so on account of its exemplary clarity and conciseness. In a "note on the use of the term 'experience,'" Jean-Pierre Jossua defines experience as an event or complex of events perceived and interpreted as significant for one or more subjects who were involved in these events.[57] Negatively, this definition refrains from confining the connotations of the term to sensations or to states of mind or feeling (such as joy, suffering, anguish, or fear).

Positively, the definition is intended to indicate four features. Firstly, experience is a matter of our *relationships*[58] with ourselves, with others, with the world—and with God. Secondly, to speak of experience is to speak of relationships constituted by *real* (and not merely notional) participation in an event—of love, or political struggle (to give his own examples), or whatever. Thirdly, such relationships only form part of our experience in the measure that they are *refracted* in consciousness. But such refraction is never a matter of pure "transparency": this much at least we should by now have learned from the "masters of suspicion." In other words (and here I am glossing and not paraphrasing Jossua's text), the trouble with a definition such as that offered by Richard Swinburne is not only that it is, by implication, thoroughly individualist; nor only that it seems to rest upon a Cartesian dissociation of mind from body; but also

---

56 *Essays and Addresses: First Series*, p. 52.

57 "Evénement ou ensemble d'événements perçus et interprétés après coup comme signifiants pour un ou plusieurs sujets qui y ont été impliqués" (Jean-Pierre Jossua, "Note sur l'usage du term 'expérience,'" in Jean-Pierre Jossua, P. Jacquemont, and B. Quelquejeu, *Une Foi Exposée*, 2d ed. [Paris, 1973], p. 171). "Significant" seems to me preferable to the loose and overblown term "meaningful," as a translation of "signifiant"—in spite of the risk of its being misread to mean merely "important," and in spite of the loss of the echo of much recent literature on "signifiers" and "signification."

58 Or, as von Hügel said, "contacts."

that, if only by silence, it seems to imply that there need not, in principle, be any great difficulty about *reporting* what goes on in our "minds."[59] Whereas, as Jossua insists, all talk of experience needs to be critically alert to a sense of the limits within which we are ever able to bring experience to speech. Finally, we need to bear in mind that the refraction of experience in consciousness is not a mechanical or automatic process, but the work of human agents: it is a matter of *deciphering* our circumstance, of *interpreting* the events and relationships in which we participate.[60]

The application of Jossua's definition to the instance of Christian experience is at once straightforward and dauntingly difficult. It is straightforward, inasmuch as "Christian experience" is simply a complex of particular experiences which have, for each Christian, the quality of being, at one and the same time, *their* experience—lived, refracted, and interpreted in faith—and yet not strictly singular, because the interpreting faith is no merely individual affair.[61]

Nevertheless, in *practice* the application is dauntingly difficult because, in this instance, bringing experience to speech requires the reworking into fresh, accurate, and accessible language of stories and symbols that have—through use, misuse, and dislocation from the common conversation of the culture—become, in fact (for Christians and non-Christians alike) an obstacle to that hearing and proclamation of the Gospel of which they remain, nevertheless, the indispensable medium. From this point of view, we might say that contemplative practice, or mysticism in Rowan Williams's sense, is as much a matter of *poetics* as it is (for example) of ethics.[62]

Stylistically, the formal, condensed elegance of Jossua's note could hardly be more different from von Hügel's craggy, cumbersome, cumulative attempts at description. Nevertheless, it seems to me that Jossua's definition does capture in summary most of the central features of von Hügel's account of the dialectical interplay of his "forces" and "elements."

---

59   On the other hand, of course, William James's admirable opposition to intellectualism led him to construct an account of "pure" or "raw" experience from which the element of refraction was simply excluded. Swinburne, as we saw in chap. 8, defines experience as "a conscious mental going on" (*The Existence of God*, p. 244).

60   "Tout discours de l'expérience doit donc être à la fois critique et averti de son caractère partiel et nullement normatif" (Jossua, *Une Foi Exposée*, p. 172).

61   See ibid., p. 173. To the earlier examples of love and political struggle we would now need to add liturgy, because the use, in worship, of Christian symbols, is not merely interpretative of "secular" experience (though it *is* that), but also constitutes an event, or pattern of events, participation in which is a constitutive element of what it is that makes someone's human experience *Christian* experience.

62   See Jean-Pierre Jossua, *Pour une Histoire Religieuse de l'Expérience Littéraire* (Paris, 1985).

It also has the advantage of enabling me to suggest that what I earlier called the naïveté of von Hügel's use of the language of affirmation may be attributed to insufficient sensitivity on the part of a somewhat isolated[63] thinker to the sheer difficulty of *recasting* inherited Christian language into terms at once interpretatively faithful and yet accessible to our time.

The second topic that I listed was that of the place of the doctrine of grace in von Hügel's theology. I said earlier that, on von Hügel's account, we *make* our experience "firsthand." But does this not suggest a dangerously Pelagian view of Christian experience? He was aware of the difficulty: "Have we not argued throughout as if the religious life were to be begun, and carried on, and achieved simply by a constant succession of efforts of our own?" His answer (which foreshadows a view of the relationship between divine grace and human freedom which we shall later discover to be integral to Karl Rahner's account of human experience and the knowledge of God) runs as follows: "Simply all and every one of our acts, our very physical existence and persistence, is dependent, at every moment and in every direction, upon the prevenient, accompanying and subsequent power and help of God; and still more is every religious, every truly spiritual and supernatural act of the soul impossible without the constant action of God's grace. . . . The more costly is our act of love or of sacrifice . . . and the more truly it is our own deepest self-expression, so much the more . . . is this action a thing received as well as given . . . man will never be so truly active, so truly and intensely himself, as when he is most possessed by God."[64]

Reality, it seems, has only such shape as we impose upon it. Patterns, and (at least to some temperaments) especially patterns of ideas, are dangerously seductive. In religion, as elsewhere, fascination with pattern— with, for example, the interplay and dialectic of forces and elements, woven (by von Hügel) from a vast array of information from ancient philosophy, from the history of the Christian Church, and from modern thought—can distract us from the unpatternable particularity of particular circumstance, suffering, and joy. Thus, in conclusion, von Hügel insists that "even the simplest effort, within this innumerable sequence and simultaneity of activities, will lack the fullest truth and religious depth and fruitfulness, unless two experiences, convictions and motives are in operation throughout the whole, and penetrate its every part."[65]

---

63 Both culturally, as immensely learned amateur and, as Whelan suggests, as "a victim of the isolation caused by his deafness" (*Spirituality of von Hügel*, p. 221).

64 *Mystical Element*, 1:79–80.

65 Ibid., 2: 394.

What, then (thirdly, and finally), are "these two eyes of religion and twin pulse-beats of its very heart"? They are, on the one hand, "the vivid, continuous sense that God . . . is the true originator and the true end of the whole movement" and, on the other, "the continuous sense of the ever necessary, ever fruitful . . . Cross of Christ—the great law and fact that only through self-renunciation and suffering can the soul win its true self." These, for von Hügel, are the "two conditions of the fruitfulness of the entire process" of Christian discipleship or contemplative practice.[66]

This view of the matter stands in sharp contrast with those accounts of religious experience which look to it primarily for balm and satisfaction, for relief in elevated private feeling from institutional or intellectual pressure. The following voice comes from Cambridge, Massachusetts (from James's Harvard): "The definite appeal of the Church, in times like these, when the external props fall away, is to the incarnation of the divine personality, and the ideal of character deduced from it as a pattern for life. This is the religion of ordinary people today; it has been the heart of Christianity for nineteen hundred years. Our feeling of this cosmic quality may be vague or definite, diffused or crystallized, but to those of us who sense behind our pulsing life a mystery which perplexes, sobers, and elevates us, that quality forms a permanent scenic background for our life."[67]

If, for von Hügel, Christianity was a school for the production of persons in discipleship of the crucified, in the alternative tradition of what he called "exclusive mysticism" divine personality becomes incarnate, not in Gethsemane, but as scenic background in a kind of tourism of moral and political evasion: "we can enjoy [religion] only by taking, as it were, the moral holiday into its regions when we are weary of the world of thinking and doing. It is a land to retreat into when we are battered and degraded by the dynamic world about us, and require rest and recuperation."[68]

But also from Harvard, in the person of the editor of von Hügel's letter to William James, comes a savage indictment of this tradition and its consequences: "This pietistic religion which supposes that privatized religion will itself suffice to produce a just and viable commonwealth is a fateful heritage in American life reaching from John Cotton's Letter to Lord Say and Seal (1636), to Jonathan Edwards, to Lyman Beecher, to William James, to 'piety on the Potomac,' to the New Narcissism in the age of the 'psychological man.' This heritage serves as an ideology concealing or ignoring the workings of unaccountable corporate powers political, eco-

---

66 Ibid., 395, 394.
67 Randolph S. Bourne, *Youth and Life* (Boston, 1913), pp. 200–201.
68 Ibid., p. 203.

nomic and social. . . . The cult of the psychological man is a major demonry both in the 'religion' and in the secularism of American life, prompting a spuriously self-serving abdication of corporate responsibility."[69] This is a harsh judgment but one which, as we shall shortly see, has certain striking affinities with Martin Buber's critique (issued far from the United States) of the form and function of what he called "religion."

---

69 Adams, "Letter from Friedrich von Hügel to William James," 226.

13

Buber on Conversion and The Severed I

In a BBC interview which he gave in 1961, four years before his death, Martin Buber said how glad he was that the word "religion" nowhere occurs in the Bible.[1] "The primal danger of man," he once remarked, "is 'religion.'" Religion, "'the great enemy of mankind,'" not only distracts people from their fundamental task of risking and constructing their human identity in the transformation of natural, social, and cultural relationships but, in so doing, it cuts them off from God—for God is to be found, not in religion, but in the world of those relationships. By erecting religious systems (whether linguistic, ritual, or organizational) we insulate ourselves from the voice of God: "if there is nothing that can so hide the face of our fellow-man as morality can, religion can hide us as nothing else from the face of God. . . . Dogma . . . has become the most exalted form of invulnerability against revelation."[2] Similarly, by erecting systems of moral principles, we insulate ourselves from the cry of those who call upon us in their need.

It is not altogether surprising that someone who voiced these opinions was reluctant to be described as a theologian: "For by theology is understood, certainly, a teaching about God, even if it is only a 'negative' one. . . . But I am absolutely not capable nor even disposed to teach this or that about God." This was not merely an opinion of old age: thirty

---

1 See Pamela Vermes, *Buber on God and the Perfect Man*, Brown Judaic Studies 13 (Missoula, Mont., 1980), p. 219.

2 Martin Buber, *The Origin and Meaning of Hasidism*, ed. and trans. Maurice Friedman (New York, 1960), p. 94; quoted from Maurice Friedman, *Martin Buber's Life and Work: The Middle Years, 1923–1945* (New York, 1983), p. 72; Buber, "Dialogue" in *Between Man and Man*, trans. Ronald Gregor Smith (London, 1927), p. 18.

years earlier he had remarked that the trouble with theologians is that "so long as they practice theology they do not get away from religion as a specification."[3]

Nevertheless, it is in no spirit of masochism that I turn to Buber at this stage in the construction of what is intended to be, from first to last, an argument in Christian theology. On the contrary, my aim in this chapter is to show that, notwithstanding this unpromising beginning, Buber offers an account of human experience and the knowledge of God which has interesting affinities both with von Hügel's account and with my critique of the Jamesian tradition. Buber's *I and Thou* (on which I shall concentrate) is as dense and difficult as it is suggestive. Before considering the text in any detail, therefore, I shall first offer some general indications of how it fits into the story that I am trying to tell.

Though only translated into English in 1937, *I and Thou* was first published in 1923, long before the storm clouds gathered in Germany. In chapter 14, therefore, I shall try to show that, by supplying the necessary correctives both to von Hügel's failure to appreciate and think through the social and political implications of his position and to the ease with which he issued positive descriptions of the mystery of God, Buber's thought offers the kind of Jewish corrective which much of our Christian theology still requires after (but not *only* on account of) the Holocaust.[4]

Religion, Mysticism, and the Ego

According to Buber, "all religious reality begins with what Biblical religion calls the 'fear of God.' It comes when our existence between birth and death becomes incomprehensible and uncanny, when all security is shattered through the mystery. This is not the relative mystery of that which is inaccessible only to the present state of human knowledge and is

---

3 Buber, "Replies to My Critics," in *The Philosophy of Martin Buber,* ed. Paul Arthur Schilpp and Maurice Friedman (Cambridge, 1967), p. 690; Buber, "The Question to the Single One," in *Between Man and Man,* p. 57.

4 In *A Matter of Hope,* I tried to make a case for what I called "Christian materialism." In the sense of that notion for which I argued, Buber (I believe) could be described as a "Jewish materialist." I therefore hope that the discussion of Buber, in this and the following chapter, will help to make clearer the continuity of concern between the present work and my study of Marx.

hence in principle discoverable. It is the essential mystery, the inscrutable-ness of which belongs to its very nature; it is the unknowable. Through this dark gate (which is only a gate and not, as some theologians believe, a dwelling) the believing man steps forth into the everyday which is hence-forth hallowed as the place in which he has to live with the mystery." But, because people cannot bear continual exposure to this dark wind, and can-not tolerate the defenselessness and insecurity which it brings, they take steps to *domesticate* the mystery: they "convince themselves that they 'have' God always and . . . are unassailably safe because they have faith that this is so." We build little shelters to divinity, in which we huddle in order to escape from ourselves, from each other, from the world—and from God. These are the shelters of organized religion and its comfortable theological descriptions: "'Religion' may come to be understood as one division of life next to others, even as standing on its own and having its own law—it has thereby already perverted the relation of faith."[5]

Buber's polemic against religion is, therefore, a polemic against the erection of *structures* of belief, precept, and ritual which render impossible the necessary *directness* of relation between human beings and God. "The man of religion has only to listen and read, and he will be told exactly what God said, and when, and what God's words signify." And if there are similarities between this critique of the function too often fulfilled by religious ideas and institutions and William James's polemic against that "mass of suggested feeling and imitated conduct"[6] which he excoriated as "second-hand" religion, the differences are still more striking.

Buber is a relentlessly *inclusivist* thinker. He criticizes the freezing of faith into system not in order to celebrate individual, private feeling or experience, but in order to deny that there is *any particular* "division of life" which is the privileged place of our encounter with God. Religion that is "something real" arises "when men have God in mind with the might of their being. If, on the contrary, they have religion in mind in-stead, what sorts of malformations must come together there! . . . either religion is a reality, rather *the* reality, namely the *whole* existence of the real man in the real world of God . . . or it is a phantom of the covetous human soul, and then it would be right promptly and completely to replace its rituals by art, its commands by ethics, its revelations by science." This

5 Buber, *Eclipse of God: Studies in the Relation between Religion and Philosophy,* trans. Mau-rice Friedman et al. (New York, 1957), p. 36 (we shall return to this distinction when, with Karl Rahner's help, we consider what is at issue in naming God as "mystery"); Vermes, *Buber on God,* p. 222; Buber, "On the Ethics of Political Decision," in *A Believ-ing Humanism: My Testament, 1902–1965,* trans. Maurice Friedman (New York, 1967), p. 206 (this text dates from 1932).

6 Vermes, *Buber on God,* p.

passage, which dates from 1923, reminds us of the fact that, by the time Buber came to write *I and Thou*, "Yes and No" to Feuerbach and Kierkegaard had "become a part of [his] existence." "Yes" to Feuerbach's emphasis on human relations, "No" to his reduction of religion to this alone; "Yes" to Kierkegaard's making of "the stages and conditions of life itself" the "elements of our existence 'before God,'" "No" to his acknowledging "as essential only the meeting between the individual man and God."[7]

For Buber, a God who is sought, or celebrated, or obeyed, *elsewhere* than in the everyday (in religion, for example) is a figment of our imagination destructive of our common humanity—and thereby destructive of our relations with God. In other words, Buber's account of "the two loves" is not unlike that indicated by von Hügel when he said that "the love of [God] is the 'form,' the principle of order and harmony; our natural affections are the 'matter' harmonized and set in order." This comes across strikingly in a well-known passage describing Buber's conversion, or turning away from, "the 'religious' which is nothing but the exception, extraction, exaltation, ecstasy"; a conversion which was a "turning towards community."[8]

"In my earlier years," he tells us, "'religious experience' was the experience of an otherness which did not fit into the context of life." Then, one day, "after a morning of 'religious' enthusiasm, I had a visit from an unknown young man, without being there in spirit. I certainly did not fail to let the meeting be friendly," but "omitted to guess the question which he did not put." Shortly afterwards, he heard of the young man's death. Since that day, "I possess nothing but the everyday out of which I am never taken. The mystery is no longer disclosed, has escaped or made its dwelling here where everything happens as it happens. I know no fulness but each mortal hour's fulness of claim and responsibility. . . . If that is religion then it is just *everything*, simply all that is lived in its possibility of dialogue. Here is space also for religion's highest forms."[9]

That it is not farfetched to describe this event in von Hügel's terminology, as a conversion from exclusive to inclusive mysticism, is suggested by the fact that, commenting on that passage from "Dialogue," Helmut

---

7   Buber, "Religion and God's Rule," in *A Believing Humanism*, pp. 110–11; "Autobiographical Fragments," in *The Philosophy of Martin Buber*, p. 34; "What Is Man?," in *Between Man and Man*, pp. 162–63; "A Believing Humanism," in *A Believing Humanism*, p. 120.

8   Von Hügel, *Mystical Element*, 2:353; Buber, "Dialogue," p. 13; Helmut Kuhn, "Dialogue in Expectation," in *The Philosophy of Martin Buber*, p. 656.

9   Buber, "Dialogue," pp. 13–14. "For true holiness," said Buber in 1936 (in criticism of Kierkegaard), a holiness which "hallows *everything*, there is no 'religious standpoint'" ("The Question to the Single One," in *Between Man and Man*, p. 57).

Kuhn says of the *kind* of mysticism to which Buber now turned that it was similar to that advocated by Saint Catherine of Genoa.[10] Buber and mysticism is a topic which generates much more heat than light, but it seems to me that, with the help of von Hügel's distinction, the confusion is easily clarified. Thus, for example, when Pamela Vermes insists that, in his maturity, Buber was largely successful in "clearing his mind of its mystical impedimenta," and that he "rejected mysticism," it is clear from the context that she is working with a concept of mysticism the essential features of which are just those picked out by von Hügel as the hallmarks of exclusive mysticism. (And the same may be said of Buber's own remark, in 1957, that "the clear and firm structure of the I-You relationship . . . is not mystical."[11])

Similarly, when Walter Kaufman says that "Buber taught me that mysticism need not lead outside the world," he is not contradicting Pamela Vermes (except terminologically), but reflecting Buber's own understanding of the Hasidic tradition which he loved so much and in which his thinking was steeped: "The Baal-Shem will probably be extolled as the founder of a realistic and active mysticism, i.e., a mysticism for which the world is not an illusion, from which man must turn away in order to reach true being, but rather, the reality between God and him in which reciprocity manifests itself. . . . A 'mysticism' that may be called such because it preserves the intimacy of the relation, guards the concreteness of the absolute and demands the involvement of the whole being; one can, to be sure, also call it religion for just the same reason. Its true . . . name is perhaps: presentness."[12]

Buber, said his friend Hugo Bergman, "insists that the way to God lies directly through this world." But what is required is appropriate *instruction* along the way. A further affinity between von Hügel and Buber is indicated by their shared conviction that what Christians often call "the spiritual life"—growth in maturity, wisdom, or sanctity—is a function of practical pedagogy.[13] For Buber, the model for such pedagogy was (once

---

10 See Kuhn, "Dialogue in Expectation," p. 656.

11 Vermes, *Buber on God*, p. 31; see ibid., p. 117, where she herself affirms that "the tradition to which Buber belongs" is "the Jewish mystical tradition"; Buber, "Afterword" to *I and Thou*, trans. and ed. Walter Kaufman (Edinburgh, 1970), p. 177.

12 Walter Kaufman, "Prologue" to *I and Thou*, p. 23; Buber, *Hasidism and Modern Man*, ed. Maurice Friedman (New York, 1960), quoted from Friedman, *The Middle Years*, p. 140.

13 Hugo Bergman, "Martin Buber and Mysticism," in *The Philosophy of Martin Buber*, p. 298. In Buber's case, unlike von Hügel's, this conviction found expression in a sustained interest in the practice and theory of education: see Friedman's chaps. on "Education" and "Jewish Education as Spiritual Resistance," in *The Middle Years*, pp. 21–39, 198–222.

again) Hasidism, which he described as "not a teaching, but a mode of life, a mode of life that shapes a community. . . . The Baal-Shem belongs to those central figures of the history of religion . . .[who] did not proceed *from* a teaching, but moved *to* a teaching, in such a way that their life worked as a teaching."[14]

And what was thus concretely taught was that "holy insecurity" by which Buber set such store, and which he persistently contrasted with "gnosis." Gnosis, he wrote shortly before his death, "not only offends the transcendent but also human existence because it constructs a structure of knowledge which passes from now on as complete."[15] Thus, for example, the fascination of religious experience for those who hope to find, *in* such experience, some relief from the Cartesian anxiety, some point of fixed certainty and unshakable reassurance in our most unstable and insecure world, would be a good illustration of what Buber meant by "gnosticism," and an indication of why he was so hostile to it. All gnosticism is egocentric, and egocentricity subverts relationship.

Without unduly anticipating my discussion of *I and Thou*, that last point can be spelled out a little (in reference to earlier stages in my argument) by considering why it is that Buber asserts, more than once, that "the I of the basic word I-You is different from that in the basic word I-It." There is, he insists, "no I as such," no "I-in-itself," and he speaks disparagingly of those who "pronounce the severed I"—of the individual in whom the "mania of his detached I-hood chases it ceaselessly around an empty circle." How, he asks, "can the buried power to *relate* be resurrected in a being" in whom this "vigorous ghost" lurks? "The spook of the soul and the nightmare of the world," he remarks bitterly, "get along with each other."[16] *I and Thou* is not the kind of text that is well furnished with references, but we have surely met this "severed I" before?

During the two and a half years that passed between the completion, in the autumn of 1919, of the first draft of *I and Thou*, and the finishing of the book in the spring of 1922, Buber tells us that he worked almost exclusively on Hasidic material. With one exception, he did not, during this crucial period, read the philosophers. And the exception? Descartes's *Discours de la Methode*. The point is of more than anecdotal interest because, according to Franz Rosenzweig, "I-It" cannot *also* be a "basic" word and, in arguing as if it could, Buber showed himself to be partly in thrall to "'the great deception in Europe' of the last three hundred years: [to] the

---

14 Buber, *The Origin and Meaning of Hasidism*, pp. 24–25.

15 Buber, "Replies to My Critics," in *The Philosophy of Martin Buber*, p. 743.

16 Buber, *I and Thou*, pp. 53 (cf. p. 111), 54, 65, 115, 108.

rationalism and idealism which has typified philosophical thought since Descartes."[17]

A more positive verdict is returned by Herbert Schneider, according to whom Buber stands squarely in a tradition of religious empiricism which includes such "noteworthy examples" as Jonathan Edwards, Schleier-macher, and William James. For Schneider, however, "what makes Buber's contribution to religious empiricism so striking and unambiguous is his definite turning from introspective psychology with its search for the sense of the Divine Presence to a social psychology of interpersonal experience."[18]

I shall return to Rosenzweig's criticism in the next section. My purpose in mentioning the matter at this point is to suggest, firstly, that Buber, in *I and Thou,* was consciously struggling against the Cartesian legacy and, secondly, that his way of doing so is closer to that which James *sought* to do (with his doctrine of "radical empiricism") than to that which, hampered by his individualism (especially in the matter of religious experience), he in fact succeeded in doing.

I and Thou

The first problem for the English-speaking reader of the book is to know how to take the title. Buber is writing about personal relationships between human beings, and between human beings and their world—about (we might say) friendship and friendliness. What pronoun shall we use for friendship's address? In many languages, the choice would be straightforward. Thus, in Buber's German, "*Du* is spontaneous and unpretentious, remote from formality, pomp, and dignity." It is no longer so with "Thou." "Thou can mean many things, but it has no place whatever in the language of direct, nonliterary, spontaneous human relationships."[19]

Moreover, in modern English, "Thou" brings God to mind and yet, until the third and final part of the book, Buber speaks hardly at all of address to God, of the "You" of "unconditional relation."[20] For the most

17 Rivka Horwitz, *Buber's Way to "I and Thou": An Historical Analysis and the First Publication of Martin Buber's Lectures "Religion Als Gegenwart"* (Heidelberg, 1978), p. 229; cf. the extract from the postscript to "The History of the Dialogical Principle" which is included as "Beginnings" in the "Autobiographical Fragments," pp. 33–35.

18 Herbert W. Schneider, "The Historical Significance of Buber's Philosophy," in *The Philosophy of Martin Buber,* p. 470. By "religious empiricism," Schneider seems to mean a tradition which grounds religious discourse in "experience."

19 Walter Kaufman, "Prologue," pp. 14, 15.

20 *I and Thou,* p. 116.

part, he speaks of the problem and possibility of direct personal relations with the worlds of nature, of other human beings, of culture, artifacts, and ideas.

And yet, if "Thou" were thought appropriate for address to God, the issue would still be undecided because, although the problem of address to God is only *explicitly* treated in the third part, it is silently, implicitly present throughout. Not only was the third part of the book "the first to reach its final form," but even after agreeing with his publisher on the title *Ich and Du,* Buber still privately referred to the work as "Prolegomena to a Philosophy of Religion." Rivka Horwitz's conclusion to her painstaking historical analysis of the preparation of the book is that "the social aspects of *I and Thou* were, in fact, additions to a work whose original and primary concern was the attempt, prompted by the disillusion with mysticism, to reformulate the concept and position of religion."[21]

And yet, according to Walter Kaufman, insofar as "Thou" does bring God to mind, it brings to mind the *wrong* God: not "Abba," but "the God of the pulpits, the God of the holy tone." Hence his decision (which I shall follow) to entitle his translation *I and Thou,* for reasons of familiarity, but always in the text to use "I and You." Maurice Friedman still prefers to retain "Thou" on the grounds that "in English 'you' is all too often impersonal and means not much other than 'one.'" Nevertheless, he allows that "Kaufman has done a real service in trying to correct the tendency to regard the 'I-Thou relationship' as exclusively or mainly between man and God . . . and restoring the primordially Jewish recognition (and that of Jesus) that the love of God cannot be separated from the love of neighbour."[22]

There is one more preliminary point of terminology to be considered. The book begins with the pronouncement that "the world is twofold for man in accordance with his twofold attitude. The attitude of man is twofold in accordance with the two basic words he can speak."[23] Buber restricts the concept of "relation," or "standing in relation," to *one* of the two fundamental attitudes or ways of being in the world: namely, to that which

---

21   Horwitz, *Buber's Way to "I and Thou,"* pp. 165, 22, 29. For "mysticism," of course, read "exclusive mysticism."

22   Kaufman, "Prologue," p. 14; Maurice Friedman, *Martin Buber's Life and Work: The Early Years, 1878–1923* (New York, 1981), p. 429. Moreover, not only can the two loves not be *separated,* but the "You" of personal address between human beings is, as it were, a finite *echo* of that "You" by which God addresses his people, enabling them to respond to his address.

23   *I and Thou,* p. 53. By "attitude," Buber does not mean merely a *mental* attitude, but "how man, in the wholeness of his being, places himself before the world" (Arthur Cohen, *Martin Buber* [London, 1957], p. 49). Our deeds are just as much part of our "attitude" as our words or thoughts.

expresses the basic word "I-You." Similarly, he restricts the concept of "experience" to the world of the "I-It." All experience is of objects, of *things,* of that with which I am not in "relation." "Man," he says, "experiences what there is to things . . . I experience something," whether a physical thing or a spiritual thing, an "outer" thing or an "inner" thing, an iceberg or an idea. "The world as experience belongs to the basic word I-It. The basic word I-You establishes the world of relation." This is why he says, when commenting on the development of modern Western culture, that "the improvement of the capacity for experience and use generally involves a decrease in man's power to relate."[24] It follows that, in point of terminology, Buber could never refer to the relation of love as an *experience* of the beloved, nor to being in relation with God as a matter of our experience of God. This is not to say that either God or other people are *beyond* experience but, rather, that insofar as we make God (or other people) into objects of experience, we cease to relate to them. (We shall return, in due course, to the question of "objectification.")

This twofold restriction of terminology was intended to serve as a corrective to his own earlier usage. Having, in his youth, been content to speak of "experience" of God, he now associated the concept "with mood and superficial emotionalism rather than real response." The "radical self-correction," once made, stood to the end of his life, when he said that "'*Erlebnis*' [experience] belongs to the exclusive, individualized psychic sphere; 'meeting,' or rather, as I mostly prefer to say, precisely in order to avoid the temporal limitation, 'relationship' transcends this sphere from its origins on."[25]

It is time to stand back a little and to ask: what is this strange little book *about?* According to Walter Kaufman, "the aim of the book is . . . to diagnose certain tendencies in modern society . . . and to indicate how the quality of life might be radically changed by the development of a new sense of community." My only quarrel with that description would be the coolly clinical tone of "diagnose" and "indicate." There is much passion in the book, much urgency, and the most lasting impression that many readers probably retain of it is of being challenged to choose: to choose between a blessing and a curse, a way of life and a way of death.[26]

---

24 *I and Thou*, pp. 55, 56, 89 (cf. p. 92).

25 Friedman, *The Early Years*, p. 320; Buber, "Replies to My Critics," p. 712. In *I and Thou*, Buber speaks of "Erfahrung," or sensible experience of the phenomenal world. But both "Erlebnis" (or affective experience) and "Erfahrung" remain, as it were, *within* the experiencing individual. As such, they do not allow one human being to *meet* another *as* a human "other" (I owe this precision to Paul Mendes-Flohr).

26 Kaufman, "Prologue," p. 38; cf. Deuteronomy 11:26, 30:15.

And yet, this impression is misleading if we take it to mean that Buber presents us with the option: *either* the world of relation *or* the world of objects and things; either "I-You" or "I-It." This brings me back to Franz Rosenzweig's criticism of the page proofs of *I and Thou*. Rosenzweig detected, in the *manner* of Buber's celebration of the primacy of "I-You," a lingering tendency romantically to denigrate the "it-world"; a tendency toward forgetfulness of the God-given "happenedness" (as von Hügel might say) of history and creation. *Utterance* takes time, binds us into temporality, whereas "thought" may be thought of timelessly.[27] It is this tendency to speak as if "it" could be constituted by *thought*, rather than by *utterance*, to which Rosenzweig was referring when he complained that "I-It" (in the text as he had it) "'is not a basic *word*, it is at most a basic thought . . . a tip of a thought, a philosophical point.'" Hence his suspicion that Buber had not yet fought completely free from the myth of "the intentional constitution of the world through the *ego cogito*." Buber took this criticism very seriously and sought to accommodate it in the final text in which, though romantic *form* endures, it "hides a profoundly anti-romantic message."[28]

According to Emil Fackenheim, "the most basic of all Buber's doctrines" is the contention that "uncommitted 'objective' knowledge which observes as an It what may also be encountered as a Thou is a lesser kind of knowledge, and that the most profound mistake in all philosophy is the epistemological reduction of I-Thou to I-It, and the metaphysical reduction of Thou to It." But if knowledge arrived at from the standpoint of the basic word I-It is, indeed, true knowledge (even if a lesser kind of knowledge), then the problem is not that of choosing between the two basic words, but of establishing and sustaining the appropriate relationship between them. Buber agreed with Fackenheim that "thinking is not properly stretched into an exclusive dualism," but shrank from having a "doctrine" attributed to him: "I have no teaching, but I carry on a conversation."[29]

---

27 In this sense, "Rosenzweig's thinking is much more historical than Buber's" (Bernhard Casper, "Franz Rosenzweig's Criticism of Buber's *I and Thou*," in *Martin Buber: A Centenary Volume*, ed. Haim Gordon and Jochanan Bloch [New York, 1984], p. 144). As a reminder that what is at issue, theologically (for Rosenzweig), is the integrity of the doctrine of creation, we might add that *God's* utterance *makes* time.

28 Rosenzweig's letter is cited from Gordon and Bloch, ibid., p. 157 (the full text of the letter is included as an Appendix to Casper's paper, in a different translation from that published in Horwitz, *Buber's Way*, pp. 253–56); Casper, ibid., p. 140; Kaufman, "Prologue," p. 25.

29 Emil Fackenheim, "Martin Buber's Concept of Revelation," in *The Philosophy of Martin Buber*, p. 281; Buber, "Replies to My Critics," pp. 691, 693.

However, even if we grant to Buber that he has no doctrine, no system of ideas to peddle as remedy for the world's disease, he undoubtedly proclaimed a message. The two principal themes of that message were "presence" and "speech." If it is required of us that we be *present* with the worlds of nature, society, and ideas—that these worlds be brought to stand under the basic word of "presence" or "relation," the word "I-You"—this requirement is not an insupportable burden or unattainable task, because God is present before us. And if it is required of us that in our deeds we speak, that we so act as to speak *real* words of "relation," the conversion that would render such speech actual is, on God's side, the redemption of the world which he speaks in creation, through his Word.[30]

This summary of Buber's message may appear somewhat obscure. As a first step toward its clarification, therefore, I would remind the reader that I have already suggested that questions of knowledge (of all kinds of knowledge: whether of the world, or of each other, or of God) are more fundamentally matters of *ethics*—of who, and what, and in what circumstances, might be responsibly relied upon—than they are technical matters to be resolved by ingenious epistemological techniques or cognitive experiments. Buber once confirmed to Maurice Friedman the truth of the latter's contention that "every one of Buber's basic distinctions . . . is rooted in the presence or absence of basic trust."[31] Not *blind* trust (there are no "leaps of faith" in Buber's world), but the discriminating, clearsighted, informed courageousness, the absence of torturing anxiety, which we associate with maturity or wisdom.

But, with that mention of wisdom and maturity, we are reminded of von Hügel's account of the relationships between his "forces" and "elements," and of the crises of maturation to be surmounted, by individuals and societies alike, on the way to wisdom. My main aim, in the remainder of this chapter, is to show that there are striking similarities between von Hügel's account and the three sections of *I and Thou*, sections which (as Buber wrote to Rosenzweig in September 1922) "bear the names Word, History, God, but I am frightened to put these names down as titles."[32]

"In the beginning is the relation." This formulation is not proposed as

---

30 See Vermes, *Buber on God*, p. 75.

31 Friedman, "Martin Buber's Credo," in *A Believing Humanism*, p. 22.

32 Cited from Horwitz, *Buber's Way*, p. 228. And, given the actual circumstances of the world in which Buber issued his message, it is hardly surprising that, as Kaufman comments, "in place of 'History' the second part could also be entitled 'Alienation'" (Kaufman, "A Plan Martin Buber Abandoned," in *I and Thou*, p. 49).

"an alternative to the Johannine 'in the beginning was the Word' but as a restoration to it of the biblical dynamic and mutuality of the word as 'between.'"[33] In the story of the individual, of the species, and of the world, it is relation, or dialogue, which is primary, foundational, original. The basic word "I-It" arises from, presupposes, the primary and originating fact of relation.

But all relationship, according to Buber, is characterized by exclusiveness (we can only address one "you," *as* "you," at a time),[34] by immediacy, and by reciprocity. It is the third of these claims which is the most questionable—for how can I enjoy *reciprocal* relations of "dialogue" with a lump of granite? Before continuing the story, therefore, we must briefly consider this curious claim.

Where so-called primitive people are concerned, Buber suggests that it is the reciprocal character of all relationship which accounts for their "populating" the world, anthropomorphically, with faces and forces, magic and *mana*. "*Mana*," he says, "is a primitive abstraction, probably more primitive than numbers, but no more supernatural."[35] But we no longer inhabit such a world: there are no fairies at the bottom of our garden, no nymphs and wood sprites in our springs and forests. What can the requirement of reciprocity mean for us who live in a world that has become (in Weber's sense) comprehensively "disenchanted"?

As a first step, we might suggest that the concept of *ecology* points in the right direction. We are beginning to appreciate that the natural world is not merely a collection of things, of objects, to be used, appropriated, exhausted by us for the satisfaction of what we take to be our needs or preferences. There may be eccentricity in vegetarianism and in movements for animal rights (and no one, so far as I know, has spoken seriously of the "rights" of sandstone and sycamores), but we are beginning to acknowledge something like a mutuality of order and dignity. It is not *only* in order to save our own skins that we are required to be the "gardeners," rather than the lords or dominators, of the natural world of which we form a part.

But even if, along these lines, we were to make some sense (however tenuous and metaphorical) of Buber's claim for the comprehensiveness of the requirement of reciprocity, we would not have entirely disposed of the

---

33 *I and Thou*, p. 78; Friedman, *The Early Years*, p. 313.

34 See Vermes, *Buber on God*, p. 194.

35 *I and Thou*, p. 72.

difficulty.[36] "If," says Emmanuel Levinas, "we criticize Buber for extending the I-Thou relation to things . . . it is not because he is an animist with respect to our relations with the physical world, but because he is too much the artist in his relations to man."[37] Levinas's complaint appears to be that Buber tends to handle the I-You relation too much in terms of creative *appreciation* and insufficiently in terms of the practical exercise of responsibility.

It is undoubtedly true that "art remained for Buber one of the primary forms of the I-Thou relationship" but (to put the point somewhat paradoxically) his account of artistry is less "aesthetic," more a matter of *ethics,* than Levinas seems to allow. What is required of the artist "is a deed that a man does with his whole being," a deed that "involves a sacrifice and a risk." The artist, the craftsman, is, firstly, someone whose integrity is invested in respectful production and, secondly, someone whose work is a *response* to the inaudible "word," the invisible form, which he seeks, in his work, to bring to "speech": "Such work is creation, inventing is finding."[38] If Levinas's charge is that Buber's account of human relations is excessively tilted toward the aesthetic, then the accusation seems to me unfounded (except to the extent that, as we have already noticed, there is a certain lyricism or romanticism in the *form* of his account). And Buber is surely correct in supposing that there is, or should be, some "artistry," some reciprocal eduction of form, of *beauty,* in human relationships?

It is time to go back to the beginning, and "in the beginning is the relation." The world of the infant is a world with all the hallmarks of relationship: exclusiveness, immediacy, and reciprocity; "It is not as if a child first saw an object and then entered into some relationship with that. Rather, the longing for relation is primary, the cupped hand into which the being that confronts us nestles; and the relation to that, which is a wordless anticipation of saying You, comes second."[39]

But then, in a second stage, we begin to differentiate ourselves and our world. The possibility of differentiation, of becoming an "I," was given in

---

36 Maurice Friedman reports that "In 1958 Buber said to me that were he to write the book again, he would not deny the I-Thou relationship with nature but neither would he use the same terminology for the relationship between man and man and that between man and nature" (Friedman, *The Early Years*, p. 319).

37 Emmanuel Levinas, "Martin Buber and the Theory of Knowledge," in *The Philosophy of Martin Buber*, p. 148.

38 Friedman, *The Early Years*, p. 335; Buber, *I and Thou*, pp. 60, 61.

39 *I and Thou*, p. 78.

the very fact of being *addressed* as "you," of being *related* to, being cherished into existence. But, in becoming "I," we begin to distance ourselves from our world, we begin to put it in order, to classify and organize it, in language and action. The infant does not recognize himself or herself as "I," but the "I" that emerges, in this first necessary and dangerous transition, is the I of the basic word "I-It": "the basic word I-It is made possible only by this recognition, by the detachment of the I." Possible, and inevitable: the work now begun is a work of analysis and ordering, and "this is part of the basic truth of the human world: only It can be put in order." [40]

Once under way, this process of construction is, in some measure, cumulative: we build on past experience, on previous institution, structure, discovery, and invention. We become "experienced." The second part of the book opens with the pronouncement: "However the history of the individual and that of the human race may diverge in other respects, they agree in this at least: both signify a progressive increase of the It-world." [41]

Any nostalgic, romantic attempt to avoid, evade, or reverse this development would be absurd. And even if we could bring off this reversal, even if we could irrationally regress to superstition (in von Hügel's sense), then, says Buber, "the tremendous precision instrument of this civilisation would be destroyed at the same time." Buber is an inclusivist, not an irrationalist, and it cannot be too strongly emphasized that there are, in his thought, no pejorative connotations to "irrelation," to the complex and diverse worlds of the basic word I-It. (Quite apart from anything else, the only way from the I-You of infancy to the I-You of wisdom or sanctity runs *through* the world of the I-It.) [42]

Nevertheless, the development of the It-world presents society, as it presents the individual, with a second crisis of maturation. We *need* an ordered world, a world that is "somewhat reliable": "Without it you cannot remain alive; its reliability preserves you; but if you were to die into it, then you would be buried in nothingness." It is not the It-world *as such* that threatens our survival, imperils our humanity, and blocks the way to wisdom; it is getting *stuck* in the It-world, immured in order. For Buber, as for von Hügel, the creation and redemption of true humanness, the production of *personal* existence, requires not that the It-world be de-

---

40 Ibid., pp. 73, 81. It is worth noticing that, although theological considerations remain latent in this first part of the book, the image of God evoked by his account of infancy, and the transitions from infancy, is evidently *maternal* (see ibid., pp. 76–79).

41 Ibid., p. 87.

42 Ibid., p. 97; cf. Vermes, *Buber on God*, p. 193.

stroyed or left behind, but that it be in some measure transcended (in something like the Hegelian sense of "aufgehoben").[43]

"The I of the basic word I-You is," we remember, "different from that of the basic word I-It." The choice, at this stage, is between getting stuck in the It-world, whose I is the "Ego," or becoming *persons:* "Egos appear by setting themselves apart from other egos. Persons appear by entering into relation to other persons."[44]

The Ego, the I of the It-world, the "severed I," is, by now, too familiar to require detailed description. No reader who has followed the argument of this book thus far will be surprised to hear Buber saying that people who "stand under the basic word of separation which keeps apart I and it" characteristically divide their life with their fellow human beings "into two neatly defined districts: institutions and feelings. It-district and I-district." "Institutions," he says with savage irony, "are what is 'out there' where for all kinds of purposes one spends time, where one works, negotiates . . . organizes, administers, officiates, preaches. . . . Feelings are what is 'in here' where one lives and recovers from the institutions. Here the spectrum of the emotions swings before the interested eye; here one enjoys one's inclination and one's hatred, pleasure and, if it is not too bad, pain. Here one is at home and relaxes in one's rocking-chair." But, as Maurice Friedman, commenting on this passage, puts it in a splendidly succinct counterstatement to Jamesian anthropology: "feelings per se are no more personal than institutions."[45]

How are we to avoid getting stuck or, if stuck already, how might we be redeemed into relationship? *If* it happens, if human beings succeed, in some measure, in changing direction so fundamentally as to take responsibility, in freedom, for their existence, by *letting go,* by risking trust, reciprocity, relation, love—then, he says (in a passage which is an exceedingly condensed reconstrual of the antinomy of freedom and necessity): "this free human being encounters fate as the counter-image of his freedom. It is not his limit but his completion; freedom and fate embrace each other to form meaning; and given meaning, fate—with its eyes, hitherto severe, suddenly full of light—looks like grace itself."[46]

Buber admits that, in relationship, "measure and comparison have fled,"

---

43   *I and Thou,* pp. 82, 83. Buber's complaint against Hegel is not a complaint against the dialectic, but against Hegel's assurance that the fruitful resolution of the dialectic is *guaranteed* (see, for example, Buber, "What Is Man?," p. 145).

44   *I and Thou,* pp. 53, 112.

45   Ibid., pp. 92, 93; Friedman, *The Early Years,* p. 347.

46   *I and Thou,* p. 102.

that the world—no longer simply ordered and reliable, no longer simply structured and secure—"appears . . . unreliable, for it appears always new to you, and you cannot take it by its word." Human beings, he says elsewhere, are "the centre of all surprise in the world."[47]

This is all very well, but is it not simply *irrational* thus to trust the resolution of the antinomy? Why should we suppose that the consequence of risking relationship should be the rising of light in our darkness? If I understand Buber correctly, his answer would be that, at least in certain circumstances, *we have no option* but thus to act, or at least no option compatible with what we still glimpse the requirements of integrity to be (as Jesus, in this sense, had no option in Gethsemane but to accept the chalice placed before him). Even as early as the 1920s, Buber was clear that what he called the "psychologizing of the world," the destructive dominance of the severed I, necessitated the risk of relation: "*Community* in a time like ours can only happen out of breakthrough, out of turning. . . . If one knows this, then one also knows that community in our time must ever again miscarry. The monstrous, the dreadful phenomenon of psychologism so prevails that one cannot simply bring about healing, rescue with a single blow."[48]

And this was still the way in which, in May 1933, he envisaged the choice with which Israel was confronted: "'Israel' means to practice community for the sake of a common covenant in which our existence is founded. . . . And today this means to preserve directness in a world which is becoming more and more indirect, in the face of the self-righteousness of collectivities to preserve the mystery of relationship, without which a people must perish in an icy death."[49]

Community in a time like ours can only happen out of breakthrough, out of *turning*. What is this notion of "turn" or "turning," the German for which is *Umkehr*—which Kaufman renders as "return," thereby (according to Maurice Friedman) "losing the whole dynamic of *teshuva* or the turning, a central concept and call of the biblical prophets"? Pamela Vermes, who regards it as *the key* concept in *I and Thou*, renders it throughout her book "in its Hebrew form rather than translate it into the loaded 'conversion' or the alien 'turning.' . . . 'Turn!' has been the cry of

---

47 Ibid., p. 83; cited from Friedman, *The Middle Years*, p. 192.

48 Buber, "On the Psychologizing of the World," in *A Believing Humanism*, pp. 151–52. This draft was written in 1923.

49 Buber, "The Children," *Judische Rundschau* (quoted from Friedman, *The Middle Years*, p. 163). And Buber added: "But have we not started out ourselves on the road toward becoming a self-righteous collectivity?" (ibid., p. 164).

all the prophets. It is the word with which the Baptist's preaching began, and that of Jesus and his apostles. They have all called for *teshuvah,* the word falsely rendered as *metanoia,* with its implications of a spiritual process, a change of mind. *Teshuvah* is a turning to God of the whole man." [50]

I can understand why she should mistrust such renderings as "metanoia" or "conversion." But I can see no reason why we should simply *surrender* to their psychologistic contraction and distortion. We *need* an English word and, in spite of the risks of misuse and misunderstanding, I do not see that we can do better than to try to recover an inclusivist reading of "conversion." [51] (The problem is similar to that which we came across earlier, when I first began to talk of "contemplative" practice.)

Community in a time like ours can only *happen* out of breakthrough, out of turning. Meeting, encounter, dialogue, relation, is always (for Buber) an *event,* an opportunity that occurs and passes. It passes because our response, our utterance of the "You," takes form and shape, becomes "objectified" in new words, images, and institutions—in the new social forms which structure the postrevolutionary society or in the marriages which structure the response of love. "All response," says Buber, "binds the You into the It-world. That is the melancholy of man, and that is his greatness." [52]

But if conversion, the turn to relation, needs therefore to occur again and again, if "personal" existence has to struggle, again and again, to win through over "ego-tism," this will only happen if the memory of its possibility, the memory of its past occurrence, is kept alive. I take it that Buber, in writing *I and Thou,* in reissuing the prophetic word in a contemporary idiom, sought thus to keep its memory, and therefore its possibility, alive.

And the project is feasible, prophetic utterance is permitted, because the event of relation does not *simply* evanesce or cease to be. We continue, in fact, to be *addressed.* The silence is on our side; God is not dead but

---

50 Friedman, *The Early Years,* p. 428; Vermes, *Buber on God,* p. 227. Moreover, "in a time like ours" the turn to community is a turning (we might say) from social *form* to social *reality,* from "Gesellschaft" to "Gemeinschaft"; see Paul Mendes-Flohr's discussion of the influence on Buber of not only Ferdinand Tönnies but also Nietzsche, in Mendes-Flohr, *Von der Mystik zum Dialog: Martin Bubers Geistige Entwicklung bis hin "Ich und Du"* (Konigstein, 1978), pp. 9–10, 82.

51 Benedictine monks take three vows: not poverty, chastity, and obedience, but obedience, stability (they are to be members of one community, not wandering individuals), and *conversio morum:* a perpetual change, not of "heart," or "mind," but of "mores," of "manners," of (as Pamela Vermes might say) the whole man's way of life.

52 *I and Thou,* p. 89–90.

eclipsed. We continue to be addressed, and it is this which renders possible the recurrence of response, the reawakening of relationship. This is why Buber says that "it is not the relationship that necessarily wanes, but the actuality of its directness. Love . . . endures, but in the alternation of actuality and latency."[53]

The call to conversion is not a call *away from* ideas, objects, and institutions; it is not a call to *abandon* the world of the I-It. Buber was not an exclusivist. The problem, as I said earlier, is that of establishing and sustaining the appropriate relationship between the two basic words. Perhaps we could say (to put the point with dangerous abstractness) that "community" would be the form in which "the alternation of actuality and latency" in relationship, in the utterance of the basic word I-You, was no utopian dream or wistful memory, but was ever-present fact and possibility.[54] (We shall return, in the next chapter, to the question of the extent to which, in the world as it is, the very *notion* of such community is itself utopian.)

So far, by concentrating my remarks on the first two parts of *I and Thou,* I have allowed Buber's theology (if he will pardon the expression) to remain, for the most part, latent. In the following chapter, therefore, I shall more directly consider the question of how we may address the God whose address, whose speech and presence, constitute the creation and redemption of the world. To move a little closer to this question, I now propose briefly to indicate five aspects of the similarity between Buber's account and von Hügel's.

In the first place, it will be remembered that, according to von Hügel, when the history of Western culture is viewed from a perspective which accords to scientific and technical rationality not only the *first* word in respect of every feature of our world but the *last* word as well, then the motor impulse of affection, the "experimental-emotional strain" appears as "a perhaps inevitable disease breaking in occasionally upon the normal health of the human mind." Whereas he wished to argue that what we have been calling "intellectualism" represented, not the health or maturity of the human, but its retarded development. Similarly, Buber says that, insofar as we are induced "to consider the It-world as the world in which one has to live and also can comfortably live," then, in this "firm and

53 Ibid., p. 147; cf. Buber's discussion of the notion of the "eclipse of God" in "Replies to My Critics," pp. 715–16.

54 Cf. Robert Weltsch, "Buber's Political Philosophy," in *The Philosophy of Martin Buber,* pp. 435–49.

wholesome chronicle the You-moments appear as queer lyric-dramatic episodes."[55]

In the second place, both men set great store by the notion of the "personal." But, for Buber as for von Hügel, in order to become persons, in order to exist as persons, we *require* the structure and content of ideas and institutions, of our mental and physical "ordering" of the world. "Without It," says Buber, "a human being cannot live. But whoever lives *only* with that is not human."[56] (Moreover, the ability to relate "personally" to each other is, for both men, a precondition of the possibility of personal relationship with God.)

In the third place, it is central to both men's accounts that God is not to be found and followed in some special part or district of experience or relationship. God is not, and can never be, one of a number of possible objects of consideration and use, nor is relation with God one of a number of possible human loves. All relationships, according to Buber, are characterized by "exclusiveness," are all-absorbing: the beloved "fills the firmament. Not as if there were nothing but he; but everything else lives in *his* light." However, when this theme is restated in the context of our relations with God, Buber is every bit as insistent as von Hügel that "in the relation to God, unconditional exclusiveness and unconditional inclusiveness are one." By connecting the two loves, says Buber, "Jesus brings to light the Old Testament truth that God and man are not rivals. Exclusive love to God ('with *all* your heart') is, *because he is God,* inclusive love, ready to accept and include all love." Or, as he puts it more generally, and more laconically, in *I and Thou:* "Looking away from the world is no help toward God; staring at the world is no help either."[57]

In the fourth place, we saw how von Hügel countered the criticism that his treatment of the elements of religion made it seem "as if the religious life were to be begun . . . and achieved by a constant succession of efforts of our own" by insisting that "man will never be so truly active, so truly and intensely himself, as when he is most possessed by God." Buber's treatment of the paradoxes of grace and freedom is similar, if more cautious in tone. Insofar as we succeed in living and acting, freely and responsibly, in the "You-world," we know "this side" of the relation with God. We do not similarly know the "other side," the movement of God which enables and enfolds our movement of response. Therefore, says Buber,

---

55 Von Hügel, *Mystical Element,* 1:7; *I and Thou,* p. 84.

56 *I and Thou,* p. 85.

57 Ibid., pp. 69, 127; Buber, "The Question to the Single One," pp. 51–52 (his emphasis); *I and Thou,* p. 127.

"our concern, our care, must be not for the other side but for our own, not for grace but for will." And the book ends: "Every spiral of [history's] path leads us into deeper corruption and at the same time into more fundamental conversion. But the God-side of the event whose world-side is called conversion is called redemption."[58]

The fifth and final similarity between these two profoundly different guides and thinkers is the most difficult to indicate with accuracy and yet it is (for the overall drift and direction of my argument) by far the most important. We talked of "triangles" in chapter 10, and of the stress laid, in the inclusivist tradition, on the indispensability of *each* of the forces and elements (to use von Hügel's terminology), and on the dialectical character of their ceaseless interplay. By the time that I had finished discussing von Hügel, the theological implications were coming into clearer view. As I put it then: the pattern of a doctrine of God which seeks to sustain the dialectic between pantheism and agnosticism, presence and absence, affirmation and denial, and which finds the resources for doing so in continual reappropriation of the biblical narratives, can hardly fail to be trinitarian in character.[59]

Must not something similar be said of a writer the principal themes of whose message concerned the necessity and possibility of "presence" and "speech"; the irreducibility of "presence" to "object" or of speech ("address") to description; and who was preoccupied with the kind of pedagogy, or educative way of life, which could sustain in us the basic trust required if we are appropriately to exist and act, in holy insecurity, in a world more marked by absence than by presence, by silence than by real speech?

There is no question of an attempt, on my part, to colonize Martin Buber, the Jew, and to make of him some kind of crypto-Christian. This has been done too often in the past, hence Walter Kaufman's insistence that "the notion of so many Christians and some Jews that Buber was really closer to Christianity than he was to Judaism should not go unchallenged. In fact, *Ich und Du* is one of the great documents of Jewish faith." But, as Paul Tillich suggested in a lecture devoted to the "elaboration of those elements in religious thought, in which Judaism is a permanent corrective of Christian . . . theology," the God of Jewish experience is perhaps "not so far from the Trinitarian God as popular distortions and theological con-

---

58 Von Hügel, *Mystical Element*, 1:79–80; *I and Thou*, pp. 124, 168 (in the light of my earlier discussion of the matter, where Kaufman twice has "return" I have "conversion").

59 See the final paragraph of the section on "Clarifying the Sense of God" in chap. 12, above.

cepts seem to indicate." And Pamela Vermes, who is at least as insistent as Kaufman on Buber's Jewishness, and who asserts that "Christianity and Judaism are essentially different," nevertheless adds that "they may have help as yet unsuspected to render to one another and something as yet unsaid to say to one another." [60] In the following chapter, therefore, I want to indicate some of the correctives which Buber's thought supplies to much Christian theology, and I shall do so under the headings of *eclipse, word,* and *presence.*

---

60 "Prologue" to *I and Thou,* p. 35; Paul Tillich, "Jewish Influences on Contemporary Christian Theology," *Cross Currents* 2 (1952): 35, 40; Vermes, *Buber on God,* p. 62.

14 ❧

Eclipse of Word
And Presence

Eclipse of God

Nietzsche's proclamation of the death of God is no longer news. It has entered so deeply into modern Western experience and imagination as to be almost tediously familiar. And yet, it is still worth asking whether the message of God's death is matter for celebration or regret. There have been many different answers to this question, answers which range across the spectrum from straightforward celebration to equally straightforward regret. At one extreme, there is that assured Prometheanism (more widespread in the nineteenth century than at the end of the twentieth) which sees in the suppression of the very *question* of God the opening up of new vistas of human possibility and which therefore regards the death of God as pure benefit for humankind, facilitating the acceptance of common responsibility for shouldering the burden of making a human world.

At the other extreme, the announcement of the death of God has been construed, equally straightforwardly, as matter for regret. Atheism is the deep disease and darkness of our modern world, the source of manifold oppression and moral anarchy (it is worth remarking that, today, this view is at least as likely to be found among Muslims as among Christians). According to one widespread version of this view, human sanity and human flourishing require the *re*construction of a social order in which the question of God could be treated in the traditional way in which it *used* to be treated before the rot set in. (Reconstructionists, holding back barbarism and chaos through devotion to an imagined past, tend not to be much interested in the variety and complexity of history, and in the fragile incompleteness of all our readings of the past. They simply take for granted that there once *was* some single way in which the question was both asked and answered: that there was some single question which, in the good old days, counted as the question of God.)

Because the first of these positions has been characteristic of much left-wing thought, and because the second has been the hallmark of some forms of cultural conservatism, they are often believed to be diametrically opposed. And so they are, but cut the circle along a different diameter, and similarities appear which are at least as interesting as the differences. Thus, for example, from both points of view it is widely assumed that the status of the question of God is to be decided simply in function of human needs: either "of course we need *not* to have God," or "of course God is necessary for us." But all such functionalist reductions of the question of God, or of the place of religion in human affairs, risk losing sight of what (according to Buber) was "Nietzsche's real great theme": namely, "the questionableness of man."[1]

In their pure forms (and pure forms, admittedly, exist only in abstraction, as ideal types) neither right-wing individualism nor left-wing collectivism ask, with sustained seriousness, Buber's question: "What is Man?" They do not need to, for they know the answer. And, knowing the answer, they dedicate their energies to contesting the spurious "knowledge" claimed by the other. The contest is real enough (at present it threatens the survival of the human race) and yet, according to Buber, it is a struggle of abstractions, a warfare, both parties to which stand under the basic word I-It: "Individualism sees man only in relation to himself, but collectivism does not see *man* [i.e., human beings] at all, it sees only 'society.' With the former, man's face is distorted, with the latter it is masked." In either perspective, the human person (who only exists, *as* person, in relationship) is eclipsed, obscured from view. Hence Buber speaks of the need "to smash the false alternative with which the thought of our epoch is shot through—that of 'individualism' or 'collectivism.'"[2] In a world in which human beings can only be seen as abstractions—whether the form of that abstraction be the individual or the collectivity—the living God is eclipsed in the eclipse of human community.

It is, moreover, worth underlining the point that the living God, the God who addresses us and in whose presence we might find life, is as thoroughly eclipsed by the individualisms which suppose themselves to be in need of God as by the collectivisms which suppose themselves to have disposed of the question of God. Both systems, and the theories which they generate, are forgetful of the risk-laden possibility of social

---

1   See Martin Buber, "What Is Man?," p. 148.

2   Ibid., pp. 200–202.

relationship, of personal identity and freedom as *construct* in relationship. When God can only "appear" in our world as an object, a thing, which we either need (for the "ego" needs an "alter ego": Cartesianism requires, as Descartes knew, the God of modern theism) or which we need to *dispose* of (by criticism or religious persecution) then, indeed, the living God cannot appear at all. To illustrate the point concretely: the living God is as thoroughly eclipsed by American civil religion as by Soviet state atheism.

These two extremes do not, of course, by any means exhaust the options open to us. There are, for example, those who, although they take it for granted that "God is dead," and that the question of God is simply not a question that can any longer be seriously entertained, do not find in this state of affairs occasion for straightforward Promethean celebration. Richard Rorty, for instance, because he takes it for granted that raising the question of God is *always* expressive of an attempt to escape from or to evade the implications of our situatedness, our finitude, regards religion as something which is simply "too childish to be discussed seriously" and notes, as something too obvious to merit discussion, that we have "got rid of theology." In Rorty's case, however, the celebration of postreligious modernity is qualified by the recognition that bourgeois self-satisfaction is achieved at considerable cost: "we should be more willing than we are to celebrate bourgeois capitalist society as the best polity achieved so far, while regretting that it is irrelevant to most of the problems of most of the population of the planet."[3] If this is indeed so, then is "regret" an adequate response? Rorty's admission is (I should have thought) so large as to be tantamount to an acknowledgment of intellectual, moral, and political bankruptcy.

Buber's replacement of Nietzsche's metaphor of the "death" of God by the metaphor of God's "eclipse" is an attempt to open up a fresh position along this spectrum of responses to the question as to whether the predicament articulated by Nietzsche is matter for celebration or regret. "Eclipse of the light of heaven, eclipse of God—such indeed is the character of the historic hour through which the world is passing. But . . . an eclipse of the sun is something that occurs between the sun and our eyes, not in the sun itself."[4] What, then, is this "something" that has occurred to darken our vision? In order to understand Buber's answer to this question, we need to explore the *connections* between the "objectification" of God—the rendering of God into an "It," an *object* of our experience—and the ego-

---

3 Richard Rorty, *Consequences*, pp. 24, 34, 210.

4 Buber, *Eclipse of God*, p. 23.

tism which drives the human quest for certainty and security. And a good place from which to start is the problem of prayer.

"The fact that it is so difficult for present-day man to pray," said Buber in 1953, "and the fact that it is so difficult for him to carry on a genuine talk with his fellow men are elements of a single set of facts."[5] *Genuine* conversation with other people is only possible in an atmosphere of mutual trust (which is why East-West peace "talks" are so rarely "conversation"). In the absence of such trust, the other person—to whom we can no longer relate as "You"—becomes an *object,* an "It." And the condition is the same irrespective of whether the object is perceived as a threat to my identity, property, and freedom, or as a thing to be *used* for my particular purposes (and the same is true of the object that we may continue to call "God").

Buber's point, if I understand him, is that, in the absence of that basic trust which is the precondition of relationship, it is the lack of human community which renders prayer impossible (rather than, as preachers sometimes suggest, the other way around). "The single presupposition of a genuine state of prayer," he says in *The Eclipse of God,* "is thus the readiness of the whole man for this Presence, simple turned-towardness, unreserved spontaneity." But, to the "severed I," such spontaneity is not attainable: "in this our stage of subjectivized reflection not only the concentration of the one who prays, but also his spontaneity is assailed. The assailant is consciousness, this overconsciousness of this man here that he is praying, that he is *praying,* that *he* is praying."[6] To the self-absorbed individual "ego," the requirement of spontaneity can only appear as an invitation to some kind of irrational "leap" of faith—in which folly (if he is prudent) he properly refuses to indulge.

When the absence of human community thus renders prayer well-nigh impossible, the only route open to the knowledge of God (and, indeed, of other people) requires the construction of bridges of proof or theoretical demonstration: "To the man who is no longer able to meet [i.e., to be "in relation" with another] yet is able as ever to think, the only possible religious question is whether man can ascertain the existence of the gods. . . . Philosophy errs in thinking of religion as founded in a noetical act."[7]

But if, in our world, genuine community is so rare and fragile an attainment and if, as a result, we are largely constrained to misconceive "God" as the name of an object, a particular thing (which, if we found it, might

5   "Genuine Dialogue and the Possibilities of Peace," in *A Believing Humanism,* p. 200.

6   Buber, *Eclipse of God,* p. 126.

7   Ibid., pp. 30–32.

threaten our freedom and identity), why do some people persist in continuing the inconclusive and apparently dangerous quest for God? Perhaps
because they suppose that, if only we could *find* Him, if only we could
locate Him, if only we could "get a fix" on God, then—no longer alone in
a bleak and inhospitable universe—we would once and for ever have assured his presence in our world, brought the dead God back to life. But
this, of course, is mere delusion. If we *did* succeed in getting a fix on God,
all that we would have succeeded in doing would have been to set up some
object of our mind's construction, some idol of our imagination and desire, which, coming between us and Him whom we sought, would further
darken our vision and render the "eclipse of God" more or less total.

In that case, then, perhaps the only sensible thing to do, in the actual
circumstances of our world and culture, is simply to drop the word "God"
from our vocabulary, to give up a quest which is (apparently) for ever
doomed to be self-defeating, and concentrate our energies on fostering
conversion, in the world of social relations, from I-It to I-You: on practic-
ing community, preserving directness in the fact of dehumanizing mechanisms of individualism and collectivism.

We may try (and some people do) but, according to Buber, we shall not
get very far if we do. It does not follow, from the difficulty of prayer in
our world, the near impossibility of using the word "God" appropriately,
that *abandoning* the word would contribute significantly to the world's redemption. "It is the most heavy laden of all human words. None has become so soiled, so mutilated. Just for this reason I may not abandon it.
Generations of men have laid the burden of their lives upon this word and
weighed it to the ground; it lies in the dust and bears their whole burden. . . . But we may not give it up. How understandable it is that some
suggest we should remain silent about the 'last things' for a time in order
that the misused words may be redeemed! But they are not to be redeemed
thus. We cannot cleanse the word 'God' and we cannot make it whole; but,
defiled and mutilated as it is, we can raise it from the ground and set it
over an hour of great care."[8] The metaphors in that passage (with its overtones of the Passion narratives) are rich and allusive. Buber's central claim
(to put it more bluntly) is that "objectification" of the mystery of God is
as necessary as it is hazardous. Returning to the text of *I and Thou,* I now
propose, therefore, to examine this claim in a little more detail.

"If to believe in God means to be able to talk about him in the third
person, then I do not believe in God." It does not follow that there is
nothing to be said about God "in the third person," but that such speech

---

8   Ibid., pp. 7–9.

is not constitutive of belief. But is not such speech necessary, if not for belief, then at least for the purpose of indicating what the one who believes, or prays, supposes themselves to be doing (and not doing)? Were it not so, why should Buber himself indulge so frequently in the practice, as (to give but one example) in the case of his famous description of God as the "You that in accordance with its nature cannot become an It"? But is there not then some inconsistency here? Perhaps, and perhaps the inconsistency is unavoidable, arising (as it does) from the difficulty of giving direct expression to the difference between God and the world. Perhaps it only collapses into contradiction if such a statement is misread as an empirical claim, as furnishing some information about God which Buber has (somehow) managed to acquire. Instead, one should (I suggest) take such a statement as a grammatical comment on what (to use Schleiermacher's terminology) "is for us the really original signification of that word." Whatever is an "It," an object of (in Buber's sense) "experience," is not God: it is, at best, a metaphor, or symbol, which we are liable to misuse. And, insofar as the statement I have quoted does furnish us with information, it tells us something about *us* rather than telling us (at least in any direct or straightforward manner) something about God. Buber says as much: "The eternal you is You by its very nature; only *our* nature forces us to draw it into the It-world and It-speech."[9]

The implication is, surely, that we have no alternative, and that we are obliged, even here, "to bind the you into the It-world"? Yes, indeed, and this is why he says of "the history of God as a thing, the way of the God-thing through religion . . . through its illuminations and eclipses . . . the way from the living God and back to him again," that all this hazardous journeying is, indeed, "*the* way."[10] It seems to me that, with this insistence that (to use a different terminology) objectification does not, *of itself*, "alienate" us (whether from each other or from God), Buber is closer to Marx than to Hegel.[11] There is, as I emphasized in the previous chapter, no *disparagement* of the basic word I-It in Buber's work. Even if discourse

---

9   Buber, "Autobiographical Fragments," p. 24; *I and Thou,* p. 123; Schleiermacher, *The Christian Faith,* p. 16; *I and Thou,* p. 148.

10   *I and Thou,* pp. 89, 161.

11   Though Marx, of course, only drew this distinction in respect of social relations, not in respect of our relation with God: see Nicholas Lash, *A Matter of Hope,* pp. 169–91. Melvyn Matthews has perceptively noticed that on this issue I rather sharply part company with my colleague Don Cupitt who, in a number of recent studies, has emphasised (I think one-sidedly) the pitfalls into which "objectification" of the mystery of God can lead us: see Melvyn Matthews, "Cupitt's Context," *New Blackfriars* 56 (1985): 540. For a penetrating, and by no means unsympathetic, critique of Cupitt's position, see Rowan Williams, "On Not Quite Agreeing with Don Cupitt," *Modern Theology* 1 (1984): 3–24.

on the basis of that word furnishes us with "a lesser kind of knowledge," it is with knowledge that it furnishes us. Buber's suspicion of religion and theology, as aspects of the It-world, arose from the fear that having thus (unavoidably) "objectified" the mystery of God and the forms of his speech and presence, having thus "bound him into the It-world," we might find ourselves in circumstances in which there was, quite possibly through no fault of our own, no prospect of our finding our way *back* to God's presence. Conversion, turning, is a practical matter, a social matter, with material conditions. It cannot occur through the mere exercise of will power, or through wistfully wishing that it were so. Hence Friedman's comment that "our human existence is compounded of hope for man's turning and despair over his being able to turn." We know where the way would lie, its "place is called community," and yet that way does not simply lie open to us, to be taken as and when we will: "'No *way* can be pointed to in this desert night.' All that one can do is 'to help men of today to stand fast, with their souls in readiness, until the dawn breaks and a path becomes visible where none suspected it.'" [12]

Especially in circumstances (such as ours) in which the prospects for community, indeed for survival, seem exceedingly bleak, "the alternation of actuality and latency" which characterizes *all* relationship, including relationship with God, "does not suffice man's thirst for continuity. . . . Thus God becomes an *object* of faith. Originally, faith fills the temporal gap between the acts of relation; gradually it becomes a substitute for these acts." The heart of the matter (once again) is the possibility of prayer: "In faith and cult [form] can freeze into an object; but from the gist of the relation that survives in it, it turns ever again into presence. . . . In true prayer, cult and faith are unified and purified into living relation. . . . Degeneration of religions means the degeneration of prayer in them." [13]

The fatal temptation (to which, perhaps, the contemporary dissociation of religion from culture and politics renders us peculiarly vulnerable) is to suppose that prayer can be sustained, that address to God can occur, by turning *away* from the It-dominated darkness of the world. However, Buber's sharp comment on those who seek to divide their life "between an actual [i.e., I-You] relationship to God and an . . . I-It relationship to the world" is that "whoever knows the world as something to be utilized knows God the same way." [14]

---

12 Friedman, *The Middle Years*, p. 319; Buber, "Dialogue," p. 7; quoted from Friedman, *The Middle Years*, p. 325.

13 *I and Thou*, pp. 162, 167.

14 Ibid., p. 156.

Hence he says, at one point: "I know nothing of a 'world' and of 'worldly life' that separate us from God. . . . Whoever goes forth in truth to the world, goes forth to God." We misunderstand this remark if we read it as endorsing the kind of world-affirming spirituality which finds no place for asceticism or solitude—for what Buber calls "lonesomeness." On the contrary, his account has much in common with von Hügel's treatment of what he called a "larger asceticism." If lonesomeness means "detaching oneself from experiencing and using things," then, he says, "this is always required to achieve any act of relation." And what, in our solitude, do we turn *toward?* "If lonesomeness is the place of purification . . .[then] that is how we are constituted. But if it is the castle of separation where man becomes a dialogue with himself . . . that is the spirit's lapse into mere spirituality";[15] the autism of the ego.

Buber's reflections on the eclipse of God constitute a powerful reminder of how unreal, and ultimately *frivolous,* is any pattern of theological reflection which freewheels in abstraction from the actual historical, cultural, and political circumstances in which we find ourselves. It is, after all, God confessed (in the first article of the Christian creed) as creator of the *world,* whom we seek to address. If, in this time and in this place, prayer is impossible, then so is theology. And if it is *in* this time and place that we try to pray, then we should not be surprised if we find it (at best) dauntingly difficult to articulate our speech with accuracy and integrity.

What is it, then, that has occurred "between the sun and our eyes" to make such speech so difficult? It is, he says at the end of *The Eclipse of God,* "the I-It relation, gigantically swollen, [that] has usurped, practically uncontested, the mastery and the rule. The I of this relation, an I that possesses all, makes all, succeeds with all, this I that is unable to say Thou . . . is the lord of the hour. This selfhood that has become omnipotent, with the It around it . . . steps in between and shuts off from us the light of heaven." As a result, we may be (as many are) driven to silence. But (always with one eye on Nietzsche) Buber refused to read the darkness as betokening God's death: "One may also call what is meant here [i.e., by "eclipse of God"] a silence of God's or rather, since I cannot conceive of any interruption of the divine revelation, a condition that works on us as a silence of God."[16] But if God, in this condition that works on us as silence, continues to address us, how might we hear his word?

---

15   Ibid., pp. 143, 152.

16   *Eclipse of God,* pp. 23, 129; "Replies to My Critics," p. 716.

Word

The Christian reader may be tempted to suppose that, in the second article of the Creed, in the doctrine of the redemptive incarnation of God's eternal Word, Christians are pointed to a place of pure light which the darkness cannot eclipse or overcome. But here, too, we require from Buber the Jewish corrective, because the area or aspect of incarnation is no exception to the rule that "dogma" may come to serve as "the most exalted form of invulnerability against revelation." [17]

The heart of the problem concerns the Jewish suspicion that orthodox christological doctrines (and the patterns of ecclesial life and polity which flow from them) improperly and dangerously *isolate* one man, and the people who purport to be his followers, from all other peoples and times and places—as if it were only *here,* in Christ and Christianity, that God *addresses* his people, bringing them back, again and again, to his presence. The problem can be laid out under three headings: the *visibility* of God, the *uniqueness* of Christ, and the *completeness* of the work of our redemption.

VISIBILITY

"Israel in terms of religious history means," according to Pamela Vermes, "direct relation between man and a Being who allows himself to be seen in events and natural phenomena yet remains invisible. To this form of God, Christianity *opposed* one with a particular human face." And Walter Kaufman puts it even more sharply: "Christianity was born of the denial that God could not possibly be seen." [18]

To this, we may quite properly protest that it is a distortion of the classical Christian doctrine. If it is indeed in flesh, *as* human flesh, in poverty, weakness, and failure, that God appears in Christ, then does not the *manner* of his appearing continue to require confession of his hiddenness? Anyone who supposes that the claim of God's appearance in Christ dissolves the paradoxes of invisibility would seem not to have before their mind's eye the image of the crucified. And yet, Buber is surely correct in insisting that Christians have, again and again, so bound the word incarnate into the It-world (whether in quest of security or power) as to make of him

---

17 "Dialogue," p. 18.

18 Vermes, *Buber on God,* p. 61 (my emphasis); Kaufman, "Prologue," p. 34.

simply an "object" of belief? Is there not an ancient, widespread, and destructive *idolatry* of "the Christ of faith" which, waving (for example) the banner of Constantine, simultaneously obscures from view the unseen God and ruptures relation between Christians and other people?

And if it is also possible for the following of Christ to be a form and focusing of the following in the world of the way of the unseen God; if "cult and faith" even here, even in respect of *this* appearance, may be "unified and purified into living relation" with Him who remains incomprehensible mystery; then (ironically perhaps) it seems as if the Jewish corrective, at least under this heading, serves to bring Christianity back to the purer forms of its own constitutive conviction. "The God of Christians," says Buber, "is both imageless and imaged, but imageless in the religious idea, and imaged rather in actual experience. The image conceals the Imageless One."[19] That is the charge, and I see no reason to deny that this has often been the case. But that it should be so is not (as Buber and his Jewish commentators seem to suppose) an integral requirement of the Christian confession. On the contrary: if we were to succeed in so understanding and living our Christian discipleship as to allow the image to *reveal* "the Imageless One," this would be not a departure from Christian truth but its purification.

UNIQUENESS

The Fourth Gospel, according to Buber, "is really nothing less than the Gospel of the pure relationship . . . God and man, being consubstantial, are actually and forever Two, the two partners of the primal relationship that, from God to man, is called mission and commandment; from man to God, seeing and hearing; between both, knowledge and love." And he says of the manner of Jesus' life, his "I-saying," that "it is the I of the unconditional relation in which man calls his You 'Father' in such a way that he himself becomes *nothing but a son.*" But is this not close cousin to the recognition which classical Christian doctrine (at least since Nicea) has striven to secure? Perhaps, but Buber's next step is to say that "everyone can say Father and thus become son." At this point, we are reminded of current debates, among Christians, as to whether the difference between Jesus and the rest of us is a difference "in kind" or only "of degree." And the issue is sharpened by a remark of Maurice Friedman's that, for Buber,

---

19   *I and Thou*, p. 167; Buber, *Two Types of Faith,* trans. Norman P. Goldhawk (New York, 1951), p. 131.

"Jesus is not the exception, but the illustration, not the image of God but the image of man."[20]

The necessary context for understanding Buber's remarks about Jesus is his lifelong fascination with Hasidism. The complex history of the shifting senses of the terms *hasid* and *zaddik*, and of the groups and individuals to which the terms were applied, is not our concern. It is sufficient to notice that *zaddik* came to be applied to the leaders of those communities, in Poland and the Ukraine, which became known as "Hasidic."[21]

In seeing Jesus as *zaddik*, therefore, as "the perfected man who realizes God in the world,"[22] Buber is seeing him as one forerunner of the Hasidic leaders, guides, and teachers of Jewish community. And there is a *difference* between leaders and followers, teachers and pupils—a difference which the distinction between "kind" and "degree" is too abstract and imprecise to capture.

We get nearer the heart of the problem when we notice that, according to Buber, the true Hasidic *zaddik* did not *set himself up*, did not (as he puts it) step "out of the hiddenness of the servant of the Lord." What troubled Buber about Jesus was that he was the first, even if "the purest, the most legitimate," of those who thus fatally "clarified" (and, by clarifying, obscured) the "Messianic mystery [which] rests upon hiddenness."[23]

"The Hasidic message of redemption," says Buber, "stands in opposition to the Messianic self-differentiation of one man from other men, of one time from other times, of one act from other actions." A Christian might reply that Jesus' messiahship is appropriately understood not as *self-differentiation*, or what Buber calls "automessianism,"[24] but as the enactment of a difference *made* by God and *acknowledged* ("in the Spirit") by those who seek to be his disciples. But this, for two reasons, does not dissolve the difficulty.

In the first place, it is all too evident (and nobody is better placed than the Jew to remind us of this) that "automessianism" has surfaced, again and again, in the destructive arrogance of Christian claims and performances. Jesus may not have claimed definitive messianic status for himself, but the Church has all too often done so for *it*self, with disastrous consequences for those outside its self-differentiated uniqueness. If automessian-

---

20 *I and Thou*, pp. 133, 116 (my emphasis), 117; Friedman, *The Early Years*, p. 360.

21 For one reading of the history of the terminology, see Vermes, *Buber on God*, p. 145.

22 Buber, "Autobiographical Fragments," p. 22.

23 *The Origin and Meaning of Hasidism*, pp. 109–10.

24 Ibid., pp. 111, 110.

ism is idolatrous, rupturing the relation between human beings and God, then to such idolatry the Christian Church has been tempted whenever it has had access to public power.

In the second place, Buber sees more clearly than some Christian theologians have done that the heart of the scandal of Christianity lies (to put it in the standard terminology) not so much in the doctrine of the "person" of Christ as in the doctrine of the "work" that was done in him. Thus, in 1954, countering the criticism that, in the passages quoted just now, he had seemed to hold Jesus "guilty" of self-differentiation, Buber said: "If now, in an hour in which the question ascends from the depths, he asks the men called 'disciples' . . . who he is in their view . . . and receives the answer that he receives, then there happens as a result of it just what happens, the 'pressing of the end,' and it happens in highest innocence." [25] But that reference to the "pressing of the end" brings us to the matter of our next section.

COMPLETION

In 1921 Buber said that "the fundamental difference between Judaism's conception of history and that of Christianity (or that of another savior religion, for example, Buddhism)" does not lie in the notion of redemption itself, for "this already lived in prophetic Messianism and was developed by post-exilic Judaism to the core of its world-view. But to the savior religions redemption is a fact—one by its nature transcending history, nonetheless localized in it; to Judaism it is a pure prospect." And again, in 1930: "'to the Christian the Jew is the incomprehensibly obdurate man, who declines to see what has happened; and to the Jew the Christian is the incomprehensibly daring man, who affirms in an unredeemed world that its redemption has been accomplished.'" [26]

This, perhaps, is where the immovable difference between Judaism and Christianity is most deeply to be found. It is true, as the recovery, in recent decades, of the centrality of eschatology to the grammar of Christian speech has shown, that Christianity has its own resources for correcting a one-sided emphasis upon the "already" (or what von Hügel called "happenedness") through equal insistence upon the "not yet." [27] Nevertheless,

---

25 Ibid., p. 251.

26 Ibid., p. 129; quoted from Friedman, *The Middle Years,* p. 119.

27 On the correlation, in Christian theology, of anthropological, christological, and eschatological statements, see Karl Rahner, "The Hermeneutics of Eschatological Assertions," *Theological Investigations,* vol. 4, trans. Kevin Smyth (London, 1966), 323–46.

even if memory and hope are, or should be, dialectically related in Christian discourse, Buber is surely correct in insisting that redemption, for the Christian, can never be a matter of *pure* prospect? The Easter "Alleluia" is sung, undoubtedly, in expectation, but the song springs from a particularity of memory which the Jew does not share.

But, in that case, what is the corrective which, in this area, Buber's Jewishness supplies to Christian speech? The simplest way to indicate it might be by amplifying the point just made. The forms of Jewish and Christian hope are not identical because they spring from differences of memory. We do not feel the force of this if, as Christians, we allow our imaginations *immediately* to focus on Bethlehem or Galilee, on a cross in Jerusalem or on an empty tomb. Between those happenings and today lie two thousand years of Jewish and Christian history. That history was differently enacted and undergone by our two people, and therefore we remember it differently. I am almost tempted to say that, in the shadow cast by the Holocaust, a shadow eclipsing God in the eclipse of relationship, the Christian *requires permission* from the Jew to sing the Easter "Alleluia."

What form could such "permission" take? The answer, surely, is the form of forgiveness. Forgiveness is not forgetting. It is a matter of addressing as "You" an other who has hitherto known the one forgiving only as an "It." But the basic words cannot be uttered in monologue: they are words uttered in *mutual* relation or irrelation. Therefore, the Jewish permission, the Jewish forgiveness, is only effective if it succeeds in eliciting, from the Christian, the practical matter of conversion, thus establishing *between* them the basic word "I-You."

What is at issue here is by no means only a question of Jewish–Christian relations (even if, for historical reasons, these relations should serve as a standard and paradigm), and therefore the point can be made more generally. The victors, the rich, the powerful, those who call the tune (whether individuals, classes, nations, or alliances of nations) always require "permission" to sing the songs of Easter from the vanquished, the poor, and the weak.

But, once again, what does the metaphor mean? It does not mean that Easter *belongs* to the poor. The empty tomb belongs to nobody; it is nobody's property. But the Easter "Alleluia" is, we might say, a song of "unconditional relation"; it is a song the grammar of which is "I-You by its very nature."[28] Anyone can *say* "Christ is risen," but *if* this is said (as, in a world as darkly dominated as our own by the forces and structures of the It-world, it is *likely* to be said) as an expression of the basic word I-It, an

---

28   Cf. *I and Thou*, pp. 116, 148.

utterance of the severed I, then the words are spoken in judgment on the speaker, not in celebration of the redemption of an apparently unredeemed world.

Thus far, Buber's corrective to Christian speech at least serves as a reminder that singing the songs of Easter is a much more difficult and dangerous affair than Christians usually suppose. It follows, I suggest, that there are circumstances in which, if judgment is to be averted, the gift has to be left at the altar, the song left unsung, until the reestablishment of relation (which is a practical matter of economics and politics, and by no means merely a matter of *attitude*) renders its truthful utterance once again possible. As in the more specific case of Jewish-Christian relations, what we are talking about is the occurrence of that conversion which alone reestablishes relationship.

But, if this is right, then (by analogy with my earlier remarks on forgiveness) the point of the metaphor of permission would be to suggest that, if the chaos, the *definitive* corruption or "eclipse" of relation, the dark silencing of the world of which Buber, the prophet, warned us for more than forty years, is to be averted, then the redemptive *initiative* lies not with the rich, but with the poor, not with the powerful, but with the weak and dispossessed. And perhaps it is because the rich and the powerful have begun to perceive this that they misread any signs of life among the weak as threatening and subversive.[29]

I have not, in the last few paragraphs, been changing the subject because, in Buber's thought, the *context* of his reflections on Jewish-Christian relations is almost always the far wider issue of questions about God's presence in the world, questions which (for him) concern the possibility of human community.

Presence

The "eclipse" of God, the absence of God from the world, is the absence of relation, of human community. The presence of God in the world, therefore, would occur with the redemptive transformation of the It-world, the reestablishment of relation, the occurrence of community. But what are the prospects for such occurrence? Or, to put it differently, what *forms* of God's presence are we entitled to expect and required to work for? These are, evidently, *practical* questions that cannot be decided by arm-

---

29 Cf. Cardinal Paulo Evaristo Arns, "The Destabilizing Poverty Crisis," *New Blackfriars* 67 (1986): 169–74.

chair, utopian speculation. The difficulty of following Buber's thought on these matters arises partly from the fact that, here more than anywhere else, romantic form obscures an unromantic message.

Thus, for example, the dominance of singular personal pronouns in *I and Thou* can mislead us into supposing that the basic word "I-You" can only be uttered between individuals or, at most, in small domestic human groups. This impression is misleading, even though it is true that only gradually, with his deepening dedication to cultural Zionism, did he lay the groundwork for the political philosophy sketched in *What Is Man?*.[30]

We need to bear in mind that the assumption from which his thinking starts is that dialogue has been silenced, community rendered virtually impossible, by the antithetical dominance of individualism and collectivism. "Bundled together, men march without *Thou* and without *I,* those of the left who want to abolish memory, and those of the right who want to regulate it: hostile and separated hosts, they march into the common abyss." Or, as he put it in *What Is Man?:* both individualism and collectivism "are essentially the conclusion or expression of the same human condition. . . . This condition is characterized by the union of cosmic and social homelessness."[31]

At first sight, this bleak diagnosis of the prospects for human community is reminiscent of that despair of "modern systematic politics" which, more recently, led Alasdair MacIntyre to recommend the "construction of local forms of community within which civility can be sustained through the new dark ages which are already upon us."[32] But I hope to show that, although Buber viewed the prospects no less darkly, his position was less *resigned* and, for that reason, stood further from despair.

A central issue concerns what Buber called the "politicization of truth," which Maurice Friedman defines as "the identification of truth with what is useful." On the side of collectivism, Buber saw this identification at work in the "universal existential mistrust" which springs from a one-sided preoccupation with *necessity* at the expense of freedom.[33] Tutored by the "masters of suspicion," we know ourselves to be ineluctably bound and conditioned by the mechanisms which produce and rule us. Mechanisms, structures that operate with lawlike regularity, are *things,* items in the It-world. We may use them, we may even—within limits—manipulate

---

30   Cf. Friedman, *The Middle Years,* p. 277.

31   Buber, "Dialogue," pp. 32–33; "What Is Man?," p. 200.

32   Alasdair MacIntyre, *After Virtue* (London, 1981), pp. 237, 245. For some reflections of mine on MacIntyre's diagnosis, see *Theology on the Way to Emmaus,* pp. 197–201.

33   Friedman, *The Middle Years,* pp. 206, 193.

them (if it seems useful to do so) but, in so doing, we (the "severed us"?) remain personally aloof and disengaged.

If freedom finds no place in the manipulative operations of collectivism, in individualism it is simply the name of the space in which the severed I can fantasize at will: Disneyland is the perfect expression of a society which identifies the exercise of human freedom with the construction (at someone else's expense) of individual playgrounds furnished with as many *things* as possible.

"The man who thinks 'existentially,'" said Buber in 1933, "that is, who stakes his life in his thinking, brings into his real relation to the truth not merely his conditioned qualities but also the unconditioned nature, transcending them, of his quest, of his grasp, of his indomitable will for the truth." Only the existence of people who thus stake their lives in their thinking can redeem the "disintegration of human faith in the truth, which can never be possessed," can heal "the paralysis of the human search for the truth." Buber was no social Luddite: he was not recommending that the machinery of modern politics and economics, which are aspects of "the tremendous precision instrument of this civilization," be smashed in some orgy of anarchism. According to him, the realms of "politics, economics, and the state" become evil and destructive "only when they become independent of the aim of building genuine community to which they are legitimate means." [34] It is, once again, not a matter of *replacing* the "It-world" by the world of relation, but of setting these two worlds in their proper order, according to which things exist for people, not people for things.

What is required, therefore, is not the abolition of the objects that we have made, the things whose slaves and manipulators we have variously become, but (we might say) the transformation of "things" into "words," of fetishes and idols (which some people erect for others to buy or bow down before) into *sacraments*, symbols of human relationship which, as such, might symbolize the presence of God. [35]

For a Christian theologian, one of the most striking features of Buber's reflections on the lessons still to be learned from Hasidism is the central place which he gives to the concept of the sacramental. "Through God's

---

34 "The Question to the Single One," pp. 81–82; *I and Thou*, p. 97; Friedman, *The Early Years*, p. 341.

35 Buber rarely discussed Marx (see, however, *Paths in Utopia*, trans. R. F. C. Hull, introd. Ephraim Fischoff [Boston, 1958], and esp. the chap. on "Marx and the Renewal of Society," ibid., pp. 80–98). However, prescinding from theological considerations, there are affinities between his account of what is required for the "transcending" of our alienation and that offered by (at least) the "early" Marx.

indwelling in the world the world becomes . . . a sacrament. . . . That one has thus been given charge of the things and beings in their sacramental possibility—this constitutes the existence of man in the world."[36]

Just as von Hügel deplored the exclusivism which located the "mystical element" in feeling as *contrasted* with facts and thoughts, institutions and ideas, so Buber deplored the misreading of the Hasidic movement as "the revolt of 'feeling'" against rationalism and ritual. And just as von Hügel located the possibility of wisdom in "inclusive" mysticism, attained through the pedagogy of a "larger asceticism," so Buber saw the genius of Hasidism as springing from "a genuine vision of unity and a passionate demand for wholeness." For both men, what was at issue was the production of the personal in a world made holy without loss of "worldliness": "Everything wants to be hallowed, to be brought into the holy, everything worldly in its worldliness . . . everything wants to become sacrament."[37]

But whereas von Hügel tended to see the sacramentality of the world as a *fact*, Buber saw it as an exceedingly fragile possibility (almost, we might say, as "pure prospect"). For him, the paradigm of that possibility was the return of a holy people to a holy land. Where might a Christian look for Christian forms of its incipient occurrence? I am inclined to think that the widespread interest being shown, by Christians in Europe and the United States, in Latin American liberation theology, arises from the recognition that, in the "basic communities" of the Third World, new possibilities of human community, of *sacramental* community, are being born (and, like the Hasidic communities, being born "from below"). And governments are showing themselves more perceptive than some academics in their recognition that *what* is being born is of potentially far-reaching political (and by no means merely religious) significance.

Against the darkness of a world dominated by vast and endlessly complex, dauntingly powerful, patterns of economic, military, and political mechanism largely beyond public accountability and control, a few thousand small groups of Third World peasants and slum dwellers and what remains in Israel of the kind of Zionism Buber worked for, are flickering spots of light so scattered and fragile as to warrant dismissal on any realistic calculus. Buber was not an optimist (and neither am I): "No dialectical guarantee keeps man from falling; it lies with himself to lift his foot and take the step which leads him away from the abyss. The strength to take this step cannot come from any security in regard to the future, but only from those depths of insecurity in which man, overshadowed by de-

---

36 Buber, *Origin and Meaning of Hasidism*, p. 96.

37 Ibid., pp. 171, 172, 181.

spair, answers with his decision the question about man's being."[38] And the decision of which he speaks is not (as the context makes clear) any "decisionistic" leap of faith, but small practical steps of friendship and basic trust.

The temptation, of course, especially for those people inclined to set some store by such small and vulnerable realizations of human community, such sacraments of intimate union with God and of unity for the whole human race, is to bind them into the It-world, to try to make of them another form of private property, reliable real estate, citadels of security. But the presence of God in our world remains God's gift: if we grasp it, we have thereby rejected it. In a fascinating section of *What Is Man?*, Buber distinguishes between "epochs of habitation and epochs of homelessness."[39] Whether we like it or not, ours is an epoch of homelessness.

At an earlier period, with the collapse of "pre-Copernican space," Hegel tried "to give man a new security, to build a new house of the universe for him. . . . Hegel builds it in *time* alone. . . . Man's new house is to be in time in the form of history whose meaning can be perfectly learned and understood." That house, in turn, has now collapsed with the intellectual exhaustion of mainline Marxism. Time, or "history," or "progress," is no more *secure* a dwelling than space once seemed to be. After Einstein, says Buber, "no new house in the universe is being planned for man, but he, as the builder of houses, is being required to know himself."[40]

Such self-knowledge would, of course, be simultaneously knowledge of the unknown God. But education in such self-knowledge is a matter of learning, together, to acquire the basic trust—in God and in each other—which enables us to live in "holy insecurity." With no new houses in prospect, we have to learn to live in tents. Christians, like Jews, are (or should be) nomads and, as such, should function as prophetic *irritants* (or, as they say, "subversives") to the builders of cities.[41] As I have put it elsewhere: "it is not, I think, fanciful to suggest that . . . a not unimportant responsibility for the future of humanity could be exercised by a transcultural, global 'network' of local communities, each of which conceived its primary duty to be that of sustaining, in its particular place, the memory of him in whose dying we discern the transformative presence of God; com-

---

38 "What Is Man?," p. 145.

39 Ibid., p. 126.

40 Ibid., pp. 139, 137.

41 And especially, perhaps, to the builders of Jewish and Christian cities?

munities which, in that act and process of remembrance, sustain an absolute hope for all humanity in the light of which to stimulate resistance to those dreams and nightmares in which individual nations and destinies, individual projects and policies, are destructively idolized."[42]

Conclusion

In this chapter, I have tried to do two things. On the one hand, I have tried to indicate the kind of corrective which Buber's thought supplies, firstly, to von Hügel's failure to appreciate and think through the social and political implications of his position and, secondly, to the ease with which he issued positive descriptions of the mystery of God. What I hope has come across is the extent to which these are two aspects of one single weakness or limitation. It only seems easy to speak about our experience and knowledge of God and his ways in the measure that we insulate our religious speech and theological imagination from the endlessly complex and disturbing world in which that speech finds reference.[43] Religious and theological speech have become so disconnected from the conversations of our culture that we lack the language in which to say what needs to be said simply. But at least, I think, we can learn from Buber something of the *reticence* which might make such speech possible: a reticence which, in the context of religion construed as "contemplative practice," is not an expression of *doubt* but rather of *reverence*—toward God, and hence toward particular people and particular things, the particular features of his world.

On the other hand, I have tried, without "Christianizing" Buber the Jew, to show that the pattern of the single problem that he sought to address, the problem of how to live in "exile . . .[an] unarbitrary life 'in the face of God,'"[44] is the pattern of the Christian doctrine of God's Trinity, at least insofar as that doctrine is taken to function more like a set of rules or protocols for Christian speech and less like a set of descriptive claims or propositions (a matter to which we shall return).

Buber speaks, as does the Christian, of the mystery of God, of God's "address" to us, his word, and of his "presence," or indwelling spirit. This is not (I repeat) to elide the differences, but only to highlight similarities

---

42 Lash, *Theology on the Way to Emmaus,* p. 201.

43 It may seem unfair to suggest that von Hügel's speech was thus insulated. But, although he considered an impressively wide range of ideas and states of mind, he confined his attention to a fairly narrow range of public facts.

44 Buber, *Eclipse of God,* p. 34.

too often overlooked. If I were to try, once again, to put my finger on the difference, I would take up Friedman's lapidary formula that Jesus, for Buber, "is not the exception, but the illustration, not the image of God but the image of man."[45] Might it not be the case, however, that God has so bound himself into the *human* world as to make that image of man his own self-image, the image of the Imageless One? And might it not also be the case that the transformative impact of that image was such as to breathe into our history the Spirit whose presence is, in fact, the condition of the permanent possibility of human conversion? Perhaps the Jew cannot say these things. I am only suggesting that, especially under corrective pressure from their Jewish sisters and brothers, Christians may be able so to say them as to be developing, rather than denying, their Jewish inheritance.

---

45 Friedman, *The Early Years*, p. 360; cf. Buber, *Two Types of Faith*, p. 131.

15

Difference,
Mystery,
Experience

As he grew older, Karl Rahner became fond of insisting that he was not a scholar. This was not false modesty nor even (as he saw it) necessarily matter for regret. It was simply a fact, a consequence of the uncontrollable expansion of data and the irreducible (and increasing) diversity of contexts and patterns of inquiry which combine to produce, in our contemporary situation, what he called "a quite different and new form of ignorance"[1] from those that we have hitherto experienced. The problem of knowledge has new aspects, which epistemological ingenuity does nothing to alleviate.

Even a few decades ago, it was possible for an individual to "reach the heights of the objectification that was possible *at all* at that time." It is not so today and, as a result, a choice is imposed upon us: *either,* in quest of scholarly expertise—of keeping in control of one's subject—increasingly to confine oneself to knowing more and more about less and less, *or* to accept the situation and seek to come to terms with it (which is a matter, not of simply submitting to this state of affairs, but rather of trying appropriately to live with it and to understand it). Rahner had no doubt as to the direction in which, on ethical grounds, the choice should lie: "the individual is no longer in a position adequately and positively to organise in his mind all the knowledge which is important for his picture of the world." And yet, if we are not irresponsibly to drift or wander through the world, some such picture must be formed of where we stand and what we have to do. Rahner had little sympathy with those who "mistake the

---

1 Karl Rahner, "On the Situation of Faith," in *Theological Investigations,* vol. 20, trans. Edward Quinn (London, 1981), 16.

weakness of indecision . . . for the courage of the sceptic who is devoid of illusion." "Intellectual honesty," he insisted, "commands us to have the courage to take basic human decisions however weighed down we may feel by uncertainty, darkness and danger."[2] He was not talking about "leaps" of faith (Rahner was as little prone as Buber to leaping in any direction). He was simply drawing his readers' attention to the fact that politics and religion are among those matters in respect of which every human being unavoidably *enacts* fundamental decisions, whether or not she or he is aware of the fact, and whether or not they acknowledge it to be the case.

The more contracted our account of what it is to be personally and cognitively "in relation" with God, the less urgent and intractable such considerations may seem to be. For if "God" is the name of one of a number of actual or possible objects that we may (perhaps) come across in some particular district of human experience (in the district, for example, which we name as *religious* experience), then it might seem as if whether or not we have anything to do with God is simply a matter of whether or not we inhabit (at least from time to time) some such district. It is at least possible, however, that no such object is, or ever could be, God. It is also possible that God has something to do with us, whether we know it or not. In which case, ascertaining what being in relation with God might mean becomes more than a matter of academic interest or personal preference. Why? Because this question may be one of those concerning which we unavoidably enact fundamental decisions, whether or not we are aware of the fact, and whether or not we acknowledge it to be the case.

In the last few chapters, I have tried (with the help of von Hügel and Buber) to open up a perspective on what it might mean to be "in relation" with God, of sufficient comprehensiveness as to include fundamental questions of ethics, politics, and personal identity. I hope, as a result, to have conveyed the impression that the question of God is simply not the *kind* of question in respect of which anybody is or could be an expert.[3] If the effect has been to leave the reader a little bewildered, I am not too inclined to apologize: bewilderment, in these matters, may be preferable to illusory clarity.

Nevertheless, I am trying to construct an argument, not simply to en-

---

2 Rahner, "Some Clarifying Remarks about My Own Work," ibid., vol. 17, trans. Margaret Kohl (London, 1981), 245; "The Foundation of Belief Today," ibid., vol. 16, trans. David Morland (London, 1979), 7; "Intellectual Honesty and Christian Faith," ibid., vol. 7, trans. David Bourke (London, 1971), 48, 49.

3 See Nicholas Lash, *Theology on the Way to Emmaus*, pp. 4–9.

gender confusion. What we need to do at this stage, therefore, is to stand back a little from specific and concrete issues, and consider, somewhat more *formally,* some features of the pattern of the argument. In this way we shall, I hope, begin to gather the threads together. In this chapter, therefore, I shall offer some reflections on three topics: the *difference* between God and the world, the *mystery* of God, and *experience* of God.

In discussing James and Schleiermacher, von Hügel and Buber, my intention (as I said at the beginning) was not to add to the number of learned studies of their work, but to build up the elements of my argument through a fairly close reading of their texts. In Rahner's case, however, the balance tips even further in that direction. Not only was he dauntingly prolific, not only has the accumulation of secondary studies of his work begun to accelerate since his death on 30 March 1984, but (for my purposes) there is no need to do more than to call in aid a handful of his essays.[4]

Difference

If we were to cease to try to make some sense of things, to find our way around, to order our experience, we would be acting both irrationally and irresponsibly. We not only *need* to make some sense of things but we also have a duty to do so: a duty to each other and to ourselves. And yet, things do not make much sense. Not (by any means) because we have insufficient information, but because the world in which we find ourselves is confusing, fragmentary, conflictual, and threatened by chaos. Some disaster— bereavement, unemployment, betrayal, the impact of civil disturbance or of war—may bring this *home* to us, but *unmeaning,* incomprehensibility, darkness, is always around us on every side, silently or violently threatening and encroaching upon whatever small enclave of clarity, intelligibility, and security we have succeeded in fashioning for our inhabitation. Nor is this obscurity only in the world around us. It indwells us. We do not make much sense to ourselves, and much of the sense that we do make is

---

4 I suppose that, during the last twenty-five years or so, I have read some three or four hundred of his books and articles. But this is only the tip of the iceberg. I am not an "expert" on Rahner and, anyway, he would surely have regarded the acquisition of such expertise as a distraction from more serious tasks! (The English bibliography prepared as a tribute for his eightieth birthday in 1984 contains 923 items, and much of his own work and most of the work done on him, has not been translated into English: see Christopher J. Pedley, "An English Bibliographical Aid to Karl Rahner," *Heythrop Journal* 25 [1984]: 319–65.)

fragile and illusory (nor is this only a consequence of our infinite capacity for self-deception).

Against this background, what sense is to be made of the doctrine of God's "incomprehensibility," upon which both Judaism and Christianity have insisted from the beginning? "How can the incomprehensible and nameless be the meaning that *we* have?" The problem is not that the doctrine of God's incomprehensibility *surprises* us, but that it seems to function simply as a reinforcement of the darkness. If God is incomprehensible, then (it would seem) he is either an aspect, presumably the fundamental aspect, of the threatening dark, or (being unintelligible) he is best ignored; we have *enough* to be getting on with in trying to bring up children, keep a job, and do what we can to contribute to the construction and maintenance of some kind of more or less just and tolerable social order. "How exactly," asks Rahner, "must the act of man," of the human being in quest of meaning, "be understood in which he can allow for the incomprehensibility of God without being broken by this incomprehensibility or putting it aside as irrelevant for himself?"[5]

Christians have sometimes supposed either that the revelation of God in Christ alleviates the pressure, renders the mystery of God *less* incomprehensible, or that this incomprehensibility is a temporary condition which will cease to obtain when we see God "face to face." But, on either count, this is to reduce the divine incomprehensibility to a function of our ignorance, whereas (according to the classical Jewish and Christian conviction) it is more correctly understood as pertaining to the very "essence" of God himself. Thus, for example, the first of these suppositions overlooks the fact that "revelation does not mean that the mystery is overcome by gnosis bestowed by God . . . on the contrary, it is the history of the deepening perception of God *as* the mystery." And, "when we acclaim the immediate vision of God as the one, proper and alone fulfilling goal of man," the chances are that "we have forgotten in practice that this blessedness of eternal glory means coming immediately into the presence of the *incomprehensibility* of God."[6]

Rahner's own answer to the question posed by him a little earlier runs as follows: "This act in which man can allow for and accept God's incom-

---

5 Rahner, "The Human Question of Meaning in Face of the Incomprehensible Mystery of God," in *Theological Investigations,* vol. 18, trans. Edward Quinn (London, 1984), 94, 99. Elsewhere, he describes this "putting aside," this "indifference on man's part towards something which he cannot understand," as "a kind of practical atheism" ("The Hiddenness of God," ibid., 16:231).

6 Rahner, "The Hiddenness of God," ibid., 16:238; "The Human Question of Meaning in Face of the Incomprehensible Mystery of God," ibid., 18:92.

prehensibility (and thus the comprehensive meaning of his own existence), without being broken by it and without taking refuge in the banality of clear knowledge and of a demand for meaning based solely on this complete knowledge as open to manipulation, is the act of self-surrendering love trusting entirely in this very incomprehensibility, in which knowledge surpasses itself . . . and is aware of itself only by becoming love."[7] I do not propose to comment in detail on this condensed statement, because the issues that it raises embrace the topics to be considered in all three sections of this chapter. I will, for the time being, just throw out one clue: what Rahner is saying seems to have something in common with Schleiermacher's doctrine of piety as consciousness of "absolute dependence" and with Buber's insistence on the indispensability of "basic trust."

I spoke earlier of the difficulty of making sense of God's incomprehensibility. We make sense of things by *ordering* them, by giving them names, putting their names into sentences and stories, fitting them into a larger pattern, establishing the connections and differences, the similarities and dissimilarities, among things. Things of which we can make *no* sense cannot be spoken of, cannot be fitted into sentences (except in the sense that a name may serve as a cipher for a problem that we have identified but not yet solved—but this is no help, for God is not a problem to be solved). Surely, therefore, making sense of God's incomprehensibility is not merely very difficult; it is, quite simply, impossible. If God is incomprehensible, he cannot be spoken of, and if he can be spoken of, he is not incomprehensible. Or so it would seem.

Let me put it another way. If we accept William James's sensible pragmatic postulate that "there is no difference of truth that doesn't make a difference of fact somewhere,"[8] we might ask: what difference, in fact, does God make? If he does make a difference, he ceases to be God (because particular differences are made by particular things, and God is not a particular thing). If, on the other hand, he does not, in fact, make a difference, then there is nothing useful, or intelligible, or true, that can be said about him (not even that he does or does not exist). Or so it would seem.

For William James (and many other people) the difference that God makes is the difference made by religion. There is no doubt that religion makes a difference. That is why people find it interesting. In morals and politics, in architecture, literature and art, religious beliefs and attitudes, religious language and religious institutions, have not only been influenced by, but have also exerted an influence upon, other aspects of human be-

---

7 Ibid., 18:100.

8 William James, *Essays in Radical Empiricism*, p. 81.

havior, belief, and experience. Whether, and on what grounds, the difference made by religion (in this form or that, in this period or another, in this culture or elsewhere) is judged to be beneficent or harmful, is quite another matter. Religion is a fact and, for better or worse, it makes a difference.

Now, notwithstanding the possibility of so defining "religion" as to include its secular and atheistic forms, belief in God (however God is named) has undoubtedly formed a central feature of many religions. Belief in God, therefore, frequently makes a difference, and the kinds of difference that it makes can be examined by students of morals and politics, language and architecture. And it is, of course, important that anyone studying the difference that such belief has made should never lose sight of the fact that the misleadingly abstract notion of "belief in God" covers a wide range of convictions and attitudes—from the arrogance of the theocrat to the darkest and most demanding Job-like trust or casual and notional assent to the proposition that there is some supreme being "outside" the world of our experience. The *ways* in which people believe in God, the accounts that they work with and offer of what it might mean to believe in God, vary at least as widely as do the kinds of God in which they believe. (And this is one reason why it is impossible to draw clear and unambiguous distinctions between atheists and religious believers.)

Religion, then, makes a difference, and so does belief in God. But to return to the more difficult question: does *God* make a difference? It has sometimes been suggested that he does, and that the kind of difference that he makes consists in the rearrangement of certain items in the furniture of his creation. God does indeed make a difference (so the argument might go) and the kind of difference that he makes shows up in the fact that the best explanation for certain events or occurrences is: God did it.

One version of this view is that associated with early modern notions of the miraculous. Another is that which we came across in James, whose answer to the question concerning the difference, in fact, that God makes, was: "in general I have no hypothesis to offer beyond what the phenomenon of 'prayerful communion,' especially when certain kinds of incursion from the subconscious region take part in it, immediately suggests."[9] The difference made by James's God also consists, therefore, in the rearrangement of certain items in the furniture of the world, only in his case the items in question were not physical objects but certain features of the psychic condition of privileged individuals.

Let us suppose, however, that God does not make any particular difference (in the sense that there is no event or occurrence for which the best

---

9 James, *Varieties*, pp. 411–12.

explanation would be: God did it). This is not an original suggestion. It expresses a view shared by some forms of both agnosticism and pantheism, and also by classical deism (with the qualification that, for the deist, God makes a difference inasmuch as he establishes the world's initial conditions). It is, however, a view widely regarded as incompatible with orthodox Christian accounts of the incarnation of God's Word and the outpouring of his Spirit. I suggest, however, that such judgments of incompatibility rest upon the assumption that the relations between God and the world are best pictured in terms of cause and effect. This assumption is so ancient and so widespread as to exercise something like a stranglehold on the imagination.

But what is wrong with this assumption? Do we not confess God to be the creator of the world? And is not creation some kind of "making"? And is not making the production, by causes, of effects? All very true and yet, consider the following reasons why it might be worth the effort of trying to loosen the stranglehold exercised by the picture of God as "cause."

In the first place, when we think of causes and effects, we think most easily of *physical* processes. As a result, when we think of the relations between God and the world in terms of cause and effect, we have already "bound" God into the It-world and made it that much more difficult to take seriously Buber's suggestion that "the relation to a human being is the proper metaphor for the relation to God." [10] We have thereby made it more difficult to pray because, under the influence of images of cause and effect, prayer seems to be a matter of the effect futilely attempting to exert some influence upon its cause.

In the second place, naming God as "cause," we seek to find in him some ultimate *explanation* of the world, some single explanatory center. What is the passion that drives this quest for ultimate explanation? It is, I suggest, the Cartesian anxiety, the terror or self-importance (twin faces of egotism) which leads us to suppose that we can only find identity, security, and peace in the measure that we establish ourselves as the explaining centers of a world whose center of explanation we so anxiously seek. (This is a theme we have come across before: classical modern "theism" as the counterpart of "egotism.") And so, in spite of all the evidence and argument to the contrary, we continue to sustain the illusion that we may claim and exercise "autonomous control over how things make sense." [11] Yet we can no more find an "ultimate explanation" of the world than we can

---

10 Martin Buber, *I and Thou*, p. 151.

11 Denys Turner, "De-centring Theology," *Modern Theology* 2 (1986): 142. In this admirable article, Turner argues that "a theological discourse which can qualify as truly cognitive is that which knows itself to be the decentred language of a decentred world, a

"solve the plot" of the world's history. (And to whom, incidentally, does *we* refer in such sentences: to all human beings, which seems improbable; or to some band of gnostic geniuses to which those who engage in such attempts suppose themselves privileged to belong?) God is the creator of the world, not its explanation; the world's redeemer, not its solution. To use Buber's terminology again: the relations of explainer to explanation, of solver to plot, stand resolutely under the basic word "I-It."

Those two remarks were hints and headings, rather than arguments. They may be worth bearing in mind, however, as we now retrace our steps a little in order to consider the question of how the difference between God and the world might appropriately be displayed.

That God is other than the world, that he is distinct from whatever else there is, and that the world adds nothing to his holiness or perfection, is a commonplace of Jewish, Islamic, and Christian belief. But since it is the world, the universe, the sum total of things, "which forms the context for all that we know and do," it follows that God "must be deemed unknowable" or, as we said earlier, incomprehensible. As a result, "the quintessential theological task" becomes that of so formulating the *difference* between God and the world "as to assure the required transcendence, while allowing us to have some notion of what it is we are referring to in addressing 'the Holy One,' 'our Father,' or 'Allah Akbar.'" [12]

In our attempts (which are requirements of faith, of nonidolatrous worship, and by no means simply expressions of intellectual curiosity) to distinguish God from the world, we have great difficulty in avoiding treating this distinction as though it were a distinction *in* the world, like every other distinction that we make. And this tendency to treat the difference between God and the world as though it were a difference *in* the world "has two quite opposite effects." Taken in a Platonic direction, for example, it usually results in denigrating the world that we know, in favor of a God, or Other, which alone *truly* is. Conversely, it can lead us to conjure up images or systems which simultaneously contain or comprehend both God and the world, thus obliterating the "difference." [13]

There is, of course, one easy way of avoiding either form of this mistake, and that is to hold on "quite firmly to the reality of the world in

---

discourse which is above all a moment of 'unknowing' in a contingent, semantically unstable world" (142).

12 David Burrell, *Knowing the Unknowable God: Ibn-Sina, Maimonides, Aquinas* (Notre Dame, 1986), p. 2.

13 Ibid., p. 17. Burrell's charge against "process theology" is that it tends to fall into this trap (and in this he seems to me to be correct). See David Burrell, "Does Process Theology Rest on a Mistake?" *Theological Studies* 43 (1982): 123–35.

which we live," [14] while asserting that God is *simply* other than the world. But, if God is *simply* "other," then he is simply inaccessible to our discourse: he cannot be named or mentioned, and therefore cannot be addressed. Nor could he make himself accessible to our discourse without thereby falsifying our initial assertion. If, therefore, we have reason to suppose that he has rendered himself accessible, that he has addressed us and made himself present to us, then we may not continue to assert that he is simply other than the world.

What we require, therefore, is a distinction, or difference, "which makes its appearance, as it were, within the world as we know it, yet does not express a division within that world." [15] Only thus may we, without incoherence, name the imageless one, address the incomprehensible mystery of God.

That, we may say, is the general or perennial form of "the quintessential theological task." But what the execution of this task amounts to in practice will vary from time to time, and from culture to culture, with the variation of cosmologies, worldviews, or what it is now fashionable to call "overarching narratives," because it is always a matter of seeking to display the difference between God and the world *against the background* of some "picture" of the *connections* between them.

Thus, according to Burrell, the dominant image for "picturing the connection" in the Middle Ages was that of Neoplatonic schemes of "emanation" and "return." Burrell charts the efforts of Muslim, Jewish, and Christian thinkers (represented by Avicenna, Maimonides, and Aquinas) to effect the necessary *break* or interruption in the connective images and narratives. He argues that the connection was brilliantly broken by Aquinas's handling of the distinction between *esse* and "essence," which enabled him to indicate how we might speak of God while yet insisting that, concerning God, we can only say what he is not. And if this claim is clearly consistent with Rahner's contention that Aquinas's doctrine of God's incomprehensibility "opens up all the heights and depths of Thomist theology and philosophy," [16] it may surprise those who remember that Aquinas did, after all, continue to speak of God as cause. Indeed he did but, in spite

---

14 Burrell, *Knowing the Unknowable God*, p. 17.

15 Ibid., p. 17.

16 Rahner, "An Investigation of the Incomprehensibility of God in St Thomas Aquinas," *Investigations*, 16:245. I retain *esse* because both "being" and "existence" tend to obscure the crucial *verbal* form of the Latin. If existence is not a predicate, it is certainly not a "form" or "thing"! On Aquinas's use of *analogy*, in this connection, see some remarks of mine (which owe much to earlier work of Burrell's) in Lash, *Theology on the Way to Emmaus*, pp. 106–14.

of the moves made by many of his less cautious commentators, it was clear to Aquinas that to speak of God, the creator, as "cause," is a matter of controlled metaphorical usage and not, as it were, a straightforward *extension* of the language of causality as we employ it to speak of things and processes in the world.

Aquinas's distinction, however, cannot be of direct assistance to us. Not because it is necessarily unintelligible (though recovering the sense of it may be a most demanding exercise in historical interpretation) but because the context in which *we* seek to display the difference between God and the world is not that of a culture whose imagination is shaped by Neoplatonic images of emanation. What form, then, might executing "the quintessential theological task" take in our place and time? We could, I suggest, do worse than to return to Buber's image of homelessness.

According to some accounts of the difference between our time and the times that went before, the recognition of homelessness is unique to our postmodern predicament. From a historical point of view, this judgment may merely be an expression of a dangerously self-indulgent preoccupation with *our* problems which leads us romantically or nostalgically to contrast them with the problems of earlier times. Why should we suppose that we are the *first* people to have found themselves homeless in the world? Buber referred, more cautiously, to "epochs of habitation and epochs of homelessness," which suggests that others have been homeless before us.[17]

Be that as it may, it is undoubtedly the case that "a theme common to attempts to convey the secular ethos of our time . . . highlights the absence of an enveloping tapestry in which we can locate ourselves." And Burrell, who mentions (as Buber had done) both Galileo and Freud in this connection, comments on that absence as follows:

> the "crisis in meaning" which secularity represents, embodies a crisis of imagination which only dawns upon most of us when the events of our time cumulate to challenge our capacity to imagine *evil*. Auschwitz epitomizes what has become our preoccupation: how can we retain what we deem most precious—human life with human relationships—when that very gift can be systematically *eliminated* by totalitarian regimes, or made administratively to *disappear* by their authoritarian counterparts? And are not such callous "procedures" but the political consequence of our metaphysical malaise: how sustain our

---

17 See Martin Buber, "What Is Man?," p. 126.

conviction that this is what is most precious—human life with its attendant relationships—when its origins and our imaginative hold on its sense vanish into a swirling void?[18]

How might this crisis of meaning be met? Not, it seems clear, by exercise of the imagination alone, for that would be to fill with dreams an absence which is real enough for the victims of what Burrell calls its "political consequences." The essay of Rahner's which I considered at the beginning of this section is entitled "The Human Question of Meaning in Face of the Absolute Mystery of God." And Rahner, we remember, suggested that this crisis of meaning was to be met by the *actual* establishment of self-surrendering trust—at which point I hinted at affinities with Buber's insistence on the indispensability of "basic trust."

What is the characteristically *modern* dominant image for "picturing the connection," the image whose stranglehold *we* need to break, the narrative *we* need to interrupt, if we are appropriately (which means, redemptively) to display the difference between God and the world? It is, surely, the image of mechanism, of relentless causal systems obliterative of all spontaneity, freedom, and relationship. Nor are these *merely* images, as Buber's portrayal of the nightmare collision of the forces of individualism and collectivism makes clear, and therefore (once again) their God-eclipsing dominance is not to be met in the imagination alone.

It is the *actual* occurrence of human community which, serving as "the proper metaphor for relation to God,"[19] might meet the contemporary crisis of meaning. Or, to put it more modestly, such community as we may succeed in realizing (with whatever fragility, and however fitfully in terms of its actuality) might at least serve to give us a grammar for talking of "home," might serve as sacrament of the habitation which, in our "homelessness," we lack.

Throughout my discussion of Buber, I have tried to emphasize that the distinction between "I-You" and "I-It," between relation and irrelation, does not (to use Burrell's terminology) express a division within the world. It is not a distinction between kinds of things, a distinction of districts or categories. It is not, therefore, a distinction which can be scientifically demonstrated or technologically controlled. And yet it is, undoubtedly, a distinction which "makes its appearance . . . within the world as we know it." Being in relation makes a difference, community

---

18 Burrell, *Knowing the Unknowable God,* pp. 6, 7 (where he refers to Loren Eiseley's *Firmament of Time* [New York, 1980] for a "masterful" development of this theme).

19 Buber, *I and Thou,* p. 151.

makes a difference, "address" and "presence" make a difference. And the *kind* of difference that they make *displays,* we might say, the difference— which is never identifiable with, or reducible to, any particular differ- ence—between the world and the things that there are in the world (in- cluding human beings), and the "You that in accordance with its nature cannot become an It."[20]

Does "being in relation" with another human being (being in love, for example) make any particular difference? Of course it does, it makes all the difference in the world! But that was not what I asked: I asked whether it made any *particular* difference and, at one level, the answer (surprisingly) appears to be no. Being in relation with another human being does not explain any event in the world that was previously puzzling. It does not solve any particular problem, remove any particular responsibility (though it may bring fresh problems in its wake, and certainly engenders fresh responsibilities). People who find themselves to be "in relation" to each other still need food (in spite of what romantic poets sometimes seem to imply), still get toothache, still require work and shelter, and still live under the threat of nuclear war. In some sense, then, being in relation does not, in itself, rearrange the furniture of the world or make any particular difference. And the suggestion is that the same is true of our relationship with God.

And yet, it does seem correct to say that being in relation makes *all* the difference. It makes all the difference in the world. It may even change the world (and, in that sense, come to make particular differences) because people in relation, in acknowledged mutual dependence, may find that they are newly enabled to *cope,* with fresh energy and clear-sightedness, with all the particular problems that engage their attention and responsi- bility. And this may serve as metaphor for our relation to God (except that here, of course, the dependence is not mutual).

We began by considering the doctrine of God's incomprehensibility. How might we come to know the unknown God? How might we know him with a knowledge which is, *as* knowledge of *God,* redemptive—and hence in some measure transformative of our contemporary crisis of meaning (which is a crisis of *human* meaning, of culture and politics and institutions, and by no means merely a problem about ideas)? And how might such knowledge as we can attain be knowledge that displays the *difference* between the world and its creator, and thus be knowledge of the *un*known God? How, in Rahner's formulation, "can the incomprehensible

---

20 Burrell, *Knowing the Unknowable God,* p. 17; Buber, *I and Thou,* p. 123.

and nameless be the meaning that *we* have?"[21] The answer is as easy to *state* as it is difficult and demanding to "realize" and to understand: through the occurrence of human community.

Ever since his early, more philosophical writings, Rahner's own answer to these questions took the form of trying to recast (against the background of the tradition of German idealism, and especially under the influence of Kant, Hegel, and Heidegger) Aquinas's distinction between *esse* and "essence" in terms of the distinction between spirit and matter.[22] If I have preferred to sketch my answer in language which kept closer to Buber than to Rahner, I did so because models of mechanism, of all-encompassing systems of efficient causality (and the ideal of knowledge as explanation which corresponds to them) so dominate our contemporary imagination as to make it exceedingly difficult to avoid portraying the distinction between spirit and matter as if it were a "division within the world": as if "spirit" (or "mind") and "matter" were names of classes of object, types of *thing,* or kinds of cause. Cartesianism is not easily exorcised (nor is it certain that even Rahner himself entirely kept clear of its influence). Therefore, I have preferred to work with Buber's suggestion that "the relation to a human being is the proper metaphor for the relation to God."[23] In the following chapter we shall consider what kind of doctrine of God might best correspond to the use of this metaphor. In the meantime, I want to take up, in a little more detail, two topics that we have touched upon already: namely, what is at issue in naming God as "mystery," and what might now be meant by *experience* of God.

Mystery

"God does not offer himself for observation."[24] The "nature" of God is not that of an object which could be identified, described, compared, and

---

21 Rahner, *Investigations,* 18:94.

22 In his introduction to *Spirit in the World,* trans. William Dych (New York, 1968), a work first completed in 1936, Rahner remarked that "if the reader gets the impression that an interpretation of St. Thomas is at work here which has its origins in modern philosophy, the author does not consider that such a criticism points to a defect, but rather to a merit of the book" (lii).

23 Buber, *I and Thou,* p. 151. "Many would hold that, in Rahner's ontology of knowing the Kantian, or even the Cartesian, ghost is not exorcised" (George Vass, *Understanding Karl Rahner,* vol. 1, *A Theologian in Search of a Philosophy* [London, 1985], p. 42; cf. Vass, ibid., vol. 2, *The Mystery of Man and the Foundations of a Theological System* [London, 1985], p. 48).

24 Hegel, *Lectures on the Philosophy of Religion* 1:258.

contrasted with other objects. Any "god" known this way would be a creature, not the creator of the world, for the world is the sum total of the objects that there are (and that is not an empirical claim, concerning which I might be mistaken, but a grammatical comment on the use of the word "world").[25] Therefore, the nature of God is unknown to us. It can neither be pictured, depicted, narrated, nor described. We could go a step further and say that it is far from clear what the *right* answer would be to the question: "Does God have a nature?" (It might be worth reconsidering, in the light of that question, Buber's reference to God as the "You that in accordance with its nature cannot become an It."[26] For surely, not to be able to be taken under the basic word I–It is not, as it were, to have a nature of a rather peculiar kind but, as a matter of definition, not to "have a nature" *at all*? And is not Buber's formulation in part an attempt to alert us to this possibility?)

I have been laying much emphasis upon nonknowing and denial. According to David Brown, however, I may thereby be surreptitiously issuing an alternative series of descriptions. Reacting rather sharply to what he calls my "unremitting attack on positive analogy," Brown appeals to Wittgenstein's remark that, logically, "positive and negative descriptions are on the same level" with negative propositions presupposing positive ones and vice versa.[27] Thus (to take his own example), in denying temporality to God we may, in practice, *use* that denial as the basis on which to make a number of positive affirmations concerning the character and implications of God's eternity.

I accept the warning as a reminder that the way of negation is *mis*used if

---

25 "*That* God really does not exist who operates and functions as an individual existent alongside of other existents, and who would thus be a member of the larger household of all reality. Anyone in search of such a God is searching for a false God. Both atheism and a more naive form of theism labour under the same false notion of God, only the former denies it while the latter believes that it can make sense out of it" (Rahner, *Foundations of Christian Faith: An Introduction to the Idea of Christianity,* trans. William Dych [London, 1978], p. 63).

26 Buber, *I and Thou,* p. 123; on what it is to ask whether God "has" a nature, see Burrell, *Knowing the Unknowable God,* p. 38. (It was partly because classical modern theism *takes it for granted* that this question is straightforward, and that the answer to it is: "of course he does, he has a *divine* nature," that we earlier suggested "dispensing with theism.")

27 See David Brown, "Wittgenstein against the 'Wittgensteinians': A Reply to Kenneth Surin on *The Divine Trinity,*" *Modern Theology* 2 (1986): 273. That he should have reacted sharply is not surprising because the background to his remarks was a somewhat intemperately critical review which I had written of his erudite but (as it seems to me) infuriatingly unsatisfactory study, *The Divine Trinity* (London, 1985). (For my review, see *The Times* (London), 21 Nov. 1985, p. 13.) Nevertheless, in the light of the account of analogy which I offered in *Theology on the Way to Emmaus,* pp. 95–119 (an essay which

it serves, in practice, surreptitiously to furnish us with just the kind of information about God the possibility of which it in principle denies. This is not, however, the moral that he himself draws from his warning. "Precisely because negatives are so often simply disguised positives," he says, "the only really 'disciplined way of unknowing' is to admit that one can say nothing at all." This, he goes on, is "why there is so little reference to mystery in *The Divine Trinity*. For, once you have reached the point of mystery, as you do fairly soon once the analogies start breaking down, there is nothing more that can be said. For to say anything more, even negatively, is already to make further claims. So I do not deny the existence of mystery, only the pointlessness of speaking about it."[28]

On this account, "mystery" is where we are left when the analogies break down. It is as if we were operating in a clearing, a sunlit glade, surrounded by impenetrable forest. *Within* the clearing, there are a number of things that can sensibly be said about God. However, once we reach its limits, once the analogies start breaking down, there is no further that we can go, nothing more that we can say.

In this section, I simply want to indicate that, as I understand it, the doctrine of God's incomprehensibility, a doctrine that requires us to confess God as mystery, operates with a very different *account* of mystery, and hence of the relationship between "mystery" and "clarity." It is an account according to which God is confessed *from the outset* as mystery, is *met* as mystery; an account according to which the concept of mystery functions more like a *definition* of "God," an indication of how the concept of God is and is not to be used, than it does as a marker indicating the point at which some initial clarity collapses. The holy mystery of God is not the dark shadow, surrounding and (perhaps) threatening the little clearing in the forest which we have cultivated and rendered habitable (though this may be how it appears to the self-protective nervousness of the "severed I"). That holy mystery is, rather (in Buber's metaphor), the "dark gate" through which "believing man steps forth into the everyday which is henceforth hallowed."[29]

"Mystery," says Herbert McCabe, "is a depth of meaning . . . mystery concerns what shows itself but does not show itself easily. Mysteries are not for concealment but for revelation; it is because the revelation is so

---

Brown considers in his reply to Surin), "unremitting attack" seems something of an overstatement. The remark of Wittgenstein is quoted by Brown from a conversation recorded in Friedrich Waisman, *Wittgenstein and the Vienna Circle* (Oxford, 1979), p. 87.

28 Brown, "Wittgenstein against the 'Wittgensteinians,'" 273.

29 Buber, *Eclipse of God,* p. 36.

important and so profound that we have to work to understand it." He illustrates the point with reference to *Macbeth*. The play can be appreciated at several levels: as "a good thriller," as a "piece of English political propaganda slandering the memory of a perfectly decent king who was, however, Scottish," and as "a tragedy about a man over-reaching himself; about the relationship of human life with nature and especially with time." [30]

It is *necessary* to take the play at the first level if we are more deeply to enter into its meaning. But if we stopped there, we might as well be watching Agatha Christie's *The Mousetrap*. "The job of the literary critic is, in part, to prevent you *merely* seeing *Macbeth* as a thriller. The critics are asking you not to stop there." [31]

To take the play as thriller merely requires attentiveness. To take it as propaganda requires some information about the world of Shakespeare's day. It is useful to take it at this level but, if we stopped there, we might as well be reading political history. As entertainment, or as propaganda, the meaning of *Macbeth* is exhaustible or comprehensible: at either level a point is reached at which we could reasonably say: "That's it; now I understand it." *Macbeth,* however, is a work of art, and "the mark of a great work of art [is] that it seems inexhaustible, and one reason for this is that as we understand a mystery it enlarges our capacity for understanding." And, in this enlargement, it is not only *Macbeth* that is more deeply understood: "To understand *Macbeth* is to reach into depths within ourselves which we did not suspect we had." [32] The job of the critics is to invite us (they cannot compel us) to enter more deeply into the meaning of the play and, in so doing, to enlarge our understanding of ourselves and of the world in which we live.

The critics are always harder to read than the plays, not because they try to make things difficult (that would be a mark of second-rate criticism), nor because the deeper meanings toward which they guide us are in themselves complicated. On the contrary, the deep meaning of mystery is "something simple; the difficulty lies in bringing it up from its depth. When you try to bring deep simplicities to the surface you have to be complicated about them. If you are not, then you will simply have substituted slogans . . . for the truth." [33]

McCabe's remarks about *Macbeth* can serve as a parable of the relation-

30   Herbert McCabe, "A Long Sermon for Holy Week. Part I. Holy Thursday: The Mystery of Unity," *New Blackfriars* 67 (1986): 56.

31   Ibid., 57.

32   Ibid., 56, 57.

33   Ibid., 57.

ship between, on the one hand, the use of scriptures and liturgies by those whose "trust" in these stories and symbols enables them to expect to find "deep" meaning in these things and, in that discovery, to find themselves (and to find themselves, perhaps, in the presence of God) and, on the other hand, the pedagogical function of the complexities of academic theology.[34]

More generally, McCabe's remarks invite us, firstly, to take mystery to mean, not obscurity, but deep simplicity, a simplicity that lies the other side of complication. Secondly, they suggest that the attainment of *wisdom*, of deep simplicity in our understanding of ourselves and other people, requires the effort of willing and disciplined participation in appropriate pedagogical practices. Thirdly, they suggest that, if God is to be named as mystery, or as "absolute mystery," this is because God alone is "absolutely simple." It is on account of God's simplicity that he is incomprehensible, the unknown one, and the *unity* or "oneness" of God, far from being a merely theoretical stipulation or postulate the sense of which is luminously clear from the outset, is the heart and center of Jewish, Islamic, and Christian faith.[35] The simpleness or oneness of God (which is, in part, a matter of his reliability or trustworthiness) is not *graspable* by us. It lies the other side of all the complications in the world, and it is *in* those complications that we (who do not lack complexity) have to live, and work, and suffer, and find our way.

We are now, I think, better placed than we were at the beginning of this section to hear what Rahner has to say about God as mystery. In a phrase strikingly reminiscent of Buber's view that "uncommitted 'objective' knowledge which observes as an It what may also be encountered as a Thou is a lesser kind of knowledge," Rahner asserts that the doctrine of the "incomprehensibility of God is in itself enough to show that comprehensive knowledge is a deficient mode of knowing when measured by that knowledge which is beyond all doubt the highest." Or again: "What if there be an 'unknowing,' centred on itself and the unknown, which when compared with knowledge [by which, as the context makes clear, he means 'categorial' knowledge, the knowledge of 'objects,' knowledge according to the basic word I-It] is not a pure negation . . . but a positive characteristic of a relationship between one subject and another?"[36]

---

34 For some similar remarks of my own (taking, as it happens, *King Lear* rather than *Macbeth* for the parable), see Nicholas Lash, *Theology on the Way to Emmaus*, pp. 37–46.

35 See Burrell, *Knowing the Unknowable God*, p. 111. The first chap. of Rahner's *Foundations of Christian Faith* is entitled "The Hearer of the Message," and the second, "Man in the Presence of Absolute Mystery."

36 Emil Fackenheim, "Martin Buber's Concept of Revelation," in *The Philosophy of Martin Buber*, p. 281; Rahner, "Reflections on Methodology in Theology," in *Theological Inves-*

We quite miss the point of such passages (which abound in his writings) if we take them to be expressing some romantic or "fideistic" mistrust of rationality. His concern is rather with the horizon (a favorite metaphor) within which considerations of rationality, or pure reason, require to be set.[37] And the reference to "the relationship between one subject and another" suggests that, for Rahner as for Buber, human relationships are the proper metaphor for our relation to God.

If we take an interest in other human beings, if we try to get to know them better, we do, indeed, try to find out more about them, to diminish our ignorance of them as objects or facts in the world. But getting to know people better is not simply, or even primarily, a matter of thus extending the scope of our knowledge *about* them. Getting to know people better is not simply, or even primarily, a matter of "comprehending" them, of subjecting them to procedures of cognitive explanation and control. Persons are not problems to be solved. Indeed, the *closer* we are to people, and the better we understand them, the more they evade our cognitive "grasp" and the greater the difficulty that we experience in giving adequate expression to our understanding. Other people become, in their measure, "mysterious," not insofar as we *fail* to understand them, but rather in so far as, in lovingly relating to them, we succeed in doing so.

This, I think, is the kind of consideration that Rahner has in mind when he claims that "comprehensive" knowledge, knowledge the ideal of which is explanation, is a "deficient mode of knowing." An indispensable mode of knowing (Rahner is no more interested in denigrating "categorial" knowledge, the disciplined forms of which are scientific inquiry, than Buber was in denigrating the uses of the basic word I-It), but deficient nonetheless.

It is, moreover, central to Rahner's metaphysics of the human spirit that we do not *begin* with the knowledge of "objects" and only attain to the knowledge of "mystery" on some later occasion when clarity collapses or reaches its limits. Mystery, deep meaning discovered through the labor of personal relationship, is not the penumbra which surrounds present knowledge, gradually contracting as that knowledge expands. On the contrary, it is our awareness of incomprehensible mystery which constitutes the permanent condition of possibility of our (indefinitely extendable) comprehension of contingent particulars. This is why he says that "divine incomprehensibility is of vital importance for human self-

---

tigations, vol. 11, trans. David Bourke (London, 1974), 104; Rahner, "The Concept of Mystery in Catholic Theology," ibid., 4:41.

37 See *Investigations*, 4:38–42.

understanding: it affects all man's knowing and does not only emerge when man is specifically concerned with God." And again: "Man is he who is always confronted with the holy mystery, even when he is dealing with what is within hand's reach, comprehensible and amenable to a conceptual framework. So the holy mystery is not something upon which man may 'also' stumble, if he is lucky. . . . Man always lives by the holy mystery, even if he is not conscious of it."[38]

Before moving on, however, to consider more explicitly what Rahner has to say about God as "absolute" or "holy" mystery, we need to notice a troubling inconsistency in his theological anthropology. He says at one point that "creation strictly as such can contain no absolute mysteries." Elsewhere, less cautiously, he argues that, in itself, no finite, particular reality is "mysterious." Every such reality is, in principle, comprehensible: "For this reason it constitutes as such a mere object for the sciences to investigate."[39] But are not human beings finite, particular realities? What, then, has become of his insistence (which we noted earlier) on that attentive, trustful nescience or *un*knowing in the face of mystery which was said to be a "positive characteristic of a relationship between one subject and another"?

I mentioned earlier that Rahner's distinction between "spirit" and "matter" serves as a restatement (in the light of the history of modern German thought) of Aquinas's distinction between *esse* and "essence." If this restatement is to be successful, however, it is of absolutely fundamental importance that, while the distinction should be such as to allow the difference between the world and God to appear or be displayed in our discourse, it must *not* operate as if it referred to a division *within* the world. According to George Vass, however, the individualism of Rahner's treatment, together with his use of (modified) Kantian terminology, pushes his thought in the latter direction. The tendency, in other words, is for Rahner unwittingly (because it is exactly the opposite of what he *intends* to do) to "endow spirit, or mind and soul, with substance, as distinct from the substance of matter." Rahner's thought thus remains infected (in Vass's view) with the "dualistic Cartesianism still lurking at the back of the Christian mind."[40]

---

38 Ibid., 16:253, 4:53–54.

39 Ibid., 4:62, 11:106.

40 George Vass, *Understanding Karl Rahner*, 2:48. In his two volumes (see n. 23 above; there are two further volumes to come) Vass offers the most penetratingly thorough, and fundamentally sympathetic critique of Rahner's thought that I know. Indispensable to all serious students of Rahner, his study is (I believe) a major achievement of Christian theology in its own right.

Human beings are not *bounded* in the way that rocks and rabbits are. They have more possibilities, more scope for action and discovery. The possibilities that we have, the "creatures of possibility" that we are, constitute our capacity to "go beyond." Whatever we succeed in making or stating constitutes the objects or things (classified according to categories) which we are and fashion: our history, our language, our artifacts. But there is always *more* to us than we succeed in making or stating.[41] "Spirit," for Rahner, "is the self-transcendence of the knowing subject." It is, however, all too easy (under the influence of the idealist tradition) oversharply to contrast human beings with other facts in the world, and by so doing unwittingly to treat "spirit" as if it were the name of a substance or "stuff," a thing which makes up *part* of human beings, and of them alone. It is this tendency, I believe, which accounts for the inconsistency which we noted earlier. When Rahner says that every finite, particular reality "constitutes as such a *mere* object for the sciences to investigate,"[42] he seems only to have nonhuman beings in mind. But, by thus stating the matter, it would be difficult to *bring* human beings to mind except by implying that they contained some part or feature (say, "spirit") which other things did not— and this would open the door to just that Cartesian dualism which we have sought to eradicate from our account.

The same difficulty recurs, from another angle, when we consider how Rahner handles the category of the "personal." When Rahner (according to Vass) says that "man is not yet: he becomes himself in relating to his environment," or that "personhood is not given to man like a birthmark: man *becomes* a person," we (having learned a thing or two from von Hügel) are with him all the way. Unfortunately, however, the idealist strand in his thought, the "bias for the transcendental," encourages him to speak of human beings as ("transcendentally") constituted as persons *from the outset* (for only thus, it seems, can he show them to be, *from* the outset, incipiently in relation to the mystery of a "personal" God).[43]

It is the individualism which is at the heart of the problem, for it leads him to lose sight of the fact that all statements about the individual's relationship to God are *abstract* or formal statements, abstracted from the context in which, in the concrete, such relationship occurs: namely, the individual's relationships with other people and things. As a result, Rahner

---

41 For a succinct survey of Rahner's shifting uses of the transcendental-categorial distinction, see ibid., 1:119–23.

42 Rahner, *Investigations*, 11:106 (my emphasis); on spirit as self-transcendence, see Vass, *Understanding Karl Rahner*, 1:74–75.

43 *Understanding Karl Rahner*, 1:43, 1:87, 2:125.

tends to underplay the indispensability of taking actual human relationships as the proper metaphor for the relation to God. Unlike William James, however, Rahner's individualism is not an individualism of *principle*, but what we might call an individualism of oversight or inattention. This is why Vass believes that the necessary correctives can be supplied within the framework of Rahner's own thought.[44] Specifically, Vass is not fundamentally departing from that framework when he says that "it is enough for us to state that man becomes a person *in* facing the personal other and *through* the event of his fellowship with him." The correctives may, however, be more effectively supplied if we restrict the language of "mystery" to God alone, and use some less portentous term to characterize how it is that human beings, in their relationships with each other and with the natural world, may find themselves to be "in relation" to the mystery of God. And the term that Vass proposes is "adventure."[45]

We are thus brought back (after a somewhat technical but, I think, necessary detour) to consider what Rahner has to say about how it is that, in the adventure of human existence, we have to do with the "absolute mystery" of God.

Where the knowledge of God is concerned, if it is true that God can never be met, or come across, as an object in the world—for God is only "met" as mystery—then knowledge of God (and hence, analogously, knowledge of persons and even, perhaps, of impersonal facts and things) requires a measure of that effort of trust, that "going out of oneself" or surpassing of "mere" knowledge, without which no "deep meaning" can be apprehended. Only as the fruit of such love can the everyday into which we step be hallowed,[46] and cease to be a place of terror or of sheerly trivial and evanescent "meaning."

But this insistence on what we might call the structural unity of knowledge and love (and hence of freedom, because human freedom, for Rahner, is precisely what is meant by "spirit" or "transcendence": the capacity to "go beyond" in responsible action, and lovingly to understand) calls for a corresponding amplification of the concept of God as mystery. It requires us to say that to name God as mystery is not only to name him as "incomprehensible"—as the nongraspable, nonobjectifiable ground and term of

---

44 See ibid., 1:xi. Rahner was thus able, without inconsistency, to welcome the antiindividualist "political" theology developed by his former pupil, Johann-Baptist Metz. See, for example, Rahner, *Investigations*, 11:120–21.

45 *Understanding Karl Rahner*, 2:52; see ibid., 22. Rahner himself often acknowledged that, strictly speaking, the concept of "mystery" applies only to God: "Basically speaking, there can be only *one* mystery: God as he is in himself" (*Investigations*, 11:106).

46 See Buber, *Eclipse of God*, p. 36.

all knowledge and discovery—but also as the nonspecifiable ground and term of all our loving and striving.[47] Love, like knowledge, is always a matter of response or recognition (for we do not create ex nihilo), and if "reticence" would be an appropriate expression of our acknowledgment that all knowledge occurs in the face of God's incomprehensibility, then "reverence" would be an appropriate expression of our acknowledgment that all our loving occurs in the face of God's holiness.

Hence God, for Rahner, is to be named as "holy mystery" because, "when we speak of transcendence we do not mean only . . . the transcendence which is the condition of possibility for categorial knowledge as such. We mean also and just as much transcendence of freedom, of willing, and of love." Or, more succinctly: "the two words 'holy mystery' . . . express equally the transcendentality both of knowledge and of freedom and love."[48]

It is important not to be so swept along (or perplexed) by Rahner's heady Teutonic abstractions as to lose sight of the fact that he is really saying something quite simple. If the God who always has to do with us (whether or not we advert to the fact, or have been educated to recognition of the fact) is to be named as "holy mystery," then it follows that *all* our actions and relationships—domestic and political, cultural and scientific—must be disciplined and qualified by such reticence and reverence. Respect for the creature, and precisely for the mysterious *particularity* of the creature is, we might say, the general form of the worship of God *alone*.[49] It follows that we have, as Christians, no ultimate explanations; that there are, for us, no final solutions. The Christian, says Rahner, "has less 'ultimate' answers which he could throw off with a 'now the matter's clear' than anyone else." And when he says that "all human knowing . . . is enfolded in an incomprehensibility which forms an image of the divine incomprehensibility where God reveals himself as the one without a name," he means (I think) that it is in living in "holy insecurity," in openness to each other and all truth, as not the possessors or centers of the world, that we become, in some measure, the "image of the imageless one."[50]

---

47 Nonspecifiable, of course, because God can no more be one among the objects of our love than he can be one among the objects of our knowledge. On spirit as the capacity to "go beyond," see Vass, *Understanding Karl Rahner*, 1:70–75.

48 Rahner, *Foundations of Christian Faith*, pp. 65, 66.

49 Which finds particular, explicit recognition and acknowledgment in those patterns of symbolic, interpretative action which we call "acts of worship."

50 Rahner, *Christian at the Crossroads*, trans. V. Green (London, 1975), p. 23 (though that, of course, is to overstate the matter, because the same would seem to be true at least for

Any further specification of these remarks in Christian terms would, of course, be christological, because the school in which we learn thus to live our human lives in relation to the mystery of God is the school of discipleship of the crucified. Outside the context of that school, we might have supposed that the difference between the world and God implied that there was some great *distance* between them. In fact, of course, emphasis upon the "difference" is quite compatible with affirmation of the proximity of the world to God, indeed of the *identity* between them, provided it is insisted (as certain kinds of pantheism do) that the affirmation is not so construed, monistically, as to obliterate the difference between *particular* things and the God whose reality they "differently" express and instantiate.[51] One of the functions of christology, however, in orthodox Christianity, is (as I put it in chapter 12) to sustain the dialectic between pantheism and agnosticism, proximity and distance, and to find the resources for doing so in continual reappropriation of the gospel narratives. John O'Donnell summarizes the situation as follows: "Rahner's theology is basically very simple. His key insight is that man inevitably lives in the presence of Holy Mystery and that this Mystery has drawn so near to us that He can be found in the depths of our own spirit and in the space and time of our human history. To make these affirmations is implicitly to accept the Christian doctrines of grace and Incarnation. To follow these doctrines to their logical conclusion is to recognize the Trinitarian character of our experience of God's salvation. To live this Mystery which faith proclaims is to be open to God as ever greater and to be able to find him in all things."[52]

The only difficulty that I have with that admirable summary is that it seems to me insufficiently to indicate Rahner's profound awareness of the darkness and difficulty of our circumstance. For Rahner, the acknowledgment, in faith, of God as "holy mystery," entails the recognition that, in our perplexity, we may yet hope. But the form of that hope is not such as to dissipate the darkness, because "death contains a veto against our masking or stifling this perplexity. . . . If we gaze upon the crucified Jesus, we should realise that we are to be spared nothing." This is why I have elsewhere preferred to characterize the undoubtedly consistent and (I agree) basically simple vision in Rahner's theology as "a vision of the uncontrollably diverse darkness of human existence which is, nevertheless, at all

---

our Jewish sisters and brothers); *Investigations,* 16:253; cf. Buber, *Two Types of Faith,* p. 131.

51 Vass describes Rahner as taking up, in *Foundations of Christian Faith,* "a view hovering between pantheism and, as he terms it, dualism" (*Understanding Karl Rahner,* 1:61).

52 John O'Donnell, "The Mystery of Faith in the Theology of Karl Rahner," *Heythrop Journal* 25 (1984): 318.

points 'graced' by the Spirit of God and illuminated by the Cross of Christ. From that dark place and in that light we may learn appropriate obedience, which is our freedom, to the incomprehensible mystery of God."[53]

Experience

How do human beings experience God? If the identity of "religious experience" and "experience of God" is taken to be a matter of *definition*, then the answer to the question is supplied by the account given of religious experience. The more common procedure is to suppose that, *if* we experience God, it is in *religious* experience that we do so, and then to find oneself left with the problem of demonstrating that *what* we experience, in our religious experience, is, in fact, the creator of the world.[54] For Buber, in contrast, there can be no question of our "experiencing" God because the concept of experience is restricted to the world of I-It: of our handling (in action and thought) of particular objects and things, and God is not a particular object or thing.

Not all that far from Buber (except in point of terminology) there is another tradition—which we came across in Kant, Schleiermacher, von Hügel, and Jossua—according to which the account that we render of the way things are is itself a constitutive element in what we take "experience" to mean. In this hermeneutical tradition, the suggestion is that, far from it being clear from the outset how the word "God" is to be taken, the *sense* of the word is only discoverable through the practical enterprise of bringing certain features of whatever, as human beings, we do and undergo, into mutually critical correlation with a history of discourse and behavior which is, in fact, the long and complex history of uses of the word "God."[55]

It is, we might say, a matter (on the one hand) of learning to *read* our experience—our culture and our politics, our fears and hopes, our enterprises and relationships—in the light of particular traditions of narrative and symbolic usage and (on the other hand, because interpretation is itself

---

53 Rahner, *Investigations*, 16:22; Nicholas Lash, review of Rahner, *Investigations*, vols. 18 and 19, in *Journal of Theological Studies* 37 (1986): 668.

54 Cf. Thiemann's question to Schleiermacher (see chap. 9, above) and Sherry's to von Hügel (see chap. 12).

55 As Rahner puts it, this word "comes to us in the history of language in which we are caught whether we want to be or not" (*Foundations of Christian Faith*, p. 50).

a constitutive element in experience) of changing our practice, or working to transform our culture, our politics, our relationships, in the light of that reading.[56] We may, of course, decide not to do so. We may decide that we have no use, or no prudent or proper use, for this language. But (as we have already discovered from Buber's account of conversion, and as we shall shortly see again in Rahner's account of our experience of God) the kind of choice with which we find ourselves confronted is no mere matter of aesthetics (of a preference of "worldviews," for example), but one that affects our very identity and every aspect of our way of living, working, thinking, and suffering in the world. All serious uses of theological language are ineluctably "self-involving." Or, as a friend of mine once put it, reading the scriptures is an exceedingly dangerous business.

Rahner's account of experience of God (to which I now turn) proceeds along something like the following lines. Consider the following general features of human experience. Consider them as features of *your* experience. Consider their *drift,* the kind of threat and promise that they pose and offer. Now, that to which such commonplace features of human experience *point,* in darkness, is what has in fact been meant, in the Christian tradition, by God.[57] That is what "God" means, and because we cannot "see" what it means, our human experience, as experience of God, is always experience of God the unknown. To put it in the language of the previous section, God may indeed be "met" in our experience, but it is always as holy mystery that he is met.

It is clear, of course, that such an account of what experience of God might mean embodies complex and contestable *historical* claims—concerning the uses to which, in the past, Christian language has been put—which, because (in Rahner's writings as in Schleiermacher's) they are often not made explicit, may be missed. And if we miss them, we misread Rahner (or Schleiermacher) as offering, not a particular theological interpre-

---

56 In the measure that we do so, of course, we shall then be led to *re*-read the tradition. I have spoken of *mutually* critical correlation (a phrase which I owe to Edward Schillebeeckx, *Interim Report on the Books "Jesus" and "Christ,"* trans. John Bowden [New York, 1981], p. 9) because the "hermeneutical circle" does not cease to turn.

57 "Have the courage to be alone . . . stop, be silent, wait. Do not cast furtive glances towards some strange mystical experience. . . . Perhaps you will not be aware of anything but an uneasy feeling of emptiness and deadness. Endure yourself! . . . let the silent speak in stillness. Do that, but be careful. Do not call it God. Do not try to derive enjoyment from it, as if it were a part of yourself. It is a mute pointer in the direction of God, something which . . . gives us a hint that God is more than just another thing, added to those with which we normally have to deal" (Rahner, "Thoughts on the Theology of Christmas," in *Theological Investigations,* vol. 3, trans. Karl-H. Kruger and Boniface Kruger [London, 1967], 24–28).

tation of the way things are, but a disturbingly untestable and somewhat arbitrary series of (in the popular, derogatory sense) metaphysical claims.

According to Rahner, there are features of our mundane experience, of (as von Hügel would say) "the endless contacts . . . between ourselves and objects of all kinds which act upon us, and upon which we act in some degree or way,"[58] which are "basic," both in the sense that they are present in all our experience, and in the sense that they are irreducible to particular contexts and constituents of such experience. Most of the time we do not advert to such basic experiences because our energies are concentrated on coping with particular circumstances: on paying bills, feeding children, catching trains, looking up references, and so on.

In all this necessary "busyness" we are, or seek to be, *in control* of the situation: by meeting our debts, keeping the food off the floor, getting to the station on time, or finding the reference. And yet, in all our experience, there is also that which points beyond the boundaries of the particular, simultaneously threatening our achieved identity and control and promising fulfillment and freedom unachieved and largely unimagined.

This further dimension of experience is ineluctably present in such features of common experience as joy, anxiety, fidelity, love, trust, logical thought, and responsible decision. In order to know what it is to be joyful, anxious, faithful, loving, trustful, reasonable, and responsible, it is not necessary to subject these features of experience to reflective consideration. Our awareness of them often remains (as Buber might say) latent. And, if we *do* attend to such "basic experience," the account that we give of its fact and significance may be quite "false or inadequate" and will, at best, be incomplete. There are limits to our capacity for bringing experience to interpretative speech. Not that our efforts to do so are unimportant: "The actual *experience* of love is indeed absolutely basic and absolutely indispensable. But despite this fact the experience can in itself be accepted more profoundly, more purely, and with greater freedom when we achieve a knowledge of its true nature and its implications at the explicitly conscious level."[59]

The distinction with which Rahner is working here is that between spirit and matter cast in terms of a neo-Kantian distinction between the "transcendental" and the "categorial." But, if this distinction is to work properly, it must not be taken as descriptive of a "division within the world." We do not hear what Rahner is trying to say if we suppose him to

---

58 Von Hügel, *Mystical Element* 1:52.

59 Rahner, *Investigations*, 11:151, 152.

be saying that there are basic experiences *and also* experiences of objects and things; an "experience of love" *and also* an experience of feeding the child.

Nevertheless, there are, according to Rahner, circumstances in which the invitation which basic experience brings, the simultaneous threat and promise which it represents, may be *brought home* to us in a more or less peremptory manner. Such circumstances include those in which someone is "suddenly reduced to a state of *'aloneness'* . . . when everything is 'called in question'"; when we are, for some reason, "inescapably brought face to face with [our] own freedom and *responsibility*"; when we suddenly notice that "we have been accepted [by someone else] with a love which is . . . unconditioned"; "when *death* silently directs its gaze towards a man," exposing his powerlessness. In such circumstances, we are confronted with a choice: not a categorial choice between (for example) reading the newspaper and feeding the cat or, less trivially, between taking or turning down some job that has been offered to us. It is, quite simply, a choice between acceptance or rejection. It is not (usually) a *dramatic* choice, as the forms of its rejection show. Rejection, most often, takes the form of evasion. There is so much that we have to do, and to be getting on with, that we brush the challenge aside, hardly noticing it. Sometimes, the challenge is acknowledged, but its consideration postponed: we remain modest and practical people. Sometimes, the rejection is more energetic: we bury ourselves furiously in work or play, ambition, or distraction.[60]

But what are the forms of acceptance? What is it that we are being invited to accept? Ourselves. That answer is correct, but most misleading. It is misleading because, in the measure that we imagine, or think about, the challenge of basic experience in *categorial* terms, "self-acceptance" can only be construed as egotism or complacency: self-acceptance as a matter of *settling for* the object or It that I am. But the self-acceptance of which Rahner is speaking is "transcendental" in character. It does not contain its own categorial element: for that we must look elsewhere. Thus, for example, to accept oneself as loved is to accept oneself as someone else's gift, not as their controller; as constrained by truth or responsibility, it is a matter of accepting oneself as constituted by, rather than as constituting and defining, reality; as confronted by death and "aloneness," acceptance of oneself as fragile, questionable, set in impenetrable darkness.

---

60 Ibid., 11:157–58 (for a more extended meditation on, and list of, such circumstances, see ibid., 18:200–203; Rahner is *not* talking about "religious" experience unless that notion is recast to include, as it usually does not, a sense of profound boredom and "bitter monotony" [ibid., 18:202]); cf. *Foundations of Christian Faith*, pp. 32–33.

In other words, the self-acceptance to which basic experience invites us is always a matter of "decentring," of surrendering what we took to be autonomy; a matter of that *conversion* which entails the surrender of the "false drive for self-affirmation which impels man to flee from the unreliable, unsolid, unlasting, unpredictable, dangerous world of relation into the having of things."[61] It is therefore clear (I hope) that there are affinities between Rahner's account of self-acceptance and Schleiermacher's account of piety.

The challenge of basic experience is a challenge to practical acknowledgment, not simply of our finitude, but of our *creatureliness,* of our "absolute dependence" on the mystery of God (although it will only be characterized as such by those who have learned to use such language—but we will come to that later on). There is nothing more difficult to discover, in practice, than that in *absolute* dependence consists our freedom. In order to make such discovery, we would seem to need some new grammar of dependence: a state of affairs and its description in which, with solitude and egotism transcended, dependence meant not slavery, but responsible relationship: with ourselves, with each other, with all things—and with God. We would seem, in other words, to need the fact and language of *community.* But, if this is how things are, then to characterize Christianity as "a school for the production of the personal" is to characterize it as a school the purpose of whose pedagogy is to foster the conditions in which creatureliness, construed not as slavery but as sonship, might responsibly and effectively be acknowledged. By implication, then, I am suggesting that Rahner's account of the challenge of basic experience, though fine as far as it goes, is insufficiently attentive to the problem of how those actual social circumstances might be fostered which would facilitate acceptance, rather than rejection or deferral of the challenge.

In that last paragraph, I was jumping the gun a little, because Rahner's account of experience had not, up to the point to which we had followed it, yet made mention of God. And yet, of course, the whole point of the essay "Experience of God Today" (and of many similar passages in his writings) is to suggest that *all* human experience is, in varying degrees of "latency" or "actuality," experience in relation to the mystery of God, and may be accepted as such "even if the word 'God' is never heard and is never used as the term for the direction and goal of the transcendental experiences known in this way." As he puts it at one point, in a splendidly provocative formulation: "without any experience of God . . . experience

---

61 Buber, *I and Thou*, p. 126.

of the self is absolutely impossible."[62] (A claim which will be quite unintelligible to those who take the "self" to be the "severed I.")

Theologically, it is not too difficult to indicate what the formal justification for such strange claims might be. For, if there is God, and if the God that there is is creator and redeemer of the world, then all that exists—all events, processes, circumstances, persons—is constituted by God's gracious relationship. To be "creature" is what, in fact, it *means* for anything to *be*. To be conscious of creatureliness, and to act in this consciousness and responsibility, is what it truly means to be a *human* creature. Nevertheless, if this central contention of Rahner's is to appear plausible (and if it is not to be misunderstood), there are four areas in which some comments on it are in order.

In the first place, Rahner is not attempting a proof of God's existence, but offering a Christian interpretation of human experience.

In the second place, although it is a *theological* interpretation, he does not bring the word "God" in early lest, by doing so before he has prompted us to consider, as accurately as possible, familiar predicaments in which we find ourselves, we have recourse to religious or explicitly theological categories to take *the pressure off* the practical dilemma that we *are*. For Rahner, it is *in* that dilemma, in accepting and coming to terms with our predicament, that we "meet" God in the only way in which he is, in fact, to be met in our world: namely, as "holy mystery."[63]

For this reason, I am not entirely persuaded by the contrast drawn by Fergus Kerr between Rahner's strategy and that of his teacher, Heidegger. "Whereas," says Kerr, "Rahner would say that man becomes human only as he seeks God, Heidegger would reply that man becomes human only as he learns to live within the confines of the world—and then, by a surplus or a kind of grace, God's presence might be granted."[64]

Within the confines of *which* "world" are we to live? Today's world or tomorrow's? Rahner's account is at least compatible with the recognition that acceptance of the challenge of basic experience is always (at least implicitly) acceptance of responsibility to contribute to the redemptive transformation of the world, whereas Heidegger's insistent agnosticism drew him in the direction of a (politically conservative) fatalism. And if Rahner

---

62 Rahner, "Religious Feeling Inside and Outside the Church," *Investigations,* 17:237; Rahner, "Experience of Self and Experience of God," ibid., vol. 13, trans. David Bourke (London, 1975), 126.

63 Similar considerations, I suggest, underlie Buber's strategy in postponing explicit consideration of "relation to God" to the third part of *I and Thou.*

64 Fergus Kerr, "Rahner Retrospective. 3. Transcendence or Finitude," *New Blackfriars* 62 (1981): 377.

would, indeed, say that it is in response to the mystery of God (and, in that sense, in quest of God) that we become authentically human, he would also say that the *form* of that quest lies in acceptance, not evasion, of our finitude and contingency.

I am not denying that there are deep differences between Heidegger and Rahner, differences which spring most deeply from the fact that Rahner was convinced—because he had *learned* this in the school of Christian discipleship—that (whether we recognize it or not) the world in which we live and work and make our choices is a world "graced" by God's presence as Word and Spirit, whereas Heidegger did not, I think, share this conviction.

But this brings me, in the third place, to the problem of where *explicitly* Christian proclamation and discipleship fit into Rahner's scheme of things. If the "primal, and sustaining ground of all piety outside the Church," including purely secular forms of such piety, "is the experience of God," what (to put it rather bluntly) is *the point* of being a Christian? If *all* human beings simply in virtue of the fact that they *are* human beings, may encounter the mystery of God in meeting the challenges of their basic experience, then is Rahner not offering us "just another theory about man, another anthropological *Weltanschauung*," such that, "at the end of the day the gracious God of Christianity [can] be put into brackets"? Throughout George Vass's second volume, it is clear that he finds in this question "the source of our most acute uneasiness concerning Rahner's approach to grace." [65]

Vass's uneasiness would be fully justified if it were the case that our philosophical and theological interpretations were simply *brought to* some already finished and constituted body of experience; if they were merely descriptive of completed fact, mere theoretical speculation as to why things are the way they are. (For many people, the pointlessness of theological interpretation arises from the supposition that this is, in fact, the case.) The situation is different, however, if (as I have argued) the relationship between experience and interpretation is dialectical in character, is a matter of "mutually critical correlation." For, in this case, the accounts that we give, the interpretations that we offer, *make a difference* to the experience itself, constitute an internally constitutive feature of that experience. [66] Christian experience is not the *same* experience as Jewish, or

---

65   Rahner, *Investigations*, 17:233; Vass, *Understanding Karl Rahner*, 2:108.

66   Hence Anne Carr's question, "Is the Christian revelation an interpretation of experience or its transformation?" (Anne Carr, "Theology and Experience in the Thought of Karl Rahner," *Journal of Religion* 13 [1973]: 375) seems to me to express a false antithesis.

Muslim, or secular experience, differently described, because—in every case—experience is *modified* by the interpretations that we offer, the memories to which we appeal in the stories that we tell. This, I think, is the kind of thing that Rahner has in mind when he says that "the answer given in revelation *clarifies* the question a man asks."[67] And other interpretative traditions, religious and secular, purport in various ways to offer comparable clarification (and the civilized interaction between them is what we now call "dialogue").

Another way of putting this would be to say that the framework within which Rahner envisages the relationships between human experience and a tradition of discourse and behavior which, in interpreting that experience, effectively changes it, is sacramental. The relationship of Christian memory and proclamation to the human world of which such memory and proclamation forms a part, and in which it occurs and functions, is best expressed *not* in terms of the relationship of "religion" to "secularity" (let alone of "weltanschauung" to "fact") but rather in terms of the relationship of (sacramental) "form" to "matter." It is the task of Christian community, of a network of relations defined and shaped by Christian discourse, to exist and operate in the world as "sacrament of intimate union with God and of unity for the whole human race."[68]

This is a constant theme in Rahner's writings, and it indicates why he should say that "Christian faith and theology see the historical reality of Jesus, the Church, the sacrament, and the proclaimed word, as ways of reaching God," not in the sense that God is not reached in other ways, nor "in the sense that all these things are merely elements of a subsequent reflection on the actual salvific relationship of man to God and [are] not constitutive of the relationship itself," but rather in the sense that the account given of them declares them to be "internal and constitutive elements of this salvific relationship to God."[69]

And if the claim that *any* particular fact, or sequence of facts, may be of *universal* significance (a claim by no means peculiar to Christianity) is shocking to much modern sensibility, this, I suggest, is partly due to the influence on our imagination of the scientist assumption that no particular fact, or particular person, can be more than an instance of the opera-

---

67 Rahner, *Investigations*, 16:9 (my emphasis).

68 "Dogmatic Constitution on the Church: *Lumen Gentium*," article 1, in *The Documents of Vatican II*, ed. W. M. Abbott (London, 1966).

69 Rahner, "Experience of Transcendence from the Standpoint of Catholic Dogmatics," *Investigations*, 18:179; on the sacramental theme, see, for example, Rahner, *The Church and the Sacraments*, trans. W. J. O'Hara (London, 1963); "Unity of the Church—Unity of Mankind," *Investigations*, 20:154–72.

tion of universal lawlike causal mechanisms. In a world which has no language but the abstract in which to speak of universals, all *stories* of the human world, all interpretative narratives of memory and hope, are reduced to the status of mythology or science fiction. As such, they may be allowed to *adorn* the "real world," but can hardly be supposed to constitute an element of its truth.

It is not my intention to suggest, by these remarks, that Vass's uneasiness is simply unfounded. He does, I think, put his finger on a real and abiding difficulty at the heart of the Christian theological enterprise. It is the difficulty of so telling the story, so "picturing the connection" between God and the world, as yet to allow the *difference* between the world and God to be appropriately "displayed." In the present context, the aspect of that difference which Vass fears may be obscured by Rahner's strategy for portraying the connection is that of God's sovereign *freedom*. Is not Rahner's account of human experience as experience of God in danger of making it seem as if this is how things *had* to be: as if the forms of God's appearance in the world, of his presence in the world, were *necessitated* by the form of the creature?[70] If this is the difficulty, then another way of expressing it would be to say that Rahner's strenuous intellectualism, his attempt to *understand* the way that (under God's sovereign freedom) things are, stands too close to Hegel's rationalism[71]—for the difference between the world and God's freedom is fatally obscured by all attempts (as it were) to render the ways of that freedom intellectually luminous or "comprehensible." But, if this is right, then we do not have to *choose* between Rahner and Vass, but simply to acknowledge that the quest for understanding (which is always in danger of *obscuring* the difference) and the insistent recognition of "infinite qualitative difference" (which is always in danger of making all mention of God simply impossible) are dialectically related: each stands permanently in need of corrective pressure from the other.

In the fourth place, in emphasizing the *ordinariness* of human experience of God, am I not in danger of underestimating the *theological* significance of those events and occurrences, those special moments, upon which accounts of religious experience habitually concentrate? To put it in the form of Patrick Sherry's question to von Hügel: if the experience of God is so

---

70 Are there not, in this respect, affinities between George Vass's uneasiness and what it was that troubled Karl Barth about Schleiermacher's project (notwithstanding the fact that the corrective supplied in the two cases is very different)?

71 This is implied by the (misleading) remark that Jesus Christ, for Rahner, "represents a unique example of what any man could realize theoretically" (Winfried Corduan, "Hegel in Rahner: A Study in Philosophical Hermeneutics," *Harvard Theological Review* 71 [1977]: 295).

general in character, then what would it be like for someone *not* to have such experience?[72]

The form of the question is unfortunate, in that it seems to imply that "experience of God" would be experience of some particular (categorial) kind, distinguishable as such from other kinds of experience (from the experience of feeding a child, for example, or chairing a committee, or dying of cancer). I would prefer to say, with Rahner, that "experience of God must not be conceived as though it were one particular experience *among* others."[73] (And this would be a grammatical stipulation concerning Christian uses of the concept of "God.")

Nevertheless, even if there are good theological grounds for insisting that there is no particular district of experience in which God is to be met, the question could still be asked: but are not some experiences more *important* than others, as far as our relationship with God is concerned? And the answer, of course, is yes. In denying that there are any particular districts, or places, or times, in which God is more likely to be met than in any others, I am not saying that anything that happens to us equally, or indiscriminately, facilitates relation with God—any more than anything that happens to us equally, or indiscriminately, facilitates self-discovery or acquaintance with each other. But the experiences that matter most—whether they be episodic in character (as in the case of those circumstances in which the challenge of basic experience is peremptorily brought home to us, thus prompting the shift, in Buber's terminology, from latency to actuality) or whether they be of more extended duration (such as the experience of parenthood, which matters more than most)—are at least as likely to have the character of responsibility acknowledged, or suffering endured, as they are to have the character of aesthetic satisfaction or heightened feeling. A Christian account of the "experiences that matter most" should be derived from a consideration of the ways in which Jesus came to bear the responsibility of his mission and, especially, of how it went with him in Gethsemane.

Conclusion

In this chapter, we have considered how the difference between the world and God, a difference which never appears as a division *within* the world,

---

72 See chap. 12, above.

73 Rahner, *Investigations*, 11:154.

can nevertheless be exhibited or displayed in that "going beyond," in basic trust, which is the life of the spirit lived in the presence of holy mystery. It follows from this account that the occurrence of redemptive *community* is a necessary condition of the possibility of prayer, and hence of explicitly religious activity of a kind which does not *deepen* the "eclipse of God."

To indicate why this should be so, we can consider the only form in which, in the absence of such redemptive trust, Kant's questions could be raised. Kant asked four questions: "What can I know?," "What ought I to do?," "What may I hope?," and a fourth question which he raised but did not answer: "What is man?" [74] In asking the first three questions, however, Kant did not entertain the possibility that the answer to any or all of them could be "nothing." Therefore, although he did not supply an answer to the fourth question, his exploration of the other three, in three *Critiques,* presupposed (according to Buber) the possibility of an answer being given to the fourth.

But let us suppose (and this is not, I think, an unreal supposition, in the present darkness and confusion of the Western imagination) that the first three questions *are* raised in such a manner as to expect the answer, in each case, to be "nothing": raised simply as expressions of our fear that there is no reliable knowledge, no clear lines of duty, and that all hope is illusory. Should this happen, then these questions cease, in fact, to be *questions* at all: they become simply expressions of "lostness" and despair. Such cries can in some sense briefly be *met* (by clinging to such comfort, wealth, structure, or solace as comes our way), but, because they are no longer *questions,* they cannot be answered. And, if they cannot be answered, then the fourth question simply cannot and does not arise. [75] And, *if* "the question of the human" cannot be raised, then the question of God cannot be raised either, because the holy mystery that is God only appears in the world in human words and human relationships.

It would, of course, be possible—even in the face of our acknowledged impotence to feed the world, to order it in dignity and tranquillity, and to bring the insanity of nuclear policy under effective control—still to *talk about* God, to tell stories about God, but these would now be dreams (or nightmares), not forms of "address"—to each other or to God. We might still find some place for religion, and perhaps especially for religious ex-

---

74 See Buber, "What Is Man?," pp. 118–21. These concluding comments are offered by way of reflections on this passage from Buber.

75 This is hinted at in some current discussion of the "death of the subject." What is it that died: the "ego," the "severed I" (hardly, although its plausibility may have been undermined) or the *human* possibility?

perience, but it would now only serve as pastime or narcotic, as a way of pretending that things were not as bad as we knew them to be.

It is in this sense that it seems to me that the occurrence of *community*— not exclusively conceived, as shelter from the storm, but inclusively as particular enactment of universal possibility; as exemplification (however fragile and modest) of what an answer to Kant's fourth question might *look like*—is a necessary condition of the possibility of prayer, of address to God, of living in his presence. The Christian doctrine of God is to the effect that such occurrence is permanently possible, and its furtherance permanently required, because God has indefeasibly *clarified* the question of the human in one life lived and one death undergone—in a piece of history which, for that reason, we confess to be the incarnation of God's Word; and because he continually renders possible the celebration and furtherance of that clarification in the self-gift which we call his presence as Spirit in the world of our experience. In the following chapter, therefore, I shall have something further to say about this Christian doctrine of God.

16

The Pattern
Of Christian
Pedagogy

"What Is Man?"
Revisited

To Kant's fourth question there are no true answers of such a kind that their provision would bring the inquiry to an end, for the end of the inquiry would be the end of the adventure that we are. Again and again, in each fresh set of circumstances, we have to find out what it is that we can know, that we should do, and for which we may with integrity hope. And continually, practically, and realistically to be addressing these three questions keeps the (underlying) fourth question *open*. But, in the darkness and confusion of our homelessness, in the fragility and fitfulness of our attainment of community, the pressures on us are immense to surrender the struggle between the forces and elements constitutive of our experience and, to try to find, in feeling or theory, in memory or in public order, some fixed point, some center, some locus of an overriding *absolute,* in clinging to which we may find peace.

What *sort* of question is this curious question "what is man?" It can be taken as a question about the "nature" of human beings, about the identity of the species (we are animals, but we are not the same "kind" of animals that elephants are). It may be important to take it this way, because a delineation of the elements of human nature can serve as the basis on which we may protest against the exclusion of some members of the species (Jews, blacks, slaves, women, unborn babies) from the company of those engaged in the adventure. But the danger in taking the question that way, as a question about the "nature" of human beings, is that we are then liable to overlook the fact that, being the kind of animals that we are—namely:

animals that ask questions, dream dreams, and implement policies—the nature of the human is never completely *given,* in biological constitution or historical achievement, but has again and again to be sought and struggled for, in action, affection, agreement, and understanding.

All natural kinds, and all members of each natural kind, have histories in the sense that they come into existence and eventually cease to be. There are (presumably) species which the evolutionary process has not yet produced, but some stars have died, and all the dinosaurs. It seems that only the human species also has a history in two further senses: firstly, that the members of the species are responsible for the form which that history takes, and secondly, in the sense that the nature of the species (an adequate account of which would furnish a true description of "humanity") cannot be fully known or predicted in advance of the outcome of that species' history. As human beings, it is our responsibility to *become* human beings, and to assist in the production of a common humanity. But sharing a common *human* nature is a matter of relationship, and not merely of biological affinity. Community, Bernard Lonergan has said, is "an achievement of common meaning, and there are kinds and degrees of achievement." As I have put it elsewhere, the concept of a common human nature has not only biological, but also ethical, political, and (in Christian conviction) eschatological components.[1]

It is no easy matter even heuristically to state what achieving the project of producing a common humanity would entail. On the one hand, it could be said to underlie educational and political strategies aiming to bring into relation all members of the (biological) species, and thereby refusing to relegate any group, or any individuals, to the status of "things," of *means* that exist merely to facilitate the achievement of other people's ends. And if it follows (for example) that the present generation may not be sacrificed for the sake of some imagined utopian future, it also follows that we may not so squander, today, our natural and cultural resources, as significantly to diminish the possibilities for other people's tomorrow.

On the other hand, however, the requirement to bring *all* members of the species into the community of persons in relation is a requirement in respect not only of the future but also of the past. In other words, I take it that the only form of community which would satisfy the requirement of a common humanity shared by *all* members of the species would be one which included those who have died, those whose achievements and

---

1 B. J. F. Lonergan, "*Existenz* and *Aggiornamento,*" in *Collection,* p. 245 (cf. ibid., pp. 254–55); see Lash, *Theology on the Way to Emmaus,* pp. 22–23.

sufferings helped to create *our* "possibilities"—for to suppose otherwise would be to reduce the dead to the status of *things:* of means now used by us to further what we take to be our ends.

The purpose of these remarks is simply to indicate the indispensability (implicit in everything which we have learned, in the last few chapters, from Martin Buber and Karl Rahner) of keeping the question of the human *open.* It is not the kind of question that any *words* could answer, for all our words—even the words that we address to each other or to the mystery of God—are but an aspect of the questionable project that we are. The question of the human could only be "answered," if at all, by that *deed* which would be the imperishable attainment of a common humanity. To put the point in more recognizably theological terms, the answering of Kant's fourth question requires not merely revelation (the utterance of a "word," even if it be a word of address from God) but the work of our redemption (the performance of a deed).

"What is man?" Pilate provided an answer to this question when he pointed to one particular human individual and said: "Ecce homo"; "Behold the Man." But Christians, alerted by the irony characteristic of the Fourth Gospel to judge that answer to have been (unwittingly) *correct,* may be tempted to suppose that the quest is therefore ended: that the doctrine of the incarnation of God's Word in Jesus answers Kant's fourth question. But this would be to overlook Rahner's insistence that the answer given in revelation *clarifies* the question that we are. The question remains open, and it could only be "answered"—the *request* that it contains could only be met—by the attainment of a common humanity, a community inclusive of all members of the species. In other words, a Christian account of the human, an account which corresponds to the Christian doctrine of God, must be an account which *sustains the difference* between revelation and redemption, word and deed, "logos" and "spirit."

It will, by now, be clear to the reader that the point of these introductory remarks is simply to suggest that any doctrine of God is suspect in the measure that it supplies us with ideas or images which serve, in practice, merely to obliterate the difference between our most unfinished and unsatisfactory world and the mystery in relation to which we attempt, *in that* world, to exercise our responsibilities for the construction of a comprehensively inclusive common humanity. Aquinas, in a prayer which I once quoted, requested of God the "clarification" of our twofold darkness: a darkness not merely of ignorance but of sin (or inhumanity).[2] But *such* a

---

2 "Dominus Deus ac Deus noster, qui vere fons luminis diceris, infundere dignere super animi nostri tenebras tuae radium claritatis, duplicas a nobis removens tenebras, peccati

request could only be met by that redemptive deed which entails our conversion in the work of a common humanity. It could not be met by the furnishing of some image or explanation which might appear to satisfy our minds, while leaving the *fact* of our manifest *in*humanity, our vast destructiveness and unrelatedness, untouched and untransformed.

Doctrine as Protocol

The reason offered by Buber for his reluctance to be described as a theologian was that theology is "a teaching about God" and he deemed himself neither capable nor disposed "to teach this or that about God," being unable "to talk about him in the third person."[3] The notion of "talking about" something is, however, ambiguous. We need to distinguish between *mentioning* something, making some reference to it, and furnishing some description of what it is to which we are referring.

Thus, for example, there may well be (as a matter of fact) some object in space and time which is, as I write, farther from me than all other objects that there are. If there is such an object then, by mentioning it, I have said something "about" it, and what I have said is true (namely: it is true that there is an object farther from me in space and time than all other objects that there are) even if, for lack of any further information on the matter, there is *nothing else* that I can say about it.

God is not, of course, an object in space and time nor is he, for that matter, an object "outside" of space and time (whatever that would mean). Nevertheless, if God is not a figment of our imagination, if it is truly "in relation" to his incomprehensible mystery that we, and all things, exist and have their being, then, in our worship of God, our address to God, we may (and do) make mention of him. Except, therefore, on a purely expressivist account of our use of the term, such mention as we make of God in worship has cognitive implications: it entails the conviction that there is something that we can truly say "about" God. In other words, even if the "nature" of God is unknown to us, because we cannot understand God, cannot *grasp* him in concept or image, cannot render his mystery comprehensible, we may perhaps, nevertheless, in relation to him,

---

scilicet et ignorantiae, in qua nati sumus" (quoted by me in *Theology on Dover Beach*, p. 23, from F. W. Dillistone, *C. H. Dodd* [London, 1977], p. 205).

3   Martin Buber, "The Philosopher Replies," in *The Philosophy of Martin Buber*, p. 690; "Autobiographical Fragments," p. 24.

living in his presence and responding to his address, successfully *refer* to God, make true mention of him.

It therefore follows, from this distinction between reference and description, that not all questions concerning the possibility of true speech about God are questions concerning the possibility of offering true *descriptions* of God. This latter set of questions does, indeed, inevitably arise. It arises from consideration of the implications of that relation to him in which—in all our human life and suffering and activity—we seek to stand. To keep near Buber's terminology: questions concerning the possibility of offering true descriptions of God arise from the hazardous inevitability of the "objectification" of God in our speech. And, for Buber, it is in the quality of human relationships purifying the form of our prayer that our proclivity toward idolatry—toward the binding of the mystery that is "You by its very nature" into the It-world—is corrected and restrained.[4]

Idolatry takes many different forms, but what is common to them all is setting our hearts on something less than God. This can occur, not only through the more obvious forms of egotism and self-will, but also (and perhaps especially) in religion: by grasping the forms of God's address and presence, thus misidentifying some word or sign as the mystery by which we are addressed and in whose presence we live. The suggestion that I wish to explore, arising from the distinction between reference and description, is that the Christian doctrine of God is more fundamentally a matter of ensuring correct reference than it is of attempting appropriate description. In creeds and prayers, in hymns and preaching, we frequently make mention of God. How are we to ensure that that which we mention is, indeed, the living God, the incomprehensible mystery of creation and redemption, and not something else that we mistake for him? How, in other words, are we to learn to use the word "God" correctly? As a first step toward consideration of these questions, we need to say something more about the notion of "doctrine."

Doctrine is an activity. It has its place in the family of activities that go under the general heading of "teaching and learning." It is an aspect of pedagogy. Christian doctrine, therefore, is an aspect of Christian pedagogy. But pedagogy (on the "inclusive" account of these matters with which we have been working) is by no means confined to the classroom or the seminar. If Christianity is a school for the production of persons in relation to the unknown God through discipleship of the crucified, then there is *nothing* that we do and suffer, think, or feel, or undergo, which

---

4   See my discussion of "Eclipse of God" in chap. 14, above.

may not contribute to such schooling. It follows that there is no single activity, or cluster of activities, which alone counts as "Christian teaching."

This point is worth bearing in mind when we concentrate discussion (as we often do) on only one or two aspects of such teaching: on (for example) the difference between preaching and doing theology—and on the relationship which these activities should have to each other. In such discussions, it is not uncommon for the concept of "Christian doctrine" to be taken, quite generally, to refer to what Christian teachers teach about Christian beliefs. I propose to take the concept to refer, much more narrowly, to the declaration of identity-sustaining rules of discourse and behavior.

I have emphasized that "doctrine" is the name of an activity, lest we be misled (by the more widespread use of the term as a substantive) into supposing that the Christian doctrine of God is some substance or "thing" to which some group (be it large or small: the Church universal, the congregation, or some subgroup of church authorities) might lay claim as their *possession*. But nobody *owns* the identity-sustaining rules of Christian discourse. As Christians, we acknowledge *responsibility* for their use because we acknowledge, or confess, their use to be "authorized." And even though it was people like us who *made* the rules, they did so in the conviction that they were authorized to do so. Neither the Fathers of Nicea, nor the authors of the Westminster Confession, supposed themselves to be simply "making up" the rules that they made.[5]

There are historical warrants for taking the term in this restricted sense. Thus, for example, Bernard Lonergan argued that the term *homoousios* was not used, at Nicea, to make a first-order, descriptive claim about the Son's relationship to the Father, but to make a second-order claim to the effect that whatever is to be said of the Father is to be said of the Son, save only that the Father alone is Father and the Son alone is Son. The doctrine of Nicea, on this account, does not tell us *what* to say about the mystery confessed as "Father," or about him whom we confess to be that Father's "Son."[6] It simply lays down rules of discourse, establishes the pattern

---

5 For an excellent discussion of how we might "speak of revelation or authorisation without taking the obvious ideological short-cut," a discussion which concentrates on the issue of how it is that we *learn* the language that we use, see Rowan Williams, "Trinity and Revelation," *Modern Theology* 2 (1986): 197–212 (the quoted phrase occurs on 198).

6 The doctrine "leaves the believer free to conceive the Father in scriptural, patristic, medieval, or modern terms; and of course contemporary consciousness, which is historically minded, will be at home in all four" (B. J. F. Lonergan, "The Dehellenization

within which whatever we say and do in the primary discourses of praise and story, prayer and preaching, is properly said and done. It provides, we might say, a frame of reference.

More recently, and more generally, George Lindbeck has proposed a view of church doctrine as "regulative," as the issuing of "communally authoritative rules of discourse, attitude, and action." And although such a view is very ancient, for "the notion of *regulae fidei* goes back to the earliest Christian centuries," the novel element in Lindbeck's proposal is that on his view the regulative function "becomes the *only* job that doctrines do in their role as church teachings."[7]

Lonergan's work in this area has been criticized for handling the historical evidence too woodenly and schematically, and, according to Avery Dulles, Lindbeck's theory of doctrines "unduly minimizes [their] cognitive and expressive import."[8] The legitimacy of these criticisms can be accepted without (as it seems to me) undermining the central contention that the *primary* function of Christian doctrine is regulative rather than descriptive.

I have been suggesting that the concept of the Christian doctrine of God be taken to refer to the declaration, by the Christian community, of identity-sustaining rules of discourse and behavior governing Christian uses of the word "God." It is in modes of action and speech consonant with the pattern declared in the doctrine that we discover, as Christians, how we may so speak and act as to live in relation, or in truthful reference, to the mystery in which we live, and work, and speak, and hope, and die. To take the Christian doctrine of God in this way is to take it, in Walter Kasper's phrase, as the "summary grammar" of the Christian account of the mystery of salvation and creation.[9] We *require* some such grammar for our pedagogy, because all the pressures—outside and within—both pressures applied by the structures and mind-sets of individualism and collectivism alike, and pressures derived from fear and egotism, homelessness, ambi-

---

of Dogma," in *Second Collection*, ed. W. F. J. Ryan and B. J. Tyrrell [Philadelphia, 1974], p. 23). That last remark, I think, was meant to be read ironically rather than optimistically!

7 George A. Lindbeck, *The Nature of Doctrine: Religion and Theology in a Postliberal Age* (London, 1984), pp. 18, 19. For some earlier, sympathetically critical, comments by Lindbeck on Lonergan's views, see Lindbeck, "Protestant Problems with Lonergan on Development of Dogma," in *Foundations of Theology*, ed. Philip McShane (Notre Dame, 1972), pp. 115–23.

8 Avery Dulles, "Paths to Doctrinal Agreement: Ten Theses," *Theological Studies* 47 (1986): 43.

9 See Walter Kasper, *The God of Jesus Christ*, trans. Mathew J. O'Connell (New York, 1984), p. 311.

tion, and despair, incline us to opt for "irrelation": to treat persons as things, and to bind the mystery of God into the It-world by mistakenly identifying some feature of the world—some individual, some nation, some possession, some dream, some project, or some ideal—with divinity, with the "nature" of God. We require some "set of protocols against idolatry," against the manifold forms of the illusion that the nature of God lies within our grasp.[10]

Consideration of the various mechanisms (congregational, conciliar, or other) by which such doctrines are generated, and the various procedures by which, once produced, they are or are not received by the community as doing what they purport to do: namely, establishing the rules of discourse and behavior through which, in changing circumstances, the identity of Christianity is sustained—all such ecclesiological considerations, interesting and important as they undoubtedly are, lie outside the scope of this chapter, the purpose of which is simply to indicate why it is that that doctrine of God which best corresponds to the account of Christian experience which I have sought to provide is the doctrine of God's Trinity. There are limits to the number of issues that can be even cursorily considered in one book! Nevertheless, there are four questions in this general area on which some comment seems required before the argument can be taken a stage further. Firstly, is there *one* Christian doctrine of God, or are there many? Secondly, does this doctrine change? Thirdly, is not my suggestion as to how the proper use of the word "God" is to be learned preposterously arbitrary? And, fourthly, is not my account of Christian doctrine unduly restrictive?

In the first place, then, is there one Christian doctrine of God, or are there many? If no clear distinctions are drawn between "doctrine" and "theology," then there would seem to be as many different Christian accounts of our relation to the mystery of God, as many doctrines, as there are theologies and schools of theology. But, if doctrine is taken more narrowly, as I have done, to refer to the declaration—acknowledged by the community as communally authoritative—of identity-sustaining rules of discourse and behavior governing Christian uses of the word "God," then the question as to the unity of doctrine becomes, in fact, a question concerning the unity of the Christian creed.

In view of the vast, complex, and often conflictual diversity displayed by Christianity in the course of its history, not the least remarkable thing about that history has been the extent to which Christians of East and West, Catholic, Orthodox, and Reformed, have continued to sustain their

---

10   See Nicholas Lash, "Considering the Trinity," *Modern Theology* 2 (1986): 187.

identity in the confessional use of a common creed.[11] As a people which finds in Jesus of Nazareth, and in the writings which bear witness to what was shown and done in him, "a focus for its identity,"[12] and which, in the light of that finding, seeks to ascertain and discharge its responsibilities toward all "humanness," and toward the world in which that humanness or humanity is sought, Christians have engaged in vigorous disputes about the implications—political and theological, ethical and aesthetic—of the frame of reference which the creed provides. But the extent to which such disputes occur *within* that frame of reference justifies me, I believe, in asserting that there is *one* Christian doctrine of God which finds expression in confession of a common creed.

In the second place, does this doctrine change? Or, rather, is it not obvious that it has often changed, both in that different "forms of sound words" have been taken into use (the so-called Apostles' Creed, for example, is far from being verbally identical with the so-called Nicene Creed) and in the extent to which the frame of reference which the creed provides has been *realized* in Christian life and practice?

On the first point, it can be argued that, since creeds are historical products, made by men and women in different contexts of culture and circumstance, the production and use of different verbal formulations, far from *threatening* the unity or maintained identity of the creed, is required for its insurance. And what is true historically (or diachronically) is also likely to be true synchronically in a world as culturally diverse as our own. Hence Karl Rahner's expectation that, in future, "there will no longer be any one verbal formula of the Christian faith applicable to the whole Church."[13] Historically, the unity of the creed is maintained—in the unending interpretative process of mutually critical correlation between present and past—by the production of doctrinal forms, or versions of the creed, in which Christians are able to recognize that they are (however differently)

---

11 Of course this statement is contestable, but noncontestable statements tend to be trivial. It could be argued, for example, that the introduction of the "Filioque" deprived the churches of East and West of the use of a common creed. It has often seemed so, and yet an Orthodox theologian has recently asserted that "the Filioque is not a decisive difference of dogma but a serious difference in the interpretation of dogma which awaits resolution" (Theodore Stylianopoulos, "The Orthodox Position," in *Conflicts about the Holy Spirit,* Concilium 128, ed. Hans Küng and Jürgen Moltmann (New York, 1979), p. 30.

12 Rowan Williams, "Trinity and Revelation," 202.

13 Karl Rahner, "Reflections on the Problems Involved in Devising a Short Formula of the Faith," *Investigations,* 11:233. On the general issue, of which the paragraph in the text is no more than a headline summary, see Rahner, "Pluralism in Theology and the Unity of the Creed in the Church," ibid., 11:3–23.

still *telling the same story* of human relationship to the mystery of God, and not telling a different story. Synchronically, the unity of the creed is maintained through the quest and achievement of mutual recognition, among different Christian groups, of a common confession which in their different versions finds varying expression.[14]

On the second point, that unity of the creed, that unity of confession, which is historically given to us, is not maintained merely by the *utterance* (on our part) of appropriate rules of discourse and behavior, because the community whose identity doctrine sustains does "not exist simply or exclusively in the dimension of the word." Therefore, "if we want to bring the unity of the creed to its fulness . . . then we must *express* this one creed in common, celebrate the Death of the Lord in common in the physicality belonging to this . . .[and] serve the world in common in action."[15] In this sense, the unity of the creed (like the unity, or common humanity, of the human race whose sense and destiny the creed declares) is, at one and the same time, a gift, a task, and the object of our hope. (It is, therefore, a unity sustained in the "difference" between word and deed, "logos" and "spirit.")

In the third place, is it not both arbitrary and arrogant to claim that it is in life lived within the frame of reference provided by the Christian creed that the correct use of the word "God" is to be learned? I see no reason to deny that some such claim has often been put to exceedingly arrogant and "exclusive" uses. But these, I would argue, are (on its own terms) *misuses* of the claim, and can be shown to be so.

The word "God" does not come to us from nowhere. It comes to us from the history of its uses, and only from consideration of and participation in that history can responsible decisions be reached and implemented as to its appropriate and inappropriate use. All such decisions are, indeed, *particular* decisions, but particular decisions are only threatened by arbitrariness in the measure that we fail to furnish them with more or less satisfactory warrants.

According to H. D. Lewis, F. H. Bradley's claim that "God is but an aspect, and that must mean an appearance, of the Absolute" has to be taken "quite seriously."[16] I am not sure what Bradley meant, but let us

---

14 See Nicholas Lash, "Theologies at the Service of a Common Tradition," *Theology on the Way to Emmaus*, pp. 26–31; "Credal Affirmation as a Criterion of Church Unity," in *Church Membership and Intercommunion*, ed. J. Kent and R. Murray (London, 1973), pp. 51–73. ·

15 Rahner, "Pluralism in Theology and the Unity of the Creed in the Church," 22.

16 H. D. Lewis, "The British Idealists," in *Nineteenth-Century Religious Thought*, 2:307, citing F. H. Bradley, *Appearance and Reality* (Oxford, 1897), p. 397.

suppose that he meant that any God of whom tales are told, and descriptions offered, in some particular tradition of religious practice or philosophical reflection, is but an aspect of the Absolute. Such a claim would be far from arbitrary, but it would nevertheless be a particular claim and, as such, contestable. Thus, for example, I see no reason to deny that all images, or stories, or concepts of God are but metaphors, symbols, expressive of "aspects" of that to which they purport to refer. But I should also wish (nonarbitrarily) to argue that all uses of notions of "the Absolute" are in similar circumstance. *Whatever* is bound into the It-world of descriptive speech, *including* all notions of the Absolute or "the transcendent," is no more (at best) than an aspect or "appearance" in our speech of the mystery that is "You by its very nature" and (at worst) may become *objects*—however abstract, rarified, or metaphysical—which contribute to God's eclipse.

When we remember that the "God" of modern theism was born of a deliberate decision to *break* with the Jewish and Christian traditions of "authorized" usage, it is surely evident that modern philosophical uses of the word stand in traditions which are every bit as particular (and hence contestable) as the tradition which they either discount or, in some cases, take to be marginal to their concerns.

Nevertheless, even if all decisions as to how the word "God" is to be used are decisions taken in respect of particular traditions, is it not arrogant to claim, for any one such tradition, comprehensive or universal validity? I have conceded that this may be, and has often been, the case. But I cannot see that it need necessarily be so. We do not, as Christians, own or possess our rules of discourse and behavior. But in the measure that we are brought, through experience and reflection, to endorse those rules, to acknowledge their use to be authorized and thus, in fact, required, we are thereby brought to acknowledge our responsibility to recommend them to others.[17] And (at least in the Jewish and Christian traditions) the outcome is paradoxical, because *what* is being urged or recommended is that *no* particular object, thing, history, institution, individual, or idea (and especially none that are produced in the course of *our* objectification of God's mystery) is to be identified with the mystery whose address and presence establish the history and destiny of the world. In other words, a form of Christianity purified into recognition that the Christian doctrine

---

17 All judgments of truth (and by no means only theological judgments) are issued in acknowledgment of their authorization. This contention will only seem obscure to people working with "a model of truth as something ultimately separable in our minds from the dialectical process of its historical reflection and appropriation" (Rowan Williams, "Trinity and Revelation," 197–98).

of God functions as a set of protocols against idolatry, far from "exclusively" and arrogantly imposing its claim through argument, Inquisition, or Crusade, would be obliged, *on its own terms,* to be receptive to enrichment and purification from other traditions of speech and behavior, whether religious or secular—for God's word and presence are not *confined* to that particular tradition which acknowledges responsibility sacramentally to bear witness to them.

Nevertheless, finally, is not my proposal unduly restrictive: does it not improperly narrow the range of theological inquiry? Once again, it is clear, from the history of Christianity, that theologians have often found themselves *cramped* by what they (or others) took to be the content of the doctrine which they sought to implement and to understand. But, once again, I cannot see that this need necessarily be so. The unity or identity of the creed is only maintained, in changing times and circumstances, through the unending interpretative labor of mutually critical correlation. There is therefore no way in which exegetes and historical theologians (for example) can properly be disbarred from putting fresh questions to the evidence, nor is there any way of knowing in advance what the outcome of their inquiries will be. Perhaps we could say that the Christian doctrine of God (and hence the identity of Christianity) is always necessarily *at risk* in the very execution of the projects which are required for its recovery and maintenance. The same is true, not only of interactions between present and past, but also of interactions between present patterns of Christian speech and practice and other contexts of action, utterance, assessment, and interpretation—in interreligious dialogue, in literature and politics, in science and ethics. But to suppose that it could be otherwise, to suppose that the identity of the Christian doctrine of God could ever be finally secured, definitively possessed, against all possible ravages of time and circumstance, is to forget that the creed only properly fulfils its function, as declaration of identity-sustaining rules of discourse and behavior, in the measure that, through working with these rules, we are again and again confronted with the possibility of conversion: of being brought to live our human lives in basic trust of each other and of the unknown God.

So far as I can see, the use of the creed only *restricts* the theologian in her or his work in the sense that, if the Church is to maintain its identity *at all,* if it is to have any discernible distinctiveness as a people bearing a particular message of universal import, and displaying the requirements of human community, then it must be possible for practical judgments to be reached, from time to time, to the effect that such-and-such a position or policy threatens its identity and mission. But (as I hope to indicate in the next section) the Christian doctrine of God, as the doctrine of God's

Trinity, provides the pattern within which each of its principal tendencies to self-destruction is held in check through the corrective operation of the others.

Far from the pattern of creedal declaration restricting the range of possible inquiry, the Church *requires* the complications of theology, its endless and often irresolvable disputes, its tentative and fragmentary character, not in order to render our confusion even more obscure, but because only thus, only through engagement in such complexity (whether—as for most people—primarily at the practical level, or also at more reflective levels) can we be brought to that wisdom which enables us patiently to live out our human lives in trustful relationship to the absolute simplicity of the mystery of God.

It follows that, if Christian theology "makes progress," it only does so, as Newman said, "by being always alive to its own fundamental uncertainties."[18] It therefore seems to me that my account of the function of the creed, as offering a frame of reference for, rather than as offering a description of the object of, our faith and worship, is quite neatly compatible with Stephen Sykes's insistence that the "idea" of Christianity belongs to the category of "essentially contestable concepts."[19] And if I have laid the emphasis on the identity-sustaining function of creedal declaration, whereas Sykes lays it on common participation in communal worship, these two accounts are seen to be not too far apart when we remember that it is in an act of worship, *as* an act of worship, of address to God, that the primary uses of the creed occur. As Christians, we use our rules of discourse and behavior not, shall we say, as "scientific instruments," but rather as the regulative pattern of the pedagogy of contemplative practice.

Sustaining
the Difference

It was at a much earlier stage in the discussion that I first suggested that the similarity of pattern between the Christian doctrine of God (which is the doctrine of God's Trinity, confessed in the creed) and the pervasively

---

18   J. H. Newman, *The Letters and Diaries of John Henry Newman,* vol. 29, ed. C. S. Dessain and Thomas Gornall (Oxford, 1976), p. 118. And much the same is (as I suggested in chap. 2) to be said about philosophy.

19   This is a principal thread in the argument of Stephen Sykes's admirable study, *The Identity of Christianity* (London, 1984). For some comments of mine on this book, see Nicholas Lash, "Argument, Essence and Identity," *New Blackfriars* 65 (1984): 413–19.

tripolar treatments, in Western culture, of "the intrinsic dialectics of experienced life," was hardly sheer coincidence.[20] I now want to develop the
remarks made in the previous section by offering some indications of how
the doctrine of God's Trinity[21] serves, at one and the same time, to indicate
where God is to be found and—by denying, at each point, that what we
find there is to be simply identified with God—to prevent us from getting
stuck in one-sidedness, for the effect of such one-sidedness (or exclusiveness) is always in one way or another to make us misidentify some feature
of the world with God, and this (however unwittingly and guiltlessly entered into) is idolatry. The doctrine thus leads, at every turn, to both
affirmation and denial; it enables us both to make true mention of God
and, by denying that the particular forms of our address, of our worship
of God—in action and relation, institution and feeling, thought, organization, and suffering—furnish us with some hold upon the "*nature*"
of God, it sustains our recognition of the *difference* between the world
and God.[22]

Thus, for example, in action and discourse patterned by the frame of
reference provided by the creed, we learn to find God in all life, all freedom, all creativity and vitality, and in each fresh particular beauty, each
unexpected attainment of relationship and community—for all such occurrences are forms of his presence. To speak of "spirit" as "God" is to
ascribe all creativity and conversion, all fresh life and freedom, to divinity.
Divinity, "godness," is thus not far from finitude and contingency, but is
all finitude's inmost gift and possibility, for there is nothing "outside" the
presence of such divinity. This line of thought is ancient and attractive,
and finds formal expression in varieties of pantheism.

The instinct of pantheism is sound (far sounder than the dominant
theism which takes the term "God" to refer to some strange entity outside
the world). But, by identifying the forms of God's presence with the *nature*

---

20 See the opening paragraphs of chap. 10, above.

21 I choose this formulation, in preference to the more usual phrase "the doctrine of the
Trinity," as a reminder that, on the account which I am offering, the doctrine of God's
Trinity is not some *further* teaching, additional to a teaching which would count as a
"doctrine of *God*," but simply *is* the Christian doctrine of God, the Christian account of
how the word "God" is to be used.

22 To attempt, at this point, some summary recapitulation of the unfortunate consequences
of the varieties of "exclusiveness" or "one-sidedness," as we have come across them in
our discussion of James, Schleiermacher, von Hügel, Buber, and Rahner, would be (I
think) not only an unmanageably cumbersome undertaking, but also one which would
require a quite artificial *synthesizing* of the very different treatments of the problem that
we have considered. My hope is that, having reached this stage in the construction of
my argument, no such summary is, in fact, required.

of God, with divinity, pantheism obscures the difference between the world and God, mistakes the sign and promise for the reality, and thereby leads us disastrously to misread our circumstances and responsibilities. "Pantheism," said Lukács, "is the great attempt to discover a human home in this strange cosmos."[23] But homelessness is the truth of our condition, and the "gifts of the spirit," gifts of community and relationship, forgiveness and life-giving, are at least as much a matter of promise, of prospect, and of the task that is laid upon us, as they are a matter of past achievement or present reality. The doctrine of God as "spirit" supplies us with a mode of reference, but if, in an unredeemed world, we make the exclusivist mistake of supposing that the language of spirit names the nature of God, laid hold of by us in fact or in imagination, then our use of the doctrine collapses into idolatry (the forms of which can be as varied as the worship of one's nation—as privileged bearer of the spirit—on the one hand, and on the other, the flight from the harshness of actual reality into worship of pure prospect or inward feeling).

What we require, therefore, is corrective insistence on the absolute *difference* between the world and God: an insistence that the word "God" may not be used to refer to the world, or to any feature of the world, "visible or invisible." All facts and events in the world, all institutions and ideas, all natural phenomena, all people and artifacts, are products. And it is only *as* products, and in terms of the history of their production, that we can come across them, speak about them, tell stories about them, understand them. We can, accordingly, get no imaginative or intellectual *purchase* on a God who is confessed to be creator of the world, and to create the world ex nihilo—for that is not a mode of production that could be "explained" or given narrative expression. There is no story that we could tell which begins with "nothing" (and we only suppose otherwise by supposing "nothing" to be, in fact, some kind of thing).

At least in a time like ours, a time of God's eclipse, this second aspect of the doctrine seems unsurprising. In the pain and confusion, the darkness and inhumanity, the egotism and uncontrollable destructiveness which surround us (and to which we contribute, whether energetically or by practical indifference), it is not too difficult to learn that that to which the word "God" refers is unimaginable, unknowable, ungraspable. But, as we saw in the last chapter, it is one thing to learn that God is not the world nor any part of the world, and quite another, having learned this, still to find some *use* for the word "God." The instinct of agnosticism, and

---

23 Georg Lukács, *The Ontology of Social Being*, vol. 1, *Hegel's False and His Genuine Ontology*, trans. David Fernbach (London, 1978), p. 35.

of many forms of atheism, is nevertheless sound, for the mystery of God is incomprehensible, whereas it is not too difficult to unmask the deities we worship, the gods with which we can identify and which we can describe, as products of our labor and desire, our egotism and insecurity. (Feuerbach was not wrong about this.)

But if the sole and single-minded use of this second rule for our speech about God (namely: that nothing that is may be said to be God, for God is the unoriginate, the unproduced, the creator of all that there is) ends up by depriving us, in practice, of the possibility of finding any use for the word, it is not clear why such surrender of the word should constitute idolatry. It does so, I think, indirectly, for it seems as if we *have* to set our hearts on *something,* and if we find ourselves unable to do so in reference to one who is quite other than ourselves, unable to acknowledge, in basic trust, our absolute dependence, then what we do, in resolute assertion of autonomy, is in fact to *divinize*—to ascribe divine or absolute significance to—ourselves or our plans or our possessions or some feature of our world. Expecting, perhaps, to find God at the center of the world, and not finding him there, we move into what we take to be the space vacated, thus making ourselves to be gods (the only alternative: namely that there is no single center of the world for us to occupy, being too daunting to contemplate—for it might call for conversion). This, at least, is one way of reading the strong Promethean strand in nineteenth-century thought, and it throws some light on why it is that so many forms of worship, and of the philosophies which correspond to them (including, in either case, exceedingly secular forms, in which no use is found for the *word* "God"), appear to alternate or oscillate, in practice, between strategies of one version or another of atheism and pantheism, denial and affirmation, indifference and fanaticism. But it is not in such unstable oscillation between affirmations of the absolute difference and absolute identity between the world and God that we might hope to learn true (which is to say: redemptive) uses of the word "God."

I have kept to the final place that third rule governing the use of the word "God" with which (from the standpoint of Christian theology) it might have seemed sensible to begin. I did so as a reminder that the oscillation to which I have referred is, in part, a not altogether surprising consequence of the decision (exemplified, as we have seen, in the origins of modern theism) to consider the question of God in abstraction from that history of interpretative practice which gave us the word for our use. That history has always been the history of a people fashioning and discerning its identity and its task in relation to particular past events (from Exodus to Easter) which set it on its way. "The language of revelation," says Rowan Williams, "is used to express the sense of an initiative that does not

lie with us and to challenge the myth of the self-constitution of consciousness."[24] And words were borrowed from elsewhere (words such as "theos"
and "deus") to serve as tokens of reference for that holy mystery in relation to which the people sought to live, and to the "address" and
"presence" of which initiative was ascribed. It was in that history of interpretative practice which constituted the narrative of the people's experience in the world, therefore, that people learned to refer to "God" as the
unoriginate utterer of the word addressed to them, and as the life or gift
or "spirit" the promise of whose transformative presence or donation the
word proclaims.

In other words, the third aspect of the Christian doctrine of God, according to which we refer to God as "Word," is not an *addition* to the other
two (any more than either of the first two were additions or supplements
of the other) but it is a rule of speech and action which furnishes us with
the pattern or figure according to which we are able to *correlate* the doctrines of origin and gift, creator and spirit. Or, as I put it earlier, it is in
reference to this third aspect of the doctrine that we are able to sustain the
dialectic between the other two.[25]

The most shocking feature of this third aspect of the doctrine (or so it
has often seemed to those whose ideal of knowledge is framed in terms of
systems of universal causal explanation) is its emphasis upon particular,
apparently random, historical occurrence. Prophetic testimony does not
generalize, yet Christianity (like Judaism and Islam) has fashioned its identity, as a school of interpretative practice, in relation to particular occurrences of prophetic witness. In Christianity, this scandal attained
exceptionally dramatic proportions. As the church worked out its rules of
theological speech in relation to one Word once spoken in one life lived
and one death undergone; as it affirmed its existence to be life lived "in
communion" with the risen one, it came to use of him, and of the transformative impact of *his* "spirit" upon all irrelation, servitude, and bondage
(even the bondage of death), language that had been used of no other
utterance, no earlier prophetic testimony, because it was language that
(one would have thought) could *only* be used of God. Christianity, in other
words, came to refer to him not only as prophet or bearer of God's address, but as being himself God—not as utterer, but as utterance, as Word;
not as the unoriginate, but as originated, as "the only-begotten of the
Father."

But if this new mode of reference, this unparalleled intensification of

24 Williams, "Trinity and Revelation," 200.
25 See above, pp. 172, 188-89.

the language of God's address, was, in principle, creative (for "in him were all things made"), redemptive, transformative, it became, in practice, only too easily the language of a new form of idolatry. Binding even *this* address of God (perhaps especially this address) into the It-world, Christians persuaded themselves that now, in the doctrine of the Word incarnate, they had laid hold of the *nature* of God, and made of God's truth their possession. Thus, by ascribing divine status to the language and institutions which mediate the memory of Jesus, Christians have made their own characteristic contribution to the eclipse of God.

And yet the Christian doctrine of God contains, in itself, the necessary corrective resources. If, on the one hand, the doctrine authorizes us to confess the Word as God, it only does so by also insisting that the utterance is not the utterer, that what we "see" in him is the image of the Imageless One, that though he is "God of God" and "light of light," the light illuminated in the clarification which he supplies remains (for us) impenetrable darkness which is no more dispelled for us than it was for him in Gethsemane. And if, on the other hand, the Christian doctrine of God authorizes us to confess him as God's *self*-utterance in the world, it only does so by also insisting that *what* is proclaimed in that utterance is the promise that the burden laid upon us, the task of constituting community "in the spirit," and of bearing witness to the possibility of such community for all mankind, is in God's hands, and may therefore be undertaken in tranquillity, for God himself is all finitude's inmost gift and possibility.

The function of the Christian doctrine of God, as the declaration of identity-sustaining rules of discourse and behavior, is to enable us, in every area of our ordinary human existence and experience, to live in relation to God: in other words, to pray. It does this, in part, by providing a pattern of self-correction for each of the three principal modes of our propensity to *freeze* the form of relation into an object or possessed description of the nature of God. The unceasing dialectically corrective movement which the pattern requires is, we might say, a matter of *perichoresis*.[26] It is only *in* this movement, and not apart from it, that the oneness or unity of him whom we triply worship is apprehended.

It does not follow that there is nothing that can be said about God in abstraction from consideration of the three modes or aspects of our relationship to him, but whatever is said is said, precisely, in *abstraction*. In

---

26 It is worth noting that Karl Rahner uses this patristic term in a similar context: see Rahner, "The Concept of Mystery in Catholic Theology," *Investigations,* 4:42; "Experience of Transcendence from the Standpoint of Catholic Dogmatics," ibid., 18:176.

other words, while theological consideration of the "oneness" or simplicity of God may find formal or grammatical expression (of the kind, for example, which I tried to provide in the treatment, in the previous chapter, of the difference between the world and God, and of what is at issue in confessing God as mystery) it cannot be given material or categorial descriptive expression—because God is not an object whose nature we could thus describe.[27]

Although the self-corrective movement between the three articles, articulations, or "hinges" of the creed is unceasing, there is, nevertheless, also an order or sequence between them: an order which finds expression in the narrative form of the creed, which speaks of God as the creator who sends his Son and breathes his Spirit. It is only because the absolute difference between the world and God has been bridged by *God,* in his address and presence, that we are able to live in his presence and respond to his address. But we are only able truly to do so in the measure that we do not, in our insecurity and nervous gnosticism, attempt to *overcome* that absolute difference by seeking to substitute *possession* of his word and spirit for that relationship to him which always remains relationship to holy mystery. In other words, the narrative sequence of the creed does not contradict, but permanently requires, the unceasing self-corrective movement between the three modes of reference which it supplies.

Economy and Immanence

I have been considering the way in which the Christian doctrine of God's Trinity, the declaration of identity-sustaining rules of discourse and behavior, furnishes the pattern of our pedagogy, the pattern of the Christian experience of God. But is it only "our experience" of God of which this pattern serves as regulative expression, or are we, in using this frame of reference, also saying something about God himself? In the theological literature this question is usually formulated in terms of the relationship

---

27 It would take us too far afield to consider the implications of these remarks for the textbook treatments of the treatises *De Deo Uno* and *De Deo Trino,* but it is worth noticing that there runs through Rahner's discussion of the Trinity a sense of puzzlement both as to why we should suppose these two topics to be as sharply distinct as they have often been taken to be, and as to why we should treat of them (as many, since Aquinas, have done) in that order; see Rahner, *The Trinity,* trans. Joseph Donceel (New York, 1970), pp. 15–21, 45–46; on the latter issue, see Nicholas Lash, "Considering the Trinity," 186–88.

between the "economic" and "immanent" Trinity, between (that is to say) God as he addresses us and is present with us, and God as he is "in himself."

Karl Rahner was famous (or notorious) for insisting, again and again, that "the Trinity of the economy of salvation *is* the immanent Trinity and vice versa."[28] But quite what are we to make of this claim? It is clear that, as used by Rahner, it does not mean that God only is insofar as he is in the historical "happening" of the incarnation of the Word and the sending of the Spirit. Rahner does not, in other words, collapse the difference between the world and God, reducing the story of God to a complicated mythological account of how it goes with the world. His concern is simply to insist that, in our experience of God, it is God *himself,* and not some mere "copy" or "analogy" of God, of whom we have experience, with whom we are brought into relation.[29]

In order to indicate something of what is at issue here, the first thing that needs to be said is that *of course* it is our experience of God of which, in our use of the doctrine of the Trinity, we are speaking—for what else can we sensibly and responsibly talk about, in respect of any matter that we acknowledge to be pertinent to our decisions, actions, and understanding, *except* our experience?[30]

Our experience, as Christians, is not identical with the experience of other people—of Muslims, Jews, Buddhists, or atheist humanists, for instance—nor is the account that we offer of our experience identical with the accounts offered by others. But it is, for two reasons, simply a mistake to infer from this that Christian (or Muslim, or Jewish) accounts of our experience of God constitute some peculiar, untestable, and incommunicable "religious addition" to a general, universally accessible and testable account of what human beings feel, suffer, remember, hope, fear, achieve, and undergo. It is a mistake, in the first place, because such fideistic readings of the situation presuppose that "God" is the name of some particular, unusual object, and that experience of God is an unusual condition enjoyed only by some privileged group of people. It is also a mistake because,

28 Rahner, "Remarks on the Dogmatic Treatise 'De Trinitate,'" *Investigations,* 4:87; cf. "Oneness and Threefoldness of God in Discussion with Islam," ibid., 18:114; *The Trinity,* pp. 22–24, 34–38.

29 See Rahner, *The Trinity,* p. 35. It is the danger of collapsing the difference between the world and God which leads John Milbank to speak of the atheism which threatens what he calls "the 'strong' protestant version of Rahner's axiom" (John Milbank, "The Second Difference: For a Trinitarianism without Reserve," *Modern Theology* 2 [1986]: 224).

30 In what follows, I am reworking some paragraphs from Lash, "Considering the Trinity," 188–90.

except at a level so abstract as to be uninformative (e.g., "we have all been born and we shall all surely die"), there simply is no such thing, nor could there be, as a *general* account of human experience, for the only basis on which such an account could be offered would be that universal community of all mankind which does not yet exist. There is, within human history, only an irreducible diversity of variously overlapping and interacting particular accounts, derived from particular contexts of performance and memory, speech and suffering. And because many of these particular accounts are deemed to be of general, and perhaps even of universal import, the relationships among them are frequently conflictual.

But why should we suppose that *our* account, or anyone else's, has truth enough to be worth wrestling with, worth struggling with, and (perhaps) worth dying for? In the last analysis, this is a question, not about "relativism," but about tragedy and skepticism, about *anything* being worth such expenditure. Whoever we are, and whatever the story that we tell, the experience of most of us affords sufficient evidence of failed projects and unreliable speech to give us (it would seem) good reason to be skeptical. But whereas, from the standpoint of the "severed I," as an expression of Cartesian anxiety, the question as to whether we can trust our experience is a question for *epistemology*, it is, in fact, better construed as a question concerning the *trustworthiness* of people and the *reliability* of things.

Skepticism, in other words, not as the circumspection required in particular circumstances, but as a general policy for living, is close cousin to paranoia. The question "Can anything be worth dying for?" is closely related to the question "Is anyone, or anything, sufficiently trustworthy; can anything, or anyone, be *really* trusted?" And this is a question which can only be answered practically, by the actual establishment of trust. And trust, if it is to be my possibility, must first be another's gift. To be able to trust, to be able *completely* to trust, is to be able to die. What else have we got to give our friends (and our enemies), in the last resort, except ourselves? To be able to die (as distinct from being killed) is a form of faith. And, on a Christian account of these matters, such faith, such self-gift, is *possible* because what God has given us, in a gift the terminus of which was death on Calvary, was—himself.

I suggest, then, that Rahner's axiom should be read as an acknowledgment, a recognition, that we are able to trust God's trustworthiness because what God has spoken to us is not just some particular message (behind which he might have rather different messages up his sleeve), but is his *self*-statement in the flesh and texture of our history; because what God has given us is not just some particular gift (which he might withdraw or we might exhaust), but is his imperishable *self*-gift, his joy, his Spirit.

What is at issue here, in other words, is the fact and propriety of basic trust. "The relation to a human being is the proper metaphor for the relation to God."[31] There is no way of really *getting to know* another human being except through the risk of relationship; except through that cumulative discipline of practical, mundane, and often painful dispossession in which "information" surpasses itself and becomes true knowledge as the fruit, and not merely the precondition, of love. This is how we come to know each other (not only in domestic friendship, but also in social solidarity) and, in the measure that we come to know each other in this way we may come, in that knowledge, to know the mystery of God himself.

Of course our Christian account of knowledge and love, and of how it is that, in that knowing and loving, we may come lovingly to know the holy mystery which we call "God," is (as are all other accounts and procedures) contestable. It purports to be true, but there is no neutral standpoint, no place that is not some particular place, from which competing truth claims can be tested and compared. And if, in the last analysis, problems of knowledge are problems of ethics and not of epistemology or "engineering," then it is only in the attainment of holiness, in the exercise of basic trust in working for the construction of a common humanity, that the truth of the Christian doctrine of God—of the claim that authentically human existence is life lived in response to and in the presence of the holy mystery of God—can be (perhaps persuasively) *displayed*.

Personal Problems

To say that the relation to a human being is the proper metaphor for the relation to God is at least to say that the inquiring mind's attempt to reach some understanding of the mystery of God is subordinate to the discipline of contemplative practice, for the only understanding that we can hope to attain will be a by-product of appropriate behavior. If, as I said earlier, it is the actual occurrence of community, the redemptive transformation of the dominance of "irrelation," which is the proper metaphor for the relation to God,[32] then, to the extent that, in the inhumanness of our domestic and social worlds, we are unable to relate to each other, and hence unable to pray, to *that* extent we shall be unable to attain to any proper or fruitful understanding of the mystery of God. Or, to put it another way, in the

---

31 Buber, *I and Thou*, p. 151.

32 See above, p. 229.

measure that we are *less* than "persons," the proper metaphor is likely to be misused and misunderstood. And because the work of our redemption, the labor of reconciliation and the production of the personal, is always fragile and unfinished, therefore, in our attempts to learn (within the frame of reference provided by the Creed) proper uses of the word "God," we are always more or less at the beginning. Redemption may not be *pure* prospect, but neither is it ever pure achievement.[33]

Consider, in this light, our use of personal language with respect to God. We address God as "you," and speak of God as "him," rather than as "it," not because God is "a person" (which he certainly is not, for he is not *an* anything), but because our Christian experience of the manner of God's action requires us to acknowledge ourselves to be not merely produced but addressed, not merely made but loved, and speaking and loving are *personal* characteristics. Further than this we cannot go without obscuring the difference between the world and God. God cannot be brought into our world of images, narratives, and descriptions.

But is he not, from the beginning, already *within* that world as "spirit," as that world's inmost gift and creative possibility? Yes, that is why we exist at all, and that is why we are able to live our lives and tell our stories. But, in that case, if there is something of God in the people that we are, may there not be something of God in the stories that we tell? Can God not "figure" in our story, and does he not, in *fact,* so figure when we speak of him as our lord and father, shepherd, rescuer, king, lover, and judge? Yes again, but we too easily forget that these images, and the stories in which they occur—within the complex history of conflict and clarification which is the history of the Jewish and Christian people—were usually produced in criticism of inhuman (and hence "ungodly") practices. God is *not* a king or father as other kings and fathers are; he, unlike all other shepherds, is the *good* shepherd; unlike other judges, God judges justly, and so on. In other words, it is only through the redemptive transformation of our human practices that we can acquire some sense of what the truth of these images might be when used as metaphors for our relation to the unknown God.

Perhaps we might say that the only images we have of God are not the images that his people *use,* but the images that they *are,* and—being the kind of people that we are—the imagery which we constitute is such as more likely to obscure than to clarify the sense of God. Such clarification as we are able to attain finds its full focus in Jesus and in the history of discipleship of the crucified. There is, indeed, something of God in the

---

33 Cf. Buber, *Origin and Meaning of Hasidism,* p. 129, discussed in chap. 14, above.

people that we are. God does, indeed, figure in our history. This is what we acknowledge in confessing Jesus to be God's incarnate utterance and in confessing that it is "in his Spirit" that we seek to live.

The point of these elementary observations is simply to indicate something of the *shape* or pattern which consideration of what is and is not at issue in the use of personal language with respect to God takes within the frame of reference provided by the Creed. And it is, I think, an indication of the extent to which, under the dominant influence of modern theism (and of the anthropologies which produce both this theism and its denials), the doctrine of God's Trinity has, in fact, largely ceased to function as our Christian frame of reference, that consideration of these matters usually takes the form of supposing God to be *a* person of some kind, and then going on to wonder what kind of a person he might be said to be.

Guided by our use of the "proper metaphor," we may address the mystery of God in personal terms, and use personal pronouns in what we say about God, without falling into the trap of supposing him to be "a" person. But, if God is not a person, is he perhaps (to change the subject) *three* persons?

The answer, quite simply, is *no*. It is, of course, possible for the trained theologian to jump through a series of interpretative hoops and come up with a sense of the word "person" which does not contradict what the classical expressions of the doctrine sought to say. (Indeed, it is incumbent upon her or him to do so, because only in this way can the ancient texts be understood.) But the product of this interpretative labor will be a sense of the concept so fundamentally at variance with modern English usage as to demand its replacement by some other word. Of course, if there were no other way of expressing what it was that those who brought the term into theological usage were attempting to say then, instead of replacing the term, we would perhaps be obliged to struggle to retain our (by now) strange and idiosyncratic usage. (Thus, for example, I have argued both for the retention of the word "God," and for a grammar of that word's usage which goes against the grain of much contemporary custom.) I believe this not to be the case where trinitarian uses of the word "person" are concerned, and will now try briefly to indicate why.

It is sometimes suggested that the only uses of the word "person" which are incompatible with the sense of its employment in the classical considerations of the doctrine of God's Trinity are those which express a discredited anthropological individualism. Thus, for example, if what we mean by "person" is a self-contained individual entity capable of entering into relationships of knowledge and love, then God is not three persons in this sense because (so the argument goes) *this* is not the sense with which we should be working when we describe *human beings* as persons. "The human person," said von Hügel, "begins more as a possibility than a reality." Or, as George Vass put it, a human being "becomes a person *in* facing the personal other and *through* the event of his fellowship with him."[34]

But this still does not furnish us with a sense of the term applicable to God the Father, Son, and Holy Spirit because, even in this usage, "persons" exist in *mutual* relationships of knowledge and love, and the "persons" in God are not *thus* distinguishable.[35] That unceasing dialectically corrective movement which is the pattern or *perichoresis* of the Christian creed requires us to distinguish between Father, Son, and Spirit, but any attempt to *picture* the distinctions that we draw in terms of "three different personalities with different centres of activity" is, implicitly, sheer tritheism—however much we may deny this *verbally*. Thus, for example, David Brown brushes aside the charge that his reading of the doctrine is tritheistic while yet coming up with such remarkable statements as: "it does seem a reasonable expectation that the other persons of the Trinity would exhibit some interest in the fate of the person from their number who had become a man."[36]

God is not a number of anythings, and certainly not a number of persons ("three people," as it were). When Augustine said that we use the term "person" of God "in order that there might be something to say when it was asked what the three are, which the true faith pronounces to be three, when it both declares that the Father is not the Son, and that the Holy Spirit, which is the gift of God, is neither the Father nor the Son . . . it could not say that there were not three somewhats,"[37] he did not mean that the Father was God, the Son was God, and the Spirit was God, and that Father, Son, and Spirit were *also* something else *in addition* to being God: namely, "persons." If we require some concept by the use of which to indicate that the Spirit in whose gift we live and move and have our existence and its possibilities is reducible neither to the Word by which we

---

34   Von Hügel, *Mystical Element* 1:76; George Vass, *Understanding Karl Rahner* 2:52.

35   As Newman put it: our difficulty arises from "our inability to conceive a sense of the word person, such, as to be more than a mere character [or "persona"], yet less than an individual intelligent being" (John Henry Newman, *The Arians of the Fourth Century*, 3d ed. [London, 1871], p. 155). My suggestion is that because, *whatever* our anthropology, we can hardly help hearing the word to mean "an individual intelligent being," we do better to dispense with it.

36   Rahner, *The Trinity*, p. 43; see ibid., p. 42; David Brown, *The Divine Trinity*, p. 119. Part of the reason why Brown is able to dismiss the charge as "little more than a hollow war cry" is that he has no qualms about speaking of the "separate powers," distinct "minds," "wills," and (even more striking in its anthropomorphism) "perceptions" of the three divine "persons" (see pp. 293–96).

37   Augustine, *De Trinitate*, bk. 7, chap. 4. The translation is that in *A Select Library of the Nicene and Post-Nicene Fathers of the Christian Church* 3: 109,110.

are addressed nor to him whose breathing of his Spirit enables us to hear and respond to his address, we must not be misled into supposing that whatever concept we decide to use to indicate these distinctions could furnish us with some "new extra knowledge not included in the original experience." As Newman put it: we knew, "before we began to use [the term 'person'], that the Son was God yet was not the Father . . . the word Person tells us nothing in addition to this. It is only the symbol . . . of our ignorance."[38]

Perhaps we could make the point this way. A theologian who supposes that it is more *informative* to refer to God as three "persons" than as three "hypostases" would seem to have forgotten that, as first brought into theological usage, the two terms were synonymous.[39] They were used, not as informative descriptions of what there are three of in God, not as predicates, interchangeably applicable to all three "persons"[40] but, more austerely, as reminders that the distinctions which we employ in speaking of God are no mere matter, as it were, of how things appear to be "on the surface" (beneath which surface God exists without differentiation) but that they go, we might say, to the heart of the matter. The distinctions between Father, Son, and Spirit are distinctions that are truly drawn of *God* and not merely of the way that God appears to us to be. In other words, to say that these are distinctions which operate (grammatically) in the order of "subsistence," or "hypostasis," is to say just what we earlier said when discussing Rahner's axiom concerning the identity between the economic and the immanent Trinity. To say that in God there are three "persons" is, therefore, merely to give formal or technical expression to what we take to be our justified trust that our experience of the mystery of God is truly experience of God *himself.* But, if this *is* what the language of "persons" is supposed to be doing, then surely some other expression—such as "manner of subsisting"[41]—which (as it were) wears its technicality on its sleeve, would be less misleading, nowadays, than the term "person"?

---

38 Rahner, *The Trinity*, p. 106; John Henry Newman, *The Philosophical Notebook of John Henry Newman*, ed. Edward Sillem (Louvain, 1970), 2:105.

39 See Rahner, *The Trinity*, p. 75.

40 This is a theme often stressed by Rahner: "the concept of hypostasis, when applied to God, is not a general and univocal concept which is predicated of all three persons in the same way" ("Remarks on the Dogmatic Treatise 'De Trinitate,'" *Investigations*, 4:80).

41 For Rahner's reasons for preferring "mode" or "manner" of "subsisting" to Karl Barth's "mode" or "manner" of "being" (which amounts, in intention, to much the same thing), see Rahner, *The Trinity*, pp. 73–76, 109–13. In the same sections, Rahner argues that this usage also helps us to rediscover the unity of concern which lay behind the contrasting approaches and emphases of the theologies of East and West (on which, see also "Remarks on the Dogmatic Treatise 'De Trinitate,'" p. 85).

I am only too well aware of the risks that one runs in trying to say *anything* fairly simply of matters which, for nearly two thousand years, have tested to the limit the imaginative capacity and logical power of some of the best of Christian minds—from Augustine and the Cappadocians to Hegel and Karl Barth. But it seemed to me better to take the risk than to evade the issue.

To sum up. If, in our use of the doctrine of God, we are to keep the question of the human open in sustaining our sense of the difference between the world and God, while yet making true mention of God, then we require some pattern of speech, some frame of reference, which is so structured as to sustain not only our recognition of the difference between word and gift, address and presence, meaning and life, clarification and community, but also our acknowledgment of the difference between each of these two and the "unoriginate" mystery whose twofold self-bestowal they are. For most of us, it will be sufficient for this purpose if, in our uses of the Creed, we confess that the one God whom we worship is not reducible either to his self-utterance or to his self-gift. But, because these matters strain the resources of our language to its limits, it is not improper for academic theology, reflecting on these things, to keep a watchful eye on the tendency of our speech to lapse into contradiction or incoherence. And if, in pursuit of this watchfulness, theologians call in aid quite technical tools, it would be preferable for the technicality of their treatment to be apparent in the vocabulary which they use, lest we be misled into supposing that, in meeting the requirements of rational inquiry, we were provided with some information about the mystery of God which we would not otherwise possess.

Making a Difference

Pantheism supposes that whatever can truly be said of the presence of God in the world, in nature or history, is all that can truly be said of God. It fails to refer the gift to the giver, the Spirit to the mystery whose gracious self-bestowal, in freedom and freshness, in conversion and community, that Spirit is. "Logolatry" (for want of a better word) supposes that whatever can truly be said of God, in the ideas and images, the stories and events, the *language* we are authorized to use and make our own, exhausts the meaning of God. It fails to refer the utterance to the utterer, the image to the "imageless One" whose gracious self-bestowal, in word and deed, that word or logos is. And agnosticism or atheism, knowing that all particular differences can be naturally accounted for, acknowledging the comprehensiveness of finitude—with its patterns of narrative and causal explanation—supposes there to be no uses of the word "God" that are not traces of outworn mythology. Suspicious and critical of all "heteronomy," it supposes "autonomy" to have the last word—whether that word is uttered in celebration or in acknowledgment of tragic destiny.

On this account, we might say that atheism *interrupts* the pattern or *perichoresis* of the Christian doctrine of God. It fails to make the further move (a move which both von Hügel and Buber deemed integral to the attainment of maturity, wisdom, and holiness) *beyond* autonomy into "relation," beyond both individualism and collectivism into community and *in* that movement, turning, or conversion, perhaps to find a way back into the presence of him to whose address we might again be able to respond.

Now I am moving too fast, because the attempt to *go beyond* or to "transcend" autonomy can take several different forms. Especially when autonomy, or our "aloneness" in the world, is read as fate or tragic destiny (e.g., "we are on our own, and there is nothing that we can do about it"), the attempt to transcend it may take one of two forms of *flight*. The first we might call "the flight into feeling," on the run from darkness, inhumanity, and impending chaos in the cultivation of oases of private satisfaction. A second we could call "the flight into thought," the quest for comprehensive explanation. It makes little difference whether or not the explanatory schemes that we devise do or do not make mention of "God," because all such schemes leave the bleakness of the facts largely unchanged. Pushing back the frontiers of knowledge may increase our power but (as we, by now, have good reason to know) does not necessarily contribute to the transmutation of fate into freedom. And metaphysics does not feed the hungry nor set the captives free: "The philosophers have only *interpreted* the world, in various ways; the point is to *change* it."[42] This was a thesis "on Feuerbach" but, mindful of the fact that change, *in itself,* brings no relief from tragic destiny, we need to turn to Hegel, whose shadow (at this point) looms behind both Feuerbach and Marx.

It is, of course, no coincidence that those theologians in the German-speaking world who have, in recent decades, written most illuminatingly on the doctrine of God's Trinity, have done so through critical engagement with Hegel's thought.[43] I am not (so far as I know) an Hegelian, but I willingly admit that, throughout this book, I have thrown in my lot with Hegel at least to the extent of agreeing with him that knowledge of God is not to be had by "gazing" at some real or imaginary object or idea, but

---

42 Karl Marx, *Early Writings* (London, 1975), p. 423.

43 I have in mind, for example, the work of Karl Barth, Eberhard Jüngel, Walter Kasper, Jürgen Moltmann, Wolfhart Pannenberg, and Karl Rahner.

by participating in God's self-movement of utterance and love. However, if *one* of the questions which has always to be put to Hegel asks whether he in fact succeeded in sustaining the difference between the world and God, a *second* question (and this is the question which more immediately concerns me here) asks about how he draws the *second* difference: namely, the difference between "word" and "spirit."[44]

Utterance is always particular. Words are uttered, stories are told, histories enacted, by particular people in particular times and circumstances. Jesus was a particular person, who lived a particular life and said and did particular things. And the confession that this one man *is* God's self-utterance, the Word incarnate, far from canceling or overcoming this particularity, actually *requires* it—for to go beyond or to transcend the particularity of Jesus, substituting for it some "idea" of man (or God) is to reduce him, and his history, and his people, to the status of mere instance, illustration, exemplar, or ideal. But *people* are not mere instances. All instances or illustrations stand under the basic word "I-It."

And yet, if something is to be *made* of the history of Jesus, if the incarnate Word is to "make a difference" commensurate with it being *God's* Word, *God's* address, that finds enfleshment here, then there is, indeed, a second difference to be drawn. Unless there is "more" to be seen and said and lived and suffered and done in that Word's light, incarnate utterance is reduced, as it were, to the status of an *anecdote:* a tale without enduring or universal significance. But to deny such significance to Jesus is (implicitly) to deny that he is *God's* incarnate utterance, the enactment in space and time of the mystery which establishes the world in all its difference.

Hegel may have been, as Milbank says, "the most profound meditator upon the identity of the Holy Spirit"[45] but, in Hegel's hands, the tendency is to treat the second difference as a difference between word and idea, between narrative density and conceptual transparency, between "representation" (Hegel's "Vorstellung") and "absolute" knowledge. The tendency, in other words, is to identify "spirit" with' *comprehension.* But this is, in fact, to collapse the difference between word and spirit into a distinction between two stages in a single process of knowledge or understanding. This is why I introduced my remarks on Hegel under the heading of "the flight into thought." And many Christians who have never heard of Hegel have nevertheless supposed that what we are given, in Jesus, is some kind of *explanation* to be grasped, some *answer* to all our

---

44 Throughout this section, I am indebted to John Milbank's suggestive paper on "The Second Difference."

45 Ibid., 225.

questioning, some center of security or satisfaction of the mind, some possessed assurance of the heart. But, since the facts of the world remain, with the advent of such knowledge, largely unchanged, all attempts *thus* to construe the second difference are (if not merely illusory) at best evasive of our practical responsibilities for the making of a human world. Kant's fourth question remains, in our unfinished world, an *open* question, which cannot be *closed* by revelation or by the provision of "absolute" knowledge.

It is time to go back to the beginning and to consider, once again, how we might move beyond or "transcend" autonomy without taking flight into either feeling or thought. The suggestion is that we can only do so through conversion, through the awakening of basic trust, the actualization of "relation," the occurrence of community. In such occurrence, autonomy is transcended, not only without loss of identity or dignity, but with our *true* identity and dignity, as persons, glimpsed and incipiently attained. In all relationship, all friendship, all community, there is an element of risk, because the *grammar* of relationship is trust rather than control, vulnerability rather than domination. But, in its occurrence, we may be able (with the proper metaphor now at our disposal) once again to pray. And, in our prayer, which is the movement in us of God's own Spirit, to discover that the second difference does not lie between fact and feeling, or between word and idea, but rather between "address" and "presence," clarification and community.

In other words, if my suggestion is plausible that at least some forms of atheism may be seen as "interruptions" of the movement of the Christian doctrine of God, then, on the account that I am offering, if we are not to get *stuck* in the atheism which threatens *anyone* who takes seriously the complexity and tragedy of our world (and if, at the same time, we refuse to indulge in the pastime of inventing "gods" whom we suppose might meet our needs or relieve our homelessness and insecurity), then the way "beyond" atheism does not lie through argument or self-assertion, but (once again) through that occurrence of community which makes possible the worship, "in the Spirit," of the unknown God.

It is in the occurrence of community, in the redemptive transformation of irrelation, that the breathing of God's Spirit, the movement of God's self-gift, is transcribed into the facts and possibilities of the world. "Spirit" is therefore to be construed as redemption, reconciliation, liberation, or freedom, as *life* or "authentic existence" or "new creation," and not as self-transparency or absolute knowledge. But this insistence does not entail any disparagement of the requirements of understanding, because the actual fashioning of a *human* world requires the strenuous engagement as much of mind as of heart and muscle. If we take seriously the sheer complexity of the economic, political, and cultural realms, it is surely evident that there can be no "mindless" shortcuts—through willpower, commitment, fanaticism, or demagogy—to the fashioning of human community. Nevertheless, it remains true of our relations with each other, as well as of our relation to the mystery of God, that it is "not awareness, but courageous action [which] announces the dawn of faith."[46]

There is one final remark that needs to be made. In the context of what Buber called the "public catacombs" or tomb-strewn wilderness of our expectation of God's coming, the joy, the trust, the generosity, and reconciliation which are the expressions of that expectation, the hallmarks of Easter—these things cannot *appear* in our world as in some place of peace secured from strife and suffering. Jerusalem, the city of God and the dwelling place of his people, is not a city that we can finish in time. Our business is (not restlessly or anxiously, but patiently) *making a difference.*[47]

But the kind of difference that we are required to make, and the manner of its making, against the dominant inhumanity of structure and ideology, are already indicated in the form and fate of God's address. The risen one, in the gift of whose spirit we are to make a difference, is the crucified one. It is, therefore, hardly surprising that the history of God's spirit in the world, the history of his holy people, the sacramental visibility of which we call "Israel" or "Church," should be (in the measure that the people is, in fact, faithful to its mission) a "counter-history of peace regained through atoning suffering."[48] Only through such a counterhistory (lived at all manner of levels, from political struggle to private compassion and individual endurance) could the peace of Easter, the peace made through Christ's blood on the Cross, be sacramentally displayed and actualized in our world. And yet, as I suggested earlier, we should perhaps not underestimate the difference which even such apparently fragile and certainly vulnerable enactments or parables of God's Kingdom might make.

Is there not much more that needs to be said? Undoubtedly, but if it is in all the world's confusion, savagery, self-indulgence, and sheer "impossibility"; in a world in which most people go hungry and all people are threatened by the power and paranoia of a few; if it is in *this* world that, in pedagogy patterned according to the contours of the creed, Christians learn to respond to a word that sounds in silence, and to celebrate a pres-

---

46 George Vass, *Understanding Karl Rahner* 2:151.

47 And if that sounds pelagian, we should remember von Hügel's and Buber's remarks (considered in chaps. 12 and 13) concerning the paradoxes of divine grace and human effort. For Buber's "public catacombs," see "Dialogue," p. 7.

48 Milbank, "The Second Difference," 227.

ence which (in view of our expectations in these matters) has all the hall-marks of apparent absence; if it is indeed in *this* world that we bear precious knowledge of the saving mystery of God; then, however much still needs to be *said,* there is a great deal more that needs quite urgently to be *done.*

17

Easter in Ordinary

Why This Way?

In drawing his analogy between philosophy and jurisprudence, Waisman said that the philosopher was required to submit *all* the facts of his case.[1] But no books would ever end, nor would any argument ever be brought to a conclusion, if this requirement were misunderstood. The barrister does not mention *everything* that happened on the day of the crime. Much that happened, even on that day, and even to those most closely involved in the incident—to the accused, to the victim, and to the eyewitnesses, for example—will not be relevant to the case. The trial lawyer mentions in submission not "all the facts" but all the facts *of his case*. In other words, he selects just those facts which he deems relevant, as evidence, in support of his case or contention, and weaves them into a pattern, or narrative of persuasion, which invites (for it cannot compel) from the jury the issuing of the judgment that the accused is guilty, or not guilty, as the case may be.

Most books begin at page one and, although clusters of appendices may sometimes complicate the matter, it is usually not too difficult to work out where they end (it was once the custom charmingly to print "THE END" in nice large letters, in case the reader was in any doubt). But to take the jurisprudential analogy seriously is to be reminded that the end of an argument will be that argument's "conclusion" not only in the sense of termination or terminus ("reaching the end of the line") but also in the sense of achieving its purpose or "telos." The barrister concludes his argument,

---

1   See above, p. 84.

or rests his case, only when he has reason to believe that he has adduced sufficient evidence, and patterned that evidence into a sufficiently compelling narrative, to persuade the jury to reach the same conclusion.

There is, it therefore seems, a sense in which arguments can sometimes be said to "compel"—not by terrorizing, or by the use of physical coercion, or (if they are good arguments) by manipulating the emotions, but only through what we call the "force" of the argument. Arguments compel, not by steamrolling, but by eliciting responsible free acts of judgment, evaluation, and decision. But, however things may stand with jurisprudence, or with technical argument in philosophy, the conclusion of complex, large scale, cumulative arguments in theology, or in historical interpretation, or in literary criticism, is rarely, if ever, compelling even in this sense. In such areas of discourse, the most that one can hope for is so to construct the argument as to win a hearing for one's case.

This is my final chapter, and I am almost ready to rest my case. There *is,* I think, an argument in this book, but it is not the kind of argument of which it would be profitable, at this point, to attempt a summary: to do so might make it seem to be a more purely *theoretical* argument than I intend it to be. Instead of attempting any such summary, therefore, I shall offer two distinct but related sets of remarks on why it was that the argument took the form that it did.

Consider, in the first place, the following cluster of assumptions: that the concept of "religious experience" refers to individual, incommunicable, private states of mind or feeling; that such experience, set free from the constricting particularity of warring systems of belief and organization, may be conducive to social health and harmony; that what is meant by "God" is whatever it is (transcendent of present circumstances) with which, in such experience, we have to do; that, fearful of the structures and systems which threaten not merely our individual, personal freedom and integrity, but the very survival of the race, we may find some solace in such experience and in the conviction which it brings that there is more to life than institutions and arguments, politics and warfare, and that the more that there is is fundamentally beneficent.

That was just a random reminder (for the list could be extended, and the pattern permutated, almost indefinitely) of assumptions that have become deeply embedded in the Western imagination since the early nineteenth century (though their roots go back at least a century earlier). They have, of course, been frequently challenged by those who have regarded religion and its uses either as obsolescent or (more sharply) as inimical to human progress, freedom, and maturity. But the challenge has often been, not so much to the *descriptions* offered of what might be meant by "religious experience" or by "God," but rather to their evaluation and assessment. (I have in mind such masters of suspicion as Nietzsche, Marx, and Freud.)

Suppose that someone wished to take sides with neither the friends nor the enemies of religion, and its uses, and its objects, as thus described. Suppose that someone wished to propose a different account (the warrants for which would be at once historical and philosophical, political and theological) of what might be meant by "God" and (hence) by "experience of God." How would one win a hearing for such an alternative account? No amount of bald assertion would be much help, because all the words that one wanted to use—words such as "experience" and "person" and "knowledge" and "God"—would be already *in place:* their sense and reference, their implications, overtones, and connotations embedded and arranged in the paradigms and overarching narratives of one side or the other of the dominant debates.

In such a situation, the best thing (as it seems to me) for such a person to do would be to try to work his way, step by step, toward a different view. In case all this seems rather abstract (although I hope that, in the light of all that has gone before, it may not) consider an illustration or parable of the problem.

What Jesus underwent, in the last hours of his life, he underwent in public. His pain was his own, but it was perceptible, and would surely not have been *entirely* strange or unintelligible (to a point ruling out all possibility of com-passion) to those who had followed him and learned from him. Accounts of what he underwent and of what, in undergoing it, he did and achieved, have been many and conflictual. But no account of Jesus' experience on the way to Calvary and on that hill deserves to be taken seriously if it fails to take into consideration the religious and political factors which combined to produce this particular result. There seems little doubt but that Jesus' relation to the mystery which he called "Father" was central to his suffering, and was also in contention between those who engineered his death and those who came to read his failure as marking a kind of triumph for the way of God's address to and presence in the world. Surely what happened to Jesus, and to his followers, in those days and hours, and what they then and later made of what was happening, formed part of their experience, and formed part of their experience of God. But were the experiences of Jesus on Calvary and of his followers—at first dismayed and disoriented, and later refashioned in rediscovery and worked out in courageous opposition to the authorities and in painful conflict with their fellow Jews—were they instances of "religious" experience? Not only do I not know quite what to *do* with this question, but it strikes me as both tasteless and wide of the mark.

I am trying to indicate why it seemed to me that, in order to try to open up the imaginative and conceptual *space* in which the kind of case that I wished to make might hope to win a hearing, it would be useful to begin by examining one influential exposition of the dominant account of "religious experience" and of "experience of God," subjecting that account to fairly close (but by no means wholly unsympathetic) critical scrutiny, so as thereby to rework some of the components which could then be gradually fitted into the pattern of a different story.

I said, at the beginning, that I proposed to argue that it is not the case that all experience of God is necessarily religious in form or content, and that not everything which it would be appropriate to characterize as "religious" experience would thereby necessarily constitute experience of God.

At the time, that proposal may have appeared to be mere paradox. But, let us suppose that psychologists have good reasons, as they map the objects of their study in order to make them manageable, for describing *some* psychological types and states (and only these) as "religious." It may well be that people who fall into these types, or enjoy such states, are more drawn than others to the use of what is called religious language in the performance of what are called religious acts. But I should wish, on theological grounds, to contest any suggestion that only people of these psychological types, or people who enjoy these psychological states, can live in relation to the creative and redemptive mystery of God. Indeed, the opposite may well be the case. It may well be that people such as these are more liable than others to bind the mystery of God into the It-world, to set up a "God-district" alongside the other districts in their life and, by so doing, to obscure the signs of God's address and presence both in that district and elsewhere.

Similarly, sociologists, as they map the districts and categories of social existence, may have good reasons for describing some types of behavior, some institutions and patterns of belief, as "religious." From these descriptions arise many of the different definitions of religion that are currently on offer. And it may well be that people who behave in these ways, inhabit these institutions, and sustain these beliefs are more likely than others to interpret their human experience in religious and (in many societies) in theistic terms. But I should wish, on theological grounds, to contest any suggestion that only people who behave in these ways, who are at home in these institutions, or who affirm these beliefs can live in relation to the creative and transformative mystery of God. Once again, the opposite may well be the case. It is easy to get stuck in the world of religion and, having done so, to fail to find one's way back to the hearing of God's address and the celebration of his presence in all the ordinary places and problems of our world.

Religion (however defined) performs a wide variety of social and psychological functions, the value of which, to individual health and social flourishing, is matter for debate. Moreover, bearing in mind the frequency with which functionalist accounts of religion go hand in hand with descriptions of religious experience that are primarily *aesthetic* in character, [2] it is not surprising that many people suppose that the difference between religious people and the rest of us is not unlike the difference between those who are "musical" and those who are (in varying degrees) "tone-deaf." And so, when "experience of God" is taken to be a particular kind or particular interpretation of "religious experience," being deaf to religion is identified with being deaf to God. And, within this general setup, it is very difficult to make room for the suggestion that deafness to God is not a deficiency in aesthetic perception or sensitivity, but is, rather, what (from within an older tradition) I have preferred to call idolatry: the dedication of our energies and the setting of our hearts on some particular object, event, individual, tradition, fact, or idea in the world. And of course, to make matters worse, many if not most of the dominant forms and instances of idolatry in our modern world have little or nothing to do with religion. This being how things stand, it is perhaps (again) not so surprising that I found it necessary to follow a somewhat lengthy and laborious route to the construction of my case.

My second set of reasons for proceeding as I did, though prima facie rather different from the first, is, I believe, related to it. In theology, as in politics, attractive and powerful slogans are not hard to come by. But slogans and catchphrases, satisfying stories and patterns of imagery (whether drawn from biblical material or, in the name of "relevance," from some more recent worldview or philosophy—from "process" thought or existentialism, from Marxism or the cosmology of natural science)—simply slide over the surface of our dark and broken world. All straightforward, tidily coherent descriptions (whether abstract in formulation or rich in imagery) of what we mean by "God," and of the manner of our relationship to him, not only obscure the difference between the world and God but, by freewheeling in abstraction from the actual historical, cultural, and political circumstances in which we find ourselves and have to make our way, are suspect of evasion and frivolity.

Theologians are often accused of making things difficult. But the theologian does not *invent* either the complexity and illegibility of our history or the pain and confusion of contemporary circumstance. I would wish (as I have said elsewhere) to go further: part of the theologian's responsi-

---

2   In the sense indicated in our discussion of Fries in chap. 9.

bility is to help discipline the propensity of the pious imagination to sim-
plify facts, texts, demands, and requirements that are resistant to any such
simplification.[3]

Serious theological reflection is always hard work, and its outcome fragmentary, tentative, and (often) quite technical in its quest for appropriate
imaginative and conceptual accuracy, not because *God* is complicated, but
because we are—and so is the world in which we live. It is not possible
without complexity to indicate, or point the way toward, the deep simplicity of the mystery of God. Divine simplicity, the integration—beyond
our experience and understanding—of complexity, diversity, conflict, and
particular truth, does perhaps find some refraction or metaphorical
expression in the attainment of the kind of wisdom which is known, in
the Jewish and Christian traditions, as holiness. But *such* simplicity is
never where we *start* from.

It was with considerations such as these in mind that I decided to make
my argument move through the quite detailed consideration of particular
texts and of the thought of some very different thinkers. The literary critic
helps the reader of the poem or novel to take the text *slowly.* To many
students, this procedure initially irritates—the text gets broken up, its first
excitement lost in technicality and detail. But it is, perhaps, only through
some such slow process of detailed and particular consideration that we
are able to go beyond the "surface" of the text. And why should it be
otherwise when the "text" that we are trying to read is written in the
experience that has brought us to where we now are?

Serious theological reflection, in other words, is, and should be made
to be, *hard work.* It might be objected, however, that this is to take an
improperly narrow and academic view of the tasks and responsibilities of
serious Christian speech. The Gospel is not the private property of the
"clerks" (whether ecclesiastical or academic). What right, therefore, have
academics to cloud by complication the simplicity of a message addressed,
a promise made, *especially* to the simple and unlettered? The interesting
thing about this objection, which quite misses the point of my remarks
about simplicity and wisdom, is that it is usually made, *not* by the so-
called "simple faithful" but, patronizingly, on their behalf by highly educated people who prefer not to have their own possessed simplicities
disturbed.

The simple and the poor, the sick or lonely, the oppressed or dispossessed, do not need to be told that the attainment of dignity and freedom,
the fashioning of patterns of personal relationship in which no group or

---

3   See Lash, *Theology on the Way to Emmaus,* x.

individual is reduced to the status of an object of another's purposes, is always hard work and that the work is always unfinished. And nobody needs to be told that the same is true of all growth in relationship, in self-understanding, and in true knowledge of each other. Theological reflection, in other words, is always hard work simply because it is the attempt to bring to speech, in interpretative patterns of inquiry and understanding, the common labor of the "production of the personal" in relation to the address and presence of the mystery of God.

There is one further consideration which points in the same direction. In the previous chapter, I referred to "the flight into thought," the attempt to *go beyond* the confusion and complexity of our unfinished business in quest of "answers" or explanations of the world. In our ordinary relations with each other, respect for other people, the refusal to *impose* our own opinions, plans, and purposes upon each other, is a permanent requirement of what was once called "courtesy" (when the word meant so much more than we nowadays usually mean by "good manners," which is little more than the observance of social convention). In order to sustain a climate of courtesy, it is not necessary to suppose that all opinions are equally valid, all plans equally sensible, or all purposes equally noble. On the contrary: it is when opinions held and purposes furthered with passionate conviction come into conflict that something like courtesy is required if the outcome is not to be the breakdown of relationship, the domination of one group or individual by another. (And there is, perhaps, something analogous to courtesy in the respect required by craftsmen for their materials, by scientists for the objects of their study, and, more generally, in all our human relationships with the natural world of which we form a part.)

There is, in other words, in all responsible human labor, including not only the labor of human relationship but also the academic labors of the mind, a necessary discipline, respect, or courtesy which imposes upon our patterns of speech and imagination not necessarily doubt or hesitation but at least a kind of reticence. It follows, bearing in mind the fact that our relations with each other constitute the proper metaphor for our relation with the mystery of God, that all serious and responsible *theological* speech will be characterized by the religious form of such discipline or reticence—and the usual name for this is "reverence." Theological investigation is, in itself, neither preaching nor prayer. Nevertheless, it seems to me that, if theology is not to lose touch with experience, if it is not to sever its links with that discipline of labor, interpretation, and suffering, that contemplative practice, of which it is a particular, educated, reflective, and critical moment, then it too needs to be characterized, in its uses of argument, by something close to (and often indistinguishable from) prayerfulness. This is not a recommendation for pietism or mindless religiosity. It is simply a suggestion that theology is not exempt from that requirement of reverence, reticence, or courtesy which is, in fact, a requirement laid upon all responsible human speech and that the *form* of such courtesy is dictated by its relationship to the incomprehensible mystery on which it seeks to reflect.

Where Have We Got To?

We have got to the end. And it is this fact which furnishes us with a final problem, for the end of an argument which purports to show how Christian experience may be considered as a way of keeping the question of the human open in relation to the mystery of God should surely reflect the open or unfinished character of the project or adventure which it seeks to describe. But what register of discourse would be appropriate for *that* kind of "ending"?

Argument proceeds by inference and assertion, and it is only too easy to give the impression that the job has been finished, the work done. Full stop. *Quod erat demonstrandum.* There is no virtue in obscurity or muddled thinking. The theologian tries to think things through, and to say clearly what has been thought. Theology, therefore, is always tempted toward the kind of *tidiness* which becomes, unless we are careful, just one more expression of the flight into thought. If, however, the end of the argument is not the assertion of an answer, but rather the clarification of the question, some sense of questioning should surely find expression in the way the argument ends.

Poetry might be a better vehicle for this than prose or, at least, than the sort of prose which theologians, for the most part, are trained to produce. Of course, *bad* poetry, self-indulgent verse, may foster the flight into feeling, but at least the metaphoric density of the poetic is some safeguard against the flight into thought, or what James called intellectualism.

I have argued, elsewhere, that the stance of Christian hope is closer to tragedy than to either optimism or despair, and that the mood of its discourse is less that of assertion and prediction than of interrogation and request.[4] This suggests that the kind of poetry which we need would be

---

4 See Lash, *A Matter of Hope*, pp. 231–80; "All Shall Be Well: Christian and Marxist Hope," *Theology on the Way to Emmaus*, pp. 202–15.

such as to keep close contact, in both form and subject matter, with that prayerfulness or courtesy that I discussed in the previous section.

Another reason for supposing that we should end in poetry is suggested by the hermeneutical account of experience which I have tried to recommend. To treat the relationship between experience and interpretation dialectically, as a matter of mutually critical correlation, is to offer a *sacramental* account of the relationship between human experience and a tradition of discourse and behavior which, in interpreting that experience, contributes effectively to its transformation. "Through God's indwelling in the world," said Buber, through God's address and presence, the world becomes "a sacrament."[5] But the language of sacramental action and speech is "sign-language" and, as such, is closer to poetry than to the conceptual transparency sought by theoretical explanation. Sacramental activity is not esoteric—it does not take place in some strange district of its own (for that would be to collapse the difference between the sign and the signified, and this is fetishism or idolatry)—but is interpretative of the ordinary. As Noel-Dermot O'Donoghue puts it: "what prayer achieves . . . is not communion with the Infinite but the illumination of the commonplace as the consequence and 'realisation' of this union."[6] What we require, therefore, is some poem or poems the mood and matter of which keep close to prayerfulness as illumination of the commonplace.

One final consideration. To talk of the "end," in Christian speech, is to talk of Easter. Easter is end both as *finis* and *telos,* as terminus and consummation. There is nothing that happens *after* resurrection, nor anything further to be said. This only makes sense, of course, if that to which the word "Easter" refers is a fact not only about the past from which we learned this language, but also about the present and about our future and the future of all mankind. But Easter would hardly have been, for two thousand years, the spring and center of Christian life and prayer, would hardly have provided the focus of Christian worship and the form of Christian hope, if the word "Easter" were *simply* the name of something that once happened in the past.[7]

To talk of the "end" is to talk of Easter. And this is not, nor can it ever be, an easy thing to do, for what can truly be *said* of Easter which respects the difference between our un-Eastered world and the God whose self-utterance in that world breaks, will break, and has already broken, all the

---

5 Buber, *Origin and Meaning of Hasidism,* p. 96.

6 Noel-Dermot O'Donoghue, *Heaven in Ordinarie* (Springfield, Ill., 1979), p. 192.

7 All of which needs saying much more carefully if it is not to be misunderstood: see Lash, "Easter Meaning," *Theology on the Way to Emmaus,* pp. 167–85.

seals of silence—even the silence of death? And what can truly be *shown* of Easter in such a way as to respect the "second difference," according to which the Spirit is not another utterance or idea, but is redemptive gift, occurrence, transformation, life, relationship, and to do so in a world the darkness and deadliness of which (if taken seriously, suffered, and not evaded) at least serves to correct our propensity to collapse giver into gift? These seem to me to be at least the *kind* of questions the poetic and prayerful expression of which would serve as a suitable ending.

It is not true, in fact, that most books begin at page one. They begin farther back, on the cover (which was the first thing that the reader saw) and on the title page. By way of conclusion, therefore, I offer two pieces of poetry which satisfy the requirements that I have outlined and which, taken together, explain my choice of title. The first is a sonnet by George Herbert on prayer:

> Prayer the Churches banquet, Angels age,
> > Gods breath in man returning to his birth,
> > The soul in paraphrase, heart in pilgrimage,
> The Christian plummet sounding heav'n and earth;
> Engine against th'Almightie, sinners towre,
> > Reversed thunder, Christ-side-piercing spear,
> > The six daies world transposing in an houre,
> A kinde of tune, which all things heare and fear;
> Softnesse, and peace, and joy, and love, and blisse,
> > Exalted Manna, gladnesse of the best,
> > Heaven in ordinarie, man well drest,
> The milkie way, the bird of Paradise,
> > Church-bels beyond the starres heard, the souls bloud,
> > The land of spices; something understood.[8]

The second is the concluding stanza of Gerard Manley Hopkins's "The Wreck of the Deutschland":

> > Dame, at our door
> > Drowned, and among our shoals,
> > Remember us in the roads, the heaven-haven of the reward:

---

8 George Herbert, "Prayer (1)," *The Works of George Herbert*, ed. F. E. Hutchinson (Oxford, 1941), p. 51. The sentence following that which I quoted just now from O'Donoghue runs: "Prayer is in George Herbert's haunting phrase, 'heaven in ordinarie'" (*Heaven in Ordinarie*, p. 192).

> *Our King back, Oh, upon English souls!*
> *Let him easter in us, be a dayspring to the dimness of us, be a*
>   *crimson-cresseted east,*
> *More brightening her, rare-dear Britain, as his reign rolls,*
>   *Pride, rose, prince, hero of us, high-priest,*
> *Our hearts' charity's hearth's fire, our thoughts' chivalry's throng's*
>   *Lord.*[9]

I do not know a better way of ending than with the conjunction of Herbert's "heaven in ordinarie" and Hopkins's use of "easter" as a verb. Living in relation, in the way that we do, to the unknown God, we do not possess, nor do we need to know, more of the form which the fullness of his eastering in all our ordinariness may take.

---

9 Gerard Manley Hopkins, "The Wreck of the Deutschland," *Poems of Gerard Manley Hopkins,* ed. W. H. Gardner (Oxford, 1948), p. 67.

Bibliography
Index

Bibliography

Adams, James Luther. "Letter from Friedrich von Hügel to William James," *Downside Review* 98 (July 1980): 214–36.

Almond, Philip C. *Mystical Experience and Religious Doctrine: An Investigation of the Study of Mysticism in World Religions*. Berlin: Mouton, 1982.

Anscombe, G. E. M. "The First Person." In *Mind and Language*. Ed. S. Guttenplan, 45–66. Oxford: Clarendon Press, 1975.

Arns, Paulo Evaristo. "The Destabilising Poverty Crisis," *New Blackfriars* 67 (April 1986): 169–74.

Augustine, Saint. "On the Holy Trinity." Trans. Arthur West Haddan; rev. W. G. T. Shedd. In *A Select Library of the Nicene and Post-Nicene Fathers of the Christian Church*. Ed. Philip Schaff. Vol. 3. Buffalo: The Christian Literature Company, 1877.

von Balthasar, Hans Urs. *The Glory of the Lord: A Theological Aesthetics*. Vol. 1, *Seeing the Form*. Ed. Joseph Fessio and John Riches; trans. Erasmo Leiva-Merikakis. Edinburgh: T. and T. Clark, 1982.

Barth, Karl. *Church Dogmatics*. Vol. 3, *The Doctrine of Creation. Part 2*. Ed. G. W. Bromiley and T. F. Torrance; trans. Harold Knight, G. W. Bromiley, J. K. S. Reid, and R. H. Fuller. Edinburgh: T. and T. Clark, 1960.

——. *Protestant Theology in the Nineteenth Century*. Trans. Brian Cozens and John Bowden. London: SCM Press, 1972.

de la Bedoyère, Michael. *The Life of Baron von Hügel*. London: Dent, 1951.

Bergeron, Richard. *Les Abus de l'Eglise d'après Newman*. Paris, 1971.

Bernstein, Richard J. *Beyond Objectivism and Relativism*. Oxford: Basil Blackwell, 1983.

Bixler, Julius Seelye. *Religion in the Philosophy of William James*. Boston: Marshall Jones, 1926.

Bourne, Randolph S. *Youth and Life*. Boston: Houghton Mifflin, 1913.

Bradley, F. H. *Appearance and Reality*. Oxford, 1897.

Brown, David. *The Divine Trinity*. London: Duckworth, 1985.

——."Wittgenstein against the 'Wittgensteinians': A Reply to Kenneth Surin on *The Divine Trinity*," *Modern Theology* 2 (1986): 257–76.

Buber, Martin. *A Believing Humanism: My Testament, 1902–1965*. Trans. Maurice Friedman. New York: Simon and Schuster 1967.

——. *Between Man and Man*. Trans. Ronald Gregor Smith. London: Kegan Paul, 1927.

——. *Eclipse of God: Studies in the Relation between Religion and Philosophy*. Trans. Maurice Friedman et al. New York: Harper Torchbooks, 1957.

——. *For the Sake of Heaven*. Trans. Ludwig Lewisohn. Philadelphia: Jewish Publication Society, 1945.

——. *Hasidism and Modern Man*. Ed. Maurice Friedman. New York: Harper, 1960.

——. *I and Thou*. Trans. with a Prologue by Walter Kaufman. Edinburgh: T. and T. Clark, 1970.

——. *The Origin and Meaning of Hasidism*. Ed. and trans. Maurice Friedman. New York: Horizon Press, 1960.

——. *Paths in Utopia*. Trans. R. F. C. Hull. Introd. Ephraim Fischoff. Boston: Beacon Press, 1958.

——. *Two Types of Faith*. Trans. Norman P. Goldhawk. New York: Macmillan, 1951.

Burrell, David B. "Does Process Theology Rest on a Mistake?" *Theological Studies* 43 (1982): 123–35.

——. *Knowing the Unknowable God: Ibn-Sina, Maimonides, Aquinas*. Notre Dame: University of Notre Dame Press, 1986.

Butler, Cuthbert. *Western Mysticism*. 3d ed. London: Constable, 1967.

Calati, Benedetto. "Western Mysticism," *Downside Review* 98 (July 1980): 201–13.

Capra, Fritjof. *The Tao of Physics: An Exploration of the Parallels between Modern Physics and Eastern Mysticism*. London: Wildwood House, 1975.

Carr, Anne. "Theology and Experience in the Thought of Karl Rahner," *Journal of Religion* 13 (1973): 359–76.

Casper, Bernhard. "Franz Rosenzweig's Criticism of Buber's *I and Thou*." In *Martin Buber: A Centenary Volume*. Ed. Haim Gordon and Jochanan Bloch, 139–50. [New York]: Ktav Publishing House, for the Faculty of Humanities and Social Sciences, Ben Gurion University of the Negev, 1984.

Cavell, Stanley. *The Claim of Reason*. Oxford: Clarendon Press, 1979.

Cohen, Arthur. *Martin Buber*. London: Bowes and Bowes, 1957.

Copleston, Frederick. *A History of Philosophy*. Vol. 7, *Fichte to Nietzsche*. Westminster, Md.: Newman Press, 1963.

Corduan, Winfried. "Hegel in Rahner: A Study in Philosophical Hermeneutics," *Harvard Theological Review* 71 (1977): 285–98.

Crouter, Richard. "Rhetoric and Substance in Schleiermacher's Revision of *The Christian Faith* (1821–1822), " *Journal of Religion* 60 (1980): 285–306.

Davis, Charles. *Body as Spirit: The Nature of Religious Feeling*. London: Hodder and Stoughton, 1976.

Dean, William. "Radical Empiricism and Religious Art," *Journal of Religion* 61 (1981): 168–87.

Dillistone, F. W. *C. H. Dodd: Interpreter of the New Testament*. London: Hodder and Stoughton, 1977.

The Documents of Vatican II. Ed. W. M. Abbott. London: Geoffrey Chapman, 1966.

Dulles, Avery. "Paths to Doctrinal Agreement: Ten Theses," *Theological Studies* 47 (1986): 32–47.

Durkheim, Emile. *Pragmatism as Sociology*. Ed. and introd. John Allcock; trans. J. C. Whitehouse. Cambridge: Cambridge University Press, 1983.

Eiseley, Loren. *Firmament of Time*. New York: Atheneum, 1980.

Evans, C. Stephen. *Subjectivity and Religious Belief: An Historical, Critical Study*. Grand Rapids: Christian University Press, 1978.

Feinstein, Howard M. *Becoming William James*. Ithaca, N.Y.: Cornell University Press, 1984.

Friedman, Maurice. *Martin Buber's Life and Work: The Early Years, 1878–1923*. New York: Dutton, 1981.

———. *Martin Buber's Life and Work: The Middle Years, 1923–1945*. New York: Dutton, 1983.

Fries, Jakob Friedrich. *Dialogues on Morality and Religion*. Ed. D. Z. Phillips; trans. David Walford; introd. Rush Rhees. Oxford: Blackwell, 1982.

Furse, Margaret Lewis. "A Critique of Baron von Hügel and Emil Brunner on Mysticism." Ph.D. diss. Columbia University, 1968.

Gutting, Gary. *Religious Belief and Religious Skepticism*. Notre Dame: University of Notre Dame Press, 1982.

Hardy, Alister. *The Spiritual Nature of Man*. Oxford: Clarendon Press, 1979.

Hauerwas, Stanley. *The Peaceable Kingdom*. Notre Dame: University of Notre Dame Press, 1983.

Hegel, Georg Wilhelm Friedrich. *Lectures on the Philosophy of Religion*. Vol. 1, *Introduction and the Concept of Religion*. Ed. Peter C. Hodgson. Berkeley: University of California Press, 1984.

——. *Phenomenology of Spirit*. Trans. A. V. Miller. Oxford: Oxford University Press, 1977.

Herbert, George. *The Works of George Herbert*. Ed. F. E. Hutchinson. Oxford: Clarendon Press, 1941.

Hopkins, Gerard Manley. *Poems of Gerard Manley Hopkins*. Ed. W. H. Gardner. Oxford: Oxford University Press, 1948.

Horwitz, Rivka. *Buber's Way to "I and Thou": An Historical Analysis and the First Publication of Martin Buber's Lectures "Religion als Gegenwart."* Heidelberg: Lambert Schneider, 1978.

von Hügel, Friedrich. *Baron Friedrich von Hügel: Selected Letters, 1896–1924*. Ed. with a Memoir by Bernard Holland. London: J. M. Dent, 1927.

——. *Essays and Addresses on the Philosophy of Religion: First Series*. London: J. M. Dent, 1921.

——. *Essays and Addresses on the Philosophy of Religion: Second Series*. London: J. M. Dent, 1926.

——. *Eternal Life: A Study of Its Implications and Applications*. Edinburgh: T. and T. Clark, 1912.

——. *Letters from Baron Friedrich von Hügel to a Niece*. Ed. and introd. Gwendolen Greene. London: Dent, 1928.

——. *The Mystical Element of Religion as Studied in Saint Catherine of Genoa and her Friends*. 2d ed. 2 vols. London: Dent, 1923.

——. "The Relations between God and Man in 'The New Theology' of Rev. R. J. Campbell," *Albany Review* (1907): 650–68.

James, William. *Letters of William James*. Ed. Henry James. 2 vols. Boston: Little, Brown, 1920.

——. *Memories and Studies*. New York: Longmans Green, 1911.

——. *Pragmatism and the Meaning of Truth*. Introd. A. J. Ayer. Cambridge: Harvard University Press, 1978.

——. *The Works of William James*. Ed. Frederick H. Burkhardt, Fredson Bowers, and Ignas K. Skrupskelis. *Essays in Philosophy*. Cambridge: Harvard University Press, 1978.

——. ——. *Essays in Radical Empiricism*. Introd. John J. McDermott. Cambridge: Harvard University Press, 1976.

——. ——. *The Meaning of Truth*. Introd. H. S. Thayer. Cambridge: Harvard University Press, 1975.

——. ——. *A Pluralistic Universe*. Introd. Richard J. Bernstein. Cambridge: Harvard University Press, 1977.

——. ——. *Pragmatism*. Introd. H. S. Thayer. Cambridge: Harvard University Press, 1975.

————. ————. *The Principles of Psychology.* Introd. Gerald E. Myers. 3 vols. Cambridge: Harvard University Press, 1981.

————. ————. *Some Problems of Philosophy.* Introd. Peter H. Hare. Cambridge: Harvard University Press, 1979.

————. ————. *The Varieties of Religious Experience.* Introd. John E. Smith. Cambridge: Harvard University Press, 1985.

————. ————. *The Will to Believe and Other Essays in Popular Philosophy.* Introd. Edward H. Madden. Cambridge: Harvard University Press, 1979.

Jantzen, Grace M. "'Religion' Reviewed," *Heythrop Journal* 26 (1985): 14–25.

Jossua, Jean-Pierre. *Pour une Histoire Religieuse de l'Expérience Litteraire.* Paris: Beauchesne, 1985.

————, with P. Jacquemont and B. Quelquejeu. *Une Foi Exposée.* 2d ed. Paris: Editions du Cerf, 1973.

Kant, Immanuel. *Kant's Critique of Judgement.* Ed. J. H. Bernard. London: Macmillan, 1931.

————. *Kant's Critique of Practical Reason and Other Writings in Moral Philosophy.* Trans. L. W. Beck. Chicago: University of Chicago Press, 1949.

Kasper, Walter. *The God of Jesus Christ.* Trans. Mathew J. O'Connell. New York: Crossroad, 1984.

Kelly, James J. *Baron Friedrich von Hügel's Philosophy of Religion.* Bibliotheca Ephemeridum Theologicarum Lovaniensum 62. Leuven: The University Press, 1983.

Kenny, Anthony. *The Legacy of Wittgenstein.* Oxford: Basil Blackwell, 1984.

Kerr, Fergus. "Rahner Retrospective. III. Transcendence or Finitude," *New Blackfriars* 62 (1981): 370–79.

————. *Theology after Wittgenstein.* Oxford: Basil Blackwell, 1986.

Kolakowski, Leszek. *Marxism and Beyond: On Historical Understanding and Individual Responsibility.* London: Pall Mall Press, 1969.

————. *Religion.* London: Fontana, 1982.

Lash, Nicholas. "Argument, Essence and Identity," *New Blackfriars* 65 (1984): 413–19.

————. "Considering the Trinity," *Modern Theology* 2 (1986): 183–96.

————. "Credal Affirmation as a Criterion of Church Unity." In *Church Membership and Intercommunion.* Ed. J. Kent and R. Murray, 51–73. London: Darton Longman and Todd, 1973.

————. *A Matter of Hope: A Theologian's Reflections on the Thought of Karl Marx.* London: Darton Longman and Todd, 1981.

————. *Newman on Development: The Search for an Explanation in History.* London: Sheed and Ward, 1975.

———. Review of *Nineteenth-Century Religious Thought in the West*. In *Journal of Theological Studies* 37 (1986): 656–62.

———. Review of Karl Rahner, *Theological Investigations,* vols. 18 and 19. In *Journal of Theological Studies* 37 (1986): 666–69.

———. *Theology on Dover Beach.* London: Darton Longman and Todd, 1979.

———. *Theology on the Way to Emmaus.* London: SCM Press, 1986.

Lenin, V. I., F. Engels, and K. Marx. *On Historical Materialism.* Moscow: Progress Publishers, 1972.

Levinson, Henry Samuel. "Religious Criticism," *Journal of Religion* 64 (1984): 37–53.

———. *The Religious Investigations of William James.* Chapel Hill: University of North Carolina Press, 1981.

Lindbeck, George A. *The Nature of Doctrine: Religion and Theology in a Postliberal Age.* London: SPCK, 1984.

———. "Protestant Problems with Lonergan on Development of Dogma." In *Foundations of Theology: Papers from the International Lonergan Congress 1970.* Ed. Philip McShane, 115–23. Notre Dame: University of Notre Dame Press, 1972.

Lindsay, A. D. Review of *Some Problems of Philosophy* by William James. *Hibbert Journal* 10 (1912): 489–92.

Ling, Trevor. *Karl Marx and Religion: In Europe and India.* New York: Barnes and Noble, 1980.

Lonergan, Bernard J. F. *Collection.* Ed. F. E. Crowe. New York: Herder and Herder, 1967.

———. *Second Collection.* Ed. W. F. J. Ryan and B. J. Tyrrell. Philadelphia: Westminster Press, 1974.

Luckmann, Thomas. *The Invisible Religion.* London: Collier Macmillan, 1967.

Lukács, Georg. *The Ontology of Social Being.* Vol. 1, *Hegel's False and His Genuine Ontology.* Trans. David Fernbach. London: Merlin Press, 1978.

McCabe, Herbert. "A Long Sermon for Holy Week. Part I. Holy Thursday: The Mystery of Unity," *New Blackfriars* 67 (1986): 56–69.

MacIntyre, Alasdair. *After Virtue.* London: Duckworth, 1981.

Marx, Karl. *Early Writings.* Introd. L. Colletti. London: Penguin, 1975.

Matthews, Melvyn. "Cupitt's Context," *New Blackfriars* 66 (1985): 533–43.

Mendes-Flohr, Paul. *Von der Mystik zum Dialog: Martin Bubers Geistige Entwicklung bis hin "Ich und Du."* Introd. Ernst Simon. Königstein: Jüdischer Verlag, 1978.

Milbank, John. "The Second Difference: For a Trinitarianism without Reserve," *Modern Theology* 2 (1986): 213–34.

Miles, T. R. *Religious Experience*. London: Macmillan, 1972.

Mourelatos, Alexander P. D. "Fries, J. F." In *The Encyclopedia of Philosophy*. Vol. 3. Ed. Paul Edwards. New York: Macmillan, 1967.

Moonan, Willard. *Martin Buber and His Critics: An Annotated Bibliography of Writings in English through 1978*. New York: Garland Publishing Co., 1981.

Mysticism and Philosophical Analysis. Ed. Stephen Katz. London: Sheldon Press, 1978.

Newman, John Henry. *The Arians of the Fourth Century*. 3d ed. London, 1871.

———. *The Letters and Diaries of John Henry Newman*. Vol. 29. Ed. C. S. Dessain and Thomas Gornall. Oxford: Clarendon Press, 1976.

———. *Newman's University Sermons*. Introd. J. D. Holmes and D. M. MacKinnon. London: SPCK, 1970.

———. *Parochial and Plain Sermons*. Vol. 1. London, 1868.

———. *The Philosophical Notebook of John Henry Newman*. Vol. 2. *The Text*. Ed. Edward Sillem; rev. A. J. Boekraad. Louvain: Nauwelaerts, 1970.

———. *Sermons Bearing on Subjects of the Day*. London, 1869.

———. *The Via Media of the Anglican Church*. 3d ed. 2 vols. London: 1877.

Niebuhr, Richard Reinhold. *Schleiermacher on Christ and Religion*. New York: Charles Scribner's Sons, 1964.

Nineteenth-Century Religious Thought in the West. Ed. Ninian Smart, John P. Clayton, Patrick Sherry, and Stephen T. Katz. 3 vols. Cambridge: Cambridge University Press, 1985.

Oakeshott, Michael. *Experience and Its Modes*. Cambridge: Cambridge University Press, 1933.

O'Donnell, John. "The Mystery of Faith in the Theology of Karl Rahner," *Heythrop Journal* 25 (1984): 301–18.

O'Donoghue, Noel Dermot. *Heaven in Ordinarie*. Springfield, Ill.: Templegate, 1979.

Otto, Rudolf. *The Idea of the Holy: An Inquiry into the Non-Rational Factor in the Idea of the Divine and Its Relation to the Rational*. Trans. John W. Harvey. Oxford: Oxford University Press, 1923.

Pedley, Christopher J. "An English Bibliographical Aid to Karl Rahner," *Heythrop Journal* 25 (1984): 319–65.

Perry, Ralph Barton. *The Thought and Character of William James*. 2 vols. Boston: Little, Brown, 1935.

The Philosophy of Martin Buber. Ed. Paul Arthur Schilpp and Maurice Friedman. The Library of Living Philosophers, no. 12. Cambridge: Cambridge University Press, 1967.

Pratt, J. B. *The Religious Consciousness: A Psychological Study.* New York, 1921.

Proudfoot, Wayne. *Religious Experience.* Berkeley: University of California Press, 1985.

Rahner, Karl. *Christian at the Crossroads.* Trans. V. Green. London: Burns and Oates, 1975.

———. *The Church and the Sacraments.* Trans. W. J. O'Hara. London: Burns and Oates, 1963.

———. *Foundations of Christian Faith: An Introduction to the Idea of Christianity.* Trans. William V. Dych. London: Darton Longman and Todd, 1978.

———. *Spirit in the World.* Trans. William Dych. New York: Herder and Herder, 1968.

———. *Theological Investigations.* Trans. Cornelius Ernst et al. 20 vols. to date. London: Darton Longman and Todd, 1961—.

———. *The Trinity.* Trans. Joseph Donceel. New York: Herder and Herder, 1970.

Reck, Andrew J. "The Philosophical Psychology of William James," *Southern Journal of Philosophy* 9 (1971): 293–312.

Redeker, Martin. *Schleiermacher: Life and Thought.* Trans. John Wallhauser. Philadelphia: Fortress Press, 1973.

Rorty, Richard. *Consequences of Pragmatism.* Minneapolis: University of Minnesota Press, 1982.

———. *Philosophy and the Mirror of Nature.* Princeton, N.J.: Princeton University Press, 1979.

Sabatier, Auguste. *Religions of Authority and the Religion of the Spirit.* Trans. Louise Seymour Houghton. New York: McClure Phillips, 1904.

Schillebeeckx, Edward. *Interim Report on the Books "Jesus" and "Christ."* Trans. John Bowden. New York: Crossroad, 1981.

Schleiermacher, Friedrich D. E. *Brief Outline on the Study of Theology.* Trans. and introd. Terrence N. Tice. Richmond: John Knox Press, 1970.

———. *The Christian Faith.* Ed. H. R. MacKintosh and J. S. Stewart. Edinburgh: T. and T. Clark, 1928.

Searle, John. *Minds, Brains and Science.* London: BBC, 1985.

Seigfried, Charlene Haddock. "The Postivist Foundation in William James's *Principles,*" *Review of Metaphysics* 38 (1984): 579–93.

Shepherd, John L. *Experience, Inference and God.* London: Macmillan, 1976.

Sherry, Patrick. "Von Hügel: Philosophy and Spirituality," *Religious Studies* 17 (1981): 1–18.

———. "Are Spirits Bodiless Persons?" *Neue Zeitschrift für Systematische Theologie und Religionsphilosophie* 24 (1982): 37–52.

Staal, Frits. *Exploring Mysticism*. London: Penguin Books, 1975.

Staten, Henry. *Wittgenstein and Derrida*. Oxford: Basil Blackwell, 1985.

Stylianopoulos, Theodore. "The Orthodox Position." In *Conflicts about the Holy Spirit*, 23–30. Concilium 128. Ed. H. Küng and J. Moltmann. New York: Seabury Press, 1979.

Suckiel, Ellen Kappy. *The Pragmatic Philosophy of William James*. Notre Dame: University of Notre Dame Press, 1982.

Swinburne, Richard. *The Coherence of Theism*. Oxford: Clarendon Press, 1979.

———. *The Existence of God*. Oxford: Clarendon Press, 1979.

———. "The Evidential Value of Religious Experience." In *The Sciences and Theology in the Twentieth Century*. Ed. A. R. Peacocke, 182–96. Notre Dame: University of Notre Dame Press, 1981.

Sykes, Stephen. *The Identity of Christianity*. London: SPCK, 1984.

Thiemann, Ronald F. *Revelation and Theology: The Gospel as Narrated Promise*. Notre Dame: University of Notre Dame Press, 1985.

Tillich, Paul. "Jewish Influences on Contemporary Christian Theology," *Cross Currents* 2 (1952): 35–42.

———. *Systematic Theology*. Welwyn: James Nisbet, 1968.

Toulmin, Stephen. *The Uses of Argument*. Cambridge: Cambridge University Press, 1958.

———. "The Genealogy of 'Consciousness.'" In *Explaining Human Behavior: Consciousness, Human Action, and Social Structure*, 53–70. Ed. Paul Secord. Beverly Hills, Calif.: Sage Publishers, 1982.

Towler, Robert. *The Need for Certainty. A Sociological Study of Conventional Religion*. London: Routledge Kegan Paul, 1984.

Turner, Denys. "De-Centring Theology," *Modern Theology* 2 (1986): 125–43.

Tyrrell, George. *The Faith of the Millions*. 2 vols. London, 1901.

Vanden Burgt, Robert J. *The Religious Philosophy of William James*. Chicago: Nelson Hall, 1981.

Vass, George. *Understanding Karl Rahner*. 2 vols. to date. London: Sheed and Ward, 1985—.

Vermes, Pamela. *Buber on God and the Perfect Man*. Brown University, Brown Judaic Studies 13. Missoula, Mont.: Scholars Press, 1980.

Waismann, Friedrich. "How I See Philosophy." In *Contemporary British Philosophy*. 3d ser. Ed. H. D. Lewis. London: George Allen and Unwin, 1956.

———. *Wittgenstein and the Vienna Circle*. Oxford: Basil Blackwell, 1979.

Whelan, Joseph P. *The Spirituality of Friedrich von Hügel*. London: Collins, 1971.

Wild, John. *The Radical Empiricism of William James*. New York: Doubleday, 1969.

Williams, Raymond, "Base and Superstructure in Marxist Cultural Theory," *New Left Review* 82 (1973): 3–16.

Williams, Robert R. *Schleiermacher the Theologian*. Philadelphia: Fortress Press, 1978.

Williams, Rowan. "Butler's *Western Mysticism:* Towards an Assessment," *Downside Review* 102 (1984): 197–215.

——. "On Not Quite Agreeing with Don Cupitt," *Modern Theology* 1 (1984): 3–24.

——. "Trinity and Revelation," *Modern Theology* 2 (1986): 197–212.

Wittgenstein, Ludwig. *Philosophical Investigations*. Ed. G. E. M. Anscombe. London: Macmillan 1953.

Index

Religion: personal and institutional, 42–
47, 52–60, 73–75, 87–89, 133–40,
164, 176; social function of, 31–33,
48, 119, 148–49, 176–77; use of
term, 39–43, 49–50. See also God,
Language, Psychology
Representation, 109, 111. See also Language
Revelation, 178, 194–95, 206, 207, 222,
248–49, 256, 259, 269–70, 283
Ritual. See Institutions
Rorty, Richard, 70n, 86n, 94n, 201
Rosenweig, Franz, 183, 187

Sabatier, Auguste, 53n
Sacrament, 214–16, 247, 249, 294. See
also Interpretation
Schillebeeckx, Edward, 243n
Schleiermacher, Friedrich D. E., 108,
110, 112, 113, 114, 116, 119, 120–
29, 131, 133, 140n, 156, 157n,
166–67, 169, 204n, 223, 243, 250;
and Hegel, 125–26; and von Hü-
gel, 166, 169; and James, 121; and
Rahner, 243–44, 246
Schneider, Herbert, 184
Scientific method, 19–21, 28, 147–53,
164. See also Empiricism, Episte-
mology
Searle, John, 36
Seigfried, Charlene, 24
Shakespeare, William: King Lear, 235n;
Macbeth, 234–35
Sherry, Patrick, 98–99, 102, 141, 143,
168–69, 170, 171, 250
Skepticism, 26
Social conventions: and experience of
God, 57–60; constitutive, 105, 115,
117; function of, 55, 57–60. See
also Institutions, Language
Sociology: of religion, 20, 96, 289
Spirit, 28, 38, 53, 71–72, 79, 95, 98–
102, 111, 118, 141, 143, 151–52,
186, 217–18, 231, 237–40, 242,
248, 253, 256, 263, 267–68, 270,
272, 274, 276–80, 282–84, 295
Staal, Frits, 106n
Staten, Henry, 10–11
Stylianopoulos, Theodore, 262n
Suckiel, Ellen Kappy, 32n, 69n

Swinburne, Richard, 91–92, 98–99,
100, 103–4, 173–74
Sykes, Stephen, 266

Theism, 78–79, 98, 103–4, 110, 129,
172, 225, 232, 264, 277
Thiemann, Ronald F., 95n, 128
Tillich, Paul, 131, 197–98
Toulmin, Stephen, 5n, 92
Towler, Robert, 20, 96–97
Transcendence, 49, 97, 99, 167–69,
210, 281–83, 287
Trinity: and tripartite treatments of reli-
gious experience, 110–11, 131–33,
135–40, 141–53, 168–70, 172, 188,
197, 207, 217, 261, 266–67, 272–
73, 277–79, 281; developmental
process, 154–61, 172
Troeltsch, Ernst, 143n
Turner, Denys, 225
Tyrrell, George, 141–42, 165n

Value. See Ethics
Vanden Burgt, Robert J., 48n, 50n, 77
Vass, George, 237, 238, 239, 240n, 248,
250, 278, 284
Vermes, Pamela, 178n, 180, 182, 193–
94, 198, 207, 209n

Waismann, Friedrich, 84, 233n, 286
Weltsch, Robert, 195
Whelan, Joseph P., 148n, 149, 162,
165–66, 175n
Wild, John, 89n
Williams, Raymond, 5n
Williams, Robert R., 125, 129
Williams, Rowan, 106, 107, 119, 204n,
259n, 269–70
Wittgenstein, Ludwig, 39n, 232
Word, 4, 188–89, 207, 248, 263; Jesus
Christ as incarnate, 253, 256, 270–
73, 277–79, 282–84. See also Inter-
pretation, Language

Zionism, 215